FOUNDATIONS OF TIBETAN MYSTICISM

AVALOKITEŚVARA
to whom is dedicated the Mantra 'OṀ MAṆI PADME HŪṀ'

FOUNDATIONS OF TIBETAN MYSTICISM

According to the Esoteric Teachings of the Great Mantra

OṀ MAṆI PADME HŪṀ

by

LAMA ANAGARIKA GOVINDA
(*Anangavajra Khamsum-Wangchuk*)

Photographic Plates by LI GOTAMI

SAMUEL WEISER
New York

First Published Rider & Co. 1960
This American Edition 1969
Seventh Impression 1975

SAMUEL WEISER, INC.
734 Broadway
New York, N. Y. 10003

ISBN 0-87728-064-9

Printed in U.S.A. by
NOBLE OFFSET PRINTERS, INC.
New York, N.Y. 10003

To the Memory of My Guru

The Venerable

TOMO GÉSHÉ RIMPOCHÉ
NGAWANG KALZANG

Great-Abbot of the Monastery of The White Conch
in the Tomo Valley (Tibet)
whose life consisted in the realization
of the Bodhisattva Ideal

CONTENTS

Part Three

'PADMA'

THE PATH OF CREATIVE VISION

Part Four

'HŪṀ'

THE PATH OF INTEGRATION

Part Five

'OṀ MAṆI PADME HŪṀ'

THE PATH OF THE GREAT MANTRA

Epilogue and Synthesis

ĀḤ

THE PATH OF ACTION

APPENDIX

ILLUSTRATIONS

PHOTOGRAPHIC PLATES
by
LI GOTAMI
(Member of the Tsaparang Expedition)

BRUSH DRAWINGS

From pictorial representations of Tibetan tradition

DIAGRAMS

SYMBOLS AND SEED-SYLLABLES

PREFACE

THE importance of Tibetan tradition for our time and for the spiritual development of humanity lies in the fact that Tibet is the last living link that connects us with the civilizations of a distant past. The mystery-cults of Egypt, Mesopotamia and Greece, of Incas and Mayas, have perished with the destruction of their civilizations and are for ever lost to our knowledge, except for some scanty fragments.

The old civilizations of India and China, though well preserved in their ancient art and literature, and still glowing here and there under the ashes of modern thought, are buried and penetrated by so many strata of different cultural influences, that it is difficult, if not impossible, to separate the various elements and to recognize their original nature.

Tibet, due to its natural isolation and its inaccessibility (which was reinforced by the political conditions of the last centuries) has succeeded not only in preserving but in *keeping alive* the traditions of the most distant past, the knowledge of the hidden forces of the human soul and the highest achievements and esoteric teachings of Indian saints and sages.

But in the storm of world-transforming events, which no nation on earth can escape and which will drag even Tibet out of its isolation, these spiritual achievements will be lost for ever, unless they become an integral part of a future higher civilization of humanity.

Anticipating the future, Tomo Géshé Rimpoché (*tro-mo dge-bśes rin-po-che*), one of the greatest spiritual teachers of modern Tibet and a real master of inner vision, left his remote mountain hermitage, in which he had practised meditation for twelve years, and proclaimed that the time had come to open to the world the spiritual treasures which had been hidden and preserved in Tibet for more than a thousand years. Because humanity stands at the cross-roads of great decisions: before it lies the Path of Power, through control of the forces of nature – a path leading to enslavement and self-destruction – and the Path of Enlightenment, through control of the forces within us – leading to liberation and self-realization. To show this path (the *Bodhisattva-mārga*) and to transform it into reality, was the life's task of Tomo Géshé Rimpoché.

The living example of this great teacher, from whose hands the author received his first initiation twenty-five years ago, was the deepest spiritual stimulus of his life and opened to him the gates to the mysteries of Tibet. It encouraged him, moreover, to pass on to others and to the world at large, whatever knowledge and experience he had thus gained – as far as this can be conveyed in words. If, in spite of all imperfections which any such attempt is bound to contain, the author should have been able to be of some help to other seekers, thanks are due first of all to the Guru who gave the highest: namely, himself. And with him the author remembers all those teachers who since the demise of his first Guru took his place, in order to bring to maturity the seeds he had sown. To them all the author owes deep gratitude.

Through all of them radiates the exalted figure of the primordial Guru, who dwells imperishably in the innermost heart of his disciples.

Honour to Him, the Enlightened One!

OṀ MUNI MUNI MAHĀ-MUNI ŚĀKYAMUNIYE SVĀHĀ!

Kasar Devi Ashram, Kumaon Himalaya, India,
in the fifth month of the year 2500 after the Buddha's
Parinirvāna (October 1956).

The Author

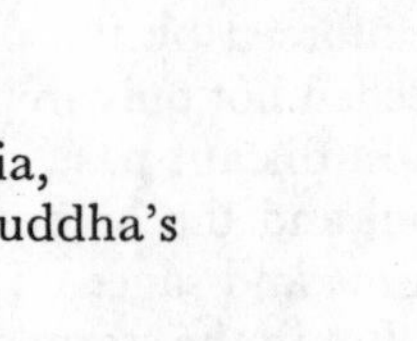

Part One

OṀ
THE PATH OF UNIVERSALITY

Plate 1

VAIROCANA

who embodies the Wisdom of the Universal Law

I

THE MAGIC OF WORDS AND THE POWER OF SPEECH

'All that is visible, clings to the invisible,
the audible to the inaudible,
the tangible to the intangible:
Perhaps the thinkable to the unthinkable.'

NOVALIS

WORDS are seals of the mind, results – or, more correctly. stations – of an infinite series of experiences, which reach from an unimaginably distant past into the present, and which feel their way into an equally unimaginable distant future, They are 'the audible that clings to the inaudible', the forms and potentialities of thought, which grow from that which is beyond thought.

The essential nature of words is therefore neither exhausted by their present meaning, nor is their importance confined to their usefulness as transmitters of thoughts and ideas, but they express at the same time qualities which are not translatable into concepts – just as a melody which, though it may be associated with a conceptual meaning, cannot be described by words or by any other medium of expression. And it is just that irrational quality which stirs up our deepest feelings, elevates our innermost being, and makes it vibrate with others.

The magic which poetry exerts upon us, is due to this quality and the rhythm combined therewith. It is stronger than what the words convey objectively – stronger even than reason with all its logic, in which we believe so firmly. The success of great speakers is not only due to *what* they say, but *how* they say it. If people could be convinced by logic and scientific proofs, the philosophers would long since have succeeded in winning over the greater part of humanity to their views.

On the other hand, the sacred books of the great world-religions would never have been able to exert such an enormous influence, because what they convey in form of thoughts is little, compared to the works of great scholars and philosophers. We are therefore justified in saying that the power of those sacred scriptures was due to the magic of the word, i.e., due to its sacred power, which was known to the Wise of the past, who were still near to the sources of language.

The birth of language was the birth of humanity. Each word was the sound-equivalent of an experience, connected with an internal or external stimulus. A tremendous creative effort was involved in this process, which must have extended over a vast period of time; and it is due to this effort that man was able to rise above the animal.

If art can be called the re-creation and formal expression of reality through the medium of human experience, then the creation of language may be called the greatest achievement of art. Each word originally was a focus of energies, in which the transformation of reality into the vibrations of the human voice – the vital expression of the human soul – took place. Through these vocal creations man took possession of the world – and more than that: he discovered a new dimension, a world within himself, opening upon the vista of a higher form of life, which is as much beyond the present state of humanity as the consciousness of a civilized man is above that of an animal.

The presentiment of the higher state of existence is connected with certain experiences, which are so fundamental, that they can neither be explained nor described. They are so subtle that there is nothing to which they can be compared, nothing to which thought or imagination can cling. And yet, such experiences are more real than anything else we can see, think of, touch, taste, hear, or smell – because they are concerned with that which precedes and includes all other sensations, and which for that reason cannot be identified with any of them. It is, therefore, only by means of symbols that such experiences may be hinted at, and these symbols again are not invented arbitrarily, but are spontaneous expressions, breaking through the deepest regions of the human mind.

'The forms of divine life in the universe and in nature break forth from the seer as vision, from the singer as sound, and are there in the spell of vision and sound, pure and undisguised. Their existence is the characteristic of the priestly power of the seer-poet (of the *kavi*, who is *drashtar*). What sounds from his mouth, is not the ordinary word, the *shabda*, of which speech is composed. It is *mantra*, the compulsion to create a mental image, power over that which IS, to be as it really is in its pure essence. Thus it is knowledge. It is the truth of being, beyond right and wrong; it is real *being* beyond thinking and reflecting.

It is "knowledge" pure and simple, knowledge of the Essential, *Veda* (Greek "oida", German "wissen", to know). It is the direct simultaneous awareness of the knower and the known. Just as it was a kind of spiritual compulsion with which the seer-poet was overpowered by vision and word, thus, for all times, wherever there are men who know how to use mantra-words, they will possess the magic power to conjure up immediate reality – be it in form of gods or in the play of forces.

In the word *mantra* the root *man* = "to think" (in Greek "menos," Latin "mens") is combined with the element *tra*, which forms tool-words. Thus *mantra* is a "tool for thinking", a "thing which creates a mental picture". With its sound it calls forth its content into a state of immediate reality. *Mantra* is power, not merely speech which the mind can contradict or evade. What the mantra expresses by its sound, exists, comes to pass. Here, if anywhere, words are deeds, acting immediately. It is the peculiarity of the true poet that his word creates actuality, calls forth and unveils something real. His word does not talk – it acts!'[1]

Thus, the word in the hour of its birth was a centre of force and reality, and only habit has stereotyped it into a mere conventional medium of expression. The mantra escaped this fate to a certain extent, because it had no concrete meaning and could therefore not be made to subserve utilitarian ends.

But while mantras have survived, their tradition has almost died out, and there are but few nowadays who know how to use them. Modern humanity is not even able to imagine how profoundly the magic of word and speech was experienced in ancient civilizations and the enormous influence it had on the entire life, especially in its religious aspects.

In this age of broadcasting and newspapers, in which the spoken and the written word is multiplied a millionfold and is indiscriminately thrown at the public, its value has reached such a low standard, that it is difficult to give even a faint idea of the reverence with which people of more spiritual times or more religious civilizations approached the word, which to them was the vehicle of a hallowed tradition and the embodiment of the spirit.

The last remnants of such civilizations may still be found in the countries of the East. But only one country has succeeded in keeping *alive* mantric traditions up to the present day, and this country is Tibet. Here not only the word, but every sound of which it consists, every letter of the alphabet, is looked upon as a sacred symbol. Even though it may serve a profane purpose, its origin is never forgotten

[1] H. Zimmer: *Ewiges Indien*, p. 81 f.

or completely disregarded. The written word is therefore always treated with respect and never thrown away carelessly, where men or animals could trample it under foot. And if it is a matter of words or scriptures of a religious nature, even the smallest fragment of them is treated with the respect of a precious relic and will not be destroyed wilfully, even though it may have ceased to serve any useful purpose, but it will be deposited in specially built sanctuaries and receptacles, or in caves, where it is left to its natural dissolution.

This may appear as primitive superstition to the outsider, who observes such actions divorced from their psychological connexions and their spiritual background. The Tibetan is not as primitive as to believe in the independent 'life' of a piece of paper or the letters written upon it (as a naïve animist might do), but he attaches the greatest importance to the attitude of one's own mind, which finds its expression in each of these actions and has its foundation in the recognition of an ever-present higher reality, which is called up and made effective in us by every contact with its symbols.

Thus the symbol is never degraded into a mere object of temporary utility, nor is it only reserved for 'Sunday use' or occasional worship, but it is a living presence, to which all profane and material things and all necessities of life are subordinated. Indeed, what we call 'profane' and 'material' is divested of its worldly and material character and becomes the exponent of a reality behind all phenomena – a reality which gives meaning to our life and actions and which integrates even the lowliest and most insignificant things into the great connexions of universal happenings.

'In the smallest you will find a master, whom the deepest in you can never satisfy.' (Rilke.) If this spiritual attitude would be interrupted anywhere, it would lose its fundamental unity and therewith its stability and its force.

The seer, the poet and singer, the spiritually creative, the psychically receptive and sensitive, the saint: they all know about the essentiality of form in word and sound, in the visible and the tangible. They do not despise what appears small or insignificant, because they can see the great in the small. Through them the word becomes *mantra*, and the sounds and signs of which it is formed, become the vehicles of mysterious forces. Through them the visible takes on the nature of symbols, the tangible becomes a creative tool of the spirit, and life becomes a deep stream, flowing from eternity to eternity.

It is good to be reminded from time to time that the attitude of the East was at home also in the West, and that the tradition of the 'inward' or spiritualized word and of the reality and actuality of the symbol had its prophets even in our time. We may only mention here Rainer Maria Rilke's mantric conception of the 'word', which reveals the very essence of mantric power:

'Wo sich langsam aus dem Schon-Vergessen,
Einst Erfahrenes sich uns entgegenhebt,
Rein gemeistert, milde, unermessen
Und im Unantastbaren erlebt:

Dort beginnt das Wort, wie wir es meinen,
Seine Geltung übertrifft uns still—
Denn der Geist, der uns vereinsamt, will
Völlig sicher sein, uns zu vereinen.'[1]

[1] Though a literal translation cannot convey the beauty of the original, the following rendering may be useful to the non-Geman-speaking reader:

'Where slowly from the long-forgotten,
Past experience rises up in us,
Perfectly mastered, mild and beyond measure,
And realized in the intangible:
There begins the word, as we conceive it,
And its meaning quietly surpasses us—
For the mind that makes us lonely, wants
To be sure that we shall be united.'

2

THE ORIGIN AND THE UNIVERSAL CHARACTER OF THE SACRED SYLLABLE OṀ

THE importance which was attached to the word in ancient India, may be seen from the following quotation:

'The essence of all beings is earth,
the essence of earth is water,
the essence of water are the plants,
the essence of the plants is man,
the essence of man is speech,
the essence of speech is the Ṛgveda,
the essence of the Ṛgveda is the Sāmaveda,
the essence of the Sāmaveda is the Udgīta (which is OṀ).
That Udgīta is the best of all essences, the highest,
Deserving the highest place, the eighth.'

(CHĀNDOGYA UPANIṢAD)

In other words: the latent forces and qualities of earth and water are concentrated and transformed into the higher organism of the plant; the forces of the plants are transformed and concentrated in man; the forces of man are concentrated in the faculties of mental reflection and expression by way of sound-equivalents, which through combination produce the inner (conceptual) and outer (audible) forms of speech, by which man distinguishes himself from all lower forms of life.

The most valuable expression of this spiritual achievement, the summary of its experiences, is the sacred knowledge (*veda*) in form of poetry (*Ṛgveda*) and music (*Sāmaveda*). Poetry is subtler than prose, because its rhythm produces a higher unity and loosens the fetters of our mind. But music is subtler than poetry, because it carries us beyond the meaning of words into a state of intuitive receptivity.

Finally, both rhythm and melody find their synthesis and their solution (which may appear as dissolution to the ordinary intellect) in the one profound and all-embracing vibration of the sacred sound OṀ. Here the apex of the pyramid has been reached, ascending from the plane of greatest differentiation and materialization (in the 'gross elements': *mahābhūta*) to the point of ultimate unification and spiritualization, which contains the latent properties of all the previous stages, just as a seed or germ (*bīja*) does. In this sense OṀ is the quintessence, the seed-syllable (*bīja-mantra*) of the universe, the magic word par excellence (that was the original meaning of the word *brahman*), the universal force of the all-embracing consciousness.

Through the identification of the sacred word with the universe, the concept *brahman* became an equivalent for the universal mind, the ever-present power of consciousness, in which men, gods and animals partake, which however can be experienced in its fulness only by the saint and the Enlightened One.

OṀ had already been used in the cosmic parallelism of the Vedic sacrificial ceremonies and became one of the most important symbols of *yoga*. After it had been freed from the mysticism and the magic of sacrificial practices as well as from the philosophical speculations of early religious thought, it became one of the essential means in the practice of meditation and inner unification (which is the actual meaning of the term *yoga*). Thus, from a metaphysical symbol OṀ became a kind of psychological tool or medium of concentration.

'Just as a spider climbs up on its thread and gains freedom, so the yogin climbs towards liberation by means of the syllable OṀ.' In the *Maitrâyaṇa Upaniṣad* OṀ is compared to an arrow with *manas* (thought) as its point, which is laid upon the bow of the human body, and which, after penetrating the darkness of ignorance, reaches the light of the Supreme State.

A similar passage is found in the *Muṇḍaka Upaniṣad*:

'Having taken as a bow the great weapon of the Secret Teaching (*upaniṣad*)
One should fix in it the arrow sharpened by constant Meditation.
Drawing it with a mind filled with That (Brahman)
Penetrate, O good-looking youth, that Imperishable as the Mark.
The *praṇava* (OṀ) is the bow; the arrow is the self;
Brahman is said to be the mark.
With heedfulness is It to be penetrated;
One should become one with It as the arrow in the mark.'[1]

In the *Māṇḍūkya Upaniṣad* the sound-values of OṀ and their symbolic interpretation are described in the following manner: 'O' is a combination of 'A' and 'U'; the whole syllable, therefore, consists of three elements, namely, A-U-M. Since OṀ is the expression of the highest faculty of consciousness, these three elements are explained accordingly as three planes of consciousness: 'A' as the waking consciousness (*jāgrat*), 'U' as the dream-consciousness (*svapna*) and 'Ṁ' as the consciousness during deep sleep (*suṣupti*). OṀ as a whole represents the all-encompassing cosmic consciousness (*turīya*) on the fourth plane, beyond words and concepts – the consciousness of the fourth dimension.

The expressions 'waking consciousness', 'dream-consciousness' and 'deep-sleep-consciousness' should however not be taken literally, but as: 1. the subjective consciousness of the external world, i.e., our ordinary consciousness; 2. the consciousness of our inner world, i.e., the world of our thoughts, feelings, desires and aspirations, which we may also call our spiritual consciousness; and 3. the consciousness of undifferentiated unity, which is no more split into subject and object and rests completely in itself. In Buddhism it is described as the state of unqualified emptiness (*śūnyatā*).

The fourth and highest state, however (*turīya*), is described in different ways by different schools of thought, according to their conception of what should be regarded as the highest aim or ideal. To some it is a state of isolation (*kevalatva*), of pure self-existence, to others a merging into a higher being (*sāyujyatva*) or into the impersonal state of the universal *brahman*, and again to others it is unqualified freedom and independence (*svātantrya*), etc. But all agree that it is a deathless, sorrowless state, where there is neither birth nor old age; and the

[1] Srî Krishna Prem's translation in his *Yoga of the Bhagavat Gîta*.

nearer we get to the Buddhist era, the clearer it becomes that this aim cannot be reached without giving up whatever constitutes our so-called self or ego.

Thus OṀ is associated with liberation, either as a means to it, or as a symbol of its attainment. In spite of the different ways in which liberation was sought and defined, OṀ never became the exclusive property of any particular school of thought, but remained true to its symbolical character, namely to express what is beyond words and forms, beyond limitations and classification, beyond definition and explanation: *the experience of the infinite within us*, which may be felt as a distant aim, as a mere presentiment, a longing – or which may be known as a growing reality, or realized in the breaking down of limitations and bondage.

There are as many infinities as there are dimensions, as many forms of liberation as there are temperaments. But all bear the same stamp. Those who suffer from bondage and confinement, will experience liberation as infinite expansion. Those who suffer from darkness, will experience it as light unbounded. Those who groan under the weight of death and transitoriness, will feel it as eternity. Those who are restless, will enjoy it as peace and infinite harmony.

But all these terms, without losing their own character, bear the same mark: 'infinite'. This is important, because it shows us that even the highest attainments may retain some individual taste – the taste of the soil from which they grew – without impairing thereby their universal value. Even in these ultimate states of consciousness there is neither identity nor non-identity in the absolute sense. There is a profound relationship between them, but no dull equality, which can never be an outcome of life and growth, but only a product of lifeless mechanism.

Thus the experience of infinity was expressed by the early *Vedas* in terms of cosmology, by the *Brāhmaṇas* in terms of magic ritual, in the *Upaniṣads* in terms of idealistic monism, in Jainism in terms of biology, in Buddhism in terms of psychology (based on the experiences of meditation), in Vedantism in terms of metaphysics, in Vaishnavism in terms of *bhakti* (mystic love and devotion), in Shaivaism in terms of 'non-duality' (*advaita*) and asceticism, in the Hindu *Tantras* in terms of the female creative power (*śakti*) of the universe, and in Buddhist Tantrism in terms of the transformation of psycho-cosmic forces and phenomena by penetrating them with the light of transcendental knowledge (*prajñā*).

This does not exhaust the different possibilities of expression, nor does it exclude their combination and their mutual penetration. On the contrary: generally many of these features are combined, and the different systems of religious thought and practice are not strictly separated, but penetrate each other more or less. However, the emphasis of the one or the other of these features gives to each of these systems its own character and its particular 'flavour'.

Consequently OṀ appears to the one as a symbol of a divine universe, to the other as a symbol of infinite power, to the next as boundless space, to another one as infinite being or as eternal life. There are some to whom it represents omnipresent light, others to whom it means universal law, and again others who interpret it as omnipotent consciousness, as all-pervading divinity, or in terms of all-embracing love, cosmic rhythm, ever-present creativeness, or unlimited knowledge, and so *ad infinitum.*

Like a mirror which reflects all forms and colours, without changing its own nature, so OṀ reflects the shades of all temperaments and takes the shapes of all higher ideals, without confining itself exclusively to any one of them. Had this sacred syllable been identified with any conceptual meaning, had it entirely yielded to any particular ideal, without retaining that irrational and intangible quality of its kernel, it would never have been able to symbolize that super-conscious state of mind, in which all individual aspirations find their synthesis and their realization.

3

THE IDEA OF CREATIVE SOUND AND THE THEORY OF VIBRATION

As every living thing, so also symbols have their periods of waxing and waning. When their power has reached its zenith, they descend into all paths of daily life, until they become conventional expressions, which have no more connexion with the original experience, or which have become either too narrow or too general in meaning, so that their depth is lost when this happens. Then other symbols take their place, while they retire into the inner circle of initiates, from where they will be reborn when their time has come.

By 'initiates' I do not mean any organized group of men, but those individuals who, in virtue of their own sensitiveness, respond to the subtle vibrations of symbols which are presented to them either by tradition or intuition. In the case of mantric symbols, the subtle vibrations of sound play a very important role, though mental associations, which crystallize around them through tradition or individual experience, help greatly to intensify their power.

The secret of this hidden power of sound or vibration, which forms the key to the riddles of creation and of creativeness, as it reveals the nature of things and of the phenomena of life, had been well understood by the seers of olden times: the Rishis who inhabited the slopes of the Himalayas, the Magi of Iran, the adepts of Mesopotamia, the priests of Egypt, and the mystics of Greece – to mention only those of whom tradition has left some traces.

Pythagoras, who himself was an initiate of Eastern wisdom and who was the founder of one of the most influential schools of mystic philosophy in the West, spoke of the 'Harmony of Spheres', according to which each celestial body – in fact, each and every atom – produced a particular sound on account of its movement, its rhythm, or vibration. All these sounds and vibrations formed a universal harmony in which each element, while having its own function and character, contributed to the unity of the whole.

The idea of creative sound was continued in the teachings of the logos, which were partly absorbed by early Christianity, as we can see from the Gospel of St. John, which begins with the mysterious words: 'In the beginning was the Word, and the Word was with God, and the Word was God. . . . And the Word was made flesh. . . .'

If these profound teachings, which were about to link up Christianity with Gnostic philosophy and with the traditions of the East had been able to maintain their influence, the universal message of Christ would have been saved from the pitfalls of intolerance and narrow-mindedness.

But the knowledge of the creative sound lived on in India. It was further developed in the various Yoga-systems and found its last refinement in those Schools of Buddhism which had their philosophical foundation in the doctrine of the *Vijñānavādins*. This doctrine was also known as *Yogācāra*, and its tradition has been preserved, in theory as well as in practice, in the countries of *Mahāyāna* Buddhism from Tibet to Japan.

Alexandra David-Neel describes in the eighth chapter of her *Tibetan Journey* a 'master of sound, who not only was able to produce all kinds of strange sounds on his instrument, a kind of cymbal, but who – like Pythagoras – explained that all beings or things produce sounds according to their nature and to the particular state in which they find themselves. "This is," he said, "because these beings and things are aggregates of atoms that dance, and by their movements produce sounds. When the rhythm of the dance changes, the sound it produces also changes. . . . Each atom perpetually sings its song, and the sound creates each moment dense or subtle forms. Just as there exist creative sounds, there exist destructive sounds. He who is able to produce both can, at will, create or destroy." '

We have to be careful not to misinterpret such statements in terms of materialistic science. It has been said that the power of mantras consists in the effect of 'sound-waves' or vibrations of small particles of matter which, as one can prove by experiments, group themselves into definite geometrical patterns and figures, exactly corresponding to the quality, strength and rhythm of the sound.

If a mantra would act in such a mechanical way, then it should have the same effect when reproduced by a gramophone record. But its repetition even by a human medium would not have any effect, if done by an ignorant person; though the intonation may be identical with that of a master. The superstition that the efficacy of a mantra depends on its intonation is mainly due to the superficial 'vibration-theory' of pseudo-scientific dilettanti, who confused the effects of spiritual vibrations or forces with those of physical sound-waves. If the efficacy of mantras depended on their correct pronunciation, then all mantras in Tibet would have lost their meaning and power, because they are not pronounced there according to the rules of Sanskrit but according to the phonetic laws of the Tibetan language (for instance not: OṀ MANI PADME HŪṀ, but 'OṀ MAṆI Péme HŪṀ').

This means that the power and the effect of a mantra depend on the spiritual attitude, the knowledge and the responsiveness of the individual. The *śabda* or sound of the mantra is not a physical sound (though it may be accompanied by such a one) but a spiritual one. It cannot be heard by the ears but only by the heart, and it cannot be uttered by the mouth but only by the mind. The mantra has power and meaning only for the initiated, i.e., for one who has gone through a particular kind of experience connected with the mantra.

Just as a chemical formula gives power only to those who are acquainted with the symbols of which it consists and with the laws of their application – in the same way a mantra gives power only to those who are conscious of its inner meaning, acquainted with its methods of operation and who know that it is a means to call up the dormant forces within us, through which we are capable of directing our destiny and of influencing our surroundings.

Mantras are not 'spells', as even prominent Western scholars repeat again and again, nor are those who have attained proficiency (*siddhi*) in them 'sorcerers' (as Grünwedel calls the *Siddhas*). Mantras do not act on account of their own 'magic' nature, but only through the mind that experiences them. They do not possess any power of their own; they are only the means for concentrating already existing forces—just as a magnifying glass, though it does not contain any heat of its own, is able to concentrate the rays of the sun and to transform their mild warmth into incandescent heat.

This may appear as sorcery to the bushman, because he sees only the effect, without knowing the causes and their inner connexions. Therefore those who confuse mantric knowledge with sorcery, are not very different in their point of view from the attitude of the bushman. And if there have been scholars who tried to discover the nature of mantras with the tools of philological knowledge, and came to the conclusion that they were 'meaningless gibberish'[1] because they had neither grammatical structure nor logical meaning, then we can only say that such a procedure was like pursuing butterflies with a sledge hammer.

Quite apart from the inadequacy of means, it is astonishing that such scholars, without the slightest personal experience and without ever attempting to study the nature and the methods of mantric tradition and practice under a competent spiritual teacher (*guru*), arrogate to themselves the right to judge and to pronounce opinions.

It was only through Arthur Avalon's courageous pioneer work (mainly in the realm of Hindu Tantras, which found their most gifted interpreter in the German Indologist Heinrich Zimmer) that the world was shown for the first time that Tantrism was neither degenerate Hinduism nor corrupt Buddhism, and that the mantric tradition was an expression of the deepest knowledge and experience in the realm of human psychology.

However, this experience can only be acquired under the guidance of a competent Guru (being the embodiment of a living tradition) and by constant practice. If after such preparation the mantra is used, all the necessary associations and the accumulated forces of previous experiences are aroused in the initiate and produce the atmosphere and the power for which the mantra is intended. But the uninitiated may utter the mantra as often as he likes, without producing the slightest effect. Therefore, mantras may be printed in books by the thousand, without giving away their secret or losing their value.

Their 'secret' is not something that is hidden intentionally, but something that has to be acquired by self-discipline, concentration, inner experience and insight. Like every valuable thing and every form of knowledge, it cannot be gained without effort. Only in this sense is it esoteric, like every profound wisdom, which does not dis-

[1] L. A. Waddell: *The Buddhism of Tibet or Lamaism*, London, 1895.

close itself at the first glance, because it is not a matter of surface-knowledge but of realization in the depth of one's own mind. Therefore, when the fifth Patriarch of the Chinese Buddhist Ch'an School was asked by his disciple Hui-nêng, whether he had any esoteric teachings to impart, he replied: 'What I can tell you is not esoteric. If you turn your light inward, you will find what is esoteric within your own mind.' Thus, esoteric knowledge is open to all who are willing to exert themselves sincerely and who have the capacity to learn with an open mind.

In the same way, however, as only those are admitted for higher education in universities and similar institutions, who have the necessary gifts and qualifications, so also the spiritual teachers of all times demanded certain qualities and qualifications from their disciples, before they initiated them into the inner teachings of mantric science. For nothing is more dangerous than half-knowledge, or knowledge which has only theoretical value.

The qualities which they demanded were: sincere faith in the Guru, perfect devotion to the ideal which he represents, and deep respect for all spiritual things. The special qualifications were: a basic knowledge of the main tenets of the sacred scriptures or tradition, and the readiness to devote a certain number of years to the study and practice of the inner teachings under the guidance of the Guru.

4

THE DECADENCE OF MANTRIC TRADITION

MANTRIC knowledge can be called a secret doctrine with as much or as little justification as higher mathematics, physics, or chemistry, which to the ordinary man who is not acquainted with the symbols and formulae of these sciences, appear like a book with seven seals. But just as the ultimate discoveries of these sciences can be misused for purposes of personal or political power and are therefore kept secret by interested parties (like state-governments), in the same way mantric knowledge became a victim of power-politics of certain castes or classes of society at certain times.

In ancient India the Brahmins, the priestly class, made the knowledge of mantras a prerogative or privilege of their caste, thereby forcing all those who did not belong to their class, blindly to accept the dictates of tradition. In this way it happened that what once streamed forth from religious ecstasy and inspiration, turned into dogma, and finally reacted even on the originators of this tradition as irresistible compulsion. Knowledge became mere belief; and belief, without the corrective of experience, turned into superstition.

Nearly all superstitions in the world can be traced to some truths which, by being separated from their genetic connexions, have lost their meaning. They are, as the word literally says, 'remainders', something that is 'left over' ('super-stitia'). And because the circumstances and the way in which those truths or ideas had been found, i.e., their logical, spiritual, or historical connexions, have been forgotten, they become mere beliefs which have nothing in common with genuine faith or the reasonable confidence in the truth or power of an idea or a person, a confidence which grows into inner certainty through being borne out by experience and in harmony with the laws of reason and reality. This kind of faith is the necessary precondition of every mental or spiritual activity, be it science or philosophy, religion or art. It is the positive attitude of our mind and our whole being, without which no spiritual progress can be attained. It is the *saddha* which the Buddha demanded from those who wanted to follow him on his way. '*Apārutā tesam amatassa dvārā, ye sotavantā pamuñcantu saddhaṁ.*' 'Opened are the gates of immortality, ye that have ears to hear, release your faith!' These were the words with which the Buddha began his career as a religious teacher. '*Pamuñcantu saddhaṁ*' means: 'let your faith, your inner trust and confidence stream forth, remove your inner obstacles and open yourself to the truth!'

It was this kind of faith, or inner readiness and open-mindedness, which found its spontaneous expression, its liberation from an overwhelming psychic pressure, in the sacred sound OṀ. In this mantric symbol all the positive and forward-pressing forces of the human mind (which are trying to blow up its limitations and burst the fetters of ignorance) are united and concentrated like an 'arrow-point'.

But all too soon this genuine expression of profound experience fell a victim to speculation; because those who had no part in the experience themselves, tried to analyse its results. It was not sufficient to them that by removing the causes of darkness, light would prevail. They wanted to discuss the qualities of light before they had even started penetrating the darkness; and while discussing them, they built up an elaborate theology, into which the sacred OṀ was woven so artfully, that it became impossible to extricate it.

Instead of relying on their own forces, they expected the help of some supernatural agent. While speculating about the aim, they forgot that the effort of 'shooting off the arrow' was to be made by themselves and not by some magic power within the arrow or the aim. They adorned and worshipped the arrow instead of using it, charged with all their available energy. They unbent the bow of mind and body instead of training it.

Thus it happened that at the time of the Buddha this great mantric symbol had become so much entangled in the theology of brahmanical faith, that it could not be used in a doctrine which tried to free itself as much from the tutelage of Brahmins as from superfluous dogmas and theories, and which emphasized the self-determination, self-responsibility of man and his independence from the power of gods.

It was the first and most important task of Buddhism 'to bend and to re-string the bow of body and mind' by proper training and discipline. And after the self-confidence of man had been restored, the new doctrine firmly established, and the ornaments and cobwebs of theology and speculation had withered and fallen from the sacred arrow-head OṀ, it could again be attached to the arrow of meditation.

We have mentioned already how closely OṀ was connected with the development of Yoga which, as a kind of inter-religious system of mental and bodily training methods, received and gave contributions to every school of religious thought. Buddhism, from its very beginning, had accepted and developed the practice of Yoga, and a continuous exchange of experiences between Buddhism and other religious systems took place for nearly two millenniums.

It was therefore not surprising that even though the syllable OṀ had temporarily lost its importance as a symbol, the religious practice of early Buddhism made use of mantric formulae, wherever these proved helpful as a means for the awakening of faith (*saddha*), for the liberation from inner hindrances, and for the concentration upon the supreme goal.

5

MANTRIC TENDENCIES OF EARLY BUDDHISM

ALREADY the early *Mahāsāṅghikas* possessed a special collection of mantric formulae in their Canon under the name *Dhāraṇī-* or *Vidyādhara-piṭaka. Dhāraṇīs* are means for fixing the mind upon an idea, a vision or an experience gained in meditation. They may represent the quintessence of a teaching as well as the experience of a certain state of consciousness, which hereby can be recalled or recreated deliberately at any time. Therefore they are also called supporters, receptacles or bearers of wisdom (*vidyādhara*). They are not different from mantras in their function but to some extent in their form, in so far as they may attain a considerable length and sometimes represent a combination of many mantras or 'seed-syllables' (*bīja-mantras*), or the quintessence of a sacred text. They were a product as well as a means of meditation: 'Through deep absorption (*samādhi*) one gains a truth, through a *dhāraṇī* one fixes and retains it.'

Though the importance of mantras and *dhāraṇīs* as a vehicle or instrument of meditation was not yet emphasized in *Theravāda* Buddhism, their efficacy was never doubted. In the most ancient *Pāli* texts we find protective mantras or *parittas* for warding off danger, illness, snakes, ghosts, evil influences and so on, as well as for the creation of beneficent conditions, like health, happiness, peace, a good rebirth, wealth, etc. (*Khuddakapātha; Aṅguttara-Nikāya*, IV, 67; *Āṭānāṭiya-Sutta, Dīgha-Nikāya*, 32, etc.)

In *Majjhima-Nikāya*, 86, the Buddha causes *Aṅgulimālā* (the former robber, converted by the Buddha) to cure a woman, suffering from an abortion, by an utterance of truth, i.e., through mantric power. That this consists mainly in the purity and truthfulness of the speaker, intensified and made into a conscious force by the solemn form of the utterance, cannot be emphasized too often. Though the inner attitude of the speaker is the main source of power, yet the form in which it is expressed is not irrelevant. It must be adequate to the spiritual content, melodious, rhythmic, forceful, and supported by mental and emotional associations, created either by tradition or personal experience.

In this sense not only the solemn utterances of the *Ratana-Sutta*, in which each verse ends with the assurance 'by force of this truth may there be happiness' (*etena saccena suvatthi hotu*), are to be rated as mantras, but also the ancient refuge-formulae which until the present day are recited with as much veneration in the countries of *Theravāda* Buddhism as their corresponding Sanskrit-mantras of the Northern Schools.

Their perfect parallelism of sound, rhythm and idea, their concentration on the highest symbols, like *Buddha*, *Dhamma* (doctrine; Sanskrit: *Dharma*) and *Saṅgha* (community of saints) and their underlying devotional attitude, in which *saddha* (faith) and *mettā* (love) occupy the first place, making them mantras in the best sense. That their formal expression is as important as their idea, is emphasized by their threefold repetition and by the fact that some of these formulae are repeated even *twice* three times with slightly different pronunciation within one and the same ceremony (as for instance in

Burma, at *pujā-*, *paritta-*, *upasampadā-*, *patimokkha*-ceremonies or similar occasions) in order to be sure of the proper form, the proper reproduction of the sound-symbol, sanctified by tradition, which like a living stream flows from the past into the future, thus connecting the individual with past and future generations of devotees striving towards the same goal. Herein lies the magic of the mantric word and its mystic power over the individual.

As the true Buddhist does not expect the Buddha or his disciples or the *Dharma* to accept prayers, or to act on behalf of the appellant in a miraculous way, it is clear that the efficacy of such formulae depends on the harmonious co-operation of form (sound and rhythm), feeling (devotional impulse: faith, love, veneration) and idea (mental associations: knowledge, experience) which arouse, intensify and transform the latent psychic forces (determination and conscious will-power are only small fractions of them).

Form is indispensable, because it is the vessel which holds the other qualities; feeling is indispensable because it creates unity (like heat which, by melting different metals, amalgamates them into a new homogeneous unit); while the idea is the substance, the 'prima materia' which vitalizes all the elements of the human mind and calls up their dormant energies. But it has to be noted that the term 'idea' should not be understood as representing a mere abstraction, but – as in the original Greek sense of 'eidos' – a creative picture, or a form of experience in which reality is reflected and reproduced ever anew.

While the form crystallized out of the practice of past generations, the idea which inspired it is the gift of the Buddha – and in this sense only it may be said that the Buddha's spiritual power is present in the mantra – but the impulse which amalgamates the qualities of heart and mind, and the creative forces which respond to the idea and fill it with life, this is what the devotee has to contribute. If his faith is not pure, he will not achieve inner unity; if his mind is untrained, he will not be able to assimilate the idea; if he is psychically dull, his energies will not respond to the call; and if he lacks in concentration, he will not be able to co-ordinate form, heart, and mind.

Thus mantras are not an effortless method of escaping the evil consequences of life, i.e., of our own actions, but a medium which requires exertion, just as any other way of liberation. If it is said that mantras act without fail when properly used, it does not mean that they can suspend the laws of Nature or contradict the effects of *karma*. It only means that one who is perfect in his concentration, in his faith and in his knowledge, cannot fail to achieve liberation – because he is already master of his *karma* (lit. 'action', productive of consequences), i.e., of himself.

Also in the later forms of the *Mantrayāna* (as the mantric Schools of Buddhism were called) it was well understood that *karma* could not be neutralized by merely muttering mantras or by any other kind of religious ritual or magic power, but only by a pure heart and a sincere mind. *Milarepa*, one of the great Masters of Sound, may be quoted as the best authority in this matter: 'If ye wonder whether evil karma can be neutralized or not, then know that it is neutralized by desire for goodness.'

> '*Without attuning body, speech and mind unto the Doctrine,*
> *What gain is it to celebrate religious rites?*
> *If anger be unconquered by its antidote,*
> *What gain is it to celebrate religious rites?*
> *Unless one meditate on loving others more than self,*
> *What gain is it merely from the lips to say:*
> '*O pity* [*sentient creatures*]'?'[1]

Words like these could be found in great numbers to prove that, notwithstanding the great changes which had taken place in the methods of religious practice in the course of time, the spirit of Buddhism had remained alive. It was not inconsistent with the ideas of Buddhism to utilize mantras as an additional help in meditation and devotional exercises as long as they remained means of liberation and did not assume the deadening role of a dogma, i.e., as long as people had a clear notion of the causes and effects and the inner meaning of mantras and did not make them articles of blind faith, or means for worldly gain.

In the theological dogmatism of the sacrificial ritual of Brahmanism at the time of the Buddha, this knowledge had been lost to a great extent and mantric words had degenerated to a mere convention and to a convenient means for escaping one's own responsibility by relying upon the magic power of god- and demon-compelling formulae.

The Buddha, however, who placed man into the centre of his universe, and who believed in liberation through one's own efforts, but not through divine intervention, could not build upon a theologically infected mantric system, but had to leave it to time and to the inner needs and experiences of his followers to find new forms of expression. The Buddha could only point the way by which everybody can arrive at his own experience. Because mantras cannot be made;

[1] *Tibet's Great Yogi Milarepa*, translated by Lama Dawa Samdup, edited by Dr. W. Y. Evans-Wentz, p. 263 f.

they must grow, and they grow only from experience and from the collective knowledge of many generations.

The development of a Buddhist science of mantras was therefore not a 'relapse' into brahmanical usages or a sign of 'degeneration' but the natural consequence of spiritual growth, which in each phase of its development produced with necessity its own forms of expression. And even there, where these forms had similarity with those of earlier epochs, they were never a mere repetition of the past but a new creation out of the abundance of overwhelming direct experience.

6

BUDDHISM AS LIVING EXPERIENCE

EACH new experience, each new situation of life, widens our mental outlook and brings about a subtle transformation within ourselves. Thus our nature changes continually, not only on account of the conditions of life, but – even if these would remain static – because by the constant addition of new impressions, the structure of our mind becomes ever more diverse and complex. Whether we call it 'progress' or 'degeneration', we have to admit the fact that it is the law of all life, in which differentiation and co-ordination balance each other.

Thus each generation has its own problems and must find its own solutions. The problems, as well as the means to solve them, grow out of the conditions of the past and are therefore related to them, but they can never be identical with them. They are neither completely identical nor completely different. They are the result of a continual process of adjustment.

In a similar way we have to look at the development of religious problems. Whether we regard them as 'progress' or 'deterioration' – they are necessities of spiritual life, which cannot be forced into rigid, unchangeable formulae.

Great religious and deep-rooted philosophical attitudes are not individual creations, though they may have been given their first impetus by great individuals. They grow from the germs of creative ideas, great experiences and profound visions. They grow through many generations according to their own inherent law, just like a tree or any other living organism. They are what we might call 'natural events of the spirit'. But their growth, their unfoldment and maturity need time. Though the whole tree is potentially contained in the seed, it requires time to transform itself into visible shape.

What the Buddha could teach in words was only a fraction of what he taught by his mere presence, his personality and his living example. And all these together are only a fraction of his spiritual experience. The Buddha himself was conscious of the shortcomings and limitations of word and speech, when hesitating to teach his doctrine, by putting into words something that was too profound and subtle to be grasped by mere logic and ordinary human reasoning. (Nevertheless there are still people who cannot see anything more in Buddhism than a 'religion of reason', and to whom 'reason' is strictly limited to the scientific illumination and the infallible logic of the last century or the 'latest' discoveries of science!)

When, in spite of this, the Buddha finally decided to disclose the truth, out of compassion for the few 'whose eyes were hardly covered with dust', he strictly avoided speaking about the ultimate things and refused to answer any questions concerning the supramundane state of Realization or similar problems which went beyond the capacity of the human intellect. He confined himself to showing the practical way which led to the solution of all those problems, and in showing it, he always explained his essential teachings in a form which corresponded to the capacity of his hearers. To the peasant he spoke in terms of agriculture, to artisans in similes corresponding to their profession, to Brahmins in philosophical language and in similes related to their conception of the universe or to their religious practices (like sacrificial rituals, etc.), to citizens and householders he spoke about civic duties and the virtues of family-life, while confiding the deeper aspects of his teachings and his experiences in the highest stages of meditation to a smaller circle of advanced disciples, especially to the members of his Order.

Later schools of Buddhism have remained true to this principle in modifying their methods of teaching and the means for its realization according to the needs of the individual as well as to the spiritual (or historically conditioned) development of their time. When Buddhist philosophy had become more elaborate and extensive, a greater number of teaching-methods, to suit every individual state of mind, came into existence. Just as the Buddha guided his disciples in stages, in the same way, later schools of Buddhism reserved the more difficult aspects of their teachings, which needed a higher standard of education and knowledge, for those who fulfilled these conditions and who had already gone through the preliminary forms of training.

These advanced teachings have been described as esoteric or 'secret' doctrines; however, their purpose was not to exclude anybody from the attainment of higher realizations or knowledge, but to avoid the empty talk and speculation of those who try to anticipate intellectually these exalted states of consciousness, without endeavouring to acquire them by practice.

When the Buddha denounced the secrecy and mysteriousness of pretentious priests who regarded their knowledge or their office as a prerogative of their caste, or when he declared that he made no difference between 'inside' (esoteric) and 'outside' (exoteric) teachings, and that he did not keep anything back in his closed fist, it certainly did not mean that he made no difference between a wise man and a fool, but that he was ready to teach without restriction all those who were willing to follow him. A restriction, however, existed on the part of his hearers and disciples, namely, their own capacity for understanding, and here the Buddha drew the line between what he knew and what he regarded as fit for teaching.

Once, when the Enlightened One dwelt in the *Siṁsapa* grove, he picked up a handful of leaves, showed them to his disciples and told them that just as the leaves in his hand were few in comparison with the leaves of the entire grove, in the same way that what he had taught them, constituted only a small fraction of what he knew, but that he would disclose only as much as was necessary to his disciples for the attainment of liberation.

This kind of discrimination has to be exercised by every teacher, not only in general but in each individual case. The *Dharma* should not be forced upon those who do not care for it or who are not yet ripe for it; it should be given only to those who thirst for higher knowledge, and it should be given at the proper time and at the proper place.

Applied to the development of Buddhism, this means that each epoch of time and each country had to find its own form of expression and its own methods of teaching in order to keep the idea of Buddhism alive. This 'idea' was not a philosophical thesis or a metaphysical dogma but an impetus towards a new attitude of mind, on account of which the world and the phenomenon of our own consciousness were not to be regarded from the standpoint of 'I', but from that of 'non-I'. By this reversal of the point of view all things suddenly appeared in a new perspective, in so far as the inner and the outer world became equally and mutually dependent phenomena of our consciousness – a consciousness which, according to the degree of its development, experienced a different kind of reality, a different world. The degree of development, however, depended on the degree in which the 'I'-Illusion had been overcome, and with it the egocentric perspective which distorts all things and events, and breaks up their inner relationship. The re-establishment of a perfect spiritual balance by overcoming this illusion of egohood, the source of all hatred, craving, and suffering, is the state of enlightenment. Whatever leads to the realization of this state is the path of the Buddha, a path which is not fixed once and for ever, and which does not exist independent of time and individuals, but only in the movement and progress of the pilgrim towards the aim indicated by the Buddha. It is a path which has to be realized and created anew by each pilgrim.

Even the most perfect formulation of the Buddha's doctrine would not have saved his followers from the necessity of new formulations, because, though the Buddha's doctrine was perfect, the people to whom he preached were not, and what they could understand and pass on to others suffered from the limitations which are inherent in all human thought.

Apart from this, we must not forget that the Buddha was compelled to express himself in the language and in the popular conceptions of his time, in order to make himself understood. Even if all those who preserved the words of the Buddha had been *Arahans* (saints), this would not change the fact that the teachings which they passed on in this form, were conceptually and linguistically time-conditioned formulations. Neither could they anticipate problems which did not yet exist, and even if they had been able to foresee them, they would not have been able to express them, because the language in which they could be expressed and understood, had not yet been born.

The Buddha himself would have expressed his teachings in a different way if he had lived in the sixth century A.D., instead of in the sixth century B.C. – and this was not because the *Dharma*, or the truth which he had to teach, would have been a different one, but because those who were to be taught, had added to their consciousness twelve centuries of historical, practical, mental and spiritual experience and had not only a greater store of concepts and possibilities of expression, but also a different mental attitude, with different problems and perspectives and different methods of solving them.

Those who blindly believe in words, as well as others to whom historical antiquity is more important than Truth, will never admit this. They will accuse later Buddhist schools of having gone beyond the Buddha, while in reality they only went beyond the time-conditioned concepts of the Buddha's contemporaries and their successors.

Spiritual things can be 'fixed' as little as living things. Where growth ceases, there nothing but the dead form remains. We can preserve mummified forms as historical curiosities, but not life. If, therefore, in our quest for truth, we do not rely on the factual testimony of history, it is not that we doubt the formal truthfulness, or even the truthfulness of intention on the part of those who preserved and passed on those forms, but we do not believe that forms created milleniums ago, can be taken over indiscriminately without causing serious harm to our mental constitution. Even the best food, if preserved too long, becomes poison. It is the same with spiritual ood. Truths cannot be 'taken over', they have to be rediscovered continually. They have ever to be re-formed and transformed, if they are to preserve their meaning, their living value, or their spiritual nutriment. This is the law of spiritual growth, from which results the necessity to experience the same truths in ever new forms, and to cultivate and propagate not so much the results, but the *methods* through which we obtain knowledge and experience Reality.

If this process of spiritual growth is repeated and experienced in each individual, it does not only mean that the individual will become the connecting link between the past and the present, but likewise that the past becomes revitalized and rejuvenated in the present experience and transforms itself into the creative germ of the future. In this way history is again reshaped into present life, becomes part of our own being and not merely an object of learning or veneration which, separated from its origins and the organic conditions of its growth, would lose its essential value.

As soon as we understand this organic growth, we cease to judge its various phases as 'right' or 'wrong', 'valuable' or 'worthless'; we shall rather come to the conclusion that the modulations of the same theme or 'motif' emphasize, by the very force of their contrasts, the common factor, the essential foundation.

The essential nature of a tree, for instance, is neither confined to its roots, nor to its trunk, its branches, twigs, or leaves, nor to its blossoms or its fruits. The real nature of the tree lies in the organic development and relationship of all these parts, i.e., in the totality of its spatial and temporal unfoldment.

In a similar way we have to understand that the essential nature of Buddhism cannot be found in the spaceless realm of abstract thought, nor in a dogma hallowed by antiquity, but only in its unfoldment in time and space, in the immensity of its movement and development, in its all-encompassing influence upon life in all its aspects, in short: in its universality.

7

THE UNIVERSAL ATTITUDE OF THE *MAHĀYĀNA* AND THE *BODHISATTVA* IDEAL

THE universality of Buddhism, which expressed itself first in a bewildering variety of religious and philosophical schools, was raised into a conscious principle by the *Mahāyāna*, the Great Vehicle, which was big enough to recognize the differences of all schools and ideals as necessary forms of expression of different temperaments and levels of understanding.

This became possible through the emphasis on the *Bodhisattva* ideal which placed the figure of the Buddha as the embodiment of highest realization into the centre of religious life. In whatever way one might have defined the reality or unreality of the world or its relationship to spiritual experience, or the state of liberation and of the ultimate *nirvāṇa* – one thing was sure: that the state of perfection, of enlightenment, of Buddhahood, had been achieved by a human being, and that it was open to everybody to attain this state in the same way. In this point all schools of Buddhism were united.

This way, however, was not one of running away from the world, but of *overcoming* it through growing knowledge (*prajñā*), through active love (*maitrī*) towards one's fellow-beings, through inner participation in the joys and sufferings of others (*karuṇā muditā*), and through equanimity (*upekṣā*) with regard to one's own weal and woe. This way was vividly illustrated by the innumerable forms of existence of the Buddha (up to his last as *Gautama Śākyamuni*), as told in the *Jātakas*, the stories of his previous births. Even if we do not want to attach historical value to these stories, they nevertheless demonstrate the attitude of early Buddhists and their idea of the course of development of a Perfectly Enlightened One.

In the *Ṭipitaka*, the canonical scriptures of *Pāli* Buddhism, also known as *Theravāda* or 'the Teaching of the Elders', which prevails in the southern countries of Buddhism, three kinds of liberated men are distinguished: firstly, the saint, or Arahan, who has overcome passions and the illusion of egohood, without possessing the all-embracing knowledge and the all-pervasive consciousness of Perfect Enlightenment (which would enable him to lead innumerable other beings to this exalted state, instead of winning liberation for himself alone); secondly, the Silent Enlightened One or *Paccekabuddha*, who has got the knowledge of a Buddha, but not the capacity of communicating it to others; and finally the *Sammāsambuddha*, the Perfectly Enlightened One, who is not only a saint, a knower, an enlightened one, but a Perfect One, one who has become *whole*, complete in himself, i.e., one in whom *all* spiritual and psychic faculties have come to perfection, to maturity, to a state of perfect harmony, and whose consciousness encompasses the infinity of the universe. Such a one cannot be identified any more with the limitations of his individual personality, his individual character and existence; of him it is rightly said that 'there is nothing by which he could be measured – there are no words to describe him'. ('*Atthaṅgatassa na pamāṇam atthi yena naṁ vajju taṁ tassa na 'tthi*'; *Sutta-Nipāta*, 1076.)

It seems that originally the *Arahan*, the *Paccekabuddha*, and the *Sammāsambuddha* were merely classified as types of men or states of attainment. But as, according to the Buddhist point of view, man is not 'created' once and for ever with a certain set of predispositions or a fixed character, but is what he makes out of himself, the knowledge of these three possibilities led with necessity to the formulation of three *ideals*; and from this point of view there could be no doubt, that the ideal of the Perfectly Enlightened One was the highest. Since it was able to carry innumerable beings across the dark ocean of this ephemeral world of birth and death (*saṁsāra*) to the luminous shore of liberation, it was called *Mahāyāna*, 'the Great Vehicle', while the other ideals (especially that of the *Arahan*) which were concerned with individual liberation only, were called *Hīnayāna*, 'the Small Vehicle'.

The terms *Hīnayāna* and *Mahāyāna* were coined for the first time during the Council of King *Kaniṣka* in the first century A.D., when the different ideals and ways of liberation were discussed by the representatives of different schools. Here the *Mahāyāna* ideal proved to be the only one which had sufficient width to bridge the differences of all Buddhist sects. It was, therefore, no wonder that the majority of those present at the Council voted for the *Mahāyāna* and that the small groups who favoured the *Hīnayāna*, died out soon afterwards.

The *Theravādins*, however, who were not present at this Council (since they had already disappeared from the Indian mainland), can strictly speaking not be identified with the *Hīnayāna*, because they do not reject the *Bodhisattva* ideal. *Nārada Mahā-Thera*, one of the acknowledged leaders of the Ceylonese Buddhism, convincingly expressed the point of view of the *Theravādins* in the following words:

'Buddhism is a teaching that appeals equally to those who wish to gain their personal salvation and to those who wish to work both for their personal salvation and for the salvation of others.

'There are some amongst us, who understand the vanity of worldly pleasures, and who are so thoroughly convinced of the universality of suffering that they seek the earliest opportunity to escape this cycle of birth and death and obtain their emancipation.

'There are some others who not only understand but feel all the sufferings of life; so boundless is their love and so pervasive is their compassion that they renounce their personal salvation and dedicate their lives for the lofty purpose of serving humanity and perfecting themselves.

'Such is the noble ideal of a *Bodhisattva*. This *Bodhisattva* ideal is the most refined and the most beautiful that was ever presented to the world, for what is nobler than a life of selfless service and perfect purity.

'The *Bodhisattva* ideal, it should be said, is exclusively Buddhistic.'

It would, however, be a great misunderstanding to think that serving one's fellow-beings would imply a postponement or a weakening to realize the highest aim. *Milarepa*, who himself realized it, warned his disciples against this error when saying: 'One should not be *over-anxious and hasty* in setting out to serve others before having oneself realized Truth in its fullness; to be so, would be like the blind leading the blind. As long as the sky endureth, so long there will be no end of sentient beings for one to serve; and to everyone cometh the opportunity for such service. Till the opportunity come, I exhort each of you to have but the one resolve, namely, to attain Buddhahood for the good of all living things.'

In order to achieve this, the practice of the highest virtues (*pāramitā*) of a *Bodhisattva* are required.

These do not only consist in avoiding what is evil, but in cultivating what is good: in self-sacrificing deeds of love and compassion, born in the fires of universal suffering, in which other beings' sufferings are felt with equal intensity as if they concerned one's own being. A *Bodhisattva* has not the ambition to teach others, except through his own example, and he pursues his spiritual career without ever losing sight of the welfare of his fellow-beings. Thus he ripens towards his exalted aim and inspires others to do likewise.

While proceeding on our way, no sacrifice that we make for the sake of others is in vain; even if it is not recognized or perhaps even misused by those for whose benefit it was intended. Each sacrifice is an act of renunciation, a victory over ourselves, and therefore an act of liberation. Each of these acts, whatever their external effect, brings us one step nearer to our aim and transforms the theoretical understanding of the *anātma* idea into the living knowledge and certainty of experience. The more we lose our ego and break down the walls of our self-created prison, the greater becomes the clarity and radiance of our being and the convincing power of our life. It is this through which we help others – more than through philanthropic deeds of charity, and more than through pious words and religious sermons.

Those, however, who keep aloof from the contacts of life, miss the opportunities of sacrifice, of self-negation, of relinquishing hard-earned gains, of giving up what was dear or what seemed desirable, of service to others, and of the trials of strength in the temptations and ordeals of life. Again: to help others and to help oneself, go hand in hand. The one cannot be without the other.

However, we should not force our good deeds upon others from a sense of moral superiority, but act spontaneously from that natural kind of selflessness which flows from the knowledge of the solidarity of all life and from the indescribable experience of oneness, gained in meditation – an experience whose universal character was expressed in the sacred syllable OṀ and in the general religious attitude of the *Mahāyāna*.

It was this knowledge of solidarity which *Milarepa* demanded as the foundation of morality and the *Bodhisattva* virtues. It was this knowledge which, however imperfect in its first dawning, led the Buddha in his former existences upon the path of enlightenment, and which made him renounce his own immediate liberation (when meeting the Buddha of a previous world-age), in order to gain perfect Buddhahood through the experiences and sufferings of countless rebirths in the practice of *Bodhisattva* virtues, which would enable him to reach the highest aim, not only for himself, but for the benefit of innumerable other beings as well.

It was this knowledge which made the Buddha return from the Tree of Enlightenment in order to proclaim his Gospel of Light, acccording to which the faculty of enlightenment (*bodhicitta*) is inherent in every living being. Wherever this faculty becomes a conscious force in any being, a *Bodhisattva* is born. To awaken this consciousness was the life's task of the Buddha. It was this, that caused him to take upon himself the hardships of a wandering life, for forty long years, instead of enjoying for himself the happiness of liberation.

8

THE UNIVERSAL PATH AND THE REVALUATION OF THE SACRED SYLLABLE OṀ

THE immediate successors of the Buddha, in their anxiety to preserve every word and command of the Master and every detail of the mode of living of his first disciples, created a codex of innumerable monastic rules and regulations, thereby forgetting the spirit over the letter; and out of the simple, selfless and spontaneous life of inspired apostles and homeless wanderers, grew a well-ordered, self-complacent and world-estranged monkhood which escaped the troubles and struggles of life in well-provided monasteries, separated from the life of laymen as well as from the world in general.

Nearly all schisms, dissensions, and sectarian controversies during the first centuries of Buddhist history, had their cause not in essential doctrinal or religious questions, but in differences of opinion concerning the rules of the Order, or in purely scholastic and theoretical interpretations of certain concepts, or in the greater emphasis upon the one or the other aspect of the doctrine and its corresponding scriptures.

The first schism occurred a hundred years after the Buddha's demise, at the Council of *Vaiśālī*, where the orthodox group of *Sthaviravādins* (in Pāli: *Theravādins*) separated themselves from the main body of the Buddhist Order, because they refused to recognize the majority vote in favour of a more liberal interpretation of the smaller rules of the Order. According to the decision accepted and passed by the majority of the assembly, greater stress was laid upon the spirit of the teaching and the individual sense of responsibility. Here are the opinions of two prominent historians:

'How much is true of the story of the Council of *Vaiśālī* cannot be decided, because the accounts known to us contradict each other in many points and are generally prejudiced in favour of the *Sthaviravādins*. Important, however, is one fact: the Buddhists attribute the schism not to differences of dogma but to differences concerning the discipline of the Order.' (H. von Glasenapp.)[1]

Most of the points of difference, as reported by the *Theravādins* (who regarded the adherents of the Great Assembly, the *Mahāsāṅghikas*, as heretics) were so trivial that one wonders how they could

[1] *Der Buddhismus in Indien und im Fernen Osten*, p. 51.

have created such a stir. But Mrs. C. A. F. Rhys Davids rightly remarks:

'The real point at issue was the rights of the individual, as well as of those of the provincial communities, as against the prescriptions of a centralized hierarchy. Not only as a unit, but also in the smaller groups, the man would have more weight; he would count as a man, and not just as the mere unit he would be, if his life, even his life in an Order of monks, were to be the carrying out of this Rule and that with the monotony of herd life. He would be able as man to wayfare in the Way *atta-dhammo*: choosing, deciding according to his "conscience".[1]

It was only when the Buddhists again began to turn more consciously towards the figure of the Buddha, whose life and deeds were the most vital expression of his teachings, that Buddhism emerged from a number of quarrelling sects as a world-religion. In the cross-fire of conflicting views and opinions, what greater certainty could there be than to follow the example of the Buddha? His words, according to changing times, may be interpreted in various ways: his living example, however, speaks an eternal language, which will be understood at all times, as long as there are human beings. The exalted figure of the Buddha and the profound symbolism of his real as well as his legendary life, in which his inner development is portrayed – and from which grew the immortal works of Buddhist art and literature – all this is of infinitely greater importance to humanity than all the philosophical systems and all the abstract classifications of the *Abhidharma*. Can there be a more profound demonstration of selflessness, of the Non-Ego Doctrine (*anātma-vāda*), of the Eightfold Path, of the Four Noble Truths, of the Law of Dependent Origination, enlightenment and liberation, than that of the Buddha's way, which comprised all the heights and depths of the universe?

'Whatever be the highest perfection of the human mind, may I realize it for the benefit of all that lives!' This is the gist of the *Bodhisattva* vow.

Just as an artist will hold before himself the greatest masters as worthy examples, irrespective of whether he will be able to reach their perfection or not, thus, whosoever wants to progress spiritually, must turn towards the highest ideal within the range of his understanding. This will urge him to ever higher achievements. For nobody can say from the beginning, where the limits of one's capacities are – in fact, it is more probable that it is the intensity of our striving that determines these limits. He who strives for the highest, will partake of the highest forces, and thereby he himself will move his

[1] *Sākya*, p. 355

limits into the infinite: he will realize the infinite in the finite, making the finite the vessel of infinity, the temporal the vehicle of the timeless.

In order to impress this universal attitude of the *Mahāyāna* upon the devotee or *Sādhaka* with the suggestive power of a concentrative symbol, the sacred syllable OṀ opens every solemn utterance, every formula of worship, every meditation.

This attitude could not have been expressed more perfectly by any other symbol as through the sacred syllable OṀ, which, as Rabindranath Tagore so beautifully said, 'is the symbolic word for the infinite, the perfect, the eternal. The sound as such is already perfect and represents the wholeness of things. All our religious contemplations begin with OṀ and end with OṀ. It is meant to fill the mind with the presentiment of eternal perfection and to free it from the world of narrow selfishness.'

And so it happened that in the moment in which Buddhism became conscious of its world-mission and entered the arena of world-religions, the sacred syllable OṀ became again the 'leitmotif' of religious life, the symbol of an all-embracing urge of liberation, in which the experience of oneness and solidarity are not the ultimate aim but the *precondition* of real liberation and perfect enlightenment. It was the symbol for an urge of liberation, which was no more anxiously concerned with one's own salvation or the union of one's own soul (*ātman*) with the soul of the universe (*brahman*), but which was based upon the understanding that all beings and things are inseparably connected and interwoven with each other, so that all discrimination of 'own' and 'other' is illusion, and that we first have to destroy this illusion by penetrating to the universal consciousness within us, before we can accomplish the work of liberation.

OṀ, therefore, is not the ultimate and the highest in the mantric system of Buddhism, as we shall see in the course of this work, but it is the fundamental, that which stands at the beginning of the *Bodhisattva* Way and therefore at the *beginning* of nearly every mantra, every formula of worship, every meditation of religious contemplation, etc., but not at the end. The Buddhist way, as we may say, begins there, where that of the *Upaniṣads* ended; and though the same symbol (OṀ) is shared by both systems, its evaluation is not the same, since this depends on the position which the symbol occupies in the particular system and in relationship to other symbols belonging to it. Therefore it would be a complete misunderstanding to interpret the use of the sacred syllable OṀ in Buddhism as a relapse into brahmanical tradition or an assimilation of or a return to the teachings of the *Upaniṣads*. This would be as great an error as the conclusion that because the term '*nirvāṇa*' is used both by Buddhists and by the followers of brahmanical systems, the meaning of this term would be the same for Buddhists and Hindus.

The revaluation of the syllable OṀ in *Mahāyāna* Buddhism can only be understood properly when viewed from the standpoint of the entire system and practice of mantras. For the present it may suffice to point out the liberating mind- and soul-opening nature of the sacred syllable. Its sound opens the innermost being of man to the vibrations of a higher reality – not a reality outside himself, but one which was for ever present within him and around him – from which he excluded himself, however, by building up arbitrary frontiers around his illusory egohood. OṀ is the means by which to destroy these artificial limitations and to become conscious of the infinity of our true nature and of our oneness with all that lives.

OṀ is the primordial sound of timeless reality, which vibrates within us from the beginningless past and which reverberates in us, if we have developed our inner sense of hearing by the perfect pacification of our mind. It is the transcendental sound of the inborn law of all things, the eternal rhythm of all that moves, a rhythm, in which law becomes the expression of perfect freedom.

Therefore it is said in the *Śūraṅgama Sūtra*: 'You have learned the Teachings by listening to the words of Lord Buddha and then committing them to memory. Why do you not learn from your own self by listening to the sound of the Intrinsic Dharma within your own Mind and then practising reflection upon it?'[1]

The sound OṀ if pronounced in the heart and from the lips of a sincere devotee in full faith (*śraddha*; Pāli: *saddha*), is like the opening of the arms to embrace all that lives. It is not an expression of self-expansion, but rather of universal acceptance, devotion and receptivity – comparable to that of a flower, that opens its petals to the light and to all who partake of its sweetness. It is a giving and taking at the same time; a taking that is free from greediness and a giving that does not try to force gifts upon others.

Thus OṀ became the symbol of the universal attitude of Buddhism in its *Mahāyāna* ideal, which knows no difference of sects, just as a *Bodhisattva*, who resolves to save all beings without distinction and who at the same time helps everyone according to his own needs, his own nature and his own way. Such an ideal distinguishes itself from a dogma, in so far as it invites and encourages the freedom of individual decision. It does not depend for its justification on historical documents, but only on its value for the present – not on logical proofs, but on its faculty to inspire and on its creative influence on the future.

[1] Translated by Bhikshu Wai-tao and Dwight Goddard in *A Buddhist Bible*, p. 258.

Part Two

MANI

THE PATH OF UNIFICATION AND OF INNER EQUALITY

Plate 2

RATNASAMBHAVA
who embodies the Wisdom of Equality

I

'THE PHILOSOPHER'S STONE' AND 'THE ELIXIR OF LIFE'

While mantric symbols have their origin within the cultural realm of a certain language or civilization, there are other symbols of figurative and conceptual nature, the origin of which cannot be traced to any particular place, tribe, or race, and which are not bound to any particular period of human civilization or to any religion, but which are the common property of humanity. These symbols may disappear in one place – in fact, they may be buried for centuries – only to reappear at another place, and to rise resurrected in a new and more brilliant garb. They may change their names and even their meaning, according to the emphasis laid upon the one or the other of their aspects, without losing their original direction: because it is in the nature of a symbol to be as manifold as the life from which it grew, and yet to retain its character, its organic unity within the diversity of its aspects.

The most popular of these symbols are those which assume visible form, either as abstract (geometrical) figures or designs, or as objects of religious cult. But there are also invisible symbols which exist only as mental pictures, i.e., as ideas.

'The Philosopher's Stone' is one of these invisible symbols, and perhaps one of the most interesting and mysterious, because it has given rise to many visible symbols, great thoughts and discoveries in the realms of philosophy and science. The eternal vision behind it, is that of the *prima materia*, the original substance, the ultimate principle of the world. According to this idea, all existing elements or phenomena are only variations of the same force or substance, which can be restored to its purity by reducing and dissolving the manifold qualities which have imposed themselves upon it through differentiation and subsequent specialization. Therefore, he who succeeds in penetrating to the purity of its undifferentiated primordial form, has gained the key to the secret of all creative power, which is based on the mutability of all elements and phenomena.

This idea, which only yesterday was ridiculed by Western science as a phantasmagoria of mediaeval thought, has today again become an acceptable theory, borne out by recent discoveries in the realm of nuclear physics. The repercussions of these discoveries already make themselves felt in all branches of modern thought and have led to a new conception of the universe.

From the beginning of human thought, the investigation into the nature of the world started from two opposite ends; one was the exploration of matter, the other the exploration of the human soul. Apparently these were two absolutely different things; but they were not so different as they may sound to us. It was not man alone who was thought of as being gifted with soul forces, but matter as well (not to speak of plants and animals). The belief in 'psychic' influences of precious and semi-precious stones and metals survives to the present day.

It was therefore of secondary importance whether those forces were pursued within the psychic realm of men or within the elements of nature, of which man, after all, was only a part. In both cases the result would be the same and would affect both sides. He who succeeded in discovering the *prima materia* would have therewith not only solved the mystery of nature and obtained power over the elements, but also found the *elixir of life*. Because, having reduced matter to its origin, he could then produce whatever he desired through the modification or addition of certain qualities.

While the Greek, and later on the Arab and mediaeval alchemists of Europe (to whom this science was transmitted by the Arabs), based their theory of the transmutation of metals and other elements on this idea and tried to prove it experimentally, there was a group of mystics in India who applied this principle to their own spiritual development and declared that he who could penetrate to the origin and ultimate principle of unity within himself, would not only transform the elements of the external world, but those of his own being. And in doing this, he would obtain that miraculous power which in the Buddhist Scriptures has been called *siddhi* (Pāli: *iddhi*; Tibetan: *grub-pa*), a power that is equally effective in the spiritual as in the material world. It is said, therefore, that highly advanced Yogins test their attainments by exercising their powers of transmutation on material elements.

Tibetan tradition has preserved for us the life-stories, legends and teachings of a great number of mystics, who had obtained those miraculous powers and who were therefore called '*Siddhas*' (Tibetan: *grub-thob*, pronounced 'dub-t'hob'). Their literary works and the records of their lives were so thoroughly destroyed when the Mohammedans invaded India, that only few traces of their activities have been preserved in Indian literature. In Tibet, on the other hand, they are well known as the 'Eighty-four Siddhas'. Their works, however, as well as their biographies, are written in a kind of symbolical language, which was known in India as *Sandhyābhāṣā*. This Sanskrit term means literally 'twilight language' and indicates that its words bear a double meaning, in accordance with whether they are understood in their ordinary or in their mystic sense.

This symbolic language is not only a protection against the profanation of the sacred through intellectual curiosity and misuse of yogic methods and psychic forces by the ignorant or uninitiated, but has its origin mainly in the fact that everyday language is incapable of expressing the highest experiences of the spirit. The indescribable that can only be understood by the initiate or the experiencer, can only be hinted at through similies and paradoxes.

A similar attitude is to be found in Chinese *Ch'an* or Japanese *Zen* Buddhism, whose spiritual and historical connexions with the *Siddhas* have been pointed out by me in previous publications. Both these movements make use of paradoxes and abound in descriptions of grotesque situations in order to prevent the one-sidedness of purely intellectual explanations to which even the most subtle parables and legends are exposed.

In the symbolic language of the *Siddhas* experiences of meditation are transformed into external events, inner attainments into visible miracles and similies into factual, quasi-historical events. If, for instance, it is said of certain *Siddhas* that they stopped the sun and the moon in their course, or that they crossed the Ganges by holding up its flow, then this has nothing to do with the heavenly bodies or the sacred river of India, but with the 'solar' and 'lunar' currents of psychic energy, and their unification and sublimation in the body of the Yogin, etc. In a similar way we have to understand the alchemistic terminology of the *Siddhas* and their search for the 'Philosopher's Stone' and the 'Elixir of Life'.

2

GURU NĀGĀRJUNA AND THE MYSTIC ALCHEMY OF THE *SIDDHAS*

GURU NĀGĀRJUNA

(Brush-drawing by the Author after an ancient Tibetan stone-engraving)

IN the centre of the stories which deal with the mystic alchemy of the *Eighty-four Siddhas*, stands the *Guru Nāgārjuna* (Tibetan: *ḥPhags-pa klu-sgrub*), who lived around the middle of the seventh century A.D. and should not be confused with the founder of the *Mādhyamika* philosophy, who bore the same name but lived 500 years earlier. It was said of him that he had changed an iron mountain into copper, and it was thought he would have transformed it into gold, if the *Bodhisattva Mañjuśrī* had not warned him that gold would only cause greed and quarrel among men, instead of helping them, as the *Siddha* had intended.

The justification of this warning, which from the Buddhist point of view had deprived the material side of alchemy of its *raison d'être*, very soon became apparent. In the course of the Guru's experiments it happened that even his iron begging-bowl turned into gold. One day, while he was taking his meal, a thief passed by the open door of his hut and, seeing the golden bowl, immediately decided to steal it. But *Nāgārjuna*, reading the mind of the thief, took the bowl and threw it out of the window. The thief was so perplexed and ashamed that he entered the Guru's hut, bowed at his feet and said:

'Venerable sir, why did you do this? I came here as a thief. Now that you have thrown away what I desired and made a gift of what I intended to steal, my desire has vanished and stealing has become senseless and superfluous.'

The Guru, however, replied: 'Whatever I possess should be shared with others. Eat and drink and take whatever you like, so that you need never more steal.'

The thief was so deeply impressed by the magnanimity and kindliness of the Guru, that he asked for his teachings. But *Nāgārjuna* knew that, though the other's mind was not yet ripe to understand his teachings, his devotion was genuine. He therefore told him: 'Imagine all things you desire as horns growing on your head (i.e., as unreal and useless').[1] If you meditate in this way, you will see a light like that of an emerald.'

With these words he poured a heap of jewels into a corner of the room, made the pupil sit down before it, and left him to his meditation.

The former thief threw himself assiduously into the practice of meditation, and as his faith was as great as his simplicity, he followed the words of the Guru literally – and lo! – horns began to grow on his head!

[1] This phrase has its origin in the well-known Sanskrit metaphor of 'the horns of a hare', which is used to indicate unreality.

At first he was elated at his success and filled with pride and satisfaction. With the passage of time, however, he discovered with horror that the horns continued to grow and finally became so cumbersome that he could not move without knocking against the walls and the things around him. The more he worried the worse it became. Thus his former pride and elation turned into dejection, and when the Guru returned after twelve years and asked the pupil how he was faring, he told the Master that he was very unhappy.

But *Nāgārjuna* laughed and said: 'Just as you have become unhappy through the mere imagination of horns upon your head, in the same way all living beings destroy their happiness by clinging to their false imaginations and thinking them to be real. All forms of life and all objects of desire are like clouds. But even birth, life and death can have no power over those whose heart is pure and free from illusions. If you can look upon all the possessions of the world as no less unreal, undesirable and cumbersome than the imagined horns on your head, then you will be free from the cycle of death and rebirth.'

Now the dust fell from the Chela's eyes, and as he saw the emptiness of all things, his desires and false imaginations vanished – and with them the horns on his head. He attained *siddhi*, the perfection of a saint, and later became known as *Guru Nāgabodhi*, successor of *Nāgārjuna*.

Another *Siddha*, whose name is associated with *Guru Nāgārjuna*, is the Brahmin *Vyāli*. Like *Nāgārjuna*, he was an ardent alchemist who tried to find the Elixir of Life (*amṛta*). He spent his entire fortune in unsuccessful experiments with all sorts of expensive chemicals, and finally became so disgusted that he threw his formula book into the Ganges and left the place of his fruitless work as a beggar.

But it happened that when he came to another city farther down the Ganges, a courtesan, who was taking a bath in the river, picked up the book and brought it to him. This revived his old passion, and he took up his work again, while the courtesan supplied him with the means of livelihood.

But his experiments were as unsuccessful as before, until one day the courtesan, while preparing his food, by chance dropped the juice of some spice into the alchemist's mixture – and lo! – what the learned Brahmin had not been able to achieve in fourteen years of hard work, had been accomplished by the hands of an ignorant low-caste woman!

The symbolical character of the story is plain. The essence of life and nature, the secret of immortality, cannot be found by dry intellectual work and selfish desire, but only by the touch of undiluted life: in the spontaneity of intuition.

The story then goes on to tell, not without humour, how the Brahmin, who spiritually was apparently not prepared for this unexpected gift of luck, fled with his treasure into solitude, because he did not like to share it with anyone, or to let others know about his secret. He settled down on the top of an inaccessible rock which rose up in the midst of a terrible swamp.

There he sat with his Elixir of Life, a prisoner of his own selfishness – not unlike Fafner, the giant of Nordic mythology, who became a dragon in order to guard the treasure, for which he had slain his brother, after they had won it from the gods!

But *Nāgārjuna*, who was filled with the ideals of *Bodhisattva*, wanted to acquire the knowledge of this precious elixir for the benefit of all who were ripe for it. Through the exertion of his magic power he succeeded in finding the hermit and in persuading him to part with the secret.

The details of this story, in which the elements of popular phantasy and humour are mixed with mystic symbolism and reminiscences of historical personalities, are of secondary importance. But it is significant that the Tibetan manuscript,[1] in which the story is preserved, mentions mercury (*dṅul-chu*) as one of the most important substances used in the experiments of the Brahmin. This proves the connexion with the ancient alchemical tradition of Egypt and Greece, which held that mercury was closely related to the *prima materia*.

3

MAṆI, THE JEWEL OF THE MIND, AS 'THE PHILOSOPHER'S STONE' AND *PRIMA MATERIA*

In the mystic language of alchemy, mercury was identified with the *prima materia*, but what was meant in this case was not the metal but 'the mercury of the philosophers', which was the essence or soul of mercury, freed from the four Aristotelian elements, earth, water, fire and air – or rather from the qualities which these represent and in which the material world appears to us.

To the Buddhist these four elements, or elementary qualities (*mahābhūta*), are well known as the solid, the liquid, the gaseous, and the radiating principle; in other words the qualities of inertia,

[1] *Grub-thob brgyad-cu-rtsa-bźiḥi rnam-thar (bstan-ḥgyur; rgyud).*

cohesion, radiation, and vibration, as the characteristics of the four states of aggregation in which the material world appears to us.

There can be no doubt about the source from which the idea and the definition of these four elements had come into Greek philosophy. And if we learn that the problem of the alchemist was how to remove from the object of his experiments the elements of earth, water, fire and air, then we cannot help being reminded of the *Kevaddha-Sutta* in the *Dīgha-Nikāya* of the Pāli-Canon, where the very same problem – namely, the dissolution of the material elements – troubles the mind of a monk who, in a state of *dhyāna* or meditative trance, travels through all the heavenly worlds without finding a solution.

Finally he comes to the Buddha and puts this strange question before him: 'Where do earth, water, fire and air come to an end? Where are these four elements completely annihilated?' And the Buddha answers: 'Not thus, O monk, is this question to be put, but: Where is it that these elements find no footing? – And the answer is: In the invisible, infinite, all-radiant consciousness (*viññāṇam anidassanam anantaṁ sabbato pabhaṁ*); there neither earth nor water, neither fire nor air can find a footing (*ettha āpo ca paṭhavi tejo vāyo na gādhati*).'

The term *anidassanam* (invisible, imperceptible) alludes to the fact that consciousness, when differentiated or objectivated, steps into visible appearance, incarnates itself, coagulates into material form, which we call our body and which in reality is the visible expression of our past consciousness, the result (*vipāka*) of previous form-creating states of consciousness.

Viññāṇam anidassanam, therefore, can only be understood as consciousness in its undivided purity, not yet or no more split into the duality of subject and object. *Buddhaghosa*, the author of the *Visuddhimagga*, declares this consciousness to be identical with *Nirvāṇa*. The term *anantaṁ* confirms this idea, because consciousness can be infinite only when it is not limited by objects, when it has overcome the dualism of ego and non-ego. The purity of this state of consciousness is also emphasized by the expression *sabbato pabhaṁ*: radiating towards all sides, penetrating everything with light (*bodhi*). In other words: this is the consciousness in the state of Enlightenment (*sambodhi*).

The Buddha alludes to the same state, when saying in *Udāna* VIII: 'Verily, there is a realm, where there is neither the solid nor the fluid, neither heat nor motion, neither this world nor any other world, neither sun nor moon. . . . There is, O monks, an Unborn, Unoriginated, Uncreated, Unformed. If there were not this Unborn, this Unoriginated, this Uncreated, this Unformed, escape from the world of the born, the originated, the created, the formed, would not be possible.'

He who has realized this, has truly found the Philosopher's Stone, the precious jewel (*maṇi*), the *prima materia* of the human mind, nay, of the very faculty of consciousness in whatever form of life it might appear. This was the real aim of all great alchemists, who knew that 'mercury' stood for the creative forces of higher consciousness, which had to be freed from the gross elements of matter in order to attain the state of perfect purity and radiance, the state of Enlightenment.

This idea is illustrated in the story of *Guru Kaṅkanapa*, one of the *Eighty-four Siddhas*. There once lived a king in the East of India who was very proud of his wealth. One day a Yogi asked him: 'What is the value of your kingship, when misery is the real ruler of the world? Birth, old age, and death revolve like a potter's wheel. Nobody knows what the next turn may bring. It may raise him to the heights of happiness or throw him into the depths of misery. Therefore do not let yourself be blinded by your present riches.'

The king said: 'In my present position I cannot serve the *Dharma* in the garb of an ascetic. But if you can give me advice, which I can follow according to my own nature and capacity, and without changing my outer life, I will accept it.'

The Yogi knew the king's fondness for jewels. So he chose the king's natural inclination as a starting-point for, and a subject of, meditation, thus – in accordance with Tantric usage – turning a weakness into a source of strength.

'Behold the diamonds of your bracelet, fix your mind upon them, and meditate thus: They are sparkling in all the colours of the rainbow; yet, these colours which gladden my heart, have no nature of their own. In the same way our imagination is inspired by multifarious forms of appearance, which have no nature of their own. *The mind alone is the radiant jewel*, from which all things borrow their temporal reality.'

And the king, while concentrating upon the bracelet of his left arm, meditated as he was told by the Yogi, until his mind attained the purity and radiance of a flawless jewel.

The people of his court, however, who noticed some strange change coming over him, one day peeped through a chink in the door of the royal private apartment and beheld the king surrounded by innumerable celestial beings. Now they knew that he had become a *Siddha*, and they asked for his blessings and guidance. And the king said: 'It is not the wealth that makes me a king, but what I have acquired spiritually through my own exertion. My inner happiness is my kingdom.'

GURU KAṄKANAPA

(Brush-drawing by the Author after an ancient Tibetan stone-engraving)

Since then the king was known as *Guru Kaṅkanapa.*

Already in the earliest forms of Buddhism the jewel was made the symbol of the three vessels of enlightenment, namely, the Enlightened one (*Buddha*), the Truth (*dharma*) in the realization of which enlightenment consists, and the community (*saṅgha*) of those who have entered or trodden the Path of Enlightenment. It is for this reason that the jewel is spoken of as the 'three-fold jewel' (*tri-ratna*).

He who possesses this shining jewel overcomes death and rebirth, and gains immortality and liberation. But this jewel cannot be found anywhere except in the lotus (*padma*) of one's own heart.

Here *maṇi* is indeed the Philosopher's Stone, the *cintamaṇi*, the wish-granting jewel of innumerable Buddhist legends, which in Tibet until the present day stands in the centre of folklore and religious poetry.

In later forms of Buddhism the idea of the jewel took the form of the Diamond Sceptre, the *Vajra*, and became as such the most important symbol for the transcendental qualities of Buddhism. The *Vajra* was originally an emblem of the power of *Indra*, the Indian Zeus, the god of thunder and lightning, who is often mentioned in the Pāli texts.

It is significant for the spiritual attitude of Buddhism that, without rejecting the cosmological and religious ideas of its time, it succeeded in creating a complete re-valuation of those ideas, merely by shifting the centre of spiritual gravitation.

4

MAṆI AS THE DIAMOND SCEPTRE

THUS it happened that, though *Indra* (like all the other gods) became a mere background-figure for the towering personality of the Buddha, the symbol of *Indra's* power was raised from the sphere of nature and physical forces to that of spiritual supremacy by becoming an attribute of the Enlightened One.

In this connexion the *vajra* is no more a 'thunderbolt', an expression to which many translators stubbornly cling and which would be adequate only if one were dealing with the *vajra* as the emblem of the Thunder-God. In Buddhist tradition, however, no such association persists. The *vajra* is regarded as the symbol of highest spiritual power which is irresistible and invincible. It is therefore compared to the diamond, which is capable of cutting asunder any other substance, but which itself cannot be cut by anything.

Likewise the properties of preciousness – nay, of supreme value – of changelessness, purity and clarity, were further reasons why in Buddhism the *vajra* was equated with the diamond. This is expressed in such terms as 'Diamond Throne' (*vajrāsana*), for the place on which the Buddha attained Enlightenment, 'Diamond Saw' (*vajracchedika*) for one of the most profound philosophical scriptures of the *Mahāyāna*, which ends with the words: 'This sacred exposition shall be known as *Vajracchedika-Prajñā-Pāramitā-Sūtra* – because it is hard and sharp like a diamond, cutting off all arbitrary conceptions and leading to the other shore of Enlightenment.'

Those Schools of Buddhism which placed this teaching in the centre of their religious life and thought are therefore known under the collective term '*Vajrayāna*', the 'Diamond Vehicle'. In all these terms the concept 'thunderbolt' is completely excluded, and the same is true for *pāli* names, like *Vajirañāa* (di amond-knowledge), etc.

The ideas which were associated with the term *vajra* by the Buddhists of the early *Vajrayāna* are clearly demonstrated by the Tibetan equivalent for *vajra*, i.e., '*rdo-rje*' (pronounced 'dorjay'): '*rdo*' means 'stone', '*rje*' means 'ruler', 'master', 'lord'. The *dorje*, therefore, is the king of stones, the most precious, most powerful and noble of all stones, i.e., the diamond.

As a visible symbol the *vajra* takes the shape of a sceptre (the emblem of supreme, sovereign power), and therefore it is correct to call it 'diamond sceptre'. This sceptre assumes a form corresponding to its function. Its centre is a sphere which represents the seed or germ of the universe in its undifferentiated form as '*bindu*' (dot, zero, drop, smallest unit). Its potential force is indicated in pictorial representations by a spiral issuing from the centre of the sphere.

From the undifferentiated unity of the centre grow the two opposite poles of unfoldment in form of lotus-blossoms, which represent the polarity of all conscious existence. From this originates space, i.e., our three-dimensional world, symbolized by the 'four quarters of the universe', with Mount Meru as its centre or axis. This spatial unfoldment corresponds to the spiritual differentiation of the principle of Enlightenment in form of the five transformed constituents of consciousness and their corresponding *Dhyāni-Buddhas*, in whom the consciousness of Enlightenment appears differentiated like rays of light passing through a prism.[1] Therefore we see that from each of the two lotus-blossoms issue five 'rays of power' (represented by five metal ribs or spokes), which again converge upon a point of higher unity (forming on each side a tip of the *vajra*), just as in meditation all conscious forces of the *Sādhaka* (or adept) are gathered in one

[1]More about this in the following chapters.

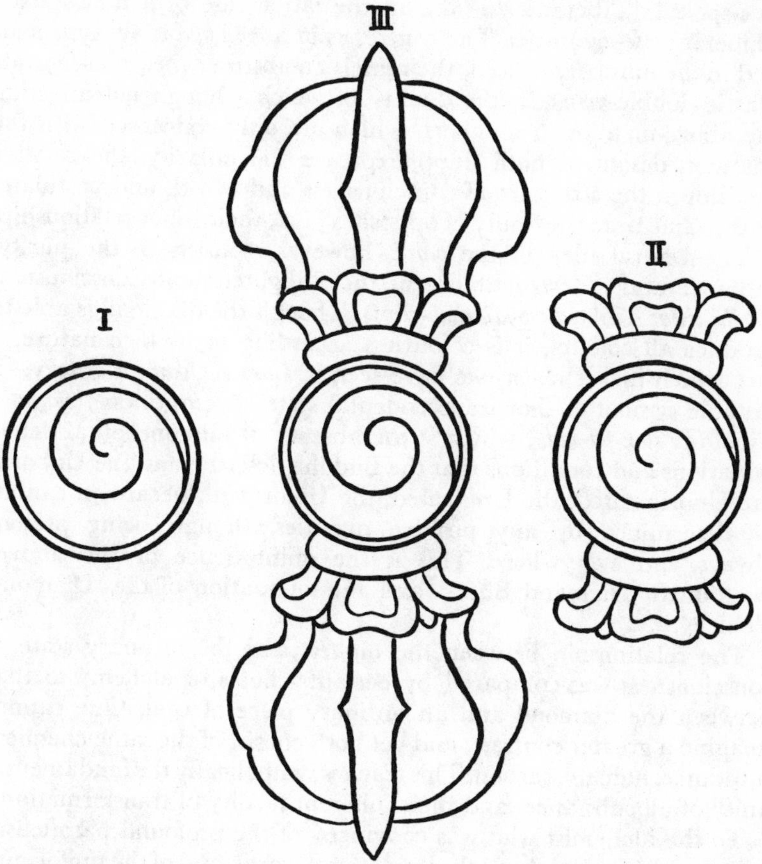

The *VAJRA* in its three stages of unfoldment

point. And in the same way as in a *maṇḍala*[1] the number of lotus petals can be raised from four to eight, by indicating the intermediate directions – thus too the rays or spokes of the *vajra*, converging upon the axis, can be raised from four to eight. In the first case one speaks of a five-spoked (Tibetan: *rtse-lṅa*), in the latter case of a nine-spoked (Tibetan: *rtse-dgu*) *vajra*. The centre, as in a *maṇḍala* is always included in the number. Indeed, the *vajra* is an abstract (i.e., non-figural) plastic double-*maṇḍala*, the duality of which (though not affecting the above-mentioned numbers, which are only concerned with the common design of both sides) expresses the polarity, the relative dualism in the structure of consciousness and world, and postulates at the same time the 'unity of opposites', i.e., their inner relationship.

The central idea of the *vajra*, however, consists in the purity, radiance and indestructibility of the Enlightenment-Consciousness (*bodhi-citta*; Tibetan: *byaṅ-chub-sems*). Though the diamond is able to produce all colours, it is colourless according to its own nature, a fact which makes it – as we have seen in *Guru Kaṅkanapa's* story – a suitable symbol of that transcendental state of 'emptiness' (*śūnyatā*; Tibetan: *stoṅ-pa-ñid*), which is the absence of all conceptual determinations and conditions that the Buddha described as 'the Unborn, the Unoriginated, the Uncreated, the Unformed', because it cannot be determined by any positive qualities, though being present always and everywhere. This is the quintessence of the above-mentioned 'Diamond Sūtra' and the foundation of the 'Diamond Vehicle'.

The relationship between the highest and the ordinary state of consciousness was compared by certain schools of alchemy to that between the diamond and an ordinary piece of coal. One cannot imagine a greater contrast, and yet both consist of the same chemical substance, namely, carbon. This teaches symbolically the fundamental unity of all substances and their inherent faculty of transformation.

To the alchemist who was convinced of the profound parallelism between the material and the immaterial world, and of the uniformity of natural and spiritual laws, this faculty of transformation had a universal meaning. It could be applied to inorganic forms of matter as well as to organic forms of life, and equally to the psychic forces that penetrate both.

Thus, this miraculous power of transformation went far beyond what the crowd imagined to be the Philosopher's Stone, which was supposed to fulfil all wishes (even stupid ones!), or the Elixir of Life, which guaranteed an unlimited prolongation of earthly life. He who

[1] A concentric diagram or plastic model, used for purposes of meditation, which will be the subject of Part III (*Padma*).

experiences this transformation has no more desires, and the prolongation of earthly life has no more importance for him who already lives in the deathless.

This is emphasized over and over again in the stories of the *Siddhas*. Whatever is gained by way of miraculous powers loses in the moment of attainment all interest for the adept, because he has grown beyond the worldly aims which made the attainment of powers desirable. In this case, as in most others, it is not the end which sanctifies the means, but the means which sanctify the end, by transforming it into a higher aim.

A robber who, in order to acquire the invincible magic sword, submitted to a strict practice of meditation, could not make use of that sword, after he had gained it, because the practice of meditation had transformed him into a saint.

And in a similar way it happened to *Guru Nāgārjuna* who, after having rescued the Elixir of Life from the selfish hermit, refused to make use of it for the prolongation of his own bodily existence, but passed it on to his disciples, while he himself sacrificed his life for the benefit of his fellow-beings when great distress had come over his country.

His main disciple, King *Salabāndha*, tried to dissuade him from his sacrifice, but the Guru answered: 'Whatever is born must die; all composed things must decay, all worldly aims are perishable. How can one enjoy them? – Go thou and fetch the Elixir of Life!' (*amṛta*). But the king answered: 'I shall only take it together with my Guru. If the Guru does not remain, how can *amṛta* help me? What value has life without spiritual guidance?' And when the Guru, who had sacrificed everything he possessed, gave away his body as his last gift, the king died at the feet of his Guru.

Thus the wise ones do not use the Elixir of Life to preserve the body beyond its time, but to attain the higher life, which does not know the fear of death. He who would utilize it only for the preservation of his physical existence, would die from within and continue to exist merely as a 'living corpse'. In selfish hands even the Elixir of Life turns into poison, just as truth in the mouth of a fool turns into falsehood and virtue into bigotry in the narrow-minded.

However, he who has found the Philosopher's Stone, the radiant jewel (*maṇi*) of the enlightened mind (*bodhi-citta*) within his own heart, transforms his mortal consciousness into that of immortality, perceives the infinite in the finite and turns *Saṁsāra* into *Nirvāṇa* – this is the teaching of the Diamond Vehicle.

5

MIND AND MATTER

In order to find the jewel (*maṇi*) – the symbol of highest value – within our own mind, we must consider more closely the nature of our consciousness, as described in the canonical texts of Buddhism. The first verse of the *Dhammapada*, the most popular verse collection of the Pāli Canon, begins with the words: 'All things are preceded by the mind, led by the mind, created by the mind', and in the less popular but all the more profound teachings of the *Abhidhamma*, the earliest attempt at a systematic representation of Buddhist philosophy and psychology, the world is viewed exclusively from the point of view of a phenomenology of consciousness.

The Buddha himself had already defined the world as that which appears as world within our consciousness – without going into the problem of objective reality. Since, however, he rejected the concept of substance, this – even when he spoke of material or physical conditions – could not be understood in the sense of an essential contrast to psychic functions, but rather in the sense of an inner and outer form of appearance of one and the same process, which was of interest to him only in so far as it fell within the realm of direct experience and was concerned with the living individual, i.e., the process of consciousness.

'Verily, I declare unto you, that within this very body, mortal though it be, and only a fathom high, but conscious and endowed with mind, is the world, and the waxing thereof, and the waning thereof, and the way that leads to the passing away thereof.' (*Aṅguttara-Nikāya II*, *Saṁyutta-Nikāya I*.)

In consequence of this psychological attitude, the Buddhist does not inquire into the essence of matter, but only into the essence of the sense-perceptions and experiences which create in us the idea of matter. 'The question regarding the essence of the so-called external phenomena is not decided beforehand; the possibility remains that the sensuous (*rūpa*) and the mental, though correlatives, cannot be dissolved into each other, but may have nevertheless the same source. In any case, the Old Scholastics also took the external world, according to the theory of *karma*, to be a constituent of personality.'[1]

In this way Buddhism escapes the dilemma of dualism, according to which mind and matter remain accidentally combined units, the

[1] Otto Rosenberg: *Die Probleme der buddhistischen Philosophie*, Heidelberg, 1924, p. 148.

relationship of which has to be specially motivated. It is for this reason that we agree with Rosenberg that the term '*rūpa*' in this connexion should not be rendered by 'matter' or the principle of materiality, but rather as 'the sensuous', which includes the concept of matter from a psychological point of view, without establishing a dualistic principle, in which matter becomes the absolute opposite of mind (*nāma*). The external, material world is actually 'the world of the senses', as Rosenberg points out, 'irrespective of whether we regard it as an object of physics or an object of psychological analysis'.

Rūpa (Tibetan: *gzugs*) literally means 'form', 'shape', without indicating whether this form is material or immaterial, concrete or imagined, apprehended by the senses (sensuous) or conceived by the mind (ideal). The expression '*rūpa-skandha*' (with which we shall deal in the next chapter) has been rendered generally as 'corporeal group', 'material aggregate', 'aggregate of bodily form', etc. – while in terms like '*rūpāvacara-citta*', 'consciousness of the realm of form', or *rūpadhyāna* (Pāli: *-jhāna*), the state of spiritual vision in meditation, *rūpa* signifies an awareness of pure, immaterial or ideal form. Worlds (*loka*) or realms (*avacara*) of existence corresponding to those ideal forms, have been called 'fine-material spheres' (*rūpāvacara*), but since they are invisible to the human eye and are only perceived clairvoyantly, they certainly do not correspond to our human concept of materiality nor to that of physics. 'The concept "*rūpa*", therefore, is much wider than the concept "matter": the so-called material things belong to the realm of the sensuous, but the sensuous is not exhausted by the quality of materiality. That, upon which matter is based, need not be necessarily material as such; matter or materiality is not necessarily something original; it can be traced back to forces or points of energy, and, as in the present case, to elements which, from the standpoint of the subject, are regarded as the sum of tactile experiences.'[1]

These elements have no substantial reality, but are ever-recurring phenomena, which appear and disappear according to certain laws of succession and co-ordination. They form a continuous stream, which partly becomes conscious in living beings in conformity with their tendencies, their development, their sense-organs, etc. Thus the doctrine of the momentariness of all phenomena does not stop short before the concept of matter. According to the *Abhidhamma* (of the Pāli Canon) seventeen thought-moments (each being shorter than a flash of lightning) form the longest process of consciousness caused

[1] "This is not contradicted by the fact that the 'great elements' (*mahābhūta*, which we mentioned previously) are sometimes conceived in a grossly materialistic sense." Rosenberg, op. cit., p. 160.

by sense-perceptions; and in accordance with this theory, seventeen thought-moments (Pāli: *cittakkhana*) are accepted as the duration of material phenomena in Buddhist philosophy. This – even as a hypothesis – is of great interest, as it connects the physical with the psychical, and asserts the fundamental unity of spiritual and material law. From this it follows that what we call matter, can only be defined as a particular kind of sense-impression or mental experience which accordingly takes its place among the elements or faculties of consciousness.[1]

The principle of materiality can be considered under two points of view: 1. as a phase in the process of perception, i.e., as the starting-point of a process of consciousness arising from a sense-impression (Pāli: *phassa*, Sanskrit: *sparśa*) or a combination of sense-impressions;

2. As the result (*vipāka*) of repeated sense-impressions of this kind and of the attachment arising from it, on account of which the individual takes bodily form.

In the first case we are dealing with the sense-impressions of hardness and softness, humidity and dryness, heat and cold, stability and movement – i.e., as resistance-impression in the consciousness of touch, as light- and colour-impression in the consciousness of sight, as sound in the consciousness of hearing, as smell in the olfactory consciousness, as taste in the 'tongue-consciousness' – while the concept of matter or of a material object arises only in the co-ordinating and interpreting mental consciousness.

We, therefore, can touch 'matter' as little as we can touch a rainbow. And just as a rainbow, though being an illusion, is by no means an hallucination, because it can be observed by all who are endowed with a sense of sight, can be recorded by cameras and is subject to certain laws and conditions; so in a similar way all inner and outer objects of our consciousness, including those which we call 'material' and which make up our apparently solid and tangible world, are real only in a relative sense (in that of an 'objective' illusion).

The same is true of our own corporeality, the psycho-physical organism (*nāma-rūpa*) of the individual. This organism, according to Buddhist conception, is so to say the coagulated, crystallized, or materialized consciousness of the past. It is the active principle (*karma*) of consciousness which as effect (*vipāka*) steps into visible appearance.

Thus, the body is a product of our consciousness, while the latter is not, or only to a very small extent, a product of the body, in so far as it transmits through its sense-organs the impressions of the

[1] Cf. Anagarika Govinda: *The Psychological Attitude of Early Buddhist Philosophy* (Abhidhamma-Tradition), Patna University, 1937; Rider, London, 1961.

outer world. The acceptance and digestion of these impressions depends on the emotional and intellectual reactions of our inner consciousness and our volitional attitude or decision depending on those reactions. It is only the latter which becomes effective as deed (*karma*) and which subsequently appears as visible and tangible effect (*vipāka*).

What appears as form does thus belong essentially to the past, and is therefore felt as alien by those who have developed spiritually beyond it (and yet not far enough to see the past in its entirety and in its universal aspect). The whole misunderstanding of the dualistic conception of mind and matter, body and soul, etc., is based upon this feeling, and precisely on this account the spiritually advanced are more susceptible to it than the average man. Because for the majority of men, whose consciousness has not yet grown beyond the past from which their visible form sprang, the body may rightly be claimed as belonging to the present. It corresponds to the existing state of mind.

However, the greater the spiritual progress and the quicker the psychic growth within one and the same span of life, the greater will be the distance between bodily form and spiritual attainment, because the body, due to its greater density, has a lesser degree of movability and therefore a longer amplitude of vibration, which cannot keep pace with that of the mind. The body adapts itself only slowly and within certain limits, which depend on the conditions of organic growth, the structural laws of matter and the nature of its primary elements.

The corporeal form may be compared to a heavy pendulum which, even after the original impulse has ceased, goes on swinging for a long time. The longer and heavier the pendulum, the slower the rate of oscillation. When the mind has already reached a state of peace and harmony by having balanced or counteracted through a change of attitude the after-effects of previous actions, the karmic effect (*vipāka*) crystallized in the bodily form can still oscillate for a long time before complete harmonization has been achieved in the form of bodily perfection. This can only be hastened by a conscious penetration, spiritualization and transfiguration of the body, as it has been reported of certain *Siddhas* and, above all, of the Buddha, whose body is said to have been of such unearthly beauty and radiance, that even the golden robes which were offered to him, lost their lustre.

One of the greatest religious thinkers of modern India described the role of the body in spiritual development in the following words: 'The obstacle which the physical presents to the spiritual is no argument for the rejection of the physical; for in the unseen providence of things our greatest difficulties are our best opportunities. Rather the perfecting of the body also should be the last triumph.'[1] 'Life has to change into a thing vast and calm and intense and powerful that can no longer recognize its old blind eager narrow self or petty impulse and desire. Even the body has to submit to a mutation and be no longer the clamorous animal or the impeding clod it now is, but become instead a conscious servant and radiant instrument and living form of the spirit.'[2]

Only from this intimate relationship of body and mind is it possible to understand the *siddhis* of bodily perfection, which have been reported again and again in the biographies of Buddhist saints – very much in contrast with the generally accepted idea of a body-reviling, ascetically-intellectual Buddhism, which has crept into the historical and philosophical representations of the *Buddha-Dharma*.

6

THE FIVE *SKANDHAS* AND THE DOCTRINE OF CONSCIOUSNESS

WHEN in Buddhism the human personality or what we call an 'individual' has been defined as a collaboration of five groups or *skandhas*, then this is but the description of the individual's active and reactive functions of consciousness in the sequence of their increasing density or 'materiality' and in proportion to their increasing subtlety, de-materialization, mobility, and spiritualization (i.e., their increasing revitalization). These *skandhas* are:

1. *Rūpa-skandha* (Tib.: *gzugs-kyi phuṅ-po*): the group of corporeality or, more correctly, the group of the sensuous, which comprises the past elements of consciousness, represented by the body; the present elements, as the sensation or idea of matter; and the future or potential sensuous elements (*dharmāḥ*) in all their forms of appearance.[3] This definition includes sense-organs, sense-objects, their mutual relationship and psychological consequences.

2. *Vedanā-skandha* (Tib.: *tshor-baḥi phuṅ-po*): the group of feelings, which comprises all reactions derived from sense-impressions as well

[1] Sri Aurobindo: *The Synthesis of Yoga*, Pondicherry, 1955, p. 10.

[2] Op. cit., p. 82.

[3] The division in past, present, and future is mentioned in *Vasubandhu's 'Abhidharma-kośa-śāstra'*, i, 14 b (Cfr. Rosenberg, op. cit., p. 134).

as from emotions arising from inner causes, i.e., feelings of pleasure and pain (bodily), joy and sorrow (mental), indifference and equanimity.

3. *Saṁjñā-skandha* (Tib.: *ḥdu-śes-kyi phuṅ-po*): the group of perceptions of discriminating awareness and representation, which comprises the reflective or discursive (*savicāra*; Tib.: *rtog-bcas*) as well as the intuitive (*avicāra*; Tib.: *rtog-med*) faculty of discrimination.

4. *Saṁskāra-skandha* (Tib.: *ḥdu-byed-kyi phuṅ-po*): the group of mental formations, of form-creating forces or tendencies of will, representing the active principle of consciousness, the character of the individual; namely the karmic consequences caused by conscious volition.

5. *Vijñāna-skandha* (Tib.: *rnam-par śes-paḥi phuṅ-po*): the group of consciousness which comprises, combines, and co-ordinates all previous functions or represents the potentiality of consciousness in its pure, unqualified form.

In this group, according to the earliest canonical texts, six kinds of consciousness can be discerned, namely:

1. The consciousness of sight (literally: 'eye-consciousness');
2. The consciousness of hearing (lit.: 'ear-consciousness');
3. The consciousness of smell (lit.: 'nose-consciousness');
4. The consciousness of taste (lit.: 'tongue-consciousness');
5. The tactile consciousness (lit.: 'body-consciousness');
6. The mental consciousness (lit.: 'mind-consciousness') *mano-vijñāna* (Tib.: *yid-kyi rnam-par-śes-pa*).

While these six kinds of consciousness can be clearly defined according to their objects, this cannot be said of the five *skandhas*. These latter correspond obviously to the five phases which occur in every complete process of consciousness, namely:

1. Contact (of the senses with their objects: *sparśa*);
2. Feeling (identical with the definition given under *vedanā-skandha*);
3. Perception (identical with the definition given under *saṁjñā-skandha*);
4. Volition (*cetanā*, which creates mental formations [*saṁskāra*]);
5. Full awareness, belonging to one of the six classes of consciousness, according to the nature of the object.

As, however, the *skandhas* are functionally connected with each other, they cannot be regarded as separate 'parts', out of which an individual is 'composed', but only as different aspects of an indivisible process to which neither the quality of 'being' nor of 'non-being' can be attributed. Feeling, perception, and volition, as integral parts of consciousness are therefore similarly divided into six classes, according to their dependence on visual objects or impressions, on sounds, odours, tastes, on bodily and mental impressions.

The mutual relationship of the *skandhas* is expressed in *Majjhima-Nikāya* 43 of the Pāli Canon, where it is said: 'Whatever there is of feeling, perception, and mental formations is mutually connected, not disconnected; and it is impossible to separate the one from the other and to show up their difference. Because what one feels, that one perceives, and what one perceives, that one is conscious of.'

In the same way the different colours of a rainbow cannot be separated from it or from each other, and have no existence or reality in themselves, although they are perceived by the senses.

The problem of the reality of the external world was, however, not yet touched by this analysis, for even if all the elements of sense-perception, including the organs of the material body, are ultimately based on consciousness, then the question arises whether each individual consciousness is an independent reality and whether what we feel or perceive as outer objects, can be traced to causes outside or beyond ourselves.

This question was answered in different ways by different Schools of Buddhism. The Buddha himself merely declared the idea of a separate personal self or of an eternal unchangeable individual ego to be illusion and taught the principle of impermanence (*anityatā*) as being the nature of all phenomena and all forms of life. In *Visuddhi-magga* VIII, we find the following: 'Strictly speaking, the duration of the life of a living being is exceedingly brief, lasting only while a thought lasts. Just as a chariot-wheel in rolling rolls only at one point of the tyre and in resting rests only at one point; exactly in the same way, the life of a living being lasts only for the period of one thought. As soon as that thought has ceased the being is said to have ceased. As it has been said: "The being of a past moment of thought has lived, but does not live, nor will it live. The being of a future moment of thought will live, but has not lived, nor does it live. The being of the present moment of thought does live, but has not lived, nor will it live." '[1]

This is reminiscent of Heraclitus' famous saying: 'We do not enter the same stream twice.' It shows not only the impermanence of all things and phenomena, but indicates the *nature* of the change – the continuous streaming in one direction, the irreversibility of the movement and its dependence on certain laws. The Buddha taught that changeability is not identical with chaos or arbitrariness, but is subject to a certain order, i.e., to the law of the mutual dependence of phenomena or what is generally known as causality.

[1] *Visuddhi-Magga,* VIII; translated by H. C. Warren.

From this follows the dynamic nature of consciousness and existence, which can be compared to a river which, in spite of its continually changing elements, keeps up the direction of its movement and preserves its relative identity. The *Theravādins* called this stream in their *Abhidhamma* Commentaries '*bhavaṅga-sota*', the subconscious stream of existence or, more correctly, of becoming – in which all experiences or contents of consciousness have been stored since beginningless time, in order to reappear in active, waking consciousness whenever the conditions and mental associations call them forth.

In spite of the incessant flow and the continual change of its elements, the existence of the stream cannot be questioned. Its factual reality consists in its continuity (*santāna*) and in the steadiness and regularity of the relations prevailing within its changing components.

The observation of this continuity is what gives rise to our self-consciousness, which is described by the *Vijñānavādins* as a function of *manas*, the seventh class of consciousness, which is thus distinguished from the mere co-ordinating and integrating of sense-impressions in the 'thought-consciousness' (*mano-vijñāna*).

7

THE DOUBLE ROLE OF THE MIND (*MANAS*)

THUS the object of the seventh class of consciousness (*manas*) is not the sense-world, but that ever-flowing stream of becoming or 'depth-consciousness', which is neither limited by birth and death nor by individual forms of appearance. For, since birth and death are only the communicating doors between one life and another, the continuous stream of consciousness flowing through them does not only contain on its surface the causally conditioned states of existence, but the totality of all possible states of consciousness, the sum total of all experiences of a beginningless 'past', which is identical with a limitless 'future'. It is the emanation and manifestation of the basic universal consciousness, which the *Vijñānavādins* called the eighth or 'Store-Consciousness' (*ālaya-vijñāna*).

In the *Laṅkāvatāra-Sūtra* the sixth consciousness (*mano-vijñāna*) is defined as intellectual consciousness, which sorts out and judges the results of the five kinds of sense-consciousness, followed by attraction or repulsion and the illusion of an objective world to which one gets bound by action.

The universal consciousness, on the other hand, is compared to the ocean, on the surface of which currents, waves and whirlpools are formed, while its depth remains motionless, unperturbed, pure and clear. 'The Universal Mind (*ālaya-vijñāna*) transcends all individuation and limits. Universal Mind is thoroughly pure in its essential nature, subsisting unchanged and free from faults of impermanence, undisturbed by egoism, unruffled by distinctions, desires and aversions.'[1]

Mediating between the universal and the individual-intellectual consciousness is the spiritual consciousness (*manas*), which takes part in both sides. It represents the stabilizing element of the mind, the central point of balance, upholding the coherence of its contents by being the centre of reference. But for the same reason it is also the cause for the conception of egohood in the unenlightened individual, who mistakes this relative point of reference for the real and permanent centre of his personality. This is what the *Mahāyāna-Samparigraha-Śāstra* calls the 'defiled mind' (*kliṣṭa manas*) the nature of which consists in an uninterrupted process of ego-creating thought or egocentric discrimination – while the *Laṅkāvatāra-Sūtra* shows the positive and intuitive side of *manas*, consisting in its liberating knowledge:

'Intuitive-mind (*manas*) is one with Universal Mind (*ālaya-vijñāna*) by reason of its participation in Transcendental Intelligence (*ārya-jñāna*) and is one with the mind-system (the five senses and the intellect) by its comprehension of differentiated knowledge (according to the six classes of *vijñāna*). Intuitive-mind has no body of its own nor any marks by which it can be differentiated. Universal mind is its cause and support but it is evolved along with the notion of an ego and what belongs to it, to which it clings and upon which it reflects.'[2]

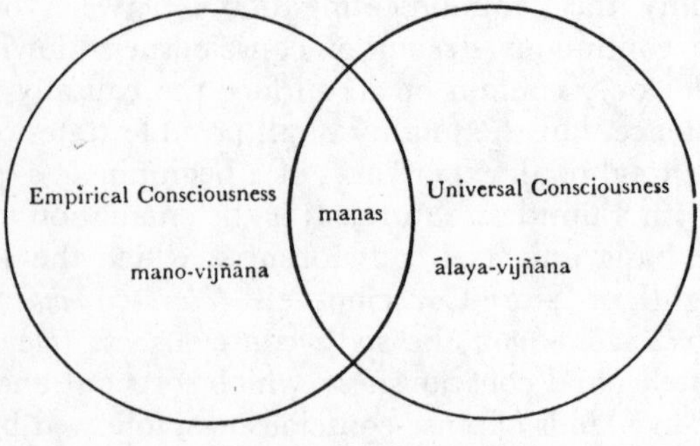

[1] Translated from the Chinese by D. T. Suzuki and D. Goddard in *A Buddhist Bible*, edited and published by Dwight Goddard, 1938; p. 306.

[2] Op. cit., p. 307.

When it is said that *manas* has no body of its own and is one with the universal as well as with the individual empirical consciousness, *manas* can only be conceived as the 'overlapping' of the universal and the individual empirical consciousness. This also explains the double character of *manas* which, though being without characteristics of its own, becomes a source of error if it is directed from the universal towards the individual or self-consciousness, while in the experience of the opposite direction, from the individual towards the universal, it becomes a source of highest knowledge (*ārya-jñāna*).

The difference in the effect of these two directions may be compared to the vision of a man, who observes the manifold forms and colours of a landscape and feels himself different from it (as 'I' and 'here') – and the vision of another one who gazes into the depth of the firmament, which frees him of all object-perception and thus from the awareness of his own self as well, because he is only conscious of the infinity of space or of 'emptiness'. His 'I' here loses its position through lack of contrast or opposition, finding neither anything to grasp nor from which to differentiate itself.

Manas is that element of our consciousness which holds the balance between the empirical-individual qualities on the one side and the universal-spiritual qualities on the other. It is that which either binds us to the world of the senses or which liberates us from it. It is the 'base metal' of the alchemists, which through magic power (*siddhi*) is turned into gold, the 'coal' that is turned into diamond, the poison that is transformed into the Elixir of Life.

The real *siddhi*, however, consists in inner conversion, in the 'turning-about in the deepest seat of consciousness', as it is called in the *Laṅkāvatāra Sūtra*. It is the re-orientation, the new attitude, the turning away from the outside world of objects to the inner world of oneness, of completeness – the all-embracing universality of the mind. It is a new vista, 'a direction of the heart' (as Rilke calls it), an entering into the stream of liberation. It is the only miracle which the Buddha recognized as such and besides which all other *siddhis* are mere playthings.

Therefore it happens again and again in the lives of the *Siddhas* that the initially desired magic power becomes worthless in the moment of its attainment; because in the meantime the much greater miracle of the inner 'turning-about' has been achieved. That by which we fall is just that by which we can rise again. This is demonstrated in all the stories of the *Siddhas*, where the Guru always transforms the weakness of the disciple into a source of strength.

Manas is the principle through which the universal consciousness experiences itself and through which it descends into the multiplicity of things, into the differentiation of senses and sense-objects, out of which arises the experience of the material world. What we call the process of becoming, is therefore, as the Pythagoreans put it, 'the progressive limitation of the unlimited'. Liberation, consequently, consists in the reversal of this process, namely, in the progressive annihilation of limitations.

In the *Aggañña-Suttanta* of the *Dīgha-Nikāya* the gradual process of self-limitation of our boundless, radiating consciousness has been described in the form of a profound myth, which almost appears like an anticipation of the *Vijñānavāda* teachings, and which shows, like the above-mentioned passage ('*viññānam anidassanam* . . .'), that the ideas of the *Vijñānavādins* already had their roots in the early Pāli Buddhism and represent a logical development of thoughts, which were already present but not yet clearly defined.

'In the past,' says the *Aggañña-Sutta*, 'we were mind-created spiritual beings, nourished by joy. We soared through space, self-luminous and in imperishable beauty. We thus remained for long periods of time. After the passage of infinite times the sweet-tasting earth rose from the waters. It had colour, scent, and taste. We began to form it into lumps and to eat it. But while we ate from it our luminosity disappeared. And when it had disappeared, sun and moon, stars and constellations, day and night, weeks and months, seasons and years, made their appearance. We enjoyed the sweet-tasting earth, relished it, were nourished by it; and thus we lived for a long time.' But with the coarsening of the food the bodies of beings became more and more material and differentiated, and hereupon the division of sexes came into existence, together with sensuality and attachment. 'But when evil, immoral customs arose among us, the sweet-tasting earth disappeared, and when it had lost its pleasant taste, outcroppings appeared on the ground, endowed with scent, colour, and taste.' Due to evil practices and further coarsening of the nature of living beings, even these nourishing outcroppings disappeared, and other self-originated plants deteriorated to such an extent that finally nothing eatable grew by itself and food had to be produced by strenuous work. Thus the earth was divided into fields, and boundaries were made, whereby the idea of 'I' and 'mine', 'own' and 'other' was created, and with it possessions, envy, greed and enslavement to material things.

8

THE 'TURNING-ABOUT IN THE DEEPEST SEAT OF CONSCIOUSNESS'

WHILE *manas* reflects the empirical consciousness of this materialized world, it is felt as the actor and experiencer of this world, as the 'I' or self-consciousness. But in the moment in which *manas* turns away from sense-consciousness and from the intellect and directs its attention upon the primordial cause of its being, upon the universal source of all consciousness, the illusion of the ego-concept becomes apparent and the experience of *śūnyatā* reveals itself in all its depth and magnitude.

This revelation does not come about through discursive thought, intellectual analysis, or logical conclusions, but through the complete coming to rest and relinquishing of all thought-activities, whereby we create the necessary conditions under which a direct vision of reality can arise, namely the intuitive experience of the infinity and the all-embracing oneness of all that is: of all consciousness, of all life, or however we may call it. For here end all names and definitions of our three-dimensional conceptual world. Here we become aware of an infinite succession of higher dimensions (in which those we know are contained), for which we have not yet found adequate means of expression, though we may sense the existence of those dimensions and feel them with the yet undeveloped organs of our intuitive consciousness, into which *manas* is transformed, if it turns away from the activities of the outer senses and the discriminations of the intellect.

These organs can only be developed through meditation, through pacification of our thought-activities (our incessant inner soliloquy and reasoning) and the reversal of the direction of our inner vision from the manifold to the unified, from the limited to the unlimited, from the intellectual to the intuitive (in which case the intuitive may be active on all levels, from the sensuous to the highest spiritual experience), from the individual to the universal, from the 'I' to the 'non-I', from the finiteness of objects to the infinity of space – until we are so pervaded by this boundlessness and universality, that when we return to the contemplation of the small, the single, the individual, we shall never lose the meaning of and the connexion with the whole and shall not fall back into the error of egohood.

Meditation, through which we try to free ourselves from the

empirical world by analytical methods of contemplation and intellectual dissection, gets us more and more involved in it, because instead of reversing the direction of our mind, we concentrate our whole attention upon the phenomena of this world, thus strengthening our own illusory conceptions of it. The dissection of empirical phenomena does not free us from their fundamental claim of representing reality, but only succeeds in depriving them of their meaning, their essential relationships, without gaining thereby any positive insight into the ultimate nature of all phenomena.

By dissecting the body into its constituent parts or by mentally creating a system of artificial divisions (into members, organs, and various substances) with complete disregard of their organic unity and the arbitrary negation of the spiritual forces which create, form and sustain them – by such utterly untruthful, self-deceptive methods we do not overcome the body of its functions; we merely reduce it to the status of gross matter and ourselves to a state of inanity by getting further enmeshed in the most primitive kind of materialism.

The same happens with the dissection of our mental functions. We may succeed in isolating and objectivating certain phenomena, but that does not mean that we have freed ourselves from them; we have only deprived them of their spontaneity and their meaning within the greater frame of conscious development – while in fact we are exercising and strengthening those very functions of our intellect which we hoped to overcome.

According to the *Laṅkāvatāra-Sūtra* it is just this 'objective' occupation with the phenomena of the world, this rationalization and intellectual analysis which leads us deeper into *saṁsāric* illusion. For, the more we try to fight against this world with its own weapons, the more seriously we believe in the reality of worldly phenomena and methods and thus become their slaves. Therefore it is said in the *Laṅkāvatāra-Sūtra*: 'It is because of the activities of the discriminating-mind that error rises, an objective world evolves and the notion of an ego-soul becomes established.'[1]

This discriminating consciousness is *mano-vijñāna*, the intellect, which conceives *manas* as the ego, because it is the apparently constant centre of reference, in which the previous moment of consciousness is reflected. This follows from the *Laṅkāvatāra-Sūtra*, where it is said that *manas*, like *ālaya-vijñāna* or universal consciousness, cannot be the source of error.

In other words, though *manas* contributes to the arising of the ego-concept, since it has the function of self-consciousness (by keeping up the connexion between past and present moments of consciousness

[1] *A Buddhist Bible*, p. 307.

and thus creating a sense of stability), it cannot be called the cause or the actual source of error, but merely a contributing factor or condition – just as a mirror which, by reflecting objects, may lead to the error that the reflections are the actual objects. But this error does not lie in the mirror, but in the mind of the observer. In a similar way the error is not committed by *manas* but by the intellect, which therefore is also called *kliṣṭa-mano-vijñāna*, 'afflicted' (namely, by error) 'intellectual consciousness'.

The double-nature of *manas* which, as we have seen, participates in the empirical-intellectual as well as in the universal (intuitive) consciousness, is the reason why *manas* and *mano-vijñāna* are often mixed up or treated as synonyms[1] and that even in the non-buddhistic Sanskrit literature a higher and lower aspect of *manas* is discerned, depending on whether *manas* is turned towards the empirical world or not.

Therefore it is said in the *Mahāyāna-Śraddhotpāda-Śāstra*: 'The mind (*manas*) has two doors from which issue its activities. One leads to a realization of the mind's Pure Essence[2], the other leads to the differentiations of appearing and disappearing, of life and death. What, however, is meant by the Pure Essence of Mind? It is the ultimate purity and unity, the all-embracing wholeness, the quintessence of Truth. Essence of Mind belongs neither to death nor rebirth, it is uncreated and eternal. The concepts of the conscious mind are being individualized and discriminated by false imaginations. If the mind could be kept free from discriminative thinking there would be no more arbitrary thoughts to give rise to appearances of form, existences and conditions.'

But in order that these hints might not become a hunting-ground for speculating philosophers and hair-splitting commentators, there follows the warning that no words, with which we may try to describe the nature of the mind, can be adequate, 'for in Mind-essence there is nothing to be grasped nor named. But we use words to get free from words until we reach the pure wordless Essence.'[3]

According to the *Laṅkāvatāra-Sūtra* the arbitrarily discriminating intellect can only be overcome if a complete 'turning-about' has taken place in the deepest seat of consciousness. The habit of looking outwards, i.e., towards external objects, must be given up and a new spiritual attitude established of realizing truth or ultimate reality within the intuitive consciousness, by becoming one with reality. So long as this intuitive self-realization of highest knowledge and wisdom

[1] In Tibetan both are rendered with '*yid*', respectively with *yid* and *yid-kyi-rnam-par-śes-pa.*
[2] *ālaya-vijñāna*
[3] Op. cit., p. 362–3.

has not been attained, the process of progressive self-limitation of the empirical consciousness will continue.

This does not mean an annihilation of sense-activities or a suppression of sense-consciousness, but a new attitude towards them, consisting in the removal of arbitrary discriminations, attachments and prejudices, in other words, in the elimination of karmic formations which fetter us to this world – or, more correctly, which create the illusion of *saṁsāra*: the world of birth and death.

'Discrimination' means here the biased judgement of things from the standpoint of an ego, in contrast to an attitude which is able to view those things in a bigger context, namely from the point of view of that fundamental oneness or wholeness, which is at the bottom of all consciousness and its objects. For only through the experience or the knowledge that we are not only parts of a whole, but that each individual has the whole as its basis, being a conscious expression of the whole – only through this experience are we awakened into reality, into a state of utter freedom. The unenlightened individual is like a dreamer who gets deeper and deeper enmeshed in the net of his self-created illusions.

9

TRANSFORMATION AND THE REALIZATION OF COMPLETENESS

THE experience of infinity which is expressed in the sacred syllable OṀ, and which forms the basis and starting-point of the Great Vehicle, is thus deepened and counterbalanced by the experience of the inner unity and solidarity of all life and consciousness. This unity, which is not brought about by an arbitrary identification of one's own consciousness with that of other living beings (i.e., not from the outside), but which results from the profound knowledge that the conception of 'self' and 'not-self', 'I' and 'not-I', 'own' and 'other', rests on the illusion of our surface consciousness, and that the knowledge and the experience of the equality (*samatā*) of beings consists in the realization of that ultimate completeness which is latent in every being.

The Buddhist, therefore, does not endeavour to 'dissolve his being in the infinite', to fuse his finite consciousness with the consciousness of the all, or to unite his soul with the all-soul; his aim is to become *conscious* of his ever-existing, indivisible and undivided completeness. To this completeness nothing can be added, and from it nothing can be taken away. It may only be experienced or recognized in a more or less perfect way. The differences in the development of beings are due to the greater or lesser degree of this knowledge or experience. The Perfectly Enlightened Ones are those who have been awakened to the perfect consciousness of completeness. Therefore all the Buddhas possess the same qualities, though they may give more prominence to the one or the other quality of their nature according to the requirements of time and circumstances.

Maṇi has been interpreted poetically as the 'dew-drop in the lotus', and Edwin Arnold's 'Light of Asia' ends with the words: 'The dew-drop slips into the shining sea.' If this beautiful simile is reversed, it would probably come nearer to the Buddhist conception of ultimate realization: it is not the drop that slips into the sea, but the sea that slips into the drop! The universe becomes conscious in the individual (but not vice versa), and it is in this process that completeness is achieved, in regard to which we neither can speak any more of 'individual' nor of 'universe'. Here, in a certain way, we may say that we go beyond the OṀ, the highest aim of Vedic endeavour, based on the notion that there does not exist a point of contact between the finite and the infinite. The one has to be left for the sake of the other, just as the arrow has to leave the bow in order to become one with the transcendental aim, after having penetrated the abysmal space which yawns between the 'here' and the 'there'.

The *Yogācārins*, however, who tried to put into practice the teachings of the *Vijñānavāda* – and among them especially the Masters of the Mystic Path, the *Siddhas* – endeavoured to build a bridge between the 'here' and the 'there', thus not only spanning the abyss, but investing our earthly life with the aura of the supreme goal towards which this life was directed and thereby making it into an inspired tool of liberation.

'Selfhood' and 'universe' are only the 'inside' and 'outside' of the same illusion. The realization of completeness, however, has all the characteristics of universality, without presuming an external cosmos, and has likewise all the characteristics of individual experience without presuming an ego-entity. The idea of the realization of completeness escapes the dualistic concepts of unity and plurality, of 'I' and 'not-I', or whatever we may call the pairs of opposites, as long as we move on the plane of our empirical consciousness. It is an idea which is applicable to all planes of experience and existence, from the material to the highest spiritual, from the empirically given to the metaphysically sensed. The way of completeness is not one of suppression and annihilation, but the way of development and sublimation of all our faculties: a way which avoids premature judgement and which examines the *fruits*.

A modern Master of the Mystic Path in the West has put this idea into immortal words: 'Transiency hurls itself everywhere into a deep state of being. And therefore all forms of this our world are not only to be used in a time-bound (time-limited) sense, but should be included in those phenomena of superior significance in which we participate (or of which we are a part). However, it is not in the Christian sense, but in the purely earthly, profoundly earthly, joyfully earthly consciousness, that we should introduce, what we have seen and touched *here*, into the widest circumference. Not into a "beyond" whose shadow darkens the earth, but into the whole, into the universe. Nature, the things of our daily contact and use, all these are preliminaries and transiencies: however, they are, as long as we are here, our possessions, our friendships, participants of our pain and pleasure, in the same way as they were the trusted friends of our ancestors. Therefore we should not only refrain from vilifying and depreciating all that belongs to this our world, but on the contrary, on account of its very preliminary nature which it shares with us, these phenomena and things should be understood and transformed by us in the innermost sense. – Transformed? – Yes, because it is our task to impress upon ourselves this preliminary, transient earth in so deep, so painful, so passionate a manner, that its essential nature is "invisibly" resurrected within us. *Within* us alone can this intimate and constant transformation of the visible into the invisible take place. . . .' (R. M. Rilke: *Letters from Muzot*, p. 371 f.)

Completeness can only be established *within* ourselves through a thorough transformation of our personality or, as expressed in Buddhist terminology, through a transformation of the *skandhas*, i.e., through a change or reversal (*parāvṛtti*) of the very foundations (*āśraya*) of our existence into a state of universality by dematerializing the hard crust of our individual selfhood. This comes about through the awakening of our faculties of enlightenment, the inner urge towards light and freedom, latent in every living being. Just as in a plant the urge towards sun and air compels the germ to break through the darkness of the earth, so the germ of Enlightenment (*bodhi-citta*) breaks through the twofold veil: the obscuration caused by passion (*kleśāvaraṇa*) and by the illusion of an objective world (*jñeyāvaraṇa*).

The path of Enlightenment is the path towards completeness, and the fact that we can tread this path – as the Buddha and innumerable of his followers have demonstrated through their example – proves that potentially every being possesses the faculty of converting the transient elements of his empirical personality into the organs of a higher reality, in which 'neither earth nor water, neither fire nor air can find a foothold'. It is the path of the great transformation, which has been described in the mystic alchemy of the *Siddhas* as the transmutation of base metals, i.e., substances exposed to decay and dissolution, into the pure uncorruptible gold of the *prima materia*, into the imperishable jewel (*maṇi*) of the adamantine mind.

How does this transformation come about? It is *manas*, as we saw, which holds the balance between the limited and the unlimited, between becoming and dissolving, between the finite and the infinite. And for this reason it is *manas* from which the transformation of the human personality (*āśraya-parāvṛtti*) proceeds by changing from the role of self-consciousness, the *principium individuationis* and cause of all differentiation, into the principle of the essential oneness of life, the cause of the experience of the inner equality (*samatā*) of all living beings.

Thus it happens that *manas* in the moment of the inner reversal or 'conversion', becomes the jewel, the consciousness of Enlightenment (*bodhi-citta*), the Philosopher's Stone, whose touch converts all the elements of consciousness into means or tools of Englightenment (*bodhyaṅga*). Then selfish volition and sensual desire (*kāma-chanda*; a synonym for *tṛṣṇa*, the thirst for life) turn into the will for liberation, the striving after realization (*dharma-chanda*); similarly individual consciousness (*vijñāna-skandha*) turns into the knowledge of the universal law and ultimate reality (*dharma-dhātu-jñāna*)[1] represented by the *Dhyāni-Buddha*[2] *Vairocana*, 'The Radiating One', and symbolized by his emblem, the Wheel of the Law (*dharma-cakra*).

Then our vision will be turned back from the world of sense-objects to the source, the Store Consciousness (*ālaya-vijñāna*), in which the primordial forms, the archetypes, the seeds or germs (*bīja*) of all things are stored. Then the waves on the surface of this ocean-like universal consciousness, which contains the treasures of all that has been and can be experienced, will be smoothed and converted into a shining mirror, 'in which the images of all forms (*rūpa*)' are reflected undistorted, in pristine purity. The 'sensuous', appearing as 'material'

[1] Tib.: *chos-kyi-dbyiṅs-kyi ye-śes*.

[2] The term *Dhyāni-Buddha* was coined by Western scholars in order to distinguish the spiritual or symbolical figures of Buddhas and Bodhisattvas, visualized in meditation (*dhyāna*) from the historical Buddha and his predecessors or successors on earth. In Tibet the historical Buddha is always referred to as *śākyamuni* (*bcom-ldan-ḥdas śākya-thub-pa*).

form (*rūpa-skandha*), thus becomes the exponent of the transcendental, of that which goes beyond the senses. It becomes the starting-point of the experience of *śūnyatā*, the formless which is the basis of all form: just as a sound may lead to the awareness of stillness, while fading into silence. Therefore it is said in the *Mahā-Prajñāpāramitā-Hṛdaya*:

'Form (*rūpa*) is emptiness (*śūnyatā*), and emptiness is not different from form, nor is form different from emptiness: indeed, emptiness is form.'

The manifold forms of existence, of becoming and dissolving, of spiritual inhalation and exhalation, become here symbols of a reality which goes beyond all form, but which at the same time becomes conscious through form: just as hieroglyphic pictures reveal to the knowing one a meaning which goes beyond that of the concrete objects depicted in them.

Thus, according to the *Vijñapti-mātra-siddhi-śāstra*[1] the *ālaya*- consciousness is transformed into the consciousness connected with the Knowledge of the Great Mirror (*mahādarśa-jñāna-samprayukta-citta-varga*), which in Tibetan is called the Mirror-like Wisdom (*me-loṅ lta-buḥi ye-śes*) and is represented in the *Dhyāni-Buddha Akṣobhya*, who is the embodiment of the immutability of this wisdom. With him are associated the element water (the *ālaya*-consciousness as ocean in a state of tranquillity with mirror-like surface), *rūpa-skandha*, and as emblem the *vajra*.

Feeling (*vedanā*), which is self-centred, as long as *manas* plays the role of self-consciousness and produces the illusion of the separateness and difference of beings, now turns into the feeling for others, into the inner participation and identification with all that lives: into the consciousness connected with the Knowledge of Equality (*samatā-jñāna-samprayukta-citta-varga*), the Equalizing Wisdom of the essential identity of all beings,[2] embodied in the figure of the *Dhyāni-Buddha Ratnasambhava*, who is represented in the gesture of giving (*dāna-mudrā*) and with the emblem of the jewel (*ratna*=*maṇi*). For nowhere is the inner unity of all beings felt more deeply than in the emotions of love (*maitrī*) and sympathy, in the sharing of others' sorrows and joys (*karuṇā-muditā*), out of which grows the urge to give, not only one's possessions but oneself.

The empirical thought-consciousness (*mano-vijñāna*), the discriminating, judging intellect, turns into the intuitive consciousness of inner vision, in which 'the special and general characteristics of all

[1] Cr. Jiryo Masuda: *Der individualistische Idealismus der Yogācāra-Schule*, Heidelberg, 1926; and Louis de La Vallée Poussin: *Vijñaptimātrasiddhi*, Paris, 1928.

[2] Tib.: *mñam-pa-ñid-kyi ye-śes*.

things (*dharmas*) becomes clearly visible, spontaneously (lit.: "without hindrance": *asaṅga*)', and in which 'the unfoldment of various spiritual faculties takes place'. It is called 'the consciousness connected with Retrospective Knowledge' (*pratyavekṣaṇa-jñāna-samprayukta-citta-varga*) or as the Distinguishing Wisdom.[1] Through this wisdom the functions of *saṁjñā-skandha*, the group of discriminating processes, which we sum up under the general term of perception, are turned inwards and become transformed and intensified into intuitive vision (*dhyāna*), in which the individual characteristics of all phenomena and their general and universal relations become apparent.

The embodiment of this Distinguishing Wisdom of inner vision is the *Dhyāni-Buddha Amitābha*, who is represented in the gesture of meditation (*dhyāna-mudrā*) and whose emblem is the fully opened lotus-blossom (*padma*).

The remaining five classes of consciousness, which can be summed up into one category namely, as sense-consciousness, become the means or tools of the *Bodhisattva* life, a life dedicated to the realization of Enlightenment, in which actions and motives are no more egocentric, and therefore selfless in the truest sense (which, in a way, is more than 'altruistic', a term based on the distinction of 'self' and 'other', and quite different in motive from the idea of Christian charity or modern social service). They are not binding or karma-creating, but liberating for the doer as well as for those who are influenced by his actions.

The functions which are characterized by the group of mental formations (*saṁskāra-skandha*) are thus transformed into 'the consciousness connected with the Knowledge of the Accomplishment of that which ought to be done' (*kṛtyānuṣṭhāna-jñāna-samprayukta-citta-varga*). 'This kind of consciousness manifests itself for the benefit of all living beings in the ten regions (of the universe) in the three kinds of transformed actions and accomplishes the deeds that ought to be done according to the vow.' (*Vijñaptimātra-siddhi-śāstra.*)

The vow, which is mentioned here, is the *Bodhisattva* vow to work for the benefit of all beings; in other words, not only to be concerned with one's own salvation but with that of all beings, by realizing Perfect Enlightenment (*samyak-saṁbodhi*). The three kinds of transformed actions are those of body, speech, and mind. Here 'body' is the universal body (*dharma-kāya*) that includes all beings, 'speech' the word of power, the sacred word (*mantra*), and 'mind' the universal consciousness, the consciousness of Enlightenment. They act or manifest themselves everywhere 'in the ten directions' of space, namely, in the four cardinal and the four intermediate directions, the zenith

[1] Tib.: *so-sor-rtogs-paḥi ye-śes.*

and the nadir – symbolized by the double-*vajra* (*viśva-vajra*), the emblem of the *Dhyāni-Buddha Amoghasiddhi*, the embodiment of the 'All-accomplishing Wisdom'.[1]

The unfoldment of these transcendental wisdoms in the transformed consciousness of spiritual vision, is the subject of the next main part, which deals with PADMA, the third symbol of the Great Mantra.

[1] Tib.: *bya-ba-grub-paḥi ye-ses*, lit. 'work-accomplishing wisdom'.

Part Three

པ་དྨ

PADMA

THE PATH OF CREATIVE VISION

Plate 3

AMITĀBHA
who embodies the Wisdom of Discriminating Vision

I

THE LOTUS AS SYMBOL OF SPIRITUAL UNFOLDMENT

THE lotus is the symbol of spiritual unfoldment, of the holy, the pure.

The Buddha-legend reports that when the newly born infant *Siddhārtha*, who later became the Buddha, touched the ground and made his first seven steps, seven lotus-blossoms grew up from the earth. Thus each step of the Bodhisattva is an act of spiritual unfoldment. Meditating Buddhas are represented as sitting on lotus-flowers, and the unfoldment of spiritual vision in meditation (*dhyāna*) is symbolized by fully-opened lotus-blossoms, whose centre and whose petals carry the images, attributes or mantras of various Buddhas and Bodhisattvas, according to their relative position and mutual relationship.

In the same way the centres of consciousness in the human body (which we shall discuss later on) are represented as lotus-flowers, whose colours correspond to their individual character, while the number of their petals corresponds to their functions.

The original meaning of this symbolism may be seen from the following simile: Just as the lotus grows up from the darkness of the mud to the surface of the water, opening its blossom only after it has raised itself beyond the surface, and remaining unsullied from both earth and water, which nourished it – in the same way the mind, born in the human body, unfolds its true qualities ('petals') after it has raised itself beyond the turbid floods of passions and ignorance, and transforms the dark powers of the depths into the radiantly pure nectar of Enlightenment-consciousness (*bodhi-citta*), the incomparable jewel (*maṇi*) in the lotus-blossom (*padma*). Thus the saint grows beyond this world and surpasses it. Though his roots are in the dark depths of this world, his head is raised into the fullness of light. He is the living synthesis of the deepest and the highest, of darkness and light, the material and the immaterial, the limitations of individuality and the boundlessness of universality, the formed and the formless, *Saṁsāra* and *Nirvāṇa*. *Nāgārjuna*, therefore, said of the perfectly Enlightened One: 'Neither being nor not-being can be attributed to the Enlightened One. The Holy One is beyond all opposites.

If the urge towards light were not dormant in the germ that is hidden deep down in the darkness of the earth, the lotus would not turn towards the light. If the urge towards a higher consciousness and knowledge were not dormant even in a state of deepest ignorance, nay, even in a state of complete unconsciousness, Enlightened Ones could never arise from the darkness of *saṁsāra.*

The germ of Enlightenment is ever present in the world, and just as (according to all Schools of Buddhism) Buddhas arose in past world-cycles, so Enlightened Ones arise in our present world-cycle and will arise in future world-cycles, whenever there are adequate conditions for organic and conscious life.

The historical Buddha is therefore looked upon as a link in the infinite chain of Enlightened Ones and not as a solitary and exceptional phenomenon. The historical features of *Buddha Gautama* (*Śākyamuni*), therefore, recede behind the general characteristics of Buddhahood, in which is manifested the eternal or ever-present reality of the potential Enlightenment-consciousness of the human mind, in fact, of all conscious life – which includes in its deepest aspect every single individual.

Superficial observers try to point out the paradox that the Buddha, who wanted to free humanity from the dependence on gods or from the belief in an arbitrary God-Creator, became deified himself in later forms of Buddhism. They do not understand that the Buddha, who is worshipped, is not the historical personality of the man *Siddhārtha Gautama*, but the embodiment of the divine qualities, which are latent in every human being and which became apparent in *Gautama* as in innumerable Buddhas before him. Let us not misunderstand the term 'divine'. Even the Buddha of the *Pāli* texts did not refrain from calling the practice of the highest spiritual qualities (like love, compassion, sympathetic joy, equanimity) in meditation a 'dwelling in God' (*brahmavihāra*), or in a 'divine state'.

It is, therefore, not the man Gautama, who was raised to the status of a god, but the 'divine' which was recognized as a possibility of human realization. Thereby the divine did not become less in value, but more; because from a mere abstraction it became a living reality, from something that was only believed, it became something that could be experienced. It was thus not a descending to a lower level, but an ascending, a rising from a plane of lesser to a plane of greater reality.

Therefore the Buddhas and Bodhisattvas are not merely 'personifications' of abstract principles – like those gods who are personified forces of nature or of psychic qualities which primitive man can conceive only in an anthropomorphic garb – but they are the prototypes of those states of highest knowledge, wisdom, and harmony which have been realized in humanity and will ever have to be realized again and again.

Irrespective of whether these Buddhas are conceived as successively appearing in time – as historically concrete beings (as in *Pāli*-tradition) – or as timeless images or archetypes of the human mind, which are visualized in meditation and therefore called *Dhyāni-Buddhas*: they are not allegories of transcendental perfections or of unattainable ideals, but visible symbols and experiences of spiritual completeness in human form. For wisdom can only become reality for us, if it is realized in life, if it becomes part of human existence.

The teachers of the 'Great Vehicle', especially of the *Tantric Vajrayāna*, were never tired of emphasizing this, because they recognized the danger of dwelling in mere abstractions. This danger was all the more real in a highly developed philosophy like that of the *Śūnyavādins*, with which the intricate depth-psychology of the *Yogācārins* and *Vijñānavādins* was combined.

2

THE ANTHROPOMORPHIC SYMBOLISM OF THE *TANTRAS*

THE abstractness of philosophical concepts and conclusions requires to be constantly corrected by direct experience, by the practice of meditation and the contingencies of daily life. The anthropomorphic element in the *Vajrayāna* is therefore not born from a lack of intellectual understanding (as in the case of primitive man), but, on the contrary, from the conscious desire to penetrate from a merely intellectual and theoretical attitude to the direct awareness of reality. This cannot be achieved through building up convictions, ideals, and aims based on reasoning, but only through conscious penetration of those layers of our mind which cannot be reached or influenced by logical arguments and discursive thought.

Such penetration and transformation is only possible through the compelling power of inner vision, whose primordial images or 'archetypes' are the formative principles of our mind. Like seeds they sink into the fertile soil of our subconsciousness in order to germinate, to grow and to unfold their potentialities.

One may object, that such visions are purely subjective and therefore nothing ultimate. However, words and ideas are nothing ultimate either; and the danger of getting attached to them is all the greater, as words have a limiting, narrowing tendency, while experiences and symbols of true visions are something that is alive, that is growing and ripening within us. They point and grow beyond themselves. They are too immaterial, too 'transparent', too elusive, to become solid or 'thingish', and to arouse attachment. They can neither be 'grasped' nor defined, nor circumscribed exactly. They have the tendency to grow from the formed to the formless – while that which is merely thought-out has the opposite tendency, namely, to harden into lifeless concepts and dogmas.

The subjectivity of inner vision does not diminish its reality-value. Such visions are not hallucinations, because their reality is that of the human psyche. They are symbols, in which the highest knowledge and the noblest endeavour of the human mind are embodied. Their visualization is the creative process of spiritual projection, through which inner experience is translated into visible form, comparable to the creative act of an artist, whose subjective idea, emotion, or vision, is transformed into an objective work of art, which now takes on a reality of its own, independent of its creator.

But just as an artist must gain perfect control over his means of expression and makes use of a variety of technical aids in order to achieve the most perfect expression of his idea, in the same way the spiritually creative man must be able to master the functions of his mind and use certain technical aids in order to embue his vision with the power and value of reality. His technical aids are *yantra*, *mantra*, and *mudrā*: the parallelism of the visible, the audible and the tangible (i.e., what can be felt). They are the exponents of mind (*citta*), speech (*vāk*, *vācā*), and body (*kāya*).

Here the term '*yantra*' is used in the sense of *maṇḍala* (Tib.: *dkyil-ḥkhor*), the systematic arrangement of symbols on which the process of visualization is based. It is generally built upon the shape of a four-, eight-, or sixteen-petalled lotus-blossom (*padma*) which forms the visible starting-point of meditation.

Mantra (Tib.: *gzuṅs*, *sṅags*), the word-symbol, is the sacred sound, transmitted from *guru* to *chela* (disciple) during the ritual of initiation and in the course of the spiritual training. The inner vibrations set up by this sacred sound and its associations in the consciousness of the initiate, open his mind to the experience of higher dimensions.

Mudrā (Tib.: *phyag-rgya*) is the bodily gesture (especially of the hands) which accompanies the ritual act and the mantric word, as well as the inner attitude, which is emphasized and expressed by this gesture.

Only through the co-operation of all these factors can the adept build up his spiritual creation bit by bit and realize his vision. This is not a matter of emotional ecstasy or unrestrained imagination, but a consciously directed creative process of realization, in which nothing is left to chance and in which there is no place for vague emotions and confused thinking.

'The old Buddhist idea, that actions carried out "*kāyena, vācāya uda cetasā*" [in body, speech or thought] produce transcendental effects, in so far as they are *karma*-producing expressions of the human will, gets a new meaning in the *Vajrayāna*. It corresponds to the new conviction of the immense importance of ritual acts: the co-ordination of the actions of body, speech and mind (thought) enables the *sādhaka* to insert himself into the dynamic forces of the cosmos and to make them subservient to his own purposes.' (H. von Glasenapp.)[1]

The dynamic forces of the universe, however, are not different from those of the human soul, and to recognize and transform those forces in one's own mind – not only for one's own good, but for that of all living beings – is the aim of the Buddhist Tantras.

The Buddhist does not believe in an independent or separately existing external world, into whose dynamic forces he could insert himself. The external world and his inner world are for him only the two sides of the same fabric, in which the threads of all forces and of all events, of all forms of consciousness and of their objects, are woven into an inseparable net of endless, mutually conditioned relations.

The word '*tantra*' is related to the concept of weaving and its derivatives (thread, web, fabric, etc.), hinting at the interwovenness of things and actions, the interdependence of all that exists, the continuity in the interaction of cause and effect, as well as in spiritual and traditional development, which like a thread weaves its way through the fabric of history and of individual lives. The scriptures which in Buddhism go under the name of *Tantra* (Tib.: *rgyud*) are invariably of a mystic nature, i.e., trying to establish the *inner* relationship of things: the parallelism of microcosm and macrocosm, mind and universe, ritual and reality, the world of matter and the world of the spirit.

This is the essence of Tantrism, as it developed with logical necessity from the teachings and the religious practice of *Vijñānavādins* and *Yogācārins* (the former name emphasizes more the theoretical or

[1] *Die Entstehung des Vajrayāna*, Zeitschrift der Deutschen Morgenländischen Gesellschaft, Band 90.

philosophical, the latter more the practical aspect of the same School of Mahāyāna-Buddhism). Like a gigantic wave the Tantric conception of the world swept over the whole of India, penetrating and modifying Buddhism and Hinduism alike and obliterating many of their differences.

3

KNOWLEDGE AND POWER: *PRAJÑĀ* VERSUS *ŚAKTI*

THE influence of Tantric Buddhism upon Hinduism was so profound, that up to the present day the majority of Western scholars labour under the impression that Tantrism is a hinduistic creation which was taken over by later, more or less decadent, Buddhist Schools.

Against this view speaks the great antiquity and consistent development of Tantric tendencies in Buddhism. Already the early *Mahāsāṅgikas* had a special collection of mantric formulas in their *Dhāraṇī-Piṭaka*, and the *Mañjuśrīmūlakalpa*, which according to some authorities goes back to the first century A.D., contains not only *mantras* and *dhāraṇīs*, but numerous *maṇḍalas* and *mudrās* as well. Even if the dating of the *Mañjuśrīmūlakalpa* is somewhat uncertain, it seems probable that the Buddhist Tantric system had crystallized into a definite form by the end of the third century A.D., as we can see from the well-known *Guhyasamāja* (Tib.: *dpal-gsaṅ-ḥdus-pa*) Tantra.

To declare Buddhist Tantrism as an off-shoot of Shivaism is only possible for those who have no first-hand knowledge of Tantric literature. A comparison of the Hindu Tantras with those of Buddhism (which are mostly preserved in Tibetan and which therefore have long remained unnoticed by Indologists) not only shows an astonishing divergence of methods and aims, in spite of external similarities, but proves the spiritual and historical priority and originality of the Buddhist Tantras.

Śankarācārya, the great Hindu philosopher of the ninth century A.D., whose works form the foundation of all śaivaite philosophy, made use of the ideas of *Nāgārjuna* and his followers to such an extent that orthodox Hindus suspected him of being a secret devotee of Buddhism. In a similar way the Hindu Tantras, too, took over the methods and principles of Buddhist Tantrism and adapted them to their own purposes (just as the Buddhists had adapted the age-old principles and techniques of yoga to their own systems of meditation). This view is not only held by Tibetan tradition and confirmed by a study of its literature, but has been verified also by Indian scholars after a critical investigation of the earliest Sanskrit texts of Tantric Buddhism and their historical and ideological relationship to the Hindu Tantras.

Thus Benoytosh Bhattacharyya in his *Introduction to Buddhist Esoterism* has come to the conclusion that 'it is possible to declare, without fear of contradition, that the Buddhists were the first to introduce the Tantras into their religion, and that the Hindus borrowed them from the Buddhists in later times, and that it is idle to say that later Buddhism was an outcome of Śaivaism' (p. 147).

One of the main propagators of this mistaken idea, which was built upon the superficial similarities of Hindu and Buddhist Tantras, was Austin Waddell who is often quoted as an authority on Tibetan Buddhism.[1] In his estimation Buddhist Tantrism is nothing but 'śaivaite idolatry; śakti worship and demonology'. Its 'so-called mantras and dhāraṇīs' are 'meaningless gibberish', 'its mysticism a silly mummery of unmeaning jargon and "magic circles" ', and its Yoga a 'parasite whose monster outgrowth crushed and cankered most of the little life of purely Buddhist stock yet left in the Mahāyāna (p. 14). 'The Mādhyamika doctrine was essentially a sophistic nihilism' (p. 11); 'the Kāla-cakra unworthy of being considered a philosophy' (p. 131).

As it was mainly from such 'authorities' that the West got its first information of Tibetan Buddhism, it is no wonder that up to the present day numerous prejudices against Buddhist Tantrism are firmly entrenched in the Western mind as well as in the minds of those who have approached the subject through Western literature.

To judge Buddhist Tantric teachings and symbols from the standpoint of Hindu Tantras, and especially from the principles of Śaktism is not only inadequate but thoroughly misleading, because both systems start from entirely different premisses. As little as we can declare Buddhism to be identical with Brahmanism, because both make use of Yoga methods and of similar technical and philosophical terms, as little is it permissible to interpret the Buddhist Tantras in the light of the Hindu Tantras, and vice versa.

Nobody would accuse the Buddha of corrupting his doctrine by accepting the gods of Hindu mythology as a background of his teachings or by using them as symbols of certain forces or meditative experiences or as the exponents of higher states of consciousness – but if the

[1] L. A. Waddell: *Buddhism of Tibet or Lamaism.*

Tantras follow a similar course, they are accused of being corrupters of genuine Buddhism.

It is impossible to understand any religious movement, unless we approach it in a spirit of humility and reverence, which is the hallmark of all great scholars and pioneers of learning. We therefore have to see the various forms of expression in their genetic connexions and against the spiritual background from which they developed in their particular system, before we start comparing them with similar features in other systems. In fact the very things which appear similar on the surface are very often just those in which the systems differ most fundamentally. The same step that leads upwards in one connexion may well lead downwards in another one. Therefore, philological derivations and iconographical comparisons, valuable though they may be in other respects, are not adequate here.

'The developments in Tantra made by the Buddhists, and the extraordinary plastic art they developed, did not fail to create an impression also in the minds of the Hindus, who readily incorporated many ideas, doctrines, practices and gods, originally conceived by the Buddhists for their religion. The literature, which goes by the name of the Hindu Tantras, arose almost immediately after the Buddhist ideas had established themselves' (p. 50).

At the end of his convincing historical, literary, and iconographical proofs, which substantiate what is evident to every student of Buddhist Tantras and Tibetan tradition, Bhattacharyya concludes: 'It is thus amply proved that the Buddhist Tantras greatly influenced the Hindu Tantric literature, and it is, therefore, not correct to say that Buddhism was an outcome of Saivaism. It is to be contended, on the other hand, that the Hindu Tantras were an outcome of Vajrayāna, and that they represent baser imitations of Buddhist Tantras' (p. 163).

We therefore fully agree with Bhattacharyya when he says: 'The Buddhist Tantras in outward appearance resemble the Hindu Tantras to a marked degree, but in reality there is very little similarity between them, either in subject matter or in philosophical doctrines inculcated in them, or in religious principles. This is not to be wondered at, since the aims and objects of the Buddhists are widely different from those of the Hindus' (op. cit., p. 47).

The main difference is, that Buddhist Tantrism is not Śaktism. The concept of *Śakti*, of divine *power*, of the creative female aspect of the highest God (*Śiva*) or his emanations does not play any role in Buddhism. While in the Hindu Tantras the concept of power (*śakti*) forms the focus of interest, the central idea of Tantric Buddhism is *prajñā*: knowledge, wisdom.

To the Buddhist *śakti* is *māyā*, the very power that creates illusion, from which only *prajñā* can liberate us. It is therefore not the aim of the Buddhist to acquire power, or to join himself to the powers of the universe, either to become their instrument or to become their master, but, on the contrary, he tries to free himself from those powers, which since aeons kept him a prisoner of *saṁsāra*. He strives to perceive those powers which have kept him going in the rounds of life and death, in order to liberate himself from their dominion. However, he does not try to negate them or to destroy them, but to transform them in the fire of knowledge, so that they may become forces of Enlightenment which, instead of creating further differentiation, flow in the opposite direction: towards union, towards wholeness, towards completeness.

The attitude of the Hindu Tantras is quite different, if not opposite. 'United with the *Śakti*, be full of power', says the *Kulacūḍāmaṇi-Tantra*. 'From the union of *Śiva* and *Śakti* the world is created.' The Buddhist, however, does not want the creation and unfoldment of the world, but the coming back to the 'uncreated, unformed' state of *śūnyatā*, from which all creation proceeds, or which is prior and beyond all creation (if one may put the inexpressible into human language).

The becoming conscious of this *śūnyatā* (Tib.: *stoṅ-pa-ñid*) is *prajñā* (Tib.: *śes-rab*): highest knowledge. The realization of this highest knowledge in life is enlightenment (*bodhi*; Tib.: *byaṅ-chub*), i.e., if *prajñā* (or *śūnyatā*), the passive, all-embracing female principle, from which everything proceeds and into which everything recedes, is united with the dynamic male principle of active universal love and compassion, which represents the means (*upāya*; Tib.: *thabs*) for the realization of *prajñā* and *śūnyatā*, then perfect Buddhahood is attained. Because intellect without feeling, knowledge without love, reason without compassion, leads to pure negation, to rigidity, to spiritual death, to mere vacuity – while feeling without reason, love without knowledge (blind love), compassion without understanding, lead the confusion and dissolution. But where both sides are united, where the great synthesis of heart and head, feeling and intellect, highest love and deepest knowledge have taken place, there completeness is reestablished, perfect Enlightenment is attained.

The process of Enlightenment is therefore represented by the most obvious, the most human and at the same time the most universal symbol imaginable: the union of male and female in the ecstasy of love – in which the active element (*upāya*) is represented as a male, the passive (*prajñā*) by a female figure – in contrast to the Hindu Tantras, in which the female aspect is represented as *Śakti*, i.e., as the active principle, and the male aspect as *Śiva*, as the pure state of divine consciousness, of 'being', i.e., as the passive principle, the 'resting in its own nature'.

In Buddhist symbolism the Knower (Buddha) becomes one with his knowledge (*prajñā*), just as man and wife become one in the embrace of love, and this becoming one is highest, indescribable happiness (*mahāsukha*; Tib.: *bde-mchog*). The *Dhyāni-Buddhas* (i.e., the ideal Buddhas visualized in meditation) and *Dhyāni-Bodhisattvas* as embodiments of the active urge of enlightenment, which finds its expression in *upāya*, the all-embracing love and compassion, are therefore represented in the embrace of their *prajñā*, symbolized by a female deity, the embodiment of highest knowledge.

This is not the arbitrary reversal of Hindu symbology, in which 'the poles of the male and the female as symbols of the divine and its unfoldment had to be exchanged apparently, as otherwise the gender of the concepts which they were intended to embody in Buddhism, would not have been in harmony with them',[1] but it is the consequent application of a principle which is of fundamental importance for the entire Buddhist Tantric system.

In a similar way the Hindu Tantras are an equally consistent application of the fundamental ideas of Hinduism, even though they have taken over Buddhist methods wherever they suited their purpose. But the same method, when applied from two opposite standpoints, must necessarily lead to opposite results. There is no need to resort to such superficial reasons as the necessity to comply with the grammatical gender of *prajñā* (feminine) and *upāya* (masculine).

Such reasoning however was only the consequence of the wrong presupposition that the Buddhist Tantras were an imitation of the Hindu Tantras, and the sooner we can free ourselves from this prejudice, the clearer it will become that the concept of *śakti* has no place in Buddhism.

Just as the Theravādin would be shocked if the term *anattā* (Skt.: *anātman*) were turned into its opposite and were rendered by the brahmanical term *ātman* or were explained in such a way as to show that the Theravādin accepted the *ātman*-idea (since Buddhism was only a variation of Brahmanism!), so the Tibetan Buddhist would be shocked by the misinterpretation of his religious tradition by the Hindu term *śakti*, which is never used in his scriptures and which means exactly the opposite of what he wants to express by the term *prajñā* or by the female counterparts of the Dhyāni-Buddhas and Bodhisattvas.

One cannot arbitrarily transplant termini of a theistic system,

[1] H. Zimmer: *Kunstform und Yoga im Indischen Kultbild*, p. 75.

centred round the idea of a God-Creator into a non-theistic system which emphatically and fundamentally denies the notion of a God-Creator. From such a confusion of terminology arises finally the mistaken idea that the *Ādibuddha* of the later Tantras is nothing but another version of the God-Creator, which would be a complete reversal of the Buddhist point of view. The *Ādibuddha*, however, is the symbol of the universality, timelessness and completeness of the enlightened mind, or as Guenther puts it more forcefully: 'The statement that the universe or man is the *Ādibuddha* is but an inadequate verbalization of an all-comprehensive experience. The *Ādibuddha* is assuredly not a God who plays dice with the world in order to pass away his time. He is not a sort of monotheism either, superimposed on an earlier, allegedly atheistic Buddhism. Such notions are the errors of professional semanticists. Buddhism has no taste for theorization. It attempts to delve into the secret depths of our inmost being and to make the hidden light shine forth brilliantly. Therefore the *Ādibuddha* is best translated as the unfolding of man's true nature.'[1]

4

THE POLARITY OF MALE AND FEMALE PRINCIPLES IN THE SYMBOLIC LANGUAGE OF THE *VAJRAYĀNA*

By confusing Buddhist Tantrism with the Śaktism of the Hindu Tantras an enormous confusion has been created, which until now has prevented a clear understanding of the *Vajrayāna* and its symbolism, in iconography as well as in literature, especially in that of the *Siddhas*. The latter used, as we have mentioned already, a kind of secret language, in which very often the highest was clothed in the form of the lowest, the most sacred in the form of the most ordinary, the transcendent in the form of the most earthly, and the deepest knowledge in the form of the most grotesque paradoxes. It was not only a language for initiates, but a kind of shock-therapy, which had become necessary on account of the over-intellectualization of the religious and philosophical life of those times.

Just as the Buddha was a revolutionary against the narrow dogmatism of a privileged priestly class, so the *Siddhas* were revolutionaries

[1] H. V. Guenther: *Yuganaddha, the Tantric View of Life* (Chowkhamba Sanskrit Series), Banaras, 1952, p. 187.

against the self-complacency of a sheltered monastic existence, that had lost all contact with the realities of life. Their language was as unconventional as were their lives, and those who took their words literally, were either misled into striving after magic powers and worldly happiness or were repelled by what appeared to them to be blasphemy. It is therefore not surprising that, after the disappearance of Buddhist tradition in India, this literature fell into oblivion or degenerated into the crude erotic cults of popular Tantrism.

Nothing could be more misleading than to draw inferences about the spiritual attitude of the Buddhist Tantras (or of genuine Hindu Tantras) from these degenerated forms of Tantrism. The former cannot be fathomed theoretically, neither through comparisons nor through the study of ancient literature, but only through practical experience in contact with the still existing Tantric traditions and their contemplative methods, as practised in Tibet and Mongolia, as well as in certain Schools of Japan, like Shingon and Tendai. With regard to the latter two, Glasenapp remarks: 'The female Bodhisattvas figuring in the Maṇḍalas, like *Prajñāpāramitā* and *Cuṇḍī*, are sexless beings, from whom, quite in accordance with the ancient tradition, associations of a sexual nature are strictly excluded. In this point these Schools differ from those known to us from Bengal, Nepal, and Tibet, which emphasize the polarity of the male and female principles.'[1]

The fact that Bengal, Nepal, and Tibet are mentioned here side by side, shows that the Tantrism of Bengal and Nepal is regarded to be of the same nature as that of Tibet, and that the author, though seeing the necessity of distinguishing between Tantrism and Śaktism has not yet drawn the last conclusion – namely, that even those Buddhist Tantras which build their symbolism upon the polarity of the male and female, *never* represent the female principle as *śakti*, but always as its contrary, namely *prajñā* (wisdom), *vidyā* (knowledge), or *mudrā* (the spiritual attitude of unification, the realization of *śūnyatā*). Herewith they reject the basic idea of Śaktism and its world-creating eroticism.

Though the polarity of male and female principles is recognized in the Tantras of the *Vajrayāna* and is an important feature of its symbolism, it is raised upon a plane which is as far away from the sphere of mere sexuality as the mathematical juxtaposition of positive and negative signs, which is as valid in the realm of irrational values as in that of rational or concrete concepts.

In Tibet, the male and female *Dhyāni-Buddhas* and *-Bodhisattvas*

[1] H. von Glasenapp: *Die Entstehung des Vajrayāna*, Zeitschr. d. Deutsch. Morgenländ. Gesellschaft, Vol. 90, p. 560. Leipzig, 1936.

are regarded as little as 'sexual beings' as in the above-mentioned Schools of Japan; and to the Tibetan, even their aspect of union (Skt.: *yuganaddha*; Tib.: *yab-yum*) is indissolubly associated with the highest spiritual reality in the process of enlightenment, so that associations with the realm of physical sexuality are completely ignored.

We must not forget that the figural representations of these symbols are not looked upon as portraying human beings, but as embodying the experiences and visions of meditation. In such a state, however, there is nothing more that could be called 'sexual'; there is only the super-individual polarity of all life, which rules all mental and physical activities, and which is transcended only in the ultimate state of integration, in the realization of *śūnyatā*. This is the state which is called *Mahāmudrā* (Tib.: *phyag-rgya-chen-po*), the 'Great Attitude' or the 'Great Symbol', which has given its name to one of the most important systems of meditation in Tibet.

In the earlier forms of Indian Buddhist Tantrism *Mahāmudrā* was represented as the 'eternal female' principle, as may be seen from *Advayavajra's* definition: 'The words "great" and "mudrā" together form the term "*mahāmudrā*". She is not a something (*niḥsvabhāvā*); she is free from the veils which cover the cognizable object and so on; she shines forth like the serene sky at noon during autumn; she is the support of all success; she is the identity of *saṁsāra* and *nirvāṇa*; her body is Compassion (*karuṇā*) which is not restricted to a single object; she is the uniqueness of Great Bliss (*mahāsukhaikarūpa*).'[1]

If in one of the most controversial passages of Anaṅgavajra's *Prajñopāyaviniścayasiddhi*[2] it is said that *all* women should be enjoyed by the *Sādhaka* in order to experience the *Mahāmudrā*, it is clear that this cannot be understood in the physical sense, but that it can only be applied to that higher form of love *which is not restricted to a single object* and which is able to see all 'female' qualities, whether in ourselves or in others, as those of the 'Divine Mother' (*prajñāpāramitā:* 'Transcendental Wisdom').

Another passage, which by its very grotesqueness proves that it is meant to be a paradox and not to be taken literally, states that 'the Sādhaka who has sexual intercourse with his mother, his sister, his daughter, and his sister's daughter, will easily succeed in his striving for the ultimate goal (*tattvayoga*)'.[3]

To take expressions like 'mother', 'sister', 'daughter' or 'sister's

[1] Advayavajra, *Caturmudrā*, p. 34, quoted in *Yuganaddha*, p. 116.

[2] In *Two Vajrayāna Works*, G.O.S., No. XLIV, p. 22 f.

[3] *Anaṅgavajra: 'Prajñopāyaviniścayasiddhi'*, V, 25, quoted in '*Yuganaddha*', p. 106. A similar passage is found in the *Guhyasamāja-Tantra*, from where *Anaṅgavajra* took this quotation.

daughter' literally in this connexion is as senseless as taking the well-known *Dhammapada* verse (No. 294) literally, which says that, after having killed father and mother, two Kṣattriya kings, and having destroyed a kingdom with all its inhabitants, the Brahmin remains free from sin. Here 'father and mother' stands for 'egoism and craving' (Pāli: *asmimāṇa* and *taṇhā*), the 'two kings' for the erroneous 'views of annihilation or eternal existence' (*uccheda vā sassata diṭṭhi*), the 'kingdom and its inhabitants' for 'the twelve spheres of consciousness' (*dvādasāyatanāni*) and the Brahmin for the 'liberated monk' (*bhikkhu*).

It is a strange coincidence, if not a conscious allusion to this famous simile of the *Dhammapada*, that 'the destruction of a kingdom with its king and all its inhabitants' is also ascribed to *Padmasambhava*, the great scholar and saint, who brought Buddhism to Tibet in the middle of the eighth century A.D. and founded the first monastery there. In his symbolical biography (about which we shall hear more later on), written in *Sandhyābhāṣā*, it is said, that *Padmasambhava*, in the guise of a terrible deity, destroyed a king and his subjects, who were enemies of the religion, and that he took all their women to himself in order to purify them and to make them mothers of religious-minded children. It is obvious that this cannot be taken in the sense that *Padmasambhava* killed the population of a whole country and violated all codes of sex-morality. This would be in blatant contradiction to the works attributed to him, which are of the highest moral and ethical standard and of profound spiritual insight, based on the strictest sense-control. It is one of the characteristics of the *Sandhyābhāṣā*, as of many ancient religious texts, to represent experiences of meditation (like the Buddha's struggle with *Māra* and his hosts of demons) in the form of outer events. The remark, that *Padmasambhava* took the form of a wrathful deity, shows that the fight with the forces of evil took place within himself and that the 'recognition' of the female principles in the process of inner integration consisted in the unification of the two sides of his nature, namely, the male principle of activity (*upāya*) and the female principle of wisdom (*prajñā*), as we shall see in the following paragraphs.

To maintain that Tantric Buddhists actually encouraged incest and licentiousness is as ridiculous as accusing the *Theravādins* of condoning matricide and patricide and similar heinous crimes. If we only take the trouble to investigate the still living traditions of the Tantras in their genuine, unadulterated forms, as they exist up to the present day in thousands of monasteries and hermitages of Tibet, where the ideals of sense-control and renunciation are held in highest esteem, then only can we realize how ill-founded and worthless are the current theories, which try to drag the Tantras into the realm of sensuality.

From the point of view of Tibetan Tantric tradition, the above-mentioned passages can only have meaning in the context of yoga-terminology: 'All women in the world' signifies all the elements which make up the female principles of our psycho-physical personality which, as the Buddha says, represents what is called 'the world'. To these principles correspond on the opposite side an equal number of male principles. Four of the female principles form a special group, representing the vital forces (*prāṇa*) of the Great Elements (*mahābhūta*) 'Earth', 'Water', 'Fire', 'Air', and their corresponding psychic centres (*cakra*) or planes of consciousness within the human body. In each of them the union of male and female principles must take place, before the fifth and highest stage is reached. If the expressions 'mother', 'sister', 'daughter', etc., are applied to these forces of these fundamental qualities of the *mahābhūtas*, the meaning of the symbolism becomes clear.

In other words, instead of seeking union with a woman outside ourselves, we have to seek it *within ourselves* ('in our own family') by the union of our male and female nature in the process of meditation. This is clearly stated in Nāropā's famous 'Six Doctrines' (Tib.: *chos-drug bsdus-paḥiḥzin-bris*), upon which the most important *yoga*-method of the *Kargyütpa* School is based, a method which was practised by *Milarepa*, the most saintly and austere of all the great masters of meditation (whom, certainly, nobody could accuse of 'sexual practices'!). Though we need not go here into the details of this *yoga*, a short quotation may suffice to prove our point:

'The vital-force (*prāṇa*; Tib.: *śugs*, *rluṅ*) of the Five Aggregates (*skandha*; Tib.: *phuṅ-po*) in its real nature, pertaineth to the *masculine* aspect of the Buddha-principle manifesting through the left psychic nerve (*iḍā-nāḍī*; Tib.: *rkyaṅ-ma rtsa*). The vital force of the Five Elements (*dhātu*; Tib.: *ḥbyuṅ-ba*) in its real nature, pertaineth to the feminine aspect of the Buddha-principle manifesting through the right psychic nerve (*piṅgala-nāḍī*; Tib.: *ro-ma rtsa*). As the vital force, with these two aspects of it *in union*, descendeth into the median nerve (*suṣumṇā*; Tib.: *dbu-ma rtsa*) gradually there cometh the realization . . .' and one attains 'the transcendental boon of the Great Symbol (*mahāmudrā*; Tib.: *phyag-rgya-chen-po*)',[1] the union of male and female principles (as *upāya* and *prajñā*) in the highest state of Buddhahood.

Thus sexual polarity becomes a mere incident of universal polarity, which has to be recognized on all levels and has to be overcome

[1] W. Y. Evans-Wentz: *Tibetan Yoga and Secret Doctrine*, p. 200 ff (Oxford University Press, London, 1935).

through knowledge: from the biblical 'knowing of the woman' to the knowledge of the 'Eternal Feminine', *Mahāmudrā* or *Śūnyatā*, in the realization of highest wisdom.

Only if we are able to see the relationship of body and mind, of physical and spiritual interaction in a universal perspective, and if in this way we overcome the 'I' and 'mine' and the whole structure of egocentric feelings, opinions, and prejudices, which produce the illusion of our separate individuality, then only can we rise into the sphere of Buddhahood.

The Tantras brought religious experience from the abstract regions of the speculating intellect again down to earth, and clothed it with flesh and blood; not, however, with the intention of secularizing it, but to realize it: to make religious experience an active force. The authors of the Tantras knew that knowledge based on vision is stronger than the power of subconscious drives and urges, that *prajñā* is stronger than *śakti*. For *śakti* is the blind world-creating power (*māyā*), which leads deeper and deeper into the realm of becoming, of matter and differentiation. Its effect can only be polarized or reversed by its opposite: inner vision, which transforms the power of becoming into that of liberation.

5

VISION AS CREATIVE REALITY

THE perfect transformation of that blind world-creating urge into the force of liberation, depends on the perfection of inner vision, on the universality of inner knowledge. By becoming conscious of the world and of those forces which create it, we become their master. As long as these forces remain dormant and unperceived within us, we have no access to them. For this reason it is necessary to project them into the realm of the visible in the form of images. The symbols which serve this purpose act like a chemical catalyst, through which a liquid is suddenly converted into solid crystals, thus revealing its true nature and structure.

The spiritual process of crystallization which forms the productive phase of meditation is called the process of unfoldment or creation (*sriṣṭi-krama; utpanna-krama;* Tib.: *bskyed-rim*).

However, the forms of conscious representation, solidified and made visible by this process, would have a spiritually petrifying, deadening effect, if there did not exist a method of dissolving again the crystallized forms into the normal stream of life and consciousness.

This method is called the process of dissolving, of integration (*laya-krama*) or the state of perfection (*sampanna-krama;* Tib.: *rdzogs-rim*). It demonstrates the egolessness (*pudgala-nairātmya*) and non-substantiality (*dharma-nairātmya*), the mutability and relativity of all form, its emptiness (*śūnyatā*) of any abiding or absolute quality. This is taught in every Tibetan training of meditation, so that there is absolutely no room for misunderstandings or for getting attached to one's own experiences and achievements (the danger of most non-Buddhist mystics).

He who realizes that actuality (or what we call 'reality') is the product of our own actions (which start in the mind: '*mano pubbaṅgamā dhammā*'), will be thoroughly freed from the materialistic conception of the world as a self-existing or 'given' reality. This is, by far, more convincing than all theoretical or philosophical arguments. It is practical experience – and this has an infinitely deeper-going effect than the strongest intellectual conviction, because 'the act of spiritual vision transforms the seer; which obviously demonstrates the extreme opposite to the act of perception, which differentiates the perceiver from the object of perception and thus makes him conscious of his narrow separateness.' (Ludwig Klages.)

'The process of transformation, which the human consciousness brings about in the material qualities of the *yantra*, is achieved in the act of worship, the *pūjā*. The image is not the deity; nor does the divine essence, after having been called up magically, enter into the kernel of the image from somewhere outside during the ritual of worship; it is the devotee who produces within himself the vision of the divine being and projects it upon the image before him, in order to experience the divine being visibly in the state of duality that corresponds to the devotee's consciousness. It goes without saying that this inner vision is beyond all arbitrariness; a divine being beyond the external human eye is made to appear in the inner field of vision, a super-human reality is to be mirrored in the human consciousness.'[1]

A thing exists only in so far as it acts. Reality is actuality. An active symbol or image of spiritual vision is reality. In this sense the *Dhyāni-Buddhas*, visualized in meditation, are real (as real as the mind that creates them), while the merely thought-conceived historical personality of the Buddha is unreal in this sense. A non-acting symbol or image is empty form, at the best a decorative construction or the

[1] H. Zimmer: *Kunstform und Yoga*, p. 29.

remembrance of a concept, a thought, or an event, belonging to the past.

Therefore, all important Tibetan Tantric meditations presuppose the conception of a universal aim, the great mystic synthesis, the anticipation of the ideal state of Buddhahood in the mind of the devotee; and only after he has identified himself with the aim, is he left to the manifold forms of meditative experiences and methods.

Just as an archer keeps his eye upon the aim, in order to hit the mark with certainty, so the *sādhaka* must first visualize his aim and identify himself with it completely. This gives the direction and impetus to his inner urge. Whatever ways and methods he may choose after having done this, he will always progress towards the aim and never lose himself, neither in the dreariness of pure analysis, nor in the attachment to the products of his imagination. The latter danger is avoided, as already mentioned, by the liquifying, dissolving action of the process of integration. The ability to create a world and to dissolve it again, demonstrates better than any intellectual analysis the true nature of all phenomena and the senselessness of all clinging and craving.

However, before we penetrate to this stage, we have to deal with the creative stage of building up the visual image within us. It is based upon the concentric diagram or *maṇḍala* of the four-petalled lotus (*padma*). This lotus represents the unfoldment of the perfect mind or the ideal Buddhahood, in which the qualities of Enlightenment or of the Buddha, which are the *sādhaka's* aim, are differentiated in visible form.

In order to understand the qualities of sunlight or the nature of the sun, we have to separate its rays in the spectrum. Likewise, if we want to understand the nature of an Enlightened One or of the consciousness of Enlightenment, we have to spread out before our inner eye the various qualities of such a state. Because an unenlightened being cannot grasp an enlightened mind in its totality, but only in separate aspects, which – according to the plane on which they are experienced and the range of their manifold relations and mental associations – lead to an ever wider and deeper understanding.

The establishing of inner relations between spiritual qualities, psychological principles, planes of consciousness and of knowledge, elements of existence and their symbolical figures, gestures, colours and spatial positions, etc., are not an idle play of imagination or arbitrary speculations, but the visible representation of experiences, collected and confirmed by the religious practice of countless generations. They represent a quasi-symphonic or multi-dimensional awareness of reality, in so far as they depict the co-ordination of all active forces on the planes of material, physical, psychological, mental, and spiritual activity.

This co-operation, however, is harmonious only when no impure (i.e., selfish) vibrations disturb the relationship or the inner connexions between these forces. For this reason it requires a clear knowledge and a purposeful effort, directed towards a definite aim; so as to subordinate those forces to a guiding principle and to keep them in tune with each other. The instrument of human consciousness, like a musical instrument has to be tuned anew continually, and this tuning depends on the knowledge of right vibrations, on the capacity of perceiving their relationship, which requires a high degree of sensitivity and devotion.

To impart this knowledge on the various planes of experience is the aim of all Tantric methods of inner visualization. The actual coexistence and interpenetration of these planes and the simultaneousness of their functions is converted by the intellect into something that exists in different dimensions or as a sequence in time, which therefore can only be experienced and expressed piecemeal and in separate phases.

The philosophical and spiritual consequences can therefore only be revealed by approaching the given problems from different sides and points of view, so to say, by a 'concentric attack' upon them. The incommensurable remainder, which is left by each partial view and each partial solution, can only be eliminated by a total vision or an experience of the whole, which combines all aspects in the unity of a higher dimension. If, therefore, we pursue this principle to its last consequence, we shall find that the perfect solution of the problem of our existence can only consist in perfect Enlightenment – and not in a mere negation of the world and its problems, an attitude which can only lead to pure nihilism, to spiritual stagnation and death.

We, therefore, must be conscious of the insufficiency of words and all intellectual attempts of explanation, in which we should never see more than approximations and preliminaries, which prepare us for deeper forms of experience – just as the theoretical knowledge of the laws of musical harmony and counterpoint are only preliminaries, but can never be a substitute for the enjoyment or creation of music.

The relationship of the five *skandhas* (*rūpa*, *vedanā*, *saṁjñā*, *saṁskāra*, *vijñāna*) to the five qualities of the consciousness of Enlightenment and their corresponding Wisdoms, revealed already a fundamental principle, namely, that the highest qualities are potentially contained in the lower ones (like the blossom in the seed). Thus, good and bad, the sacred and the profane, the sensual and the spiritual, the worldly and the transcendental, ignorance and Enlightenment, *saṁsāra* and *nirvāṇa*, etc., are not absolute opposites, or concepts of entirely different categories, but two sides of the same reality.

6

THE FIVE *DHYĀNI-BUDDHAS* AND THE FIVE WISDOMS

THUS the world is neither condemned in its totality, nor torn into the irreconcilable opposites, but a bridge is shown, which leads from the ordinary temporal world of sense-perception to the realm of timeless knowledge – a way which leads beyond this world not through contempt or negation, but through purification and sublimation of the conditions and qualities of our present existence.

From the point of view of the five groups (*skandha*) or aspects of individual existence, this means, as we have seen already, that in the process of Enlightenment, or on the way towards it, the principles of corporeality (*rūpa*), feeling (*vedanā*), perception (*saṁjñā*), karmically decisive mental formations or volitional tendencies (*saṁskāra*), and consciousness (*vijñāna*) are transformed into the corresponding qualities of Enlightenment-consciousness (*bodhi-citta*).

Through the knowledge and realization of the universal law (*dharma*), the narrow, ego-bound individual consciousness grows into the state of cosmic consciousness, as represented in the figure of *Vairocana*, the Radiating One, the Illuminator (Tib.: *rnam-par-snaṅ-mdzad*). At the same time the principle of individual corporeality is converted into the universal body, in which the forms of all things are potentially present and are recognized, according to their true nature, as exponents of the Great Void (*śūnyatā*) by the consciousness of the Mirror-like Wisdom, which reflects the forms of all things without clinging to them, without being touched or moved by them.

This is represented by the figure of *Akṣobhya*, the Immutable (Tib.: *mi-bskyod-pa*). As a sign of his unshakable, steadfast nature, he is touching the earth (*bhūmisparśa-mudrā*) with the finger-tips of his right hand, because the earth is the symbol of the immutable, the solid, the concrete, the formed. And yet he is one with the 'Wisdom of the Great Mirror', which is *Akṣobhya's* '*Prajñā*', the wisdom which is as inseparable from him as the Divine Mother (Tib.: *yum*) *Locanā*, the Seeing One, who embraces him. Her Tibetan name is 'The Buddha-Eye' (*saṅs-rgyas-spyan-ma*). She is the embodiment of the Great Plenum-Void, in which things are neither 'existing' nor 'non-existing' – in which things appear, though one could not say either that they are within or outside the mirror.

In a similar way, self-centred feeling is converted into the feeling for others, into the compassion for all that lives, through the Wisdom of Equality, as embodied in the figure of *Ratnasambhava* (Tib.: *rin-chen-ḥbyuṅ-gnas*[1]), the 'Origin of Jewels', namely, the cause for the appearance of the Three Jewels (*triratna*) in the world: the Buddha, his teaching (*dharma*), and his community (*saṅgha*). Also *Ratnasambhava* is touching the ground with his right hand, however, his hand is reversed, with the palm turned outwards, in the gesture of giving (*dāna-mudrā*), as the bestower of gifts. He gives to the world the three precious things, in which *Akṣobhya's* wisdom of *śūnyatā* or egolessness becomes the basis of the solidarity of all beings. He, therefore, is inseparably united with his '*Prajñā*', the Equalizing Wisdom, who embraces him in the form of the Divine Mother *Māmakī* ('mineness'). Her name indicates that she looks upon all beings as her own children, i.e., as essentially identical with her.

This feeling of identity which is born from the knowledge of inner unity is, as the *Vijñapti-mātra-siddhi-śāstra* says, 'the special foundation (*āśraya*) of the investigating knowledge (*pratyavekṣaṇa-jñāna*).' That is, only on the basis and with full awareness of the great synthesis, can we devote ourselves to the analytical knowledge of details, without losing sight of the greater connexions.

Thus it comes to pass that sense-perception and intellectual discrimination are converted into the transcendental faculties of inner vision and spiritual discernment in the practice of meditation, which is the special function of *Amitābha*, the *Dhyāni-Buddha* of 'Infinite Light' (Tib.: *ḥod-dpag-med*) or of 'Infinite Splendour' (Tib.: *snaṅ-ba-mthā-yas*). His hands rest in the gesture of meditation (*dhyāna-mudrā*). He is one with the Wisdom of Discriminating Clear Vision, his '*Prajñā*', who embraces him in the form of the Divine Mother *Pāṇḍaravāsinī* (Tib.: *gos-dkar-mo*), the 'White-robed'.

In *Indrabhūti*'s '*Jñānasiddhi*' it is said that this wisdom is called *pratyavekṣaṇa-jñāna*, because it is pure from beginning, uncreated, self-luminous, and all-pervading.

This definition shows that we are not concerned here with intellectual analysis, but with *intuitive* clear vision, uninfluenced by logical or conceptual discriminations. It is the *pure* spontaneity of inner vision, without prejudice and without arbitrary conclusions. Also in

[1] Or *rin-chen-ḥbyuṅ-ldan*, the 'Jewel-possessing One'.

the Pāli scriptures the expression *paccavekkhaṇa-ñāṇa* is connected with the visions of meditation (*jhāna*), namely, as 'retrospective knowledge', in which the memory-images of spiritual impressions and experiences are called up.

If, therefore, we call the Wisdom of *Amitābha* 'analytical', in contrast to the 'reflective' Wisdom of the Great Mirror, or the 'synthetic' Wisdom of Equality – terms like 'analytical', 'discriminating' or 'investigating', with which *pratyavekṣaṇa* may be rendered, are not meant to be a logical *reductio ad absurdum* of the phenomenal world by way of a philosophical or scientific analysis. The insufficiency of such methods had already been recognized by the Buddha, on account of which he rejected the speculations of the metaphysicians and philosophers of his time – a fact which led some Indologists of the last century to the conclusion that Buddhism is a purely intellectual doctrine without any metaphysical background.[1]

The Buddha, certainly, was no enemy of logical thinking, of which indeed he made the fullest use, but he perceived its limitations and therefore taught what goes beyond it: the direct awareness of spiritual vision (*dhyāna*) which surpasses mere ratiocination (*vitarka-vicāra*). This is expressed in the figure of *Amitābha* and his '*Prajñā*' in the pure, stainless white raiment of intuition.

On the basis of such visions the ego-bound karma-creating volition is converted into the karma-free activity of the saint, like that of a Buddha or *Bodhisattva*, whose life is no more motivated by desire or attachment but by universal compassion. This is embodied in the figure of *Amoghasiddhi* (Tib.: *don-yod-grub-pa*), the 'Realizer of the Aim'. His '*Prajñā*' is the All-accomplishing Wisdom in the form of the Divine Mother *Tārā* (Tib.: *sgrol-ma*, pron. 'dölma'), the Saviouress, with whom he is inseparably united, while he himself bestows blessings on all beings in the gesture of fearlessness (*abhaya-mudrā*).

If here and in other connexions we use the word 'divine', it is not

[1] 'When getting acquainted with the scholastic literature of ancient Buddhism, the assertion, that it maintained a negative attitude towards metaphysical questions, is quite untenable.' Buddhism 'rejected these questions *not because they are metaphysical, but because* from the metaphysical point of view of the Buddha, *it is logically imposible to answer them*'. (O. Rosenberg: *Die Probleme der buddhistischen Philosophie*, p. 58 ff.)

Rosenberg explains the fact, that European authors with such insistence dispute the existence of metaphysics in primitive Buddhism, by pointing out that on the one hand Christian Missionaries in their works involuntarily, and sometimes perhaps also with intention, emphasized the absence of metaphysics from Buddhism, in order to prove its imperfection as a religious system; and that, on the other hand, the absence of metaphysics in view of the modern scientific conception of the universe, with which it was thought possible to bring Buddhism into harmony, was regarded as an excellence. 'It must not be forgotten that the beginning of Buddhist research in Europe coincided with the collapse of metaphysical philosophy and the rise of materialistic systems.'

to be understood in a theistic sense, but as 'exalted', as going beyond the range of human sense-perception, belonging to the highest spiritual experience. We therefore render the Tibetan word '*yum*' or '*yum-mchog*', which signifies the female aspect of *Dhyāni-Buddhas*, as 'Divine Mother'. In a similar way the Tibetan word '*lha*', which generally corresponds to the Indian word '*deva*', i.e., an inhabitant of higher planes of existence (comparable to the Christian hierarchies of angels), is used also for *Dhyāni-Buddhas* and *-Bodhisattvas*. The word '*lha*' can therefore not be equated with the Western concept 'God', for nothing could be more inadequate than to call the various Buddhas 'gods', as this unfortunately has frequently been done. The meaning of the word '*lha*' depends on the context in which it is used and can have accordingly the following definitions:

1. Inhabitants of higher planes of existence (*deva*) who, though superior to man in certain ways, yet are subject to the laws of the world;
2. Earth-bound spirits, demons and genii of certain places or elements;
3. Mind-created forms or forces, like *Dhyāni-Buddhas*, etc.

7

TĀRĀ, *AKṢOBHYA*, AND *VAIROCANA* IN THE TIBETAN SYSTEM OF MEDITATION

AMONG the female embodiments of Wisdom ('*Prajñā*') *Tārā* occupies a special position because she is not only of importance as the female aspect of a *Dhyāni-Buddha*, but plays an outstanding role in the religious life of Tibet, on account of her special qualities. She represents the very essence of loving devotion, which is the foundation of all religious practice, from the simplest act of veneration (*pūjā*) to the most developed training of meditation. She is therefore one of the most popular, approachable, and attractive figures of the Tibetan pantheon. She unites in herself all human and divine traits of a Madonna, whose motherly love embraces all living beings, irrespective of their merits. She extends her loving care to the good and the bad, the wise and the foolish, like the sun that shines for sinners as well as for saints.

Tibetans, therefore, call her '*dam-ishig-sgrol-ma*', the Faithful Dölma,

She is the embodiment of that faithful devotion, which is born of love and strengthened by the *Bodhisattva* vow to liberate all living beings. '*Dam-tshig*' means literally 'a sacred or solemn vow', but in the mystic language of the Tantras it is the force generated by such a vow through faith and complete self-surrender. It is 'the faith that moves mountains', the wisdom of the heart. It corresponds in a certain way to the Sanskrit term '*bhakti*', which in the theistic religions of India signifies the loving devotion to and the ultimate self-identification with God. It is therefore more than *śraddha*, more than simple faith, because it is inspired by love. A '*bhakta*' is a devotee as well as a lover.

'*Dam-tshig*' is the devotion for the Buddha in one's own heart. The syllable '*dam*' means 'bound', 'fixed'; as, for instance, 'bound by oath, promise, agreement or convention (Skt. *samaya*)'. But in this connexion it is a bond of inner relationship through the power of loving devotion, by which the devotee dedicates himself to the *Dharma* and identifies himself with the Buddha who forms the centre of his *maṇḍala* of meditation or the object of his devotional practice (*sādhanā*).

'*Dam-tshig*' is in the truest sense the religious principle (the 'inner bond', in the sense of the Latin 'religio', which is derived from 'ligare', to bind), without which no meditation and no ritual has any meaning or value. It is an attitude of deep reverence for that which surpasses words and reason, an attitude without which symbols would lose their power and their significance.

In the religious life of Tibet '*dam-tshig*' plays indeed a central role and is one of the main reasons for the silence and secrecy maintained by initiates concerning the rites of initiation and their experiences of meditation. The *sādhaka* is exhorted not to speak about these things with uninitiated or merely curious people. This is not because these things are secrets, but because he would lose his '*dam-tshig*', the power of his inner devotion, by trying to 'explain' what goes beyond words and by dragging down the sacred upon the level of the profane.

By glibly talking about the mystery we destroy the purity and spontaneity of our inner attitude, and the deep reverence which is the key to the temple of revelations. Just as the mystery of love can only unfold when it is withdrawn from the eyes of the crowd, and as a lover will not discuss the beloved with outsiders, in the same way the mystery of inner transformation can only take place if the secret force of its symbols is hidden from the profane eyes and the idle talk of the world.

In the Tibetan systems of meditation the divine forms, appearing in the creative phase of visualization and filling the concentric circles of the *maṇḍala*, are divided in '*ye-śes-pa*' and '*dam-tshig-pa*', i.e., in

Knowing Ones (Skt.: *jñānī*) and Devotional Ones (Skt.: *bhakta*). They represent the two main forces of meditation, feeling and knowledge, *ethos* and *logos*, the unification of which constitutes Liberation and Enlightenment.

The four outer *Dhyāni-Buddhas* of the basic fivefold *maṇḍala* can correspondingly be divided into two groups: *Akṣobhya-Amitābha* (east-west axis) as those in whom knowledge is emphasized (*ye-śes-pa*), *Amoghasiddhi-Ratnasambhava* (north-south axis) as those in whom feeling stands in the foreground (*dam-tshig-pa*). *Vairocana*, in the centre, represents their combination: either their origin or their integration – according to the point of view from which we start our contemplation of the *Dhyāni-Buddhas*.

Since, according to the view of the *Vijñānavādins*, there is in reality only one *skandha*, namely *vijñāna* – the other four *skandhas* were conceived as modifications of *vijñāna*, and the four (or eight) classes of consciousness as ephemeral phenomena of the universal consciousness. For this reason the *Vijñapti-mātra-siddhi-śāstra* speaks only of four Wisdoms; for, with the transformation of the four kinds of consciousness or of the four *skandhas* (which depend on them) the transformation of the basic principle of consciousness is achieved. In other words: the fifth Wisdom, the pure transcendental Buddha-knowledge, the realization of the universal law (*dharma-dhātu-jñāna*) is the sum total as well as the origin of the four Wisdoms. It can be placed at the beginning as well as at the end of the sequence, according to whether we regard the four Wisdoms as an unfoldment of the Buddha-knowledge from the centre of undifferentiated Suchness (*tathatā*) towards an active, differentiated existence – or as a progressive approach from the active aspects of knowledge (the All-accomplishing Wisdom and the Wisdom of Creative Inner Vision) towards the ultimate realization of perfect Buddhahood.

In the former case *Akṣobhya* represents the first step of the unfoldment of Buddha-knowledge, in which all things from the state of emptiness step into visible appearance without losing their connexion with the nature of their origin (*śūnyatā*). In the second case *Akṣobhya* represents the highest state of integration in the realm of human experience, in which is reflected the reality of the *dharma*-sphere, which is empty of all conceptual limitations. In this case *Akṣobhya* becomes a reflex of *Vairocana* in the experience of *śūnyatā* on the highest plane of individual consciousness.

With regard to the Mirror-like Wisdom (*ādarśa-jñāna*) *Indrabhūti's* '*Jñānasiddhi*' says: 'Just as one sees one's own reflection in a mirror, so the *dharma-kāya* is seen in the Mirror of Wisdom.'

Thus *Akṣobhya*, when turned towards the world, reflects the true nature of things beyond 'being' and 'non-being' (*dharma-nairātmya*), when turned towards the *dharma-dhātu*, however, he reflects the nature of *Vairocana*.

In those schools of the *Vajrayāna*, which follow the mystic or 'inner path of *Vajrasattva* (the Adamantine Being)' – the *Dhyāni-Bodhisattva* or the active reflex of *Akṣobhya* – in whom the rays of the combined Wisdoms are integrated, the roles of *Akṣobhya* and *Vairocana* are therefore reversed. Thus *Vajrasattva-Akṣobhya* becomes the exponent of all transformed *skandhas* integrated into the purified aggregate of consciousness (Tib.: *rnam-par-śes-paḥi-phuṅ-po gnas-su dag-pa*), while *Vairocana* becomes the exponent of the purified aggregate of bodily form (Tib.: *gzugs-kyi phuṅ-po gnas-su dag-pa*), i.e., the principle of spatial extension, or of space as precondition of all bodily existence. Herewith *Vairocana* is put more or less into the role of the latent (*śūnyatā*-aspect of) universal 'store-consciousness', the primordial cause of all form – existing before its manifestation – while *Vajrasattva-Akṣobhya* represents the conscious awareness of this state.

The subtlety of these differentiations is such, that it is difficult to put them into words without concretizing them too much and thus defeating one's own purpose. Words have a tendency to coarsen such matters, especially as the reasons for the changes in emphasis do not depend on logical necessities, but on the individual starting-point of meditation and on the spiritual and emotional attitude resulting from it.

A meditation, for instance, starting with the idea or the experience of *Amitābha*, instead of *Vairocana* or *Akṣobhya*, is governed by a different principle and can put *Amitābha* in the place of *Vairocana* and vice versa,[1] whereby the whole *maṇḍala* appears under a different perspective. In the terms of music: the same composition can be set in a different key.

The *Nyingmapas* (*rñiṅ-ma-pa*), the adherents of the oldest school of Buddhism in Tibet, introduced by *Padmasambhava*, the author of the *Bardo Thödol* (*bar-do thos-grol*), follow the tradition of the *Vijñānavādins*, in which *Vairocana* is the exponent of the undifferentiated universal principle of consciousness. He is inseparably united with his '*Prajñā*', the Divine Mother of Infinite Space (Tib.: *nam-mkhaḥi-dbyiṅs-dbaṅ-phyug-ma*; Skt.: *ākāśadhātīśvarī*): the embodiment of the all-embracing Great Void.

[1] This is demonstrated in the design on the title-page of this part. It represents the *maṇḍala* of *Amitābha*, which contains *Amitābha's* seed-syllable (*bīja-mantra*) HRĪḤ in the centre, while *Vairocana's* OṀ has been placed on the uppermost (western) petal, the original place of *Amitābha*. It may be noted here that in Tibetan *maṇḍalas* the directions of space are arranged in such a way that the west is on top, the east below, the south to the left and the north to the right.

The *Kargyütpas*, however, favour the other above-mentioned view, according to which *Vairocana* is associated with the aggregate of matter resolved into its primordial state' (as Lama Dawa Samdup puts it),[1] while *Akṣobhya* is given the more active and important role of the pure consciousness-principle. This traditional attitude explains the difference of Lama Dawa Samdup's manuscript from the generally acknowledged and authorized version of the Tibetan woodblock edition of the *Bardo Thödol*. The latter is apparently based on the older tradition, which attributes the consciousness-principle to *Vairocana*, and it is out of this principle that the aggregates of form, feeling, perception and volition can arise, according to the teachings of the *Vijñānavādins*.

On the other hand, we must bear in mind, that the tradition of the *Kargyütpas* was not in the nature of an arbitrary innovation, but was due to a stronger emphasis on the metaphysical aspect of *śūnyatā*, which was taken over by the early *Vajrayāna* from the tradition of the *Śūnyavādins* and remained an essential undercurrent in the spiritual life of the Buddhist Tantras.

8

THE SYMBOLISM OF SPACE, COLOURS, ELEMENTS, GESTURES, AND SPIRITUAL QUALITIES

THE forms in which the *Dhyāni-Buddhas* appear in the creative phase of inner vision in the process of meditation, have been compared by us with the different colours into which the rays of the sun are separated, when passing through a prism, thus revealing in each colour a particular quality of the light. This comparison is all the more adequate, as colours play an important role in the appearances of the *Dhyāni-Buddhas*. Their colours indicate certain properties and spiritual associations, which to the initiate are as significant and meaningful as notes to the musically trained. They convey the particular vibration, characteristic for each aspect of transcendental knowledge or Wisdom, which in the realm of sound is expressed by the corresponding vibration of the *mantra*, in the

[1] See *The Tibetan Book of the Dead* (translated by Lama Kazi Dawa Samdup, edited by W. Y. Evans-Wentz), pp. 106 and 109.

realm of corporeality by the corresponding gesture or *mudrā*, and in the innermost realm by the corresponding spiritual attitude.

The net of relations spreads over all realms of spiritual, mental, and sensuous perception and their conceptual derivatives, so that from the chaos of mundane consciousness there arises gradually a well-ordered, clear, intelligible and controllable cosmos.

The fundamental element of this cosmos is space. Space is the all-embracing principle of higher unity. Its nature is emptiness; and because it is empty, it can contain and embrace everything. In contrast to space is the principle of substance, of differentiation, of 'thingness'. But nothing can exist without space. Space is the pre-condition of all that exists, be it in material or immaterial form, because we can neither imagine an object nor a being without space. Space, therefore, is not only a *conditio sine qua non* of all existence, but a fundamental property of our consciousness.

Our consciousness determines the kind of space in which we live. The infinity of space and the infinity of consciousness are identical. In the moment in which a being becomes conscious of his consciousness, he becomes conscious of space. In the moment in which he becomes conscious of the infinity of space, he realizes the infinity of consciousness.

If, therefore, space is a property of our consciousness, then it may be said with equal justification that the experience of space is a criterion of spiritual activity and of a higher form of awareness. The way in which we experience space, or in which we are aware of space, is characteristic of the dimension of our consciousness. The three-dimensional space, which we perceive through our body and its senses, is only *one* among the many possible dimensions. When we speak about a 'space of time', we already hint at a higher dimension, i.e., a type of space which cannot be felt any more bodily or through the senses, but as a possibility of movement in a completely different direction.

And if we speak of the space-experience in meditation, we are dealing with an entirely different dimension (in connexion with which our familiar 'third dimension' only serves as a simile or a starting-point). In this space-experience the temporal sequence is converted into a simultaneous co-existence, the side by side existence of things into a state of mutual interpenetration, and this again does not remain static but becomes a living continuum, in which time and space are integrated into that ultimate incommensurable 'point-like' unity, which in Tibetan is called '*thig-le*' (Skt.: *bindu*). This word, which has many meanings, like 'point, dot, zero, drop, germ, seed, semen', etc., occupies an important place in the terminology and practice of meditation. It signifies the concentrative starting-point in the unfoldment of 'inner space' in meditation, as also the last point of its ultimate integration. It is the point from which inner and outer space have their origin and in which they become *one* again.

When men look up into the space of heaven and invoke heaven, or a power that is supposed to reside there, they invoke in reality forces within themselves, which, by being projected outwards, are visualized or felt as heaven or cosmic space. If we contemplate the mysterious depth and blueness of the firmament, we contemplate the depth of our own inner being, of our own mysterious all-comprising consciousness in its primordial, unsullied purity: unsullied by thoughts and mental representations, undivided by discriminations, desires, and aversions. Herein lies the indescribable and inexplicable happiness which fills us during such contemplation.

From such experiences we begin to understand the significance of the deep blue as the centre and starting-point of meditative symbolism and vision: it is the light of the transcendental Wisdom of the *Dharma-dhātu* – the origin of the very faculty of consciousness and knowledge, undifferentiated, potential, all-embracing, like infinite space – which as a blue radiance issues from the heart of *Vairocana*, occupying the centre of the *maṇḍala* of the five *Dhyāni-Buddhas*, the pericarp of the four-petalled lotus.

Therefore it is said in the *Bardo Thödol* that from the 'potential (lit. "expanding": *brdal-ba*) seed (*thig-le*) in the central realm (of deep blue space) the Blessed *Vairocana* appears. The colour of his body is white. He is seated upon a lion-throne, holding the eight-spoked wheel (of the *Dharma*) in his hand, and he is embraced by the Divine Mother of Infinite Space'. The deep blue light of the *Dharma-dhātu Wisdom*, which is identified with the primordial state, or the pure element, of consciousness (*rnam-par-śes-paḥi phuṅ-po gnas-su dag-pa*), symbolizes at the same time the potentiality of the Great Void, which is so beautifully expressed in the poetical words of the Sixth Patriarch (Hui-neng) of the *Ch'an* School:

'When you hear me speak about the void, do not fall into the idea that I mean vacuity. It is of the utmost importance that we should not fall into that idea, because then when a man sits quietly and keeps his mind blank, he would be abiding in a state of the "voidness of indifference". The illimitable void of the universe is capable of holding myriads of things of various shapes and forms, such as the sun and the moon, and the stars, worlds, mountains, rivers, rivulets, springs, woods, bushes, good men, bad men, laws pertaining to goodness and to badness, heavenly planes and hells, great oceans and all the mountains of the *Mahāmeru*. Space takes in all these, and so does the voidness of our nature. We say that Essence of Mind is great because it embraces all things since all things are within our nature.'[1]

But just as space – though, apparently, we live in it, are filled with it, are surrounded by it, and carry its whole infinity in our heart – cannot be described, explained or defined as a whole, but only in partial aspects and in relationship to the *experiencing individual*: in the same way the nature of consciousness and of Buddhahood can only be brought nearer to our understanding by a specification of their qualities and by individualizing their various aspects.

In order to orient ourselves in space, we speak of an eastern, southern, western and northern quarter, associating with each of these directions a particular phase of the sun's course, without hereby negating the unity of space or disputing the fact that the source of light remains the same throughout all its phases. Similarly we discern in the space of our inner experience, according to the sequence of phases in its unfoldment, an eastern, southern, western or northern direction or form of awareness, expression or attitude, without thereby denying the unity and the simultaneous co-existence of all these spatial aspects and qualities of consciousness. Though root, trunk, branches, leaves, blossoms, and fruits are potentially present in the undifferentiated oneness of the seed, it is only when they are unfolded in space and time, that they become reality to us.

In order to experience the reality of Universal Mind, the figures and luminous radiations of the *Dhyâni-Buddhas* arise from the deep blue space of undifferentiated consciousness. In the east appears the space-blue *Akṣobhya*, from whose heart shines the yet unqualified, colourless, pure, white (*Vairocana-like*)[2] light of the Mirror-like Wisdom, in which the forms of all things (*rūpa*) are differentiated, so to say, for the first time (to remain in the temporal simile of 'unfoldment'), in order to be reflected with the clarity, steadfastness, and impartiality of a mirror, which remains unaffected and untouched by the objects it reflects.

It is the attitude of the impartial observer, the pure, spontaneous awareness (the spontaneity of '*satori*' in Zen-Buddhism), in which our habitual, preconceived thinking is eliminated, together with its seemingly objective, but in reality arbitrary, isolation of time-conditioned events or aspects of organic processes. Hereby momentary

[1] 'Sūtra of the Sixth Patriarch,' translated from the Chinese by Wong Mou-lam, published in *A Buddhist Bible* by Dwight Goddard.

[2] *Vairocana's* body-colour is white, his light blue, while *Akṣobhya's* body-colour is blue and his light white. This indicates their complementary nature.

phenomena are torn out of their living relationship and concretized into mere 'things' or material objects.

In the light of the Mirror-like Wisdom, however, things are freed from their 'thingness', their isolation, without being deprived of their form; they are divested of their materiality, without being dissolved, because the creative principle of the mind, which is at the bottom of all form and materiality, is recognized as the active side of the universal Store Consciousness (*ālaya-vijñāna*), on the surface of which forms arise and pass away, like the waves on the surface of the ocean, and which, when stilled, reflects the pure emptiness of space (*Vairocana* in his female aspect: *śūnyatā*) and the pure light (*Vairocana* in his male aspect, as illuminator) of heaven.

Therefore it is said in the *Bardo Thödol*, that 'on the second day of the "experiencing of reality" the pure form of the element water shines as a white light. At the same time there appears from the blue eastern realm of happiness the Blessed *Vajrasattva-Akṣobhya*. The colour of his body is deep blue. He is holding a five-pronged *vajra* in his hand and is seated on an elephant-throne,[1] embraced by the Divine Mother *Locanā* (Tib.: *saṅs-rgyas-spyan-ma*: "the Buddha-Eye"). The pure principle of form (*gzugs-kyi phuṅ-po gnas-su dag-pa*), the pure, white, radiant light of the Mirror-like Wisdom issues forth from the heart of *Vajrasattva* in his Father-Mother aspect (*yab-yum*)....'

The *Dhyāni-Buddha* of the southern direction is, like the sun at noon, the symbol of giving from the abundance of spiritual force. *Ratnasambhava*, whose colour corresponds to the warm light of the sun, appears in the gesture of giving (*dāna-mudrā*) the Three Jewels (*triratna*). From his heart shines forth the golden light of the Wisdom of the essential Equality of all beings. The pure principle of feeling which is attributed to him is converted by him into the love and compassion for all living beings, into the feeling of identity.

On the elementary plane *Ratnasambhava* corresponds to the earth, which carries and nourishes all beings with the equanimity and patience of a mother, in whose eyes all beings, borne by her, are equal. The traditional symbolical colour of the element earth is yellow. In its purest form it appears as gold or as a jewel (*ratna*), in the mystic terminology of alchemy as *prima materia* or as the 'Philosopher's Stone' (*cintamaṇi*).

The *Bardo Thödol*, therefore, says: 'On the third day the pure form of the element earth shines forth as a yellow light. At the same time there appears from the yellow southern realm of glory the Blessed *Ratnasambhava*. The colour of his body is yellow. He is holding

[1] A throne carried or supported by elephants, symbols of steadfastness, and therefore emblems of *Akṣobhya*, 'The Immutable'.

a jewel in his hand and is seated on a horse-throne,[1] embraced by the Divine Mother *Māmakī* (*yum-mchog mā-ma-ki*). . . .'

The pure principle of feeling (*tshor-baḥi phuṇ-po dbyiṅs-su dag-pa*) radiates forth as the yellow light of the Wisdom of Equality. . . .'

Amitābha, the *Dhyāni-Buddha* of the western direction, appears in the colour of the setting sun (red) and, in accordance with the most contemplative hour of the day, his hands rest in his lap, in the gesture of meditation (*dhyāna-mudrā*). The deep red light of discriminating inner vision shines forth from his heart and the fully opened lotus (*padma*) of unfolding, creative meditation rests upon his hands. The faculty of intuitive vision develops from the purified principle of perception, which is attributed to *Amitābha*. On the elementary plane the fire corresponds to him and thus, according to the ancient traditional symbolism, the eye and the function of seeing.[2]

The *Bardo Thödol*, accordingly, says: 'On the fourth day the pure form of the element fire shines forth as a red light. At the same time there appears from the red western realm of happiness the Blessed *Amitābha*. The colour of his body is red. He is bearing a lotus in his hand, and is seated upon a peacock-throne, embraced by the Divine Mother *Pāṇḍaravāsinī*, the "White-robed" (*gos-dkar-mo*). The pure principle of perception (*ḥdu-śes-kyi phuṅ-po gnas-su dag-pa*) shines forth as the red light of the Wisdom of Discriminating Clear Vision. . . .'

Amoghasiddhi, the *Dhyāni-Buddha* of the northern direction, represents what we might call 'the sun at midnight', i.e., the mysterious activity of spiritual forces, which work removed from the senses, invisible and imperceptible, with the aim of guiding the individual (or, more properly: all living beings) towards the maturity of knowledge and liberation. The yellow light of an (inner) sun (*bodhi*) invisible to human eyes, interwoven with the deep blue of the night sky (in which the unfathomable space of the universe seems to open itself), form the serene mystic green of *Amoghasiddhi*. The green light of the active, All-accomplishing Wisdom, which shines forth from his heart, combines the universality of the blue light of *Vairocana* with the emotional warmth generated by the light of *Ratnasambhava*'s Wisdom of Equality.

Thus the knowledge of the essential equality and unity of all beings is transformed into the universal, spiritualized activity for the benefit of all beings by a complete surrender of self-interest: by the power of all-embracing love (*maitrī*) and unlimited compassion (*karuṇā*). These

[1] The horse is a solar symbol, associated with the south, and the sun in its zenith.

[2] Therefore the peacock, whose feathers are adorned with *eyes*, is the animal that supports *Amitābha's* throne.

THE LOTUS OR *MAṆḌALA* OF THE FIVE *DHYĀNI-BUDDHAS*
with their female aspects, qualities and symbols, according to the teachings of the *Bardo Thödol.*

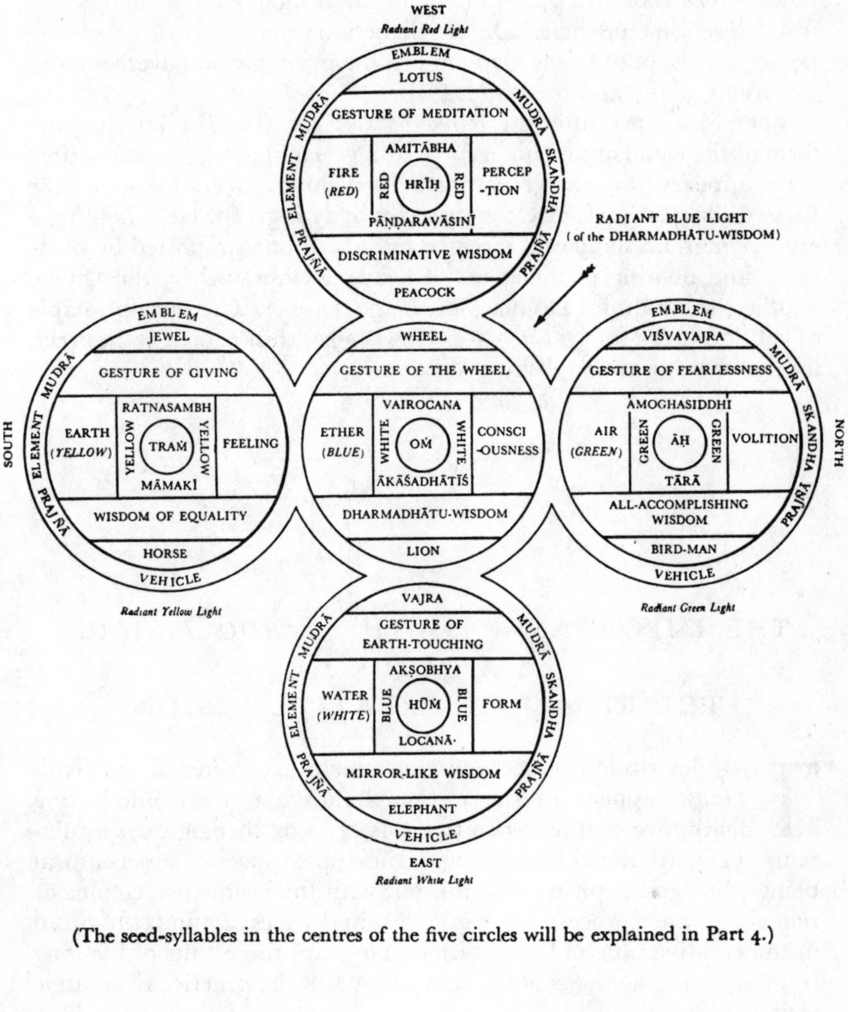

(The seed-syllables in the centres of the five circles will be explained in Part 4.)

two forces – if securely rooted in the afore-mentioned Wisdoms – are the indestructible double-sceptre (*viśva-vajra*; Tib.: *rdo-rje rgya-gram*) of *Amoghasiddhi*, which in this sense can be regarded as an intensification of *Akṣobhya*'s *vajra*. The *viśva-vajra* represents the magic spiritual power (*siddhi*) of a Buddha, in whom the principle of volition is free from all selfish tendencies. On the elementary plane this all-pervading power corresponds to the element air, the principle of movement and extension, of life and breath (*prāṇa*).

Therefore it is said in the *Bardo Thödol*: 'On the fifth day the pure form of the element air shines forth as a green light. At the same time there appears from the green northern realm of successful action the Blessed *Amoghasiddhi*. The colour of his body is green. He is holding a *viśva-vajra* in his hand and is seated upon a throne supported by bird-men[1] and floating in the space of heaven, embraced by the Divine Mother, the Faithful Dölma (*dam-tshig sgrol-ma*). The pure principle of volition (*ḥdu-byed-kyi phuṅ-po gnas-su dag-pa*) shines forth as the green light of the All-accomplishing Wisdom. . . .'

9

THE IMPORTANCE OF THE *BARDO THÖDOL* AS A GUIDE IN THE REALM OF CREATIVE VISION

THE description of these visions which, according to the *Bardo Thödol*, appear in the intermediate state (*bar-do*) following death, are neither primitive folklore nor theological speculations. They are not concerned with the appearances of supernatural beings, like gods, spirits, or genii, but with the visible projections or reflexes of inner processes, experiences, and states of mind, produced in the creative phase of meditation. They are the results of life-long training in the methods of concentration and the practice of creative vision.

The appearances of these luminous forms are like a charmed circle around the adept, protecting him from the horrors of death and the

[1] Tib.: *śaṅ-śaṅ*, pronounced 'shang-shang', a creature half man, half bird. From the waist upwards they appear in human form, male as well as female. Their feet and wings are those of birds.

dangers of sinking into lower states of existence, by calling up in his mind all that is noble, elevating, enlightening.

Such calling up of inner symbols and spiritual forces is the deeper meaning of the expression '*thö-dol*' (*thos-grol*) or 'liberation by hearing'. Only he, who has ears to hear, i.e., who has prepared himself in life for the call of liberation and has made himself receptive for it by training his inner organ of hearing, can respond to the call and follow it. Only he who has opened his inner eye can see the redeeming visions. Those, however, who have neither developed the faculty of inner hearing nor that of inner vision, cannot be benefited by merely listening to the recital of the *Bardo Thödol*.

The text, therefore, says: 'Those who have meditated on the Great Perfection (*rdzogs-chen*; Skt.: *sampannakrama*, the state of perfection, which is reached by way of perfect integration [*layakrama*]) and on the Great Symbol (*phyag-rgya chen-po*; Skt.: *mahāmudrā*, the great attitude of unification and wholeness) will see the clear light and gain illumination in the moment of death, realizing the state of liberation in the *Dharmakāya*, wherefore they will not need the recital of this *Thödol*.'

Similarly it is said at another place that *if one has meditated on the images of these divine embodiments while one was in the human world*, one would attain liberation, due to recognizing them, when they appear in the *Bardo*. 'If, however, one does not remember the teachings (concerning them) at this stage, even the hearing [of the *Bardo Thödol*] is of no avail.'

Thus the *Bardo Thödol* is first of all a book for the living, to prepare them, not only for the dangers of death, but to give them an opportunity to make use of the great possibilities which offer themselves in the moment of relinquishing the body – either for a better rebirth or for final liberation.

For all who are familiar with Buddhist philosophy, it is clear that birth and death are not phenomena that happen only once in human life, but something that happens uninterruptedly within us. At every moment something within us dies and something is reborn. The different *bardos*, therefore, are nothing other than the different states of consciousness of our life: the state of waking consciousness, the normal consciousness of a being born into our human world (*skyes-nas bar-do*); the state of dream-consciousness (*rmi-lam bar-do*); the state of *dhyāna*, or trance-consciousness, in profound meditation (*bsam-gtan bar-do*); the state of the experiencing of death (*ḥchi-kha bar-do*); the state of experiencing of Reality (*chos-ñid bar-do*); the state of rebirth-consciousness (*srid-pa bar-do*).

All this is clearly described in the 'Root-Verses of the [six]

Bardos' (*bar-doḥi rtsa-tshig*) which, together with the 'Prayers and Aspirations' (*smon-lam*),[1] form the authentic and original nucleus of the *Bardo Thödol*, around which the prose parts crystallized as commentaries. This proves that we have to do here with life itself and not merely with a mass for the dead, to which the *Bardo Thödol* was reduced in later times.

The *Bardo Thödol* is addressed not only to those who see the end of their life approaching, or who are very near death, but equally to those who are in the prime of life and who for the first time realize the full meaning of their existence as human beings. To be born as a human being is a privilege, according to the Buddha's teaching, because it offers the rare opportunity of liberation through one's own decisive effort, through a 'turning about in the deepest seat of consciousness'.

Accordingly the 'Root-Verses of the Bardo' open with the words:

'O that now, when the Bardo of Life[2] is dawning upon me,
—After having given up indolence, since there is no time to waste in life—
May I undistractedly enter the path of listening, reflecting, and meditating,
So that . . . once having attained human embodiment,
No time may be squandered through useless distractions.'

Listening, reflecting and meditating are the three stages of discipleship. The Tibetan word for 'listening' or 'hearing', *thos* in this connexion – as well as in the expression '*Thödol*' (*thos-grol*) – cannot be confused with the mere physical sense-awareness of hearing, as may be seen from the Tibetan term '*ñan-thos*' (pron. '*nä-t'hö*'), the equivalent of the Sanskrit word '*śrāvaka*', referring to a 'disciple', and, more particularly, to a personal disciple of the Buddha, and not merely to one, who by chance happened to hear the Buddha's teaching. It refers to one who has accepted this teaching in his heart and has made it his own. Thus the word 'listening' in this connexion, implies 'hearing with one's heart', that is, with sincere faith (*śraddha*). This represents

[1] The Tibetan *smon-lam* corresponds to the Sanskrit *praṇidhāna*, which is not a prayer in the sense of a supplication, but a calling up of the highest forces of our mind, of our highest ideals, and the remembrance of those who realized them (Buddhas), coupled with the firm resolution or vow to follow their example and to put into practice our aspirations.

[2] Lama Kazi Dawa Samdup has here 'Birthplace Bardo'. Apparently his manuscript has '*skyes-gnas*' instead of '*skyes-nas*', which is found in the block-print (the authorized Tibetan edition). The latter means, literally, 'having been born', that is, having been born into the state men call life. '*Skyes-gnas*' would refer to the womb, the 'place' of birth (*gnas*), and as this is the subject of the sixth verse, dealing with the *bardo* of rebirth, it cannot be meant here, for otherwise there would be only five *bardos* instead of six. Even if the word '*gnas*' is used by certain traditions, we have to keep in mind that '*gnas*' has many meanings. It can signify a place, a region, a realm, the belonging to a certain order or class, a condition, like that of human existence, the world of life and death, etc.

the first stage of discipleship. In the second stage, this intuitive attitude is transformed into understanding through reason; while in the third stage, the disciple's intuitive feeling as well as intellectual understanding are transformed into living reality through direct experience. Thus intellectual conviction grows into spiritual certainty, into a knowing in which the knower is *one* with the known.

This is the high spiritual state vouchsafed by the teachings set forth in the *Bardo Thödol.* Thereby the initiated disciple attains dominion over the realm of death, and, being able to perceive death's illusory nature, is freed from fear. For in the process of dying we pass through the same stages which are experienced in the higher states of meditation. Already Plutarch said: 'At the moment of death the soul experiences the same as those who are initiated into the great mysteries.'

The *Bardo Thödol* is such a book of initiation into one of those Great Mysteries. Under the guise of death it reveals to the initiate the secret of life. He must go through the experience of death, in order to gain liberation within himself. He must die to his past and to his ego, before he can be admitted into the community of the Enlightened Ones. Only he who looks upon every moment of his life as if it were his last, and values it accordingly, can understand the significance of the *Bardo Thödol* as a vade-mecum for initiates, a guide for the *sādhaka*, an incomparable inspiration for the unfoldment of inner vision. Herein consists for us the value of this work, one of the oldest scriptures in Tibetan language, which is looked upon as the spiritual testament of *Padmasambhava*. It contains the fundamental outlines of all later *maṇḍalas* or systems of creative visualization. For this reason we have made the *Bardo Thödol* the basis of our observations.[1]

[1] All references to the original text of the *Bardo Thödol* in the present as well as in following parts are based on the authorized Tibetan block-print edition.

For references to Lama Kazi Dawa Samdup's translation see W. Y. Evans-Wentz, *The Tibetan Book of the Dead*, Oxford University Press (Third edition, 1957).

Part Four

HŪṀ

THE PATH OF INTEGRATION

Plate 4

AKṢOBHYA
who embodies the Wisdom of the Great Mirror

I

OṀ AND HŪṀ AS COMPLEMENTARY VALUES OF EXPERIENCE AND AS METAPHYSICAL SYMBOLS

In order not to lose ourselves in a labyrinth of details, it is necessary to come back from time to time to the main features of our subject. We started from the idea of the mantric word and the principles of primordial sound, in which the power of the mind, the quintessence of all original and direct experience, is contained. As being the first and foremost of these primordial sounds, we explored the origins and the various applications of the sacred syllable OṀ in the course of its history.

In the experience of OṀ, man opens himself, goes beyond himself, liberates himself, by breaking through the narrow confines of egohood or self-imposed limitation, and thus he becomes one with the All, with the Infinite. If he would remain in this state, there would be an end of his existence as an individual, as a living, thinking and experiencing being. He would have attained perfect self-annihilation, perfect quietude, but also perfect immobility, passivity, emotionlessness, and insensibility with regard to all differentiation and individuality not only within, but also outside himself, i.e., with regard to all living and suffering beings.

But, is this the ideal which confronts us in the exalted figure of the Buddha? What then is it that attracts us so irresistibly? – Is it the Buddha's quietude, his serenity, his wisdom, the profound peace of his being? – All these properties, to be certain, co-operate in exerting upon us a strong power of attraction. However, much as we may value these properties, these alone are not sufficient to describe the nature of a Buddha. They would make him into a seer or a saint, but not a Buddha. What raises him to the status of an Enlightened One is the radiance and universality of his being, his power to reach the heart of every living being with the rays of his boundless compassion, his infinite capacity to participate in the joys and sufferings of others, without being torn or swayed by them, without losing or limiting his universality. It is this power which establishes the inner contact with all that lives, and especially with all those who approach him. He is not like a distant, intangible deity to whom one looks up with awe and fear, but like a wise friend and a loving guide, for whom one feels a spontaneous inner relationship, because he himself went the way through human errors and pitfalls, through all the heights and depths of *Saṁsāra*.

It is this *human* element in the character of the Buddha, which softens the brightness of his perfection and relieves it of the apparent distance and aloofness from ordinary human life; for his compassion is as great as his wisdom, his humanity and warmth of feeling as all-embracing as his mind.

He has returned from the experience of universality – from the sacred all-consuming and purifying flame of OṀ—to the human plane, without losing the consciousness of completeness, the knowledge of the unity of man and cosmos. And thus in the depth of his heart the primordial sound of Reality is transferred into the sound of the cosmic-human mystery (purified through suffering and compassion) which reverberates through all the scriptures of the *Mahāyāna* and *Vajrayāna*, and in the sacred seed-syllable HŪṀ.

OṀ is the ascent towards universality, HŪṀ the descent of the state of universality into the depth of the human heart. HŪṀ cannot be without OṀ. But HŪṀ is more than OṀ: it is the Middle Way which neither gets lost in the finite nor in the infinite, which is neither attached to the one nor to the other extreme.

Therefore it is said: 'In darkness are they who worship only the world, but in greater darkness they who worship the infinite alone. He who accepts both saves himself from death by the knowledge of the former and attains immortality by the knowledge of the latter.' (*Īśā Upaniśad*)[1]

OṀ, in its dynamic aspect, is the breaking through of the individual into the super-individual consciousness, the breaking through towards the 'absolute', the liberation from egohood, from the illusion of 'I'. To dwell in the 'absolute' is as impossible for a living

[1] This interpretation, which I owe to Rabindranath Tagore, seems to be nearer the original meaning than many of the more literal translations which, as often in such cases, differ considerably from each other. 'Those who worship the world,' namely, *saṁsāra*, the state of ignorance (*avidyā*), are those to whom the world is the only reality (therefore: *avidyām-upasate*); while those who have acquired knowledge (*vidyā*), but not wisdom, fall into the other extreme of devoting themselves merely to abstract, conceptual knowledge (*vidyāyāṁ ratāḥ*): 'worshipping the infinite' and despising the finite. But he who realizes that both are only the two sides of the same reality, 'overcomes death' by recognizing the nature of ignorance, which creates the illusion of death (by not knowing that life goes on incessantly, changing only its forms); and he 'attains immortality' by recognizing the relative nature of conceptual knowledge, thus going beyond its subject-object duality and arriving at the direct and spontaneous experience of reality within himself.

being as floating in a vacuum, because life and consciousness are possible only where there are relations. The experience of OṀ must be sheltered and brought to maturity in that of HŪṀ. OṀ is like the sun, but HŪṀ is like the soil, into which the sun's rays must descend in order to awaken the dormant life.

OṀ is the infinite, but HŪṀ is the infinite in the finite, the eternal in the temporal, the timeless in the moment, the unconditioned in the conditioned, the formless as basis of all form, the transcendental in the ephemeral: it is the Wisdom of the Great Mirror, which reflects the Void (*śūnyatā*) as much as the objects, and reveals the 'emptiness' in the things as much as the things in the 'emptiness'.

'To see things as parts, as incomplete elements, is a lower analytic knowledge. The Absolute is everywhere; it has to be seen and found everywhere. Every finite is an infinite and has to be known and sensed in its intrinsic infiniteness as well as in its surface finite appearance. But so to know the world, so to perceive and experience it, it is not enough to have an intellectual idea or imagination that so it is; a certain divine vision, divine sense, divine ecstasy is needed, an experience of union of ourselves with the objects of our consciousness. In that experience . . . each thing in the All becomes to us our self. . . .'[1]

Such a 'divine vision' is only possible through the realization of the universality of our higher consciousness. We, therefore, must have passed through the experience of OṀ in order to reach and to understand the still deeper experience of HŪṀ. This is why OM stands at the beginning and HŪṀ at the end of mantras. In the OṀ we open ourselves, in the HŪṀ we give ourselves. OṀ is the door of knowledge, HŪṀ is the door to the realization of this knowledge in life. HŪṀ is a sacrificial sound. The Sanskrit syllable '*hu*' means 'to sacrifice, to perform a sacrificial act or rite'. The sole sacrifice, however, that the Buddha recognizes, is the sacrifice of one's own self.

> '*I lay no wood, Brahman, for fires on altars,*
> *Only within burneth the flame I kindle.*
> *Ever my fire burns, ever composed of self*
> *. . . and the heart is the altar;*
> *The flame thereon—this is a man's self well tamed.*[2]

HŪṀ is symbolized in the Buddha's gesture of touching the earth, calling the earth as witness of innumerable acts of self-sacrifice performed by him in this and in previous existences. It is this power of supreme sacrifice, which vanquishes the Evil One (*Māra*) and drives away his hosts of demons.

It would be a complete reversal of cause and effect to define the

[1] Srī Aurobindo: *The Synthesis of Yoga*, p. 486.
[2] *Saṁyutta-Nikāya*, I, p. 169 (I. B. Horner's translation).

sound HŪṀ as an expression of anger, challenge, as an act of threatening or intimidation, or as a means of exorcising demons. Such facile explanations are due to the ignorance of mantric practice and tradition, as laid down in numerous collections of mantric formulae, which can be found in many monastic libraries and temples. These mantra-books have been neglected by Western scholars, because of their purely esoteric and untranslatable nature. A patient and careful analysis of them, however, would yield a lot of valuable information concerning the development, the structure and inner laws of these apparently arbitrary sound-forms, which neither obey the rules of grammar nor of philological word-definitions. And yet they are not devoid of meaning, because they not only correspond to certain emotional and mental attitudes, but to certain clearly defined introspective visions (mental images, symbols, etc.) which the initiate is able to call up with their help. Besides this they are a valuable aid to the study of Tibetan iconography.

If HŪṀ were the expression of anger and of a threatening attitude, it would only be applied to the mantras of the 'wrathful' or terrifying forms of *Dhyāni-Buddhas* and *-Bodhisattvas*. This, however, is not the case, as we can see from the above-mentioned collections of mantric formulae. On the contrary, HŪṀ is associated as much with the mantras of peaceful aspects, like that of *Avalokiteśvara*, the All-compassionate, whose mantra OṀ MAṆI PADME HŪṀ is the highest expression of that wisdom of the heart, that courageously descends into the world – and even into the deepest hells – in order to transform the poison of death into the Elixir of Life. Indeed, *Avalokiteśvara* himself assumes even the form of *Yama*, the God of Death and the Judge of the Dead, so as to convert the finite into a vessel of the infinite, to transfigure our mortal life in the rays of his love and to free it from the deathly rigor of separation from the greater life of the spirit.

Before dealing with the metaphysical aspects of the syllable HŪṀ and the abstract principles connected with them, we shall have to consider its purely tonal symbolism. In doing so, however, we must clearly understand, that whatever we put into words and concepts, is in no way final or exhaustive (and that holds good for all definitions of mantric sounds and formulae), but only a tentative approach, which may serve to elucidate certain aspects that appear flashlike in the experience of the sacred syllable.

HŪṀ consists of an aspirate (h), a long vowel (ū), and the closing nasal sound (ṁ), which in Sanskrit is known as *anusvara* (literally 'after-sound'), similar to a slightly nasalized 'ng' ('hūng').

The aspirate is the sound of breath, the very essence of life, the sound of *prāṇa* (Tib.: *śugs*), the subtle life-force, the 'ātman' in its original, not yet egocentrically distorted, individualized form: the ever in- and out-flowing, all-embracing vital force.

The long vowel *Ū* is the sound of the deep, vibrating forth in the *anusvara*, where it merges into the inaudible. *U* is the lower limit in the tonal scale of the human voice, the threshold of silence, or as it is expressed in Tibetan: 'the door of the inaudible' ('*U-ni thos-pa-med-paḥi-sgo*' [*bKaḥ-ḥgyur*, *myaṅ-ḥdas*, *K.*206]).

The sonorous inwardly-directed, inwardly-vibrating final sound of the *anusvara* may be said to stand (according to its nature) between consonants and vowels, being an indissoluble combination of both. In Sanskrit as well as in Tibetan it is represented, therefore, by a diacritical sign in the form of a dot, a drop, or a small circle (Skt.: *bindu;* Tib.: *thig-le*), i.e., by the symbol of unity, of totality, of the absolute, the imperishable, indestructible (*akṣara*), of the Void (*śūnyatā*), the state beyond duality, the *dharmadhātu*, etc. Every sound that is connected with it, thus becomes mantra, inner sound, psychic vibration. (In this way the plain, natural sound O becomes the mantric sound OṀ).

If, therefore, the mantric nature of the letters of the Sanskrit alphabet (which according to Indian tradition is of divine origin, and upon which the equally sacred Tibetan script is based) is to be emphasized, the *anusvara* is superimposed upon them, as we see for instance in the pictorial representations of the psychic centres or *cakras* in the human body, in which each centre is characterized by a number of seed-syllables. These are arranged like petals around the calyx or pericarp of a lotus-flower, in the centre of which appears the chief seed-syllable, corresponding to the ruling element or state of aggregation and its symbolic colour.

2

THE DOCTRINE OF THE PSYCHIC CENTRES IN HINDUISM AND BUDDHISM

THOUGH the physiological foundations of the doctrine of the psychic centres are the same in Hindu and Buddhist Tantras, we have to bear in mind that the way in which these centres are used and defined in the Buddhist system of meditation, shows considerable differences in spite of certain technical similarities. It is, therefore, not permissible to mix up these two systems and to explain the Buddhist practice of meditation, as if it were based upon or derived from the teachings and the symbolism of the Hindu Tantras, as this has been done in practically all books which have treated this subject. Due to this fundamental error the impression has been created that Buddhism has taken over something that was alien to its own character and that only subsequently had been adapted to its own use and terminology and thus fitted into the Buddhist system.

The main difference between the two systems lies in the different treatment of the same fundamental facts. Just as travellers of different temperaments or of different interests and mental attitudes would describe the same landscape in quite different ways, without contradicting thereby each other or the given facts, in the same way the Buddhist and Hindu followers of the Tantras invest the same landscapes of the human mind with different experiences.

The Hindu system emphasizes more the static side of the centres and their connexions with elementary nature, by identifying them with the fundamental elements and forces of the universe. This supplies the *cakras* with an 'objective' content in form of permanently fixed seed-syllables and their corresponding divine rulers in form of gods and goddesses.

The Buddhist system is less concerned with the static-objective side of the *cakras*, but rather with that which flows through them, with their dynamic functions, i.e., with the transformation of that current of cosmic or nature-energies into spiritual potentialities.[1] The mantric symbols of primordial sounds, represented by the letters of the alphabet are therefore not identified with or attributed to certain centres once and for ever, but they are inserted into the living flow of forces, represented as polarized currents of energy, on whose interaction, mutual penetration and combination depends the success of the Spiritual training.

The channels through which these psychic energies flow in the human body, are called *nāḍī* (Tib.: *rtsa*) and follow the fundamental structure of the body in a similar way as the nerve-system, though they cannot be identified with it, as has often been wrongly maintained. All attempts at proving it, have only shown that the experiences of Yoga can neither be measured with the yardsticks of natural science, physiology and dissecting anatomy, nor by those of experimental psychology.

[1] All methods grouped under the common name of Yoga are special psychological processes founded on a fixed truth of Nature and developing, out of normal functions, powers and results which were always latent, but which her ordinary movements do not easily or do not often manifest.' (Srī Aurobindo: *A Synthesis of Yoga*, p. 6.)

While, according to Western conceptions, the brain is the exclusive seat of consciousness, yogic experience shows that our brain-consciousness is only *one* among a number of possible forms of consciousness, and that these, according to their function and nature, can be localized or centred in various organs of the body. These 'organs' which collect, transform and distribute the forces flowing through them, are called *cakras* or centres of force. From them radiate secondary streams of psychic force, comparable to the spokes of a wheel, the ribs of an umbrella, or the petals of a lotus.

In other words, these *cakras* are the points in which psychic forces and bodily functions merge into each other or penetrate each other. They are the focal points in which cosmic and psychic energies crystallize into bodily qualities, and in which bodily qualities are dissolved or transmuted again into psychic forces. 'The seat of the soul is where the inner and outer world meet. When they penetrate each other, it is present in every point of penetration.' (Novalis.) We, therefore, can say that each psychic centre in which we become conscious of this spiritual penetration, becomes the seat of the soul, and that by activating or awakening the activities of the various centres, we spiritualize and transform our body.

In this connexion we may remember another word of Novalis: 'The active use of organs is nothing but magic, miracle-working thought' – though not in the ordinary sense: 'Thinking in the ordinary sense is thinking of thinking.' The thinking that is meant here is synonymous with creative activity. 'Thinking is making', this is the fundamental principle of all magic, especially of all mantric science. By the rhythmic repetition of a creative thought or idea, of a concept, a perception or a mental image, its effect is augmented and fixed (like the action of a steadily falling drop) until it seizes upon all organs of activity and becomes a mental and material reality: a deed in the fullest sense of the word.

'We know something only insofar as we can express it, i.e., produce it. The more perfectly and manifoldly we can produce something, the better we know it. We know it completely, if we can produce and communicate it always and in every possible way, and if we can bring about an individual expression in every organ of it.' (Novalis.)

The great secret of Tantric Yoga consists in the experience of reality on the planes of different or, if possible, *all* psychophysical centres available to us. It is only through this multidimensional awareness that our knowledge gains that depth and universal perspective which converts into inner experience and dynamic reality (actuality) what otherwise would have merely been perceived outwardly and superficially. As in a stereoscopic picture a higher degree of reality is achieved by merging two pictures of the same object, taken from slightly different points of view – or, as in a similar way, through combination of spatially different recordings of the same musical composition a more plastic and space-true sound-production becomes possible – in the same way an experience of higher dimensionality is achieved by integration of experiences of different centres and levels of consciousness. Hence the indescribability of certain experiences of meditation on the plane of three-dimensional consciousness and within a system of logic which reduces the possibilities of expression by imposing further limits upon the process of thinking.

The tacit presupposition that the world which we build up in our thought is identical with that of our experience (to say nothing of the world as such) is one of the main sources of our erroneous conception of the world. The world which we experience includes the world of our thought, but not vice versa; because we live simultaneously in different dimensions, of which that of the intellect, the faculty of discursive thought, is only one. If we reproduce in our intellect experiences which according to their nature belong to other dimensions, we do something comparable to the activity of a painter who depicts three-dimensional objects or space on a two-dimensional surface. He is doing this by consciously renouncing certain qualities belonging to the higher dimension and by introducing a new order of tonal values, proportions and optical foreshortenings which are only valid in the artificial unity of his picture and from a certain point of view.

The laws of this perspective correspond in many ways to the laws of logic. Both of them sacrifice qualities of a higher dimension and confine themselves to an arbitrarily chosen viewpoint, so that their objects are seen only from one side at a time, and in the proportions and foreshortenings corresponding to the relative position of the viewpoint. But while the artist consciously transfers his impressions from one dimension into the other, and has neither the intention to imitate nor to reproduce an objective reality, but only to express his reaction in front of it – the thinker generally falls a prey to the illusion of having grasped reality with his thought, by accepting the 'foreshortening' perspective of his one-sided logic as a universal law.

The use of logic in thought is as necessary and justified as the use of perspective in painting – but only as a medium of expression, not as a criterion of reality. If, therefore, we use logical definitions, as far as possible, in the description of meditative experiences and of the centres of consciousness, with which they are connected, we must regard these definitions only as the necessary spring-board towards the understanding of the dimensions of consciousness of a different nature, in which the various impressions and experiences of different planes or levels are combined into an organic whole.

3

THE PRINCIPLES OF SPACE AND OF MOVEMENT

According to ancient Indian tradition the universe reveals itself in two fundamental properties: as *motion*, and as that in which motion takes place, namely *space*. This space is called *ākāśa* (Tib.: *nam-mkhaḥ*) and is that through which things step into visible appearance, i.e., through which they possess extension or corporeality. As that which comprises all things, *ākāśa* corresponds to the three-dimensional space of our sense-perception, and in this capacity it is called *mahākāśa*. The nature of *ākāśa*, however, does not exhaust itself in this three-dimensionality; it comprises *all* possibilities of movement, not only the physical, but also the spiritual ones: it comprises infinite dimensions.

On the plane of spiritual activity *ākāśa* is called the 'space of consciousness', or the dimension of consciousness '*cittākāśa*', while on the highest stage of spiritual experience, on which the duality of subject and object is eliminated, it is called '*cidākāśa*'.

Ākāśa is derived from the root *kāś*, 'to radiate, to shine', and has therefore also the meaning of 'ether', which is conceived as the medium of movement. The principle of movement, however, is *ḍrāṇa* (Tib.: *śugs*), the breath of life, the all-powerful, all-pervading rhythm of the universe, in which world-creations and world-destructions follow each other like inhalation and exhalation in the human body, and in which the course of suns and planets plays a similar role as the circulation of the blood and the currents of psychic energy in the human organism. All forces of the universe, like those of the human mind, from the highest consciousness to the depths of the subconscious, are modifications of *prāṇa*. The word '*prāṇa*' can therefore not be equated with the physical breath, though breathing (*prāṇa* in the narrower sense) is one of the many functions in which this universal and primordial force manifests itself.

Though, in the highest sense, *ākāśa* and *prāṇa* cannot be separated, because they condition each other like 'above' and 'below', or 'right' and 'left', it is possible to observe and to distinguish the preponderance of the one or the other principle in the realm of practical experience.

All that is formed and that has taken spatial appearance by possessing extension, reveals the nature of *ākāśa*. Therefore the four great elements (*mahābhūta*; Tib.: *ḥbyuṅ-ba*) or states of aggregation, namely the solid ('earth'), the liquid ('water'), the incandescent or heating ('fire'), and the gaseous ('air'), are conceived as modifications of *ākāśa*, the space-ether.

All dynamic qualities, all that causes movement, change or transformation, reveal the nature of *prāṇa*. All bodily or psychic processes, all physical or spiritual forces, from the functions of breathing, of the circulation of blood and of the nervous system, to those of consciousness, of mental activities and all higher spiritual functions are modifications of *prāṇa*.

In its grossest form *ākāśa* presents itself as matter; in its subtlest forms it merges imperceptibly into the realm of dynamic forces. The state of aggregation, for instance, which we call 'fire' or the state of incandescence, is material as well as energetic. *Prāṇa*, on the other hand, appears in such bodily functions as breathing, digestion, etc., and is the cause of physical and psychic heat (Tib.: *gtum-mo*).

If this were not so, the interaction of body and mind, of spiritual and material forces, of matter and consciousness, sense-organs and sense-objects, etc., would be impossible. It is precisely this interaction of which the Yogin (irrespective whether he is Buddhist or Hindu) makes use, and upon which the technique of meditation is built. 'If the Indian saying is true that the body is the instrument provided for the fulfilment of the right law of our nature, then any final recoil from the physical life must be a turning away from the completeness of divine Wisdom and a renunciation of its aim in earthly manifestation. It can be therefore no integral Yoga which ignores the body or makes its annulment or its rejection indispensable to a perfect spirituality.'[1]

The centres of psycho-cosmic force in the human body and their respective organs correspond to the modifications of *ākāśa*, i.e., to the great, primary elements; while the currents of force, which flow through them (or are dammed up in them) and are transformed and distributed by them, represent the modifications of *prāṇa*.

The four lower centres of energy represent in their ascending sequence the various aspects of *ākāśa* (of which the following one

[1] Śrī Aurobindo: *The Synthesis of Yoga*, p. 10.

is always more subtle than the preceding one) in form of the 'elements' Earth, Water, Fire, and Air.

The lowest of these centres, which represents the Element Earth, is called *Mūlādhāra-Cakra* ('Root-support'), and is situated at the base of the spinal column. It corresponds to the *plexus pelvis* in Western physiology and contains the still unqualified, primordial vital energy, which serves either the functions of physical reproduction and rejuvenation or brings about the sublimation of these forces into spiritual potentialities.

The latent energy of this centre is depicted as the dormant force of the goddess *Kuṇḍalinī* – who as the *śakti* of *Brahma* embodies the potentiality of nature, whose effects may be either divine or demoniacal. The wise, who control these forces, may reach through them the highest spiritual power and perfection, while those who ignorantly release them, will be destroyed by them.

Just as the primordial forces, locked up in the atom, can be utilized for the benefit as well as for the destruction of humanity, so the forces, which dwell in the human body, may lead to liberation as well as to bondage, towards the light as well as into utter darkness. Only with perfect self-control and clear knowledge of the nature of these forces, can the Yogi dare to arouse them. The directions for their awakening are therefore given in religious literature in such a way, that only those, who have been initiated by a competent Guru, can practise them, in accordance with the rules which have been formulated in the course of milleniums of meditative experience.

The veil of secrecy with which certain esoteric teachings are treated, by making use of a language which can only be understood by initiates, has therefore its reason not in the intention of preventing others from obtaining such powers or knowledge, but in that of protecting the ignorant from the dangers which misuse of, or superficial experimentation with, these practices would bring about.

The Buddhist system of Tantric meditation avoids these dangers, by neither allowing the *sādhaka* to concentrate directly upon the *śakti*, nor upon the lower centres but, as we shall see later on, upon those qualities of consciousness and those psychic centres, which regulate and transform the flow of these forces. In place of the *śakti* we find in Buddhism the *ḍākinī*, i.e., in place of the power-principle the knowledge-principle in its intuitive-spontaneous form; in place of the force of nature, the unifying force of inspiration. (We shall revert to this subject in the thirteenth chapter of this part.)

4

THE PSYCHIC CENTRES OF THE *KUṆḌALINĪ-YOGA* AND THEIR PHYSIOLOGICAL COUNTERPARTS

JUST as the Root Centre, the *Mūlādhāra-Cakra*, represents the lement Earth, the next-higher one – corresponding to the *plexus hypogastricus*, which controls the organs of elimination and reproduction – represents the element water. It is called *Svādhiṣṭhāna-Cakra*.

In the Tibetan systems of meditation this Centre is usually not mentioned or regarded as an independent centre (and this holds good for the Buddhist conception of the psychic Centres in general, as may be seen from the late Ceylonese Pāli work '*Yogāvacara*'),[1] but is combined with the *Mūlādhāra-Cakra* under the name '*sang-nä*' (*gsaṅ-gnas*), the 'Secret Place' ('secret' in the sense of 'sacral', thus corresponding to the *sacral plexus* of Western physiology). This *sacral plexus* stands for the whole realm of reproductive forces, of sexual as well as of pre-sexual nature, while these functions of the *Svādhiṣṭhāna-Cakra* which belong to the negative side of the system of nutrition (like disintegration, dissolution and separation of the elements of nutrition into substances which can be accepted and assimilated by the body, and those which cannot be assimilated and have to be rejected and eliminated) are associated with the next-higher Centre, the *plexus epigastricus* or *solar plexus*.

The Centre that corresponds to the *solar plexus* is called *Maṇipūra-Cakra* or *Nābhipadma*, i.e., 'navel-lotus' (Tib.: *lte-baḥi ḥkhor-lo*). It represents the element Fire and the forces of transformation, in the physical as well as in the psychic sense (digestion, assimilation, conversion of inorganic into organic substances as well as the transmutation of organic substances into psychic energies, etc.).

The Centre that corresponds to the heart is called *Anāhata-Cakra* and represents the element Air. This Centre is not necessarily identical with the heart. It regulates and controls the organs of respiration, just as the heart does, and it is said to be situated on the vertical central axis of the body.

The three highest Centres are the Throat Centre, *Viśuddha-Cakra*, corresponding to the *plexus cervicus* – the Centre between the eyebrows,

[1] Published by the Pāli Text Society as *Manual of a Mystic* (London, 1916). Translation by F. L. Woodward.

called *Ajñā-Cakra*, which, according to modern physiology, is said to correspond to the *medulla oblongata* – and the Crown Centre, called *Sahasrāra-Padma*, the 'Thousand-petalled Lotus,' which is associated with the pituitary gland of the brain.

These last-mentioned highest Centres correspond to those forms of *ākāśa* which go beyond the gross elements (*mahābhūta*) and represent higher dimensions of space, in which finally the quality of light becomes identical with that of space and thereby merges into the psycho-energetic state of *prāṇa* and into the realm of cosmic consciousness. Just as the two lower Centres have been combined into one, so also the two upper Centres are regarded as one in the Tibetan system of Yoga: *Ājñā-Cakra* is therefore not separately mentioned in Tibetan scriptures, but regarded as part of the 'Thousand-petalled Lotus' (*ḥdab-stoṅ*).[1]

[1] In order to give readers, trained in Western physiology, an easier approach to these specifically Indian teachings concerning the psychic Centres, the following definitions of the seven systems of the human body, as found in the book *Health and Meditation* by A. M. Curtis, may be useful:

'If we now enumerate the different systems in their sequence, ascending from the basis of the spinal column to the brain, we get the following summary:

I. The *reproductive system*, represented by the *sacral plexus* of the cerebro-spinal nerve system, which controls the lower limbs and the external organs of reproduction.

II. The *negative system of nutrition*, represented by the *prevertebral hypogastric plexus* of the sympathetic nerve-system, which controls the organs of elimination, bladder, intestines, urinary ducts, and the inner organs of reproduction.

III. The *positive system of nutrition*, represented by the *prevertebral solar or hypogastric plexus* of the sympathetic system, which controls the stomach, intestines, gall-bladder, bladder, gall-ducts, urinary ducts, seminal ducts, and the gland-like organs of the liver, kidneys, spleen, and intestinal glands.

IV. The *system of blood-circulation*, represented by the heart-plexus of the *sympaticus*, which controls the heart and the blood-vessels.

V. The *respiratory system*, represented by the throat-plexus or *plexus cervicus* of the *cerebro-spinal* system, which, together with the *brachial plexus*, controls the upper limbs.

VI. The *non-volitional* (*sympathetic*) *nerve-system*, which is represented within the skull by the *medulla oblongata*, the enlarged continuation of the spinal column, forming the basis of the brain and controlling the special sense-organs, eyes, ears, nose, tongue, skin.

VII. The *volitional nerve-system*, represented by the pituitary gland, a small conical body in the depth of the central great-brain tissue, whose physiological function has not yet been discovered. Attention has to be drawn upon the close natural relationship of the pituitary gland with the optical nerves, in connexion with a higher interpretation of this organ as an undeveloped base of a consciousness of the seventh order.'

Note to I: 'The reproductive system expresses the desire for the continuity of consciousness. For the average man this desire is satisfied by the survival of his children, on a higher level of development, however, his physical energy is partially transformed into psychic energy, which finds for itself a corresponding form of expression; and with this twofold fulfilment the majority of men is satisfied. For a growing number, however, it becomes clear nowadays that this system of reproduction hints at the force which may produce the ultimate or spirit-man, and that body and soul are only the material from which, by means of transformation, the super-human state will emerge.'

(Re-translated from the German version of *Health and Meditation*, pp. 23 ff.– Niels Kampmann Verlag, Heidelberg, 1928.)

The seven Centres of the human body represent in a certain way the elementary structure and dimensionality of the universe: from the state of greatest density and materiality up to the state of immaterial multi-dimensional extension; from the organs of dark, subconscious, but cosmically powerful primordial forces to those of a radiant, enlightened consciousness. That the form-potentialities of the whole universe are latent in these centres, is hinted at by attributing to them all the sounds of the Sanskrit alphabet in the form of seed-syllables.

Each of these psycho-physical centres is depicted as a lotus-blossom, whose petals correspond to the seed-syllables (*bīja*), expressing certain qualities or forces, while the pericarp contains the symbol of the element that governs them, together with its particular (elementary) seed-syllable. Each of these elementary seed-syllables is associated with a symbolical animal as its 'vehicle' (*vahana*), by which the character of the element is expressed. Without going here into further details, like the respective gods and goddesses, connected with the centres – which would presuppose a detailed knowledge of the Hindu-Tantric pantheon – we shall confine ourselves to these elementary aspects of the centres.

The Root Centre, *Mūlādhāra*, is shown as a four-petalled lotus with the seed-syllables *Vaṁ*, *Śaṁ*, *Ṣaṁ*, *Saṁ*. Its pericarp contains a yellow square with the seed-syllable '*LAṀ*', the symbol of the element Earth. Its vehicle (*vahana*) is *Indra's* elephant *Airāvati* with seven trunks.

The next Centre, *Svādhiṣṭhāna-Cakra*, corresponding to the *plexus hypogastricus*, is shown as a six-petalled lotus with the seed-syllables *Baṁ*, *Bhaṁ*, *Maṁ*, *Yaṁ*, *Raṁ*, *Laṁ*. Its pericarp contains a white semicircle or crescent with the main seed-syllable '*VAṀ*', the symbol of the element water. Its vehicle is the crocodile (*makara*).

Maṇipūra-Cakra, the Centre corresponding to the *solar plexus*, is shown as a ten-petalled lotus with the seed-syllables *Ḍaṁ*, *Ḍhaṁ*, *Ṇaṁ*, *Taṁ*, *Thaṁ*, *Daṁ*, *Dhaṁ*, *Naṁ*, *Paṁ*, *Phaṁ*. Its pericarp contains a red triangle with its point downwards, bearing the seed-syllable '*RAṀ*', as symbol of the element Fire.

The Heart Centre, *Anāhata-Cakra*, is a twelve-petalled lotus, bearing the seed-syllables *Kaṁ*, *Khaṁ*, *Gaṁ*, *Ghaṁ*, *Ṅaṁ*, *Caṁ*, *Chaṁ*, *Jaṁ*, *Jhaṁ*, *Ñaṁ*, *Ṭaṁ*, *Ṭhaṁ*. Its pericarp contains a smoke-coloured (grey-blue) hexagram with the seed-syllable '*YAṀ*' as symbol of the element Air, or Wind. Its characteristic quality is motion, for which reason the deer, the symbol of speed, is its vehicle.

These four Centres represent the four gross elements, and in them are contained all the consonants of the Sanskrit alphabet. As we see from the increasing number of petals, the successive Centres (in ascending order) show an increasing differentiation; in other words, a higher rate of vibration or a higher degree of activity, corresponding to a higher dimension of consciousness. We observe here the development from the relatively undifferentiated subconscious state to the differentiated state of the fully-awakened consciousness, which is symbolized by the 'Thousand-petalled Lotus' (*sahasrāra padma*).

The Throat Centre, *Viśuddha-Cakra*, from which the faculty of speech and the power of the mantric sound is born, contains all the vowels of the Sanskrit alphabet on sixteen petals and is associated with the subtle element Ether, the quality of space (*ākāśa*), the substrate of sound, and the medium of vibration. Its central seed-syllable is *HAṀ*. It is depicted on a white drop or a white disc within a triangle standing on its apex and carried by a white elephant with six tusks.

Ājñā-Cakra, which is situated between the eyebrows and belongs to the realm of the Thousand-petalled Lotus (for which reason it is not regarded as a separate Centre according to Tibetan tradition) possesses only two petals (this in itself points to its dependent character) with the seed-syllables *Haṁ* and *Kṣaṁ*, while its main seed-syllable is the short or half '*A*'. We shall come back to this later.

The Crown Centre, the Thousand-petalled Lotus (*sahasrāra-padma*), has OṀ as its central seed-syllable, while its petals represent the infinite variety and sum total of all sounds and seed-syllables of all *cakras*. For this reason the Thousand-petalled Lotus is looked upon as something belonging to a higher order than the other six Centres. The term '*cakra*' in the narrower sense is applied, therefore, only to them: hence the title '*Ṣaṭcakranirūpaṇa*' (Description of the *Six* Centres), the Sanskrit text of Arthur Avalon's fundamental work on *Kuṇḍalinī-Yoga*: '*The Six Centres and the Serpent Power*'. On this work also the present observations, as far as they concern Tantric Hindu tradition, are based.

Psychic Centres
(*Cakras*)

Physiological
Counterparts

SAHASRĀRA-PADMA
Crown Centre
Seed-syllable: 'OṀ'

In the Tibetan System conceived as One Centre (*ḥdab-stoṅ*)

ĀJÑĀ-CAKRA
(between the Eyebrows)
Seed-Syllable: half or short 'A'

BRAIN
(Pituary Gland)
Volitional Nerve-system

Cerebro-spinal Nerve-system

MEDULLA OBLONGATA
Non-volitional Nerve-system

VIŚUDDHA-CAKRA
Throat Centre
Element: 'Ether' as substrate of Sound (*śabda*).
Seed-syllable: 'HAṀ'
Colour: White
Form: Circle

PLEXUS CERVICUS
Respiratory System

ANĀHATA-CAKRA
Heart Centre
Element: 'Air' (Motion)
Seed-syllable: 'YAṀ'
Colour: Grey-Blue
Form: Hexagram

PLEXUS CARDIACUS
Circulatory System
(Blood-vessels)

Physic Centres
(*Cakras*)

Physiological
Counterparts

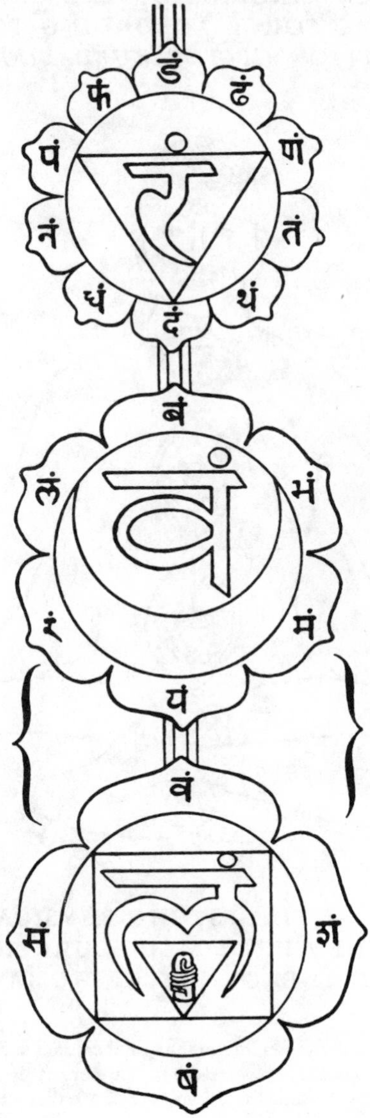

MAṆIPŪRA-
CAKRA
Navel Centre
Element: 'Fire'
Seed-syllable:
'RAṀ'
Colour: Red
Form: Triangle

PLEXUS
EPIGASTRICUS
(Solar Plexus)
System of
Nutrition

SVĀDHIṢṬHĀNA-
CAKRA
Abdominal Centre
(4 finger-widths
below the navel)
Element: 'Water'
Seed-syllable:
'VAṀ'
Colour: White
Form: Crescent

PLEXUS
HYPOGASTRICUS
Inner Organs of
Secretion and
Reproduction

In the Tibetan
System combined
under the name
'Sang-Nä' (*gsaṅ-gnas*)

Generative
System

MŪLĀDHĀRA-
CAKRA
Root Centre (in
the perineum). Its
latent primordial
force is represented
by the serpent 'Kuṇḍ-
alinī', coiled round
the 'Liṅgam' in the
centre of the
triangular 'Yonī'.
Element: 'Earth'
Seed-syllable: 'LAṀ'
Colour: Yellow
Form: Square

PLEXUS PELVIS
(Sacral Plexus)
which controls
the outer organs
of generation
(represented by
'Liṅgam', the
male, and 'Yonī',
the female symbol
of creative force
(comparable to
the 'libido')

SIMPLIFIED DIAGRAM OF THE CENTRES OF PSYCHIC FORCE ACCORDING TO THE TRADITION OF THE *KUṆḌALINĪ-YOGA*

SITUATION OF THE PSYCHO-PHYSICAL CENTRES AND THE THREE MAIN CURRENTS OF PSYCHIC ENERGY IN THE HUMAN BODY

The vertical axis, corresponding to the spinal column and shown as a simple straight line, represents the *Suṣumṇā-Nāḍī*; the curved double line *Idā-Nāḍī*, and the opposite curved single line *Piṅgalā-Nāḍī*. We shall hear more about this in the following chapters.

5

THE DOCTRINE OF THE PSYCHIC ENERGIES AND OF THE 'FIVE SHEATHS'

THE invisible channels and subtle vessels, serving as conductors of the forces, which flow through the human body, are called *nāḍīs* (Tib.: *rtsa*), as we have mentioned already.

It is better to leave this word untranslated, in order to avoid misunderstandings which would inevitably arise from translations such as 'nerves', 'veins' or 'arteries'. The mystic anatomy and physiology of Yoga is not founded on the 'object-isolating' investigations of science, but on subjective – though not less unprejudiced – observations of inner processes, i.e., not on the dissection of dead bodies or on the external observation of the functions of human and animal organisms, but on the self-observation and on the direct experience of processes and sensations within one's own body.

The discoveries of the nervous system and the circulation of the blood belong to an entirely different epoch; and even if the word *nāḍī* was adopted by a later medical science of India as being the most suitable expression for nerves and blood-vessels, this does not justify the substitution of these physiological concepts for the original meaning of the yoga-term.

What has been overlooked by most writers on the subject of *prāṇāyāma* (the *yoga* of controlling the *prāṇa*) is the fact that the same energy (*prāṇa*) is not only subject to constant transformation, but is able at the same time to make use of various mediums of movement without interrupting its course. Just as an electric current can flow through copper, iron, water, silver, etc., and can even flash through space without any such medium, if the tension is high enough, or move in form of radio-waves – in the same way the current of psychic force can utilize the breath, the blood, or the nerves as conductors, and at the same time move and act even beyond and without these mediums into the infinity of space, if efficiently concentrated and directed. For *prāṇa* is more than breath, more than nerve-energy or the vital forces of the blood-current. It is more than the creative power of semen or the force of motor-nerves, more than the faculties of thought and intellect or will-power. All these are only modifications of *prāṇa*, just as the *cakras* are modifications of the *ākāśa*-principle.

Though the *nāḍīs* may partially coincide with the courses of nerves and blood-vessels and have, therefore, often been compared with their functions, they are nevertheless *not* identical with them, but stand in similar relationship to them as the *cakras* to the organs and bodily functions with which they are associated. In other words, we are confronted here with a parallelism of bodily, psychic, and spiritual functions.

This parallelism is well demonstrated in the doctrine of the five sheaths (*kośa*) of human consciousness, which in ever-increasing density crystallize from or around the innermost centre of our being. According to Buddhist psychology this centre is the incommensurable point of relationship upon which all our inner forces converge, but which itself is empty of qualification and beyond all definitions. The densest and outermost of these sheaths is the physical body, built up through nutrition (*anna-maya-kośa*); the next is the subtle, fine-material sheath (*prāṇa-maya-kośa*), consisting of *prāṇa*, sustained and nourished by breath, and penetrating the physical body. We may also call it the *prāṇic* or ethereal body. The next-finer sheath is our thought body (*mano-maya-kośa*), our 'personality', formed through active thought. The fourth sheath is the body of our potential consciousness (*vijñāna-maya-kośa*), which extends far beyond our active thought, by comprising the totality of our spiritual capacities.

The last and finest sheath, which penetrates all previous ones, is the body of the highest, universal consciousness, nourished and sustained by exalted joy (*ānanda-maya-kośa*). It is only experienced in a state of enlightenment, or in the highest states of meditation (*dhyāna*). It corresponds in the terminology of the *Mahāyāna* to the 'Body of Inspiration' or 'Body of Bliss': the *Saṁbhoga-Kāya*.

These 'sheaths', therefore, are not separate layers, which one after another crystallize around a solid nucleus, but rather in the nature of mutually penetrating forms of energy, from the finest 'all-radiating', all-pervading, luminous consciousness down to the densest form of 'materialized consciousness', which appears before us as our visible, physical body. The correspondingly finer or subtler sheaths penetrate, and thus contain, the grosser ones.

Just as the material body is built up through nourishment, while being penetrated and kept alive by the vital forces of the *prāṇa*, in the same way the active thought-consciousness penetrates the functions of *prāṇa* and determines the form of bodily appearance. Thought, breath, and body, however, are penetrated and motivated by the still deeper consciousness of past experience, in which the infinite material from which our thought and imagination draws its substance, is stored up. For want of a better term we call it our subconsciousness or depth-consciousness.

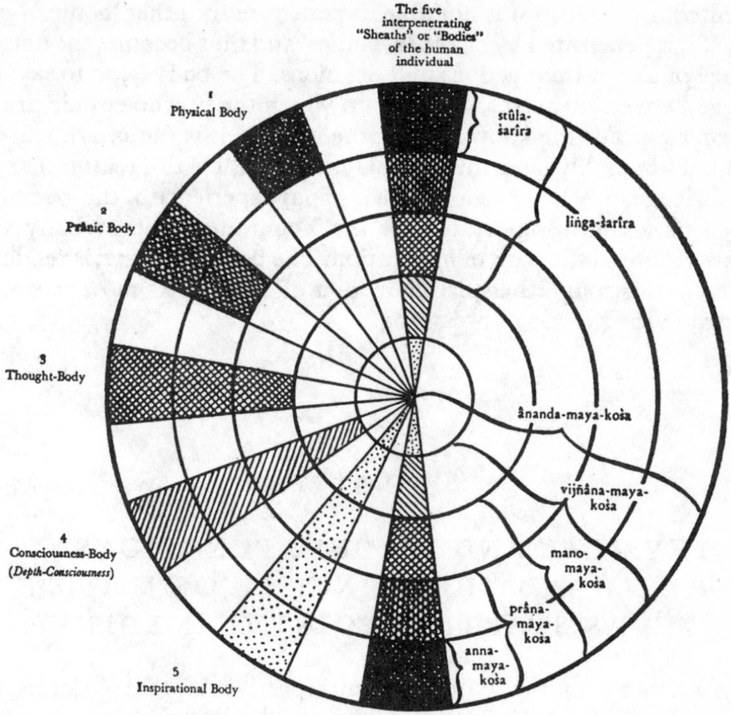

In advanced states of meditation, however, all these conscious and subconscious, fine-material, vital, and physical functions are penetrated and transformed in the flame of inspiration and spiritual joy (*ānanda*), until the universal nature of consciousness becomes apparent. This is the foundation on which rests the 'Yoga of the Inner Fire' (Tib.: *gtum-mo*), which we shall discuss in chapter 8.

It is therefore only the spiritual body, born of inspiration (No. 5 in the diagram shown above; Skt.: *ānanda-maya-kośa*), which penetrates all the five layers and thus integrates all organs and faculties of the individual into one complete whole. In this process of integration, of becoming whole and complete, lies the secret of immortality. As long as we have not attained this completeness (holiness = wholeness) and identify ourselves with lesser values, with 'parts' or partial aspects, we are subject to the laws of matter and of all component things: the law of mortality.

Yet, it would be a mistake to underestimate the value and meaning of our physical body (*sthūla śarīra*), built up through nourishment (*anna-maya*); because even though this body is by nature the most limited, in so far as it is not able to penetrate the other 'bodies' – yet, itself it is penetrated by *all* other 'bodies' and thus becomes the natural stage of all spiritual actions and decisions. The body is, so to say, the stage between heaven and earth, on which the psycho-cosmic drama is enacted. For the knowing one, the initiate, it is the sacred stage of an unfathomably deep mystery play. And it is for this reason that the knowledge, or what is more, the conscious experience of this body is of such paramount importance for the Yogin and for everybody who wants to tread the path of meditation. The body, however, is rendered conscious through the spiritualization of *prāṇa* in its most accessible form: in the process of breathing.

6

PHYSICAL AND PSYCHIC FUNCTIONS OF *PRĀṆA* AND THE PRINCIPLE OF MOTION (*VĀYU*) AS STARTING-POINT OF MEDITATION

ALREADY in the Pāli texts introspective breathing forms the basis of meditation. According to the Buddha's words in the 118th Discourse of the *Majjhima-Nikāya*, it is the conscious observation of inhalation and exhalation which causes the unfoldment of the four Foundations of Mindfulness (*sati-paṭṭhāna*), the seven Factors of Enlightenment (*sambojjhaṅga*) and, finally, the perfect knowledge and liberation.

The text says that, after the meditator has retired to a lonely place and has taken the traditional position of meditation, he consciously breathes in and out.

'Drawing in a long breath, he knows: "I am drawing in a long breath". Exhaling a long breath, he knows: "I am exhaling a long breath". Drawing in a short breath, he knows: "I am drawing in a short breath". Exhaling a short breath, he knows: "I am exhaling a short breath".'

This is the first step: the simple observation of the process of breathing, without mental interference, without compulsion, without violation of the natural functions of the body. Hereby breathing becomes conscious, and with it the organs through which it flows.

If we were concerned here only with an intellectual observation and analysis of the breathing-process, this exercise would more or less come to an end at this stage. The purpose of this exercise, however, is exactly the contrary, namely, the gaining of a synthesis: the experience of the body as a whole.

'"Experiencing the *whole body* (*sabba-kāya*) I will inhale; experiencing the whole body, I will exhale", thus he trains himself.'

Whether 'the whole body' is here meant to be the 'breath-body' (*prāṇa-maya-kośa*) or the physical body, is of secondary importance, since the former penetrates the latter in its entirety and thus does not confine itself to the organs of respiration.

The next step is the stilling of all the functions of the body through the conscious rhythm of the breath. From this state of perfect mental and physical equilibrium and its resulting inner harmony, grows that serenity and happiness which fills the whole body with a feeling of supreme bliss, like the refreshing coolness of a spring that penetrates the entire water of a mountain lake.

'"Experiencing serenity, I will breathe in, experiencing serenity, I will breathe out", thus he trains himself. "Experiencing bliss, I will breathe in, experiencing bliss, I will breathe out", thus he trains himself.'

Thus breathing becomes a vehicle of spiritual experience, the mediator between body and mind. It is the first step towards the transformation of the body from the state of a more or less passively and unconsciously functioning physical organ into a vehicle or tool of a perfectly developed and enlightened mind, as demonstrated by the radiance and perfection of the Buddha's body.

The next steps are devoted to the incorporation of spiritual functions in the process of breathing: 'Experiencing mental activities, being conscious of the mind, gladdening the mind, concentrating the mind, freeing the mind, I will inhale and exhale', thus he trains himself. In other words: whatever may be the subject of meditation, be it the body, the feelings, the mind, or that which moves the mind (phenomena and ideas), is being associated with the functions of breathing, projected into them, experienced in them, supported by them: thus becoming one with the 'breath-body'. It is a process that cannot be explained, but only experienced, and which therefore can only be understood by those who have a practical knowledge of meditation. Hence the formula-like terseness of the Pāli text in which these processes are described.

To all those who are familiar with Indian tradition, it must be clear that these formulae presuppose a knowledge common to Indian thought in general and to well-established religious practices connected therewith. In spite of their terseness these formulae were therefore able to convey a clearly defined content to those who were in touch with that tradition. It was only when Buddhism was transplanted into countries in which this tradition was not alive, that these meditative practices degenerated into mere superficialities and word-knowledge, as we can see from the commentarial literature of later Theravādins. It is, however, all the more praiseworthy that recent tendencies in Southern Buddhism show that serious efforts are being made to revive the spirit of these ancient practices.[1]

The most important result of the practice of '*ānāpāna-sati*' or 'mindfulness with regard to breathing', is the realization that the process of breathing is the connecting link between conscious and subconscious, gross-material and fine-material, volitional and non-volitional functions, and therefore the most perfect expression of the nature of all life. Those exercises that lead to the deeper states of meditation (*dhyāna* and *samādhi*) begin therefore with the observation and regulation of breath, which in this way is converted from an automatic or non-volitional function into a conscious one and, finally, into a medium of spiritual forces: of *prāṇa* in its deepest sense.

In Tibetan Buddhism, which never lost its connexion with the original tradition of the Indian mother-soil, the technique of *prāṇāyāma*, the control of *prāṇic* forces, remained alive until the present day. In order to understand the whole depth and width of this term, we must however not confuse *prāṇa* with 'breath' in the ordinary, strictly physiological sense of the word.

Though *prāṇāyāma* starts with the simple function of breathing and makes it the basis of its practice, it is far more than a mere technique for the control of breath. It is a means for the control of vital psychic energies in *all* their phenomenal forms, of which the function of breathing is the most obvious. Among all the physical activities and effects of *prāṇa*, breath is the most accessible, the easiest to influence, and therefore the most suiiable starting-point of meditation. Breath is the key to the mystery of life, to that of the body as well as to that of the spirit.

When all sense-functions, and even consciousness, have been eliminated, like in deep sleep or in a state of swoon, breathing nevertheless continues. As long as there is breath, there is life. We can do without all conscious functions of the mind and the senses for a comparatively long time, but not without breath. Breath therefore is the symbol of

[1] 'We have to admit that, in most Buddhist countries, the true understanding and the actual practice of *Satipaṭṭhāna* is lagging much behind, compared with that mainly devotional attitude. The only exception, as far as the writer's knowledge goes, seems to be present-day Burma, where the earnest practice of *Satipaṭṭhāna* is widely spread and steadily progressing.' (Nyāṇaponika Thera: *The Heart of the Buddhist Meditation*, Colombo, 1954, p. 8.) This excellent little book gives a clear and comprehensive idea of the 'New Burman Satipaṭṭhāna Method' and the importance of the 'Way of Mindfulness' in Buddhist life.

all the forces of life and stands first among the bodily functions of *prāṇa*.

Those bodily functions which represent the 'negative', i.e., gross-material side[1] of the subtle (or 'fine-material') vital energy, the invisible psychic *prāṇa* – are united under the collective term '*vāyu*'.

This term plays an important role in the Tibetan system of meditation, especially among the *Kargyüdpas* (in connexion with *rluṅ-sgom* and the creation of *gtum-mo*, the 'Inner Fire'). We, therefore, have to say a few words about it, before we proceed to the practical aspect of Buddhist Yoga.

'*Vāyu*', just like the corresponding Tibetan word '*Lung*' (*rluṅ*) means ordinarily 'air' or 'wind' and has been rendered as such in most translations into European languages, even where these words seemed to contradict all physiological facts, as for example, when it was said that the 'air' (of the breath) penetrates into the toes and finger-tips, or rises through the hollow of the spinal column up to the brain.

Just as the word 'inspiration' can be used in the sense of 'inhalation' as well as in that of direct spiritual awareness and experience, or as the Greek word '*pneuma*' can signify 'spirit' as well as 'air', so '*vāyu*' can be applied to the elementary state of aggregation (or the gaseous state) as to the vitalizing and dynamic forces of the human organism. Its nature is in both cases that of movement (the root '*vā*' expresses motion: 'wind'). Herein consists its inner relationship with the more general and wider term '*prāṇa*'.

This is also supported by the Tibetan definition of the word '*rluṅ*', which, if applied to psycho-physical or meditative processes, expresses the following functions (in perfect agreement with Indian tradition):

1. *srog-ḥdzin*: that which supports life (*ḥdzin-pa*: to support; *srog*: life); that which is the cause of breath, which forces us to inhale (Skt.: *prāṇa* in the strictest, narrowest sense of the word).

2. *gyen-rgyu*: that which is the cause (*rgyu*) of the upward movement (*gyen*) of exhalation and of the faculty of speech (Skt.: *udāna-vāyu*).

3. *thur-sel*: that which presses downwards (*thur*) and is the cause of various secretions (*sel*) (Skt.: *apāna-vāyu*).

4. *me-mñam*: the fire (*me*) that equalizes (*mñam-pa byed-pa*) everything, the faculty of assimilation, of digestion as well as of respiration, which are both heat-producing processes of oxygenation (Skt.: *samāna-vāyu*).

5. *khyed-byed*: that which penetrates the body (that which causes [*byed*] penetration [*khyed*]); i.e., the cause of muscular movement,

[1] Just as the physical body represents the reactive (*vipāka*), and in this sense, 'negative' side of consciousness.

blood-circulation and the metabolic functions of transformation (Skt.: *vyāna-vāyu*).

Réné Guénon, who deals in a deeply penetrating way with these five functions in the light of Sanskrit tradition, defines the first *vāyu* as '*aspiration*, that is, respiration regarded as ascending in its initial phase (*prāṇa* in the strictest sense) and attracting the still unindividualized elements of the cosmic environment, causing them to participate by assimilation, in the individual consciousness'.

Apāna-vāyu, which in the Tibetan definition is regarded as the cause of various secretions, is defined by Guénon as '*inspiration*, considered as descending in a succeeding phase (*apāna*) whereby these (still unindividualized) elements penetrate into the individuality'.

Vyāna-vāyu is described by Guénon as 'a phase *intermediary* between the two preceding ones, consisting on the one hand, of all the reciprocal actions and reactions which are produced upon the contact of the individual with the surrounding elements, and, on the other hand, of the various resultant vital movements, of which the circulation of the blood is the corresponding movement in the bodily organism'.

Udāna-vāyu is, according to Guénon, the function 'which projects the breath, while transforming it, beyond the limits of the restricted individuality into the sphere of possibilities of the extended individuality, viewed in its integrality. 'Breath becomes here a vehicle of the mind, namely of word and speech, and thus, in a certain sense, the medium of an enlarged individuality.

Samāna-vāyu, finally, is explained as the function of digestion or 'inner substantial assimilation, by which the elements absorbed become an integral part of the individuality. In other words: it is clearly stated that all this is not purely a matter of the operation of one or several bodily organs; it is in fact easy to realize that it refers not merely to the analogically corresponding physiological functions, but rather to the vital assimilation in the widest possible sense.'[1]

It is therefore not fundamentally important how we delineate the boundaries of these partly overlapping functions. What is important, however, is to understand the fact of the interdependence and interaction of physical and psychological, individual and universal, material and spiritual functions. Only when this has been clearly established and realized, can we understand the many-sided nature of the *cakras* and *nāḍīs* and see that they are not properties or organs of the gross-material body (*sthūla-śarīra*), but of the fine-material or ethereal body (*liṅga-śarīra*), from which this visible body has emerged.

[1] Réné Guénon: *Man and his Becoming*, pp. 77–78. Guénon, like Avalon, Coomaraswami, Heinrich Zimmer, and Richard Wilhelm, tried to convey the wisdom of the East as something alive and of vital importance to the West.

The *liṅga-śarīra* is the combination of *vijñāna-maya-*, *mano-maya-*, and *prāṇa-maya-kośa*, i.e., of the depth-consciousness, the thought-consciousness, and the vital or *prāṇic* body.

The organic relationship between the *nāḍīs* and the physiological nerve-system, or between the *cakras* and the corresponding nerve-centres, is therefore of secondary nature and need not detract us from the description of those principal *nāḍīs*, which are important for the practice of meditation and for the understanding of yogic experience.

7

THE THREE CURRENTS OF FORCE AND THEIR CHANNELS IN THE HUMAN BODY

JUST as *ākāśa* oscillates between the poles of immaterial space (a purely mental dimension) and material corporeality, in a similar way *prāṇa* reveals itself in the form of two dynamic tendencies, which condition and compensate each other like the positive and the negative poles of a magnetic or electrical field. In accordance with the view that the human body is a replica of the universe or, more correctly, a universe on a small scale, a microcosm – the polar currents of force which flow through the human body are called solar or sun-like (*sūrya-svarūpa*) and lunar or moon-like (*candra-svarūpa*) forces.

The solar energies represent the forces of the day, i.e., the centrifugal forces which tend towards conscious awareness, objective knowledge, differentiation and intellectual discrimination. The lunar energies symbolize the forces of the night, working in the darkness of the subconscious mind. They are the undifferentiated, regenerative, centripetal forces, flowing from the all-encompassing source of life and tending towards re-unification (as for instance in the impulses of love) of all that had been separated by the intellect.

These two forces flow through the human body as psychic energies in two main courses or channels: the lunar *iḍā-nāḍī* (Tib.: *rkyaṅ-ma rtsa*) and the solar *piṅgalā-nāḍī* (Tib.: *ro-ma rtsa*), from both of which issue innumerable secondary *nāḍīs*. According to the tradition of the '*ṣaṭcakranirūpaṇa*' (see page 146) *iḍā* and *piṅgalā* are represented as two spirals, starting from the left and the right nostril respectively, and moving in opposite directions around *suṣumṇā-nāḍī*, which runs like a hollow channel through the centre of the spinal column, meeting *iḍā* and *piṅgalā* in the perineum at the base of the spine.

The *suṣumṇā* (Tib.: *dbu-ma rtsa*), which is compared with the sacred Mount Meru, the mystic world-axis, establishes the direct connexion between the seven centres, and is not only able to cause a synthesis between the solar and lunar currents, but also to unite the forces of the highest and the lowest centre. The integrated solar and lunar energies are thus sublimated and raised from centre to centre until they reach the Thousand-petalled Lotus, the plane of the highest multi-dimensional consciousness.

We are dealing here, in other words, with the integration of a double polarity, which presents itself on the one hand as 'right' and 'left', i.e., as solar and lunar forms of *prāṇa* on the human or mundane plane – on the other hand as 'above' and 'below', i.e., as immaterial and material forms of *ākāśa* on the 'vertical axis' of the cosmic-spiritual realm. This integration is experienced in successive stages, namely in successive *cakras*, of which each represents a different dimension of consciousness, and in which each higher dimension includes the lower one without annihilating its qualities. In this way even the highest state of integration does not consist in the annihilation of differentiated qualities, but in their perfect interpenetration and harmonization, through which they become the qualities of one single organ: the organ of universal consciousness.

In Tibetan descriptions of meditation or yogic practices *piṅgalā* and *iḍā* are often simply called the 'right and left *nāḍī*' (*rtsa-g'yas-g'yon*). There is no mention of a spiral movement of these *nāḍīs* around the *suṣumṇā*. This seems to correspond to the original tradition, which also *Swāmi Vivekānanda* mentions in his '*Rāja-Yoga*' and in connexion with *Patañjali*'s '*Yoga Aphorisms*'. He describes there the structure of the spinal colum in the following way: 'If we take the figure eight horizontally (∞), there are two parts, which are connected in the middle. Suppose you add eight after eight, piled one on top of the other, that will represent the spinal cord. The left is the *iḍā*, the right *piṅgalā*, and that hollow canal which runs through the centre of the spinal cord is the *suṣumṇā*.'[1]

The *suṣumṇā* is closed at its lower end, as long as the latent creative forces of the *Kuṇḍalinī* (or the 'libido', as modern psychologists would say) are not awakened. In this state the *Kuṇḍalinī*, which is likened to a coiled serpent (the symbol of latent energy) blocks the entrance to the *suṣumṇā*. By awakening the *Kuṇḍalinī*'s dormant forces, which otherwise are absorbed in subconscious and purely bodily functions, and by directing them to the higher centres, the energies thus released are transformed and sublimated until their perfect unfoldment and conscious realization is achieved in the highest centre. This is the

[1] Swāmi Vivekānanda: *Raja Yoga*, p. 45.

aim and purpose of the *Kuṇḍalinī Yoga*, of *prāṇāyāma*, and of all other exercises through which the *cakras* are activated and made into centres of conscious realization.

If we define 'genius' as the faculty of becoming directly conscious of the inner relationship between ideas, facts, things, sense-data, and forces, a relationship which the ordinary intellect can only find in slow, laborious work, then we may say that these meditative practices have no other aim than the establishment of the state of a 'genius' in man. The Yogin is he who has found the central axis of his being, who has 'opened' the *suṣumṇā*, who has gained direct access to his innermost forces, and who has succeeded in establishing direct contact between the extremes of his nature, by connecting the deepest with the highest.

The *suṣumṇā* is the symbol of all the potentialities, which lie dormant in every human being, and which are realized by the Yogin. All human beings are born with the same organs, but not all make the same use of them. 'When this *suṣumṇā* current opens, and begins to rise, we get beyond the senses, our minds become super-sensuous, super-conscious – we get beyond even the intellect, where reasoning cannot reach.'[1]

According to the Tibetan text '*Chos-drug bsdus-paḥi zin-bris*'[2] (Tractate of the Six Doctrines, which are attributed to *Naropa*), the meditator is to imagine and to visualize the *suṣumṇā* (*dbu-ma rtsa*) as extending perpendicularly from the crown of the head to a place four fingers below the navel (the place of the *Mūlādhāra-Cakra*) and to the right and left of the *suṣumṇā* the right and left *nāḍīs* (*rtsa g'ya-g'yon*).

Once more: here is no mention of the spiral course of the *nāḍīs* nor is it said whether they are localized within or without the spinal column; it only is pointed out that the meditator should *visualize* them, clearly, and picture them in his mind, *as if* they extended from the nostrils over the brain and down to the base of the organs of generation (in the perineum). At the same time the meditator should imagine these *nāḍīs* as being hollow, and project into the left one the seed-syllables of all the vowels, and into the right *nāḍī* the seed-syllables of all the consonants of the Sanskrit alphabet.

This means that the seeds of all that acts and appears in the world is visualized as a living stream, which is polarized into two currents of force, of which the left one is of lunar, the right one of solar character. The seed-syllables, which are mentally projected into them, are

[1] Vivekānanda: *Rāja Yoga*, p. 54.

[2] A translation of this text, compiled by *Padma Karpo*, was made by Lama Dawa Samdup, edited and published by Dr. Evans-Wentz in *Tibetan Yoga and Secret Doctrines* under the title 'Yoga of the Six Doctrines'.

pictured as being hair-fine, in form of brilliant red letters, perpendicularly standing one upon the other, and moving alternately inwards and outwards in harmony with the rhythm of breathing in and out.

It is, however, not as if the seed-syllables were inhaled with the air and exhaled with it again, but as if they were entering the opening of the sex-organ during inhalation and leaving the body with the exhalation, without reversing their direction (which would happen, if they would simply follow the movement of the incoming and outgoing air of the breath), in a constantly rising stream. But since it is not possible to concentrate simultaneously upon two different movements, breathing takes place alternately through the right or the left nostril, by which alternately the right or the left current is made conscious and is being visualized.

What is the purpose of this exercise? The text gives a surprising and at the same time profound explanation, which throws light on the general attitude of Buddhist yoga-practices, which until now has been seen one-sidedly from the point of view of comparatively recent Hindu Tantras.[1]

The text says that these exercises can be compared to the drawing of a water-course, by digging a channel or a ditch; in other words, they are meant to create the conditions, due to which the psychic energies are made to flow and can be directed and controlled consciously. The Buddhist Tantras thus replace the static, physiologically fixed definition of the *nāḍīs*, by a spiritualized, dynamic, psychological one. The follower of the Buddhist Tantras does not commit himself as to whether the three main *nāḍīs* are within or without the spinal column, or how far the *cakras* coincide with certain organs of the body, and how many 'petals' are in each of these 'lotuses', or

[1] The text of the *Ṣaṭcakranirūpaṇa* is, according to its colophon, not older than the fifteenth or sixteenth century, i.e., more than a thousand years younger than the earliest known Buddhist Tantras. The Buddha himself described certain yoga-exercises, which show clearly that he was not only conversant with, but for a time actively practising, what may be called *Nāḍī-Yoga*. The antiquity of the *Nāḍī-Yoga* is established through the testimonial of various *Upaniṣads*, as for instance: *Chāndogya*, 8, 6, 6; *Kāṭha*, 6, 16; *Maitrāyaṇa*, 6, 21; *Yogaśikhā*, 4–7; *Kṣurikā*, 8–16.

In *Majjhima-Nikāya*, 36, the Buddha relates that through the control of breath, or, as the *Pāli* text describes it, through withholding inbreathings and outbreathings through mouth, nose, and ears, he experienced violent 'airs' (*vāta-vāyu*) piercing his head and his abdomen, and causing the sensation of a burning *fire* in his belly. That these internal 'airs' are the currents of vital force (*nāḍīs*) is all the more apparent from the fact that the Buddha was said to have stopped the ordinary breathing process. The very fact that he thus controlled his breath shows that he knew the significance of this practice. His knowledge of pre-Buddhist yoga-tradition and yoga-practice is furthermore proved by his having been the disciple of *Alāra Kālāma* and *Uddaka Rāmaputta*, whom he praised even after his enlightenment as the only people capable of understanding his *dharma*.

which quality is associated with each petal and which deity controls a particular *cakra*. He knows that these are only aids and preliminaries, and that he is not dealing with fixed facts or data, which exist unalterably and for ever, but rather with things that depend on what we make of them, things that we create ourselves – just as we have created our own body, within the frame of certain universal and immanent laws, and according to the level of our development, our karmic preconditions.

The Tibetan teacher of meditation, therefore, does not make any assertions, which the pupil has to accept as objective facts; he does not say 'the *nāḍīs* are here or there', but: 'create within yourself a vivid mental image, that a current of vital force flows from here to there'. In this way he directs the consciousness and the creative imagination of the meditator upon certain functions (for instance, the respiration) and those organs which can be influenced by them either directly or indirectly. Thus he creates the psychic and physical relations and preconditions for the flow of conscious forces. In other words he creates those channels which form the sensitive nerve-system of the spiritualized or 'fine-material' body (Skt.: *sukṣmā* or *liṅga śarīra*).

It is not important, where the *suṣumṇā* is localized, because it is there where we direct the main current of psychic force, after having made conscious the currents of the polar *nāḍīs*. The *suṣumṇā* can be as fine as a hair and at other times so wide that the whole body becomes one single current of force, a flame of highest inspiration which, annihilating all limits, grows until it fills the whole universe.

8

THE YOGA OF THE INNER FIRE IN THE TIBETAN SYSTEM OF MEDITATION (*TAPAS* AND *GTUM-MO*)

As a concrete example of what we said in the previous chapter, the following may serve as a summary of a typical meditation, in which the creation and the contemplation of the 'Inner Fire' (*gTum-mo*) forms the main subject.

After the *Sādhaka* has purified his mind through devotional exercises and has put himself into a state of inner preparedness and receptivity; after he has regulated the rhythm of his breath, filled it with consciousness and spiritualized it through mantric words, he directs his attention upon the Navel Centre (*Maṇipūra*; Tib.: *lte-baḥi ḥkhor-lo*), in whose lotus he visualizes the seed-syllable 'RAṀ' and above it the seed-syllable 'MA', from which latter emerges *Dorje Naljorma* (Skt.: *Vajra-Yoginī*) a Khadoma[1] of brilliant red colour, surrounded by a halo of flames.

As soon as the meditator has become one with the divine form of the *Khadoma* and knows himself as *Dorje Naljorma*, he places the seed-syllable 'A' into the lowest, the seed-syllable 'HAṀ' into the highest Centre (the 'Thousand-petalled Lotus' of the Crown Centre).

Thereupon he arouses, by deep conscious respiration and intense mental concentration, the seed-syllable 'A' to a state of incandescence; and this, being fanned and intensified with every inhalation, grows steadily from the size of a fiery pearl to that of a fierce flame, which through the middle *nāḍī* (Tib.: *dbu-ma rtsa*; Skt.: *suṣumṇā*) finally reaches the Crown Centre, from where now the white nectar, the Elixir of Life, issues from the seed-syllable 'HAṀ' (which the meditator has placed and visualized in this Centre) and, while flowing down, penetrates the whole body.

This exercise can be described in ten stages:[2] In the first the *suṣumṇā* with its rising flame is visualized as fine as a hair, in the second stage as thick as the little finger, in the third of the thickness of an arm, in the fourth as wide as the whole body, i.e., as if the body itself had turned into a *suṣumṇā* and had become a single vessel of fire. In the fifth stage the unfolding vision (Skt.: *utsakrama*; Tib.: *bskyed-rim*) attains its climax: the body ceases to exist for the meditator. The whole world becomes a fiery *suṣumṇā*, an infinite, raging ocean of fire.

With the sixth stage begins the reverse process of integration and perfection (Skt.: *sampanna-krama*; Tib.: *rdzogs-rim*): the storm abates and the fiery ocean is re-absorbed by the body. In the seventh stage the *suṣumṇā* shrinks to the thickness of an arm; in the eighth to the thickness of the small finger; in the ninth to that of a hair; and in the tenth it disappears altogether and dissolves into the Great Void (Skt.: *śūnyatā*; Tib.: *stoṅ-pa-ñid*), in which the duality of the knower and the known is transcended and the great synthesis of spiritual completeness is realized.

The fire of spiritual integration which fuses all polarities, all mutually exclusive elements arising from the separateness of individuation, this is what the Tibetan word *gTum-mo* means in the

[1] *Mkhaḥ-ḥgro-ma rdo-rje rnal-ḥbyor-ma*. Khadomas (Skt.: *ḍākinī*) who, according to popular conception, are divine or demoniacal beings, represent in Tantric Buddhism the inspirational force of consciousness. More about this in chapter 13 of this part.

[2] Cr. Alexandra David-Neel: *With Mystics and Magicians in Tibet*, p. 203 (Penguin).

deepest sense and what makes it one of the most important subjects of meditation. It is the all-consuming incandescent power of that overwhelming Inner Fire which since Vedic times has pervaded the religious life of India: the power of *tapas.*

Tapas, like *gTum-mo*, is what arouses man from the slumber of worldly contentment, what tears him away from the routine of mundane life. It is the warmth of spiritual emotion which, if intensified, kindles the flame of inspiration, from which is born the power of renunciation and what appears to the outsider as asceticism. But to those who are spiritually awakened or inspired, renunciation or aloofness from worldly things become a natural mode of life, because they are no more interested in the playthings of the world, whose riches appear to them as poverty and whose pleasures seem to them banal and empty.

A Buddha, who lives in the fullness of Perfect Enlightenment, does not feel that he has 'renounced' anything, for there is nothing in the world that he desires, that he regards as his possession; and therefore there is nothing left that he could renounce. The word '*tapas*', therefore, means infinitely more than asceticism or some form of self-torture, which the Buddha emphatically rejected in favour of that joyful state of liberation from the things of the world, a state which is born from the intuitive knowledge of inner vision.

Tapas is here the creative principle, which acts upon matter as well as upon mind. With regard to matter it is the forming, organizing, order-creating principle: 'Out of the flaming *Tapas* order and truth were born' (*Ṛgveda* 10, 190,1). In the spiritual realm, however, it is that force which lifts us beyond the created, beyond that which has become, originated, taken form. It lifts us beyond the boundaries of our narrow individuality and of our self-created world. It dissolves and transforms all that which has 'frozen' into rigid form.

Just as worlds are born from fire, 'through the power of inner heat' (as the hymn of creation in the *Ṛgveda* tells us) and are dissolved again through the same force of fire, in the same way *tapas* is as much creative as it is liberating; and in this sense it can be said that *tapas* is at the bottom of *kāma-chanda* (desire for sensual love) as well of *dharma-chanda* (desire for Truth, the striving after the realization of *Dharma*). Or, to remain in the frame of more generally understood expressions: it is that emotion which in its lowest form is like a straw-fire, nourished by a momentary enthusiasm and blind urges, while in its highest form it is the flame of inspiration, nourished by spiritual insight, by true vision, by direct knowledge and inner certainty.

Both have the nature of fire: but as little as the shortlivedness and the inferior force of a straw-fire negates the fact that the same element, if directed into proper channels and supplied with adequate fuel, is capable of melting the hardest steel – so we should not underestimate the force of emotion, because it may sometimes spend itself in a short-lived enthusiasm. We should recognize that the warmth of emotion is inseparable from inspiration, a state in which we truly and completely forget ourselves in the experience of higher reality, an act of self-surrender which frees and transforms our innermost being. It is what we call in religious life ecstasy, trance, absorption, vision (*dhyāna*), and so on.

The coldness of conceptual understanding is opposed by the warmth of emotion, of being 'seized' by the irresistible force of truth. Intellectual comprehension is the establishing of a subject-object relationship, in which the comprehending subject remains outside the object. Emotion, however, is a dynamic attitude, a moving towards or with the subject of our contemplation, until we have caught up with its movement, until we have become one with it and are able to experience it from within, in its intrinsic nature, in its particular rhythm. To be moved is an act of spiritual participation, a becoming one with the subject of our contemplation, and finally leads to the inner unification, the great synthesis of all spiritual, mental, emotional, and bodily qualities of man: the state of completeness. In this highest state the warmth of emotion is transmuted into the flame of inspiration.

The nature of inspiration has never been described more forcefully and graphically than by Nietzsche:

'Has anybody, at the end of the nineteenth century, an idea what poets of stronger ages called *inspiration*? If not, let me describe it.

'With the smallest residue of superstition within oneself, one would indeed hardly escape the idea of being merely the incarnation, the mouth-piece, the medium of super-human powers. The idea of revelation, in the sense that suddenly with incredible certainty and subtlety, something becomes *visible* and audible, shaking us and overpowering us in our deepest being: all this is merely a description of facts. One listens, one does not search; one accepts, one does not ask, who is giving; like lightning a thought flashes up, with necessity, without hesitation with regard to its form – I never have had a choice. An *ecstasy of joy*, whose immense tension sometimes dissolves into a stream of tears, and whose pace is sometimes like a storm and sometimes becomes slow; a state of being completely beside oneself, yet with the clearest consciousness of an infinite number of fine tremors and wave-like vibrations running *down to the very toes*; a depth of *happiness*, in which all that is painful and dark, does *not act as a contradiction* but as a necessary condition, a challenge, as a necessary colour within such an *abundance of light*; an instinct for rhythmic proportions, which spans extensive realms of form – the extension, the need for an *all-encompassing rhythm* is almost a criterion for the *power of inspiration*, a kind of compensating counter-force against its pressure and tension. . . . All this happens involuntarily in the highest degree, and yet like a storm of *freedom*, of *unconditionality*, of *power*, of *godliness*. . . . The *involuntary character of the inner image*, the simile, is the most remarkable part; one has no more the slightest idea what is image or simile, everything offers itself as the nearest, the most adequate, the simplest expression.'[1]

The words which have been put in *italics* by me, will immediately remind the reader of similar expressions used in the description of the 'trances' or states of deep absorption (*dhyāna*) in Buddhist texts:

1. The visualization of inner experiences: the immediacy and necessity of the image or symbol thus visualized;

2. The feeling of rapture and bliss, even 'down to the tips of the toes' (in the Pāli texts '*pīti-sukha*', in Tibetan '*bde*'; *Milarepa* therefore, was described as 'one whose body was filled with bliss, down to the tips of the toes'; and in *Dīgha-Nikāya* the Buddha himself says that he who dwells in the state of *jhāna* or deep absorption 'penetrates and fills his body with bliss, so that not even the smallest part of his body remains without it');

3. The bridging of contrasts through the incorporation and integration of all qualities and all Centres, by uniting the highest with the deepest;

4. The increasing luminosity of the mind and the gradual transfiguration of the body;

5. The feeling of release and freedom, beyond personal volition;

6. The awakening of 'divine' powers (*siddhi*) by awakening the psychic Centres, and the attainment of the highest realization in the state of Perfect Enlightenment.

The inclusion of the body in the process of spiritual development, which the Buddha placed into the centre of his meditative practice, is not only characterized by the already mentioned spiritualization of the breathing process (by making it a conscious function), but even more so by the fact that the duality of body and soul does not exist for him, and that therefore among bodily, mental, psychic, and spiritual functions there is only a difference in degree but not in essence. When the mind has become luminous, the body too must

[1] Translated from the original in *Kröners Taschenbuchausgabe*, Vol. 77, p. 275 f.

partake in this luminous nature.[1] This is the reason for the radiation which emanates from all saints and Enlightened Ones, the aura which surrounds them and which has been described and depicted in all religions. This radiation (Pāli: *tejasā*; Skt.: *tejas*), which is visible only to the spiritual eye, is the direct effect of *tapas*, that flame of religious devotion and self-surrender, in which the light of knowledge and the warmth of the heart are united.

Therefore it is said of the Buddha:

> '*Divā tapati adicco, rattim ābhāti candimā,*
> *Sannaddho khattiyo tapati, jhayī tapati brāhmaṇo,*
> *Attha sabbamahorattiṁ Buddho tapati tejasā.*'
>
> (DHAMMAPADA, 387)

> 'The sun shines by day, the moon shines by night,
> The warrior shines in his armour,
> The Brahmin by his meditation.
> But the Buddha shines radiant both day and night.'

These are not merely poetical metaphors, but expressions connected with an ancient tradition, whose roots lie deeper than any known form of religion.

'Sun' and 'moon' correspond to the forces of day and night, to the outwardly directed activity of the 'warrior' and the inwardly directed activity of the 'priest'. The perfect man (the Enlightened One), however, combines both sides of reality: he unites within himself the depth of the night and the light of day,[2] the darkness of all-embracing space and the light of suns and stars, the creative primordial power of life and the luminous all-penetrating power of knowledge.

[1] An interesting description of this phenomenon is contained in the diaries of Baron Dr. von Veltheim-Ostrau, who observed it in the presence of a modern saint, the late Ramana Maharshi of Tiruvannamalai. I have translated the following passage from the second volume of his 'Asian Diaries', entitled *Der Atem Indiens* (Claassen Verlag, Hamburg 1955):

'While my eyes were immersed in the golden depths of the Maharshi's eyes, something happened which I dare describe only with the greatest reticence and humility, in the shortest and simplest words, according to truth. The dark complexion of his body transformed itself slowly into white. This white body became more and more luminous, as if lit up from within, and began to radiate. This experience was so astonishing that, while trying to grasp it consciously and with clear thought, I immediately thought of suggestion, hypnosis, etc. I therefore made certain "controls", like looking at my watch, taking out my diary and reading in it, for which purpose I had first to put on my spectacles, etc. Then I looked at the Maharshi, who had not diverted his glance from me; and with the same eyes, which a moment ago were able to read some notes in my diary, I saw him sitting on the tiger-skin as a luminous form.

'It is not easy to explain this state, because it was so simple, so natural, so unproblematic. How I would wish to remember it with full clarity in the hour of my death!' (p. 264 f.)

[2] In the language of the later Tantras: the activity of the 'sun-like' *piṅgalā* and of the moon-like' *iḍā*. The former contains the elixir of mortal life, the latter the elixir of immortality.

As long, however, as these principles remain separate or, more correctly, as long as they are developed separately and one-sidedly, they remain barren, i.e., incapable of unfolding their nature and their meaning – because they are the two sides of one organic whole.

The primordial creative power of life is blind without the power of knowledge, of conscious awareness, and becomes an endless play of passions in the eternal cycle of deaths and rebirths (*saṁsāra*). The power of knowledge, without the unifying primordial force of life, turns into the deadly poison of the intellect, the demoniacal principle, aiming at the annihilation of life.

Where, however, these two forces co-operate, penetrating and compensating each other, there arises the sacred flame of the enlightened mind (*bodhi-citta*), which radiates light as well as warmth, and in which knowledge grows into living wisdom, and the blind urge of existence and unrestrained passion into the power of universal love.

The 'Yoga of the Inner Fire' is therefore not concerned with the production of bodily heat – though this as well as a number of other extraordinary qualities may be created as a by-product. It is an often repeated misunderstanding to imagine that these practices were intended to enable the *Sādhaka* to survive in the icy mountain-solitudes of Tibet. Those who advance this theory forget that this *yoga* originated in the hot plains of India, where people would give anything to keep cool. The purpose of this *yoga* is therefore purely spiritual, aiming at a state of perfect inner unity and completeness in which all dormant forces and qualities of our being are concentrated and integrated like the rays of the sun in the focus of a lens.

This process of perfect integration is represented by the symbol of the flame or the flaming drop (Skt.: *bindu*; Tib.: *thig-le*) and expressed by the seed-syllable HŪṀ (about which we shall learn more in this connexion later on). The image of the flame is however, as we must emphasize again, not merely a metaphor, but the expression of real experiences and of psycho-physical processes, in which all properties of fire, in their elementary (*tejas*) as well as in their subtle effects (*taijasa*) can make their appearance: warmth, heat, incandescence, purification and consummation by fire, fusion, upsurging flames, radiation, penetration, enlightenment, transfiguration, and so on.

9

PSYCHO-PHYSICAL PROCESSES IN THE YOGA OF THE INNER FIRE

THE most outstanding example of a life filled with the fire of *gTum-mo*, is that of the greatest Tibetan poet and saint, *Milarepa* (*Mi-la ras-pa*; 1052–1135 A.D.), the fourth patriarch[1] of the *Kargyütpa* (*bkaḥ-rgyud-pa*) School. His biography (*rje-btsun rnam-thar; rje-btsun-bkaḥ-ḥbum*) is not only one of the most beautiful literary monuments that ever was created in remembrance of a great saint, but also a historical document of the first rank, on account of which all that we know about the processes of the Yoga of the Inner Fire, is raised into the realm of living reality.

When contemplating the systems of meditation and the spiritual practices here described, the reader may sometimes wonder whether we are dealing merely with clever speculations or with facts of actual experience, and whether the results justify the expectations built upon them. The life of *Milarepa* (as also the lives of many of his numerous, mostly unknown, followers) is the greatest justification and the most convincing proof of the feasibility, the practical value and the spiritual effectiveness of the *gTum-mo* exercises. Without them *Milarepa* would hardly have been able to realize his exalted aim under the most difficult conditions, and to leave a spiritual testament which bears rich fruit up to the present day.

Only one – who like the present writer, had the good luck of visiting the places of *Milarepa*'s activities, of feeling his ineffable presence in far-off mountain-caves, where he spent years in solitary meditation and divine rapture, and of getting a glimpse of his spiritual path at the feet of masters who even now live and practise it – only one who has experienced this can get a correct idea of the tremendous possibilities of these methods of meditation, which show a practical way towards a spiritual (and physical) renovation of man.

As we may see from *Milarepa*'s biography, he received from his guru *Marpa*, who was a disciple of *Naropa*, the initiation into the esoteric teachings and practices of the *Demchog-Tantra* (Skt.: *Śrī Cakra Samvara* [*Mahāsukha*]; Tib.: *dPal ḥkhor-lo bde-mchog*, the 'Maṇ-

[1] The first three patriarchs were: *Tilopa* (*Tailopa*, *c.* 975 A.D.), *Naropa* (*Nāropā*), and the Tibetan Guru *Marpa*, 'the Translator' (*lo-tsa-ba*).

ḍala of Highest Bliss') and into the 'Six Doctrines' (Tib.: *chos-drug*) of *Nāropā*, namely:

1. The Doctrine of the Inner Fire (*gtum-mo*);
2. The Doctrine of the Illusory Body (*sgyu-lus*);
3. The Doctrine of the Dream State (*rmi-lam*);
4. The Doctrine of the Clear Light (*ḥod-gsal*);
5. The Doctrine of the Intermediate State (*bar-do*);
6. The Doctrine of the Transference of Consciousness (*ḥpho-ba*).

The common basis of these teachings, which are more or less identical with those of the *Bardo Thödol* (as can be seen from this enumeration) is the 'Yoga of the Inner Fire', the main subject of *Milarepa*'s spiritual practice. According to *Milarepa*'s own words, *Marpa* gave him as a parting gift a manuscript on *gTum-mo* (together with *Nāropā*'s mantle, as a symbol of spiritual authority), since he was convinced that *Milarepa* would attain to highest perfection by way of this particular yoga.[1]

That this was the case, has been confirmed by his disciple and biographer *Rechung*, who says of *Milarepa*, that 'his whole body was filled with bliss (*dgaḥ*) descending even to the toes (*mthe-ba-yan*) and ascending to the crown of the head (*spyi gtsug-tu*), where, due to the merging of both, the knots of the main *nāḍīs* and of the four[2] psychic Centres (*rtsa gtso-mo gsum daṅ ḥkhor-lo bźiḥi mdud-pa*) were untied until everything had been transformed into the nature of the middle-*nāḍī* (*dbu-maḥi ṅo-bor gyur-pa*).'[3]

The 'unloosening of the knots' is a very ancient and profound simile which, according to the *Śūraṅgama Sūtra*,[4] was used by the Buddha, when explaining that the process of liberation consists merely in the untying of the knots of our own being, through which we have fettered ourselves and have become slaves of our confused illusions.

In order to demonstrate this idea, as well as the way of liberation, the Budda took a silken handkerchief, tied a knot in it, held it up and asked *Ānanda*: 'What is this?' *Ānanda* replied: 'A silk-handkerchief in

[1] Cf. W. Y. Evans-Wentz: *Tibet's Great Yogī Milarepa* (*rje-btsun-bkaḥ-ḥbum*), pp. 144-156. Oxford University Press, London, 1928.

[2] The fact that in the treatises on the 'Yoga of the Inner Fire' only the *four* upper centres are mentioned throughout, should open the eyes of all those, who still confuse this system with that of the *Kuṇḍalinī-Yoga*. The *gTummo*-practice takes place on an entirely different plane. Differences like this may appear unimportant to the outsider, but they are of fundamental importance to the *sādhaka*, the practising devotee. Further details of this matter will be discussed in chapter 13 of this part.

[3] '*rJe-btsun Mi-la-ras-pahi rnam-thar*', folio *Kha* 3a.

[4] Translated by Bhikshu Wai-tao and Dwight Goddard in *A Buddhist Bible*.

which you have tied a knot.' The Buddha thereupon tied a second knot in it, and a third one, and continued doing so until he had tied in this way six knots. And each time he asked *Ānanda* what he saw, and each time *Ānanda* replied in the same way.

Thereupon the Buddha said: 'When I tied the first knot, you called it a knot; when I tied the second and third, etc., you still maintained the same answer.' *Ānanda*, not comprehending what the Buddha was driving at, became puzzled and exclaimed: 'Whether you tie a single knot or a hundred knots, they always remain knots, though the handkerchief is made of variously coloured silk-threads and woven into a single piece.'

The Buddha admitted this, but he pointed out that though the piece of silk was one, and all the knots were knots – yet, there was one difference, namely the order in which they were tied.

To demonstrate this subtle and yet important difference, the Buddha asked how these knots could be untied. And at the same time he started pulling at the knots here and there, in such a way that the knots, instead of being loosened, became even more tight, whereupon *Ānanda* replied: 'I would first try to find out how the knots were tied.'

'Well said, *Ānanda*! If you wish to untie a knot, you must first find out how the knot was tied. For he who knows the origin of things, knows also their dissolution. But let me ask you another question: Can all the knots be untied at the same time?'

'No, Blessed Lord! Since the knots were tied one after another in a certain order, we cannot untie them, unless we follow the reverse order.'

The Buddha then explains that the six knots correspond to the six sense-organs through which our contact with the world is established. If we understand that the same applies to the six Centres, which are the *conditio sine qua non* of all sense-organs, then we have already grasped the basic law of the Buddhist *yoga* and the reason why we cannot concentrate right away on the highest centres (as some modern 'mystics' naïvely believe, thinking that they can outwit the laws of nature or the originators of this *yoga*, from whom they took over the knowledge of the *cakras*) without having gained control over the lower ones.

We have to reverse the descent of the spirit into matter (or perhaps more correctly: the coagulation of consciousness into a state of materiality) by untying the knots one by one in the reverse order in which we created them. 'They are the knots tied in the essential unity of our mind,' as the Buddha says to *Ānanda* in this beautiful dialogue.

That the *cakra-* and *nāḍī-yoga* was known in the Buddha's time may be seen from the fact that it is mentioned in the *Upaniṣads*. In the *Kaṭhā-* and in the *Muṇḍaka Upaniṣad* the expression 'knots' (*granthi*; from '*granth*', to fasten, to wind round) is already used in this connexion:

'Yadā sarve prabhidyante hrdayasyeha granthayaḥ
Atha martyomṛto bhavatyetavaddhyanuśāsanam.'

(KAṬHOPANIṢAD, II, 3, 15)

'When all the knots of the heart are unloosened,
Then even here, in this human birth, the mortal becomes immortal. This is the whole teaching of the Scriptures.'

In the next verse the *suṣumṇā* is alluded to in the words, that of the 101 *nāḍīs* of the Heart-Cakra (*hṛdayasya nāḍyastāsaṁ*) only one, namely, the *suṣumṇā*, issues through the crown of the head, i.e., the *sahasrāra-padma* or the Thousand-petalled Lotus.

In the *Muṇḍaka Upaniṣad* (II, 2, 9) we read: 'When the knot of the heart is unloosened (*bhidyate hṛdaya granthiḥ*) and all doubts are cut off, and man's work is finished, then is seen That which is above and below (*tasmin dṛṣṭe parāvare*).'

Incidentally we may draw attention to the verse immediately following this, which shows a striking similarity to *Udāna* VIII (which we quoted on p. 58): 'There (in the Ultimate State, indicated by "That") neither the sun nor the moon nor the stars shine, nor do lightnings flash, how much less earthly fire!'[1]

[1] Some Pāli scholars, and especially the followers of the *Theravāda*, try to represent Buddhism as if it had originated in a spiritual vacuum, without any connexion with the immediately preceding and contemporary Upanishadic tradition, while retaining, strangely enough, some of the primitive pluralistic features of the earliest Vedic times Anybody who reads the *Upaniṣads* in the original, must be struck by the similarity of certain phrases, technical terms, religious concepts, similes and fundamental symbols, of which the latter especially point to similarities of spiritual experience which are far more important than intellectual superstructures, like 'monism' or 'pluralism'. These similarities do not take away an iota from the Buddha's greatness and originality, but only prove the objective reality of certain experiences and laws of the spirit. The Buddha gave an entirely new approach to these things by his dynamic attitude, which was neither pluralistic (like the early *Vedas*), nor monistic (like the *Upaniṣads*) – because both are static conceptions – but emphasized the idea of the Way, the Way-farer, the nature of Becoming, and the attainment of Perfect Enlightenment (*samyak-sambodhi*, which the Buddha proclaimed as the aim of his teaching in his first sermon at Benares – thus distinguishing it from the passive or static concept of *nirvāṇa*). On the other hand, we would do a grave injustice to the Buddha in assuming that he was ignorant of the greatest spiritual movement of his time, an assumption which would flatly contradict all traditional descriptions of the Buddha's life, which emphasize his acquaintance with brahmanical literature and wisdom. This is reflected in the Buddha's lifelong respect for the ideal of the *brāhmaṇa*, as may be seen from the *Brāhmaṇa-Vagga* of the *Dhammapada*, in which the term '*brāhmaṇa*' is used to represent the perfect follower of the *Dharma* (the true '*bhikkhu*'). By neglecting the spiritual and historical background, from which Buddhism grew, modern interpreters have created a rootless intellectual Buddhism.

It is therefore not a question of gaining or creating miraculous powers, but only of restoring the disturbed equilibrium of our psychic forces, by freeing ourselves from our inner tensions and our mental and spiritual crampedness. This can only be achieved through a relaxed, serene, and blissful state of body and soul, but not through self-mortification, asceticism or artificial methods of creating aversion like those of wrongly understood contemplations of corpses, through which sensuality is not overcome, but only suppressed) or through violation of body and mind by way of artificial breathing exercises and strenuous efforts to fetter the mind to preconceived ideas.

In *Milarepa's Hundred-Thousand Songs* (*mGur-ḥbum*), which forms an essential part of his biography, the following passage occurs: 'His whole body (*yoṅs lus*) is filled with bliss (*bde*) when the Inner Fire (*gtum-mo*) flames up (*ḥbar-ba*). He experiences bliss when the *prāṇic* currents (*rluṅ*) of the *piṅgalā* (*ro-ma*) [the solar force] and the *iḍā* (*rkyaṅ-ma*) [the lunar force] enter the *suṣumṇā* (*dhū-ti*) [the middle *nāḍī*]. He experiences bliss in the upper (*stod*) Centres of his body by the flowing down (*rgyun-ḥbab*) of the consciousness of enlightenment (*byaṅ-chub-sems*). He experiences bliss in the lower (*smad*) Centres on account of the penetrating (*khyab-pa*) creative energy (*thig-le*). He experiences bliss in the middle [i.e., in the Heart Centre] (*bar*) when tender compassion (*thugs-phrad-brtse-ba*) springs up on account of the union of white and red (*dkar-dmar*) [currents of sublimated lunar and solar forces]. He experiences bliss when the body [as a whole] (*lus*) is pervaded (*tsim-pa*) by unsullied happiness (*zad-med-bde-ba*). This is the sixfold bliss of the Yogi.'[1]

In order to understand this description, we have once more to come back to the above-mentioned *Tractate of the Six Doctrines*. It is said there that the meditator, after having attained the state of perfect concentration and inner devotion, identifies himself with the illusory body of *Vajra-Yoginī*, which is the subject and symbol of his meditation. He thus de-personalizes his own body and regards it as empty (*śūnya*) in its true nature, i.e., as neither being nor non-being, but as a pure product of his mind. In this transparent, insubstantial body he now visualizes and contemplates the four main Centres, namely that of the crown, the throat, the heart, and the navel – comparable to the wheels of a chariot. Through the centre of these wheels runs the *suṣumṇā* like an axle. The meditator thereupon visualizes the seed-syllable of the short (or half) 'A' at the lower end of the *suṣumṇā*

[1] 'The Biography of the Venerable Milarepa, enlarged by the Hundred-thousand Songs' (*rJe-btsun Mi-la-ras-paḥi rnam-thar rgyas-par-phye-ba mgur-ḥbum*). The Tibetan Text of this quotation is also mentioned in Jäschke's *Tibetan-English Dictionary*, p. 231.

(in the Root Centre), where *iḍā* and *piṅgalā* meet and enter the *suṣumṇā*. 'A' is the primordial sound of all speech. It is inherent in all other sounds, even in the consonants, and is therefore the *prima materia*, the womb or matrix of all sounds. This mantric syllable appears, or is visualized, as a letter of red-brown colour, fine as a hair and half a finger high, as if made of a vibrating, incandescent filament, radiating heat and emitting a sound like a cord struck by the wind.

The mantric symbol must appear perfectly alive and real on the plane of all higher sense-faculties: in the realm of thought, of sight, of sound, and of feeling. It is not a dead hieroglyph, but like a being filled with a life of its own, a mysteriously living and exceedingly real force.

In the same way the meditator must visualize the seed-syllable HAṀ of white (lunar) colour, and as if filled with nectar, appearing at the upper end of the *suṣumṇā*, in the Crown Centre. While the short 'A' is of female nature (the negative pole), the 'Ha' is conceived as being male (the positive pole). 'Ha' is the aspirate, the sound of breathing, representing the most important function of the living organism. Both together form the experience of the unity of the individual. The word '*ahaṁ*' (Skt.) means 'I'. This 'I', however, is not a static, permanent entity, but something that has to be created again and again, something that may be compared to the equilibrium of a cyclist, which can only be maintained by constant movement – or to the relative stability of atomic or planetary systems, which likewise depends on movement. The moment movement is arrested, the structure collapses and is annihilated. This is a fact of universal importance.

In the moment, therefore, in which we try to arrest, to fix, to limit, or to substantialize this experience of unity, it breaks up, turns into self-contradiction, into inner disharmony, into a deadly poison. If, on the other hand, we dissolve it in the light of higher knowledge, melt it in the fire of a super-individual consciousness, and let it flow without hindrance, then it becomes the vehicle of an all-embracing, imperishable wholeness, in which the limits of individual egohood do not exist any more.

This is demonstrated by the notion that in the moment in which the 'A' and the 'HAṀ' unite in the word-symbol 'AHAṀ', it dissolves; because in the heat of the flaming 'A' the 'HAṀ' is melted and flows down as the Elixir of Enlightenment (Skt.: *bodhi-citta*; Tib.: *byaṅ-chub-sems*) into all psychic Centres of the body, 'until not even the smallest part of it remains unpervaded'.

In the language of the Tantras 'AHAṀ' can be defined, according to the formula of the mystic 'EVAṀ'[1] in the following way: 'A' is the seed-syllable of the female principle, the 'Mother' (Tib.: *yum*), which in its full unfoldment expresses itself as wisdom or transcendental knowledge (*prajñā*); 'HA' is the seed-syllable of the male principle (Tib.: *yab*), of the 'Father', the active realization (*upāya*) of all-pervading, radiating love and all-embracing compassion; the nasal 'Ṁ' (the dot, Skt.: *bindu*; Tib.: *thig-le*) is the symbol of union, in this case that of integration of knowledge and of the means towards its realization (*prajñopāya*), the fusion of wisdom and love – because knowledge without the fertilizing power of love and compassion remains sterile.

What fans the latent qualities of the seed-syllable 'A' into a state of flaming incandescence, is the upsurge of inspiration. The inspiring muse, however, is the divine figure of *Vajra-Yoginī*, a *Ḍākinī* of highest rank. She redeems the treasures of aeons of experience, which lie dormant in the subconscious, and raises them into the realm of a higher consciousness, beyond that of our intellect.

After thus having clarified the nature of mantric seed-syllables and their functions, we continue with the description of the main features of this yoga-practice.

When inhaling consciously, the psychic energy of life-force (*prāṇa*; Tib.: *rluṅ* as well as *śugs*) enters through the right and left *nāḍī* into the middle *nāḍī* (*suṣumṇā*), strikes the hair-like short 'A' and fills it out, until it assumes its full form.

With intensified concentration, visualization, and regular, consciously rhythmic inhalation and exhalation, the seed-syllable 'A' is fanned into a state of bright-red incandescence, until a perpendicular, spindle-shaped, rotating flame shoots up from it. With each in- and out-breathing the flame rises half a finger higher. With eight in- and out-breathings it reaches the Navel Centre (8), with ten further inhalations and exhalations it fills the Navel Centre (18), with ten further breathings it moves downwards and fills the lower part of the body with fire (28). With a further ten breaths the fire, again steadily

[1] The following passage from the *Subhāsitasaṁgraha* (f. 76) of the *Devendra-paripṛcchā-Tantra*, which H. V. Guenther quotes in his illuminating work '*Yuganaddha*' (Chowkhamba Sanskrit Series, Benares, 1952), may serve here as an example:

E-kāras tu bhaven mātā	'E' is the mother (Tib.: *yum*),
va-kāras tu pitā smṛtaḥ	'VA' is the father (Tib.: *yab*),
Bindus tatra bhaved yogaḥ	the nasal (*bindu*) is their union,
sa yogaḥ paramakṣaraḥ	this union is the most sublime sound.
E-kāras tu bhaved prajñā	'E' is wisdom (*prajñā*; Tib.: *śes-rab*),
va-kāras suratādhipaḥ	'VA' is the loving husband,
Bindus anāhataṁ tattvaṁ	the *bindu* is the virgin reality;
taj-jatāny akṣarāni ca	out of it all other sounds arise.

ascending, reaches successively the Heart Centre (38), the Throat Centre (48), and finally the Crown Centre (58).

With each further set of ten inhalations and exhalations the seed-syllable 'HAṀ', visualized in the Crown Centre, is melted by the fire and transformed into the Elixir of the Englightenment-Consciousness (Tib.: *byaṅ-chub-sems*) until it fills the whole Centre (68).

From the Thousand-petalled Lotus it now flows down into the lower Centres. With each following ten breaths it reaches and fills successively the Throat Centre (78), the Heart Centre (88), the Navel Centre (98), and the whole lower body, down to the tips of the toes (108).[1]

10

THE CENTRES OF PSYCHIC FORCE IN THE YOGA OF THE INNER FIRE (*GTUM-MO*)

It goes without saying that the description, given in the previous chapter is an extreme simplification and hardly more than a skeleton of the process of meditation. But for this very reason it is suitable for a schematic representation in form of a diagram (as shown on the following page), which may illustrate the Buddhist *cakra*-system and its functions.

The Buddhist system, as we see here, confines itself to the five main Centres, which can be easily felt and recognized by everybody and which, according to Tibetan tradition, are divided into three zones: an upper one (*stod*), to which the Centres of the brain and of the throat belong; a middle one (*bar*), to which the Heart Centre belongs; and a lower one(*smad*), to which the solar plexus and the organs of reproduction belong.

These three zones are related to each other in a similar way as *iḍā*, *piṅgalā*, and *suṣumṇā* (Tib.: *rkyaṅ-ma*, *ro-ma*, *dbu-ma*). Just as *iḍā* and *piṅgalā* oppose each other as creative and perceptive, male and female principles, in the same way the lower Centres of reproduction and nutrition are opposed by the upper Centres of conscious cognition, formulation and discrimination. And just as the *suṣumṇā* stands in the middle between the two outer *nāḍīs*, establishing their inner relationship and finally uniting and absorbing them, in the same way

[1] It may be mentioned here that 108 is a highly significant number (9×12), and that both Hindu and Buddhist rosaries have 108 beads.

ASCENDING AND DESCENDING MOVEMENT OF THE INNER FIRE WITHIN THE SUṢUMṆĀ-NĀḌI

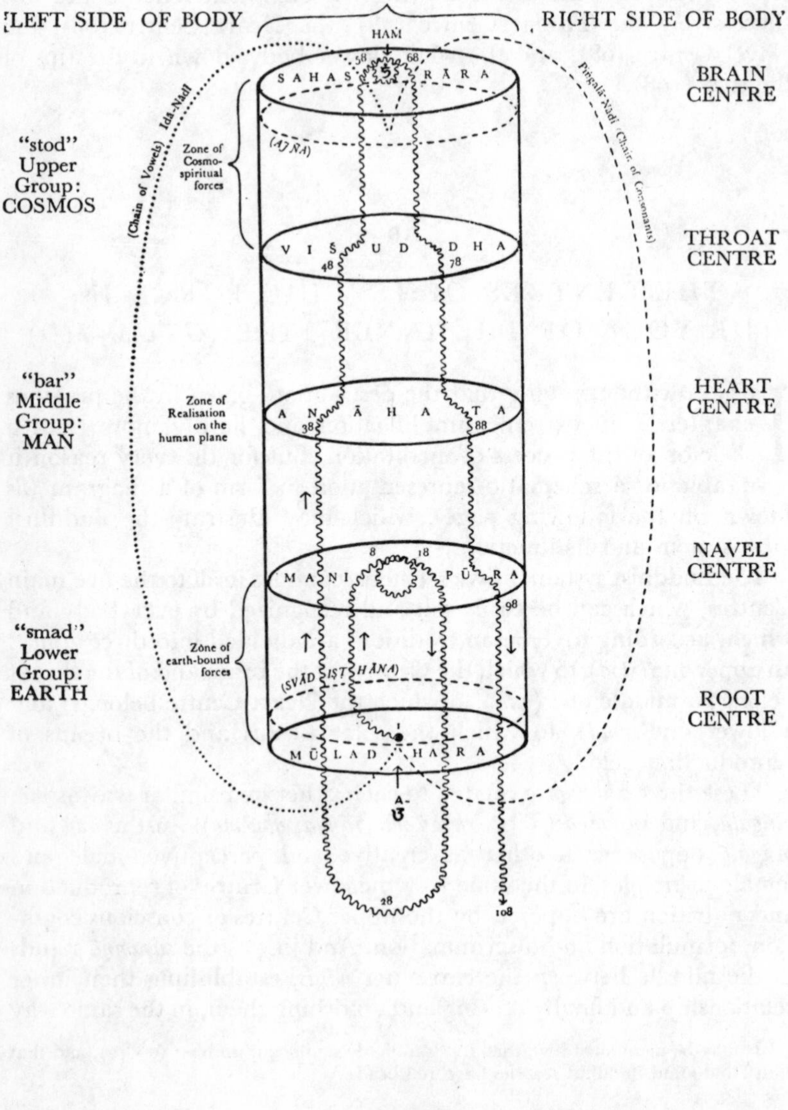

the Heart Centre mediates between the lower and the upper Centres and finally becomes the realm of realization on the human plane, after the integration of the polar forces has taken place in the highest Centre.

These three zones represent in their deepest sense:

1. The terrestial plane, namely, that of earth-bound elementary forces of nature, of materiality or corporeality (of the 'materialized past');

2. The cosmic or universal plane of eternal laws, of timeless knowledge (which from the human point of view is felt as a 'future' state of attainment, a goal yet to be attained), a plane of spontaneous spiritual awareness of the Infinite, as symbolized in the boundlessness of space and in the experience of the Great Void (*śūnyatā*; Tib.: *stoṅ-pa-ñid*), in which form and non-form is equally comprised;

3. The human plane of individual realization, in which the qualities of terrestrial existence and cosmic relationship, the forces of the earth and of the universe become conscious in the human soul as an ever-present and *deeply felt* reality. Therefore the Heart Centre becomes the seat of the seed-syllable HŪṀ in contradistinction to the OṀ of the Crown Centre.[1]

However, before we discuss the mantric qualities of the Centres, we have to devote ourselves to a further analysis of their nature. As mentioned at the beginning of this part, the Buddhist *Tantra-Yoga* does not deal with fixed magnitudes and static concepts, but with a system of dynamic functions and mutually dependent relationships whose evaluation depends on the respective position of the symbol or the Centre which we choose as our starting-point, in other words, it is our attitude, our spiritual level, that determines the direction of our inner development.

The Crown Centre is not by nature the seat of cosmic or transcendental consciousness (or whatever we may call its highest function), just as little as the Heart Centre is by nature the seat of the intuitive-spiritual consciousness, or the Root Centre the seat of psychically creative and physically wholesome forces. They may become the vehicles of these properties through conscious transformation of their functions: from those of instinctive-individual self-preservation,

[1] It is interesting to note that the philosophy of the *I-Ching*, the ancient Chinese book on 'The Principles of Nature' is based on the eternal order and inner relationship of Heaven, Earth, and Man. By uniting Heaven and Earth within him, Man achieves ultimate harmony and perfection. The *Muṇḍaka Upaniṣad* too speaks of the meeting of Heaven and Earth in Man: 'He in whom Heaven and Earth and the Middle-region are united, together with the mind and all life-currents,—know him to be the one Self; give up all other talk: this is the bridge to immortality.' (II, 2, 5.)

common to all animals, to those of spiritual self-realization. The former are directed upon material existence, the latter upon liberation from the reign of matter.

Just as the solar, centrifugal force of the *piṅgalā* (like the outward-directed 'activity of the warrior') contains the principle of individual cognition and differentiation, and therewith the poison of mortality – while *iḍā*, the lunar, centripetal force, represents the 'elixir of immortality', but at the same time also the blind urge of existence, which causes the endless round of rebirths (*saṁsāra*) – in a similar way the Brain Centre in its unsublimated form represents the mundane activity of the intellect, which separates us more and more from the sources of life and from the inner unity of all beings.

The outwardly-directed intellect entangles us ever deeper in the process of becoming, in the world of 'things' and material form and into the illusion of separate selfhood and thus of death. And if the intellect is turned inwards, it loses itself in mere conceptual thinking, in a vacuum of abstractions, in the death of mental petrification.

If, however, the intellect succeeds in catching occasional glimpses of the true nature of things, then its world collapses and ends in destruction and chaos. To the spiritually unprepared, immature mind, the nature of reality, of unveiled truth, therefore appears in terrible form. For this reason the experiences connected with the breaking-through towards highest knowledge or awareness of reality, are represented in the terrifying images of 'blood-drinking deities'. Their *maṇḍala* is associated with the Brain Centre, while the *maṇḍala* of the peaceful or benign forms of the *Dhyāni-Buddhas* are visualized as dwelling in the lotus of the Heart Centre. The blood that is drunk by the 'terrible deities', is the elixir of knowledge (the fruit from the 'Tree of Knowledge'), which in its pure, unmitigated form – i.e. without being combined with the qualities of compassion and love – acts upon man as a deadly poison.

If thus the Brain Centre of the unawakened man contains the seeds of death, the principle of mortality, the Root Centre at the opposite end of the *suṣumṇā* contains the seed of life, and thus, as we have mentioned already, the cause of the infinite cycle of rebirths, of *saṁsāra*. The consciousness of the unawakened Brain Centre has the faculty of discriminating cognition, it lacks, however, the unifying force of creative life and spontaneity. The Root Centre is the source of the unifying but blindly creating vital forces, whose functions exhaust themselves in the urge of self-preservation. It lacks the discriminating cognition, which could give meaning and direction to this blind force.

For this reason the cognizing and discriminating consciousness of the solar principle – which in the waking state is subject to our will and can be strengthened and directed by conscious respiration – must descend to the sources of life and raise its regenerative forces from the realm of sexual into that of psychic and spiritual activity.

Therefore the seed-syllable 'A', which represents the principle of cognition in the above-mentioned meditative practice, and which the Hinduistic *cakra*-system characteristically associates with the Centre of inner vision (*Ajñā-cakra*), is to be visualized in the lowest Centre, namely at the entrance of the *suṣumṇā* (the Root Centre is here not to be contemplated), while the seed-syllable 'HAṀ', here representing the creative principle or Elixir of Life, is visualized in the Crown Centre. This visualization is a symbolical anticipation of the aim, as may be seen from the fact that only when the heat of the flaming 'A' reaches the 'HAṀ' in the course of meditation, the 'HAṀ' comes to life and awakens to a state of activity. The incandescent or 'flaming' appearance of the seed-syllable 'A' is an indication of the degree of reality or experience-value it has assumed for the *Sādhaka* on account of his continued concentration. When, therefore, the heat of the flaming 'A' reaches the 'HAṀ', the latter is activated and liquefied (or 'melted') into the regenerative force of an enlightened consciousness (*bodhi-citta*), which fills the Thousand-petalled Lotus and, overflowing from it, descends into all the other Centres.

This descent marks the second transformation of the Centres: The first one consisted in making them conscious through the rising flame of inspiration – the principle of spiritual cognition, of inner awareness, or direct knowledge, fanned into a state of incandescent intensity through perfect concentration. The second and most important transformation, however, consists in making these Centres into tools of the enlightened consciousness, in which knowing and feeling, wisdom and love, the brightness of light and the warmth of life have become one. The symbol of this integration is the seed-syllable HŪṀ.

This double transformation frees the Centres from their unsublimated elementary qualities and enables them to receive new impulses and forces, provided by the mutually penetrating, ascending and descending currents of consciousness. These two streams of movements are of fiery (ascending) and liquid (descending) nature, influencing and penetrating each other. Their co-existence and simultaneous action has apparently been symbolized in the popular story of the Buddha's 'Twin Miracle' (reported in chapter XVI of *Dhammapada-Aṭṭhakathā* and mentioned in the *Nidāna-Kathā*, *Jātaka*

No. 483, *Milinda-Pañha*, as well in the introduction of *Atthasālinī*, etc.) in which it is said that the Buddha by the power of his concentration caused his body to emit simultaneously rays of fire and water, like a multi-coloured aura.

II

DHYĀNI-BUDDHAS, SEED-SYLLABLES AND ELEMENTS IN THE BUDDHIST *CAKRA*-SYSTEM

FROM what we have explained in the previous chapters, it is clear that in the Buddhist *Cakra-Yoga* the importance of the Centres depends on the particular process of meditation, on the starting-point as well as on the aim of the practice in question. Even the elementary qualities of the Centres are modified by these processes, which depend on the meditator's level of consciousness, the direction of his inner movement, and the attitude of his mind. In the Buddhist Tantric system the elements are being more and more detached from their material qualities or from their natural prototypes. Their mutual relationship is regarded to be more important than their organic functions or any other objective content associated with them. The five Centres of the Buddhist system are related to each other like the five elements; but not in the way that the same Centre would necessarily always represent the same element, or that the same element would necessarily stand for one and the same property. The symbolism of the elements moves on many planes: on that of Nature, on that of abstract concepts, on that of sense-perception, and equally so on the emotional, the psychic, the intuitional, the spiritual plane, etc.

The element 'Fire' is not only the symbol for the corresponding material state of aggregation or the physical heat resulting from it, but equally as much for light, solar force, visibility; or: destruction, transformation, purification, fusion, integration; or: psychic warmth, enthusiasm, inspiration, emotion, temperament, passion; or: desire for knowledge, devotion, self-sacrifice, and so on. In the same way 'Water' not only stands for the elementary qualities of cohesion, or the liquid state aggregation, but also for those of assimilation, equilibrium, dissolution, liquefication, unification; or for the Elixir of Life, lunar force, fertility, the female principle; or for the colourless, the reflective, the qualities of a mirror; or for the deep, the abysmal, the subconscious, etc.

Each system of symbolism has therefore its own associations, and these are dependent on development or growth. They are not built upon abstract logic, they are not intellectually thought out, but ripen and unfold in the course of time. They are like things in a state of flux: the sequence of the various phases of movement depends on many factors, from the initial direction, the original impetus, the surroundings, resistance or new impulses of movement.

The starting-point of the Buddhist *yoga* is neither of cosmological nor of theologic-metaphysical character, but psychological in the deepest sense. Thus the character of the psychic Centres is not determined by the qualities of the elements, but by the psychological functions which are ascribed or consciously attributed to them.

The intellectual Centre, in which the most immaterial qualities reside, is transformed into the organ of universal consciousness, to which the element of space or 'Ether' corresponds.

The Centre of Speech becomes the organ of mantric sound, in which physical breath is transformed into conscious *prāṇa*, the spiritualized vibration of mentally and audibly formulated knowledge. Its element is that of motion, represented by the symbol 'Wind' or 'moving air' (in the form of a semi-circular bow).

The Heart Centre becomes the organ of the intuitive mind, of spiritualized feeling (of all-embracing compassion), and the central organ of the process of meditation, in which the cosmic-abstract is transformed into human experience and realization. From the plane of the Absolute (*dharma-dhātu*) the universally valid (law, *dharma*) is first transferred upon the plane of ideal perception (*sambhogakāya*), of mantric formulation (in the Centre of Speech) and inner vision, and finally upon the plane of human realization (*nirmāṇa-kāya*) in the Heart Centre.

If, therefore, the Heart Centre is associated with the element 'Fire', we must understand that here we are dealing not with the physical element, but with the fire of inspiration, the psychic fire, the fire of religious devotion, for which reason the heart was compared with the brahmanical fire-altar.

The Navel Centre is associated with the element 'Water'. This does not mean that it could not also become the Centre of psychic heat, as for instance in the Yoga of the Inner Fire, because this 'fire', as we have seen, spreads gradually through all the Centres. The association with the element 'Water' only means that the Navel Centre is mainly to be regarded as the organ of transformation, equilibration, and assimilation of subconscious material and immaterial forces. Since in the Buddhist system the functions of the *Svādhiṣṭhāna-Cakra* are identified partly with the Navel Centre and partly with the Root Centre, the necessity of associating the element 'Water' with the Navel Centre will be obvious. These reasons, however, are not decisive for the practice of *yoga*, and least of all for the Buddhist *yoga* which, as we have seen, does not start from static data which, once given, have to be adhered to rigidly, but from dynamic principles or possibilities of psychic transmutation. The Buddhist Tantric adept does not ask 'What is there?', but 'What can be made of it?'.

It would appear plausible to conclude from this grouping of elementary qualities that the *Dhyāni-Buddhas* and seed-syllables corresponding to these elements, would be associated with the respective Centres to which those elements have been assigned. This, however, is not the case, because, as mentioned before, the elements are seen here from an entirely different point of view and belong to a different category of symbols. What connects, for instance, *Amitābha* and the element 'Fire', is not the property of heat, but the qualities of light, the faculty of making things visible, and the quality of 'redness'. What connects *Akṣobhya* with the element 'Water', are not the qualities of fluidity or cohesion, but the mirror-like surface, which reflects the pure, colourless (white) light – corresponding to the 'Wisdom of the Great Mirror' and the metaphorical relationship between the *ālayà*-consciousness and the ocean.

In all these categories of symbols we cannot count with fixed magnitudes (which have only one meaning) and from which equally definite equations (which allow only one result) can be formed, as for instance: 'if A is equal to X, and B too is equal to X, then it follows that A is equal to B'. In symbolism we are dealing with categories or sequences of mental associations, but not with equations. These categories of associations, however, are not arbitrary, but follow their own inherent laws. In this respect they are comparable to living organisms whose movements are not predictable, notwithstanding their dependence on certain laws.

In every many-sided symbolism one main point must prevail, and the more manifold and complicated a system, the more restricted are the meanings of its single constituents.

In the symbolism of meditative processes, however, the leading principle is not a theoretical point of view, but the practice and the experiences derived from it. For this reason each school of meditation and each particular sect has its own system, which is maintained by tradition and passed on from master to pupil.

Therefore in the distribution of *Dhyāni-Buddhas* and their mantras among the psycho-physical Centres of the body, there can be no single and fixed system. It depends on the meditator, which particular symbol he wants to place into the centre of his contemplation, and from this choice depends the position of all the other symbols of the *maṇḍala*. The body itself becomes a *maṇḍala* during meditation, and within it there are innumerable smaller *maṇḍalas*, because each Centre is such a one. The term '*cakra*' is in fact often used as a synonym for '*maṇḍala*'. Even the external world surrounding the body, grows into an all-embracing *maṇḍala*, whose concentric circles, like those caused by a stone thrown into a calm expanse of water, spread wider and wider, until they disappear in the infinite.

Therefore it is said in the *Demchog-Tantra* (*dpal ḥkhor-lo bde-mchog*) that 'one should regard oneself and all that is visible (*bdag daṅ snaṅ thams-cad*) as a divine *maṇḍala* (*lhaḥi-dkyil-ḥkhor*)' and that 'every audible sound (*grags-paḥi-sgra thams-cad*) is to be regarded as mantra (*sṅags*) and every thought arising in one's mind (*sems-kyi rtog-paḥi ḥdu-ḥphro thams-cad*) as a magic manifestation of the Great Wisdom (*ye-śes chen-poḥi chos-ḥphrul*)'.

In other words, the meditator must imagine himself in the centre of the *maṇḍala* as an embodiment of the divine figure of perfect Buddhahood, the realization of which is the aim of his *sādhanā*. Herewith all arbitrariness disappears. No room is left for anything that is inessential or superfluous. Nothing is left to chance or to merely subjective imagination. The things of the outer world combine and transform themselves into a sacred circle, in whose centre the *Sādhaka's* body becomes a temple. And the mere fact of being conscious and of possessing the power of spiritual creativeness becomes an inexpressible wonder. The visible becomes a symbol of deeper reality, the audible becomes *mantra*, matter a condensation of elementary forces, and the psychic Centres of the body become the five storeys of the sacred temple. And each of them contains a throne and the *maṇḍala* of a *Dhyāni-Buddha*.

The lowest storey or ground-floor is the Root Centre, represented by a yellow square or a cube, corresponding to the element 'Earth', in whose dark womb the seeds of all actions are ripening. It is the realm of karmic law, of karmically bound activity. In this bondage lies the point of comparison with the nature of the earth-element, the element of bondage to form, to a state of rigidity and inertness. *Amoghasiddhi*, who embodies the 'All-accomplishing', karma-freeing Wisdom, is therefore chosen to be the lord and the transformer of this realm. His seed-syllable is 'ĀḤ'.

The Lord of a *cakra* is therefore not a deity inherent in its nature or representing the personification of the elementary qualities of the Centre, but a symbol of those forces with which we wish to saturate and activate the Centre. The choice of this symbol depends on its particular suitability for being able to act upon the properties of the *cakra* in question, either with a view to intensify or to sublimate them. In order to achieve this, the symbol must coincide with certain features or qualities of the *cakra*, though it may be different from the elementary nature of the *cakra* in other respects.

This may be observed especially in the field of *mantras*: the seed-syllables of the elements are different from those of the *Dhyāni-Buddhas*, who in other respects correspond to them. The colours of the elements show a similar tendency, in so far as they do not coincide with the colours of the *Dhyāni-Buddhas*, who are united with them in the same Centre. This also shows that the relationship of one system cannot be transferred mechanically upon another. And if this is true within the closely related Buddhist systems, how much more is this the case with respect to Buddhist and Hindu yoga-systems! The naïvety with which these things have been mixed up by Western authors, has created an incredible confusion, the consequences of which we shall have to overcome step by step, before we can lay the foundations for a deeper understanding and an unprejudiced attitude.

Let us return to the simile of the five-storeyed temple of our body. The second storey (the Navel Centre), which is depicted as a white disc or sphere (the form of a drop), corresponds to the element 'Water', to the quality of assimilation, and to the *Dhyāni-Buddha Ratnasambhava*, the Great Equalizer. His 'Wisdom of Equality' is the knowledge of the fundamental unity of all beings. His seed-syllable is 'TRAṀ'.

The assimilating function of the Navel Centre is expressed in the *Demchog-Tantra* in the idea that the gross elements are transformed in it into vital or psychic elements. It is said there, that one should visualize in the Navel Centre a four-petalled lotus, whose petals, beginning from the east and moving clockwise, have the following qualities:

1. The *prāṇic* essence or the vital principle (*prāṇa*; Tib.: *rluṅ*) of the element 'Earth' (*sa*);
2. The vital principle of the element 'Water' (*chu-rluṅ*);
3. The vital principle of the element 'Fire' (*me-rluṅ*);
4. The vital principle of the element 'Air' (*rluṅ-gi-rluṅ*). Corresponding to these elements, one should visualize the following seed-syllables:

   1. The yellow LA(Ṁ); 2. The White VA(Ṁ);
   3. The red RA(Ṁ); 4. The green YA(Ṁ).

In the centre of the lotus one should visualize the vital principle of the 'Ether' or space-element (*nam-mkhaḥ*; Skt.: *ākāśa*) as a blue dot (*thig-le*; Skt.: *bindu*).

In another passage of the same text the vital principles of the Four Great Elements are called the 'four gates' (*ḥbyuṅ-ba bziḥi rluṅ-rgyu-ba-sgo bźi*) of the sacred temple of the body. It is important to understand that in all these visualizations we are not concerned with material elements or physical principles, but with vital and psychic forces and laws, out of which our world is built – irrespective of whether we call it the 'inner' or the 'outer' world.

The third storey, corresponding to the Heart Centre, is represented as a red triangle (also as a cone or a pyramid) and forms the central or middle-storey of the pagoda-temple. It contains the sacrificial fire-altar, the sacred flame of which transforms and purifies, melts and integrates the elements of our personality. This sacred flame corresponds to the seed-syllable HŪṀ and to the figure of *Vajrasattva-Akṣobhya.* In the following chapters we shall deal in greater detail with HŪṀ as the symbol of ultimate integration, as well as with the special role of *Vajrasattva.*

The fourth storey, corresponding to the Throat Centre, is dedicated to the element 'Air', symbolized by a semi-circular bow or a hemispherical body of green colour (the open side, or plane surface, upwards). We have already dealt with the various meanings of the Tibetan word *rluṅ* and its Sanskrit equivalent *prāṇa* and *vāyu.* The drawn bow hints at the dynamic character of this element. In connexion with the Throat Centre it does not only hint at the life-giving breath, but also at its functions as the medium of the sacred word, as the originator of all sounds and of the finest spiritual vibrations, from which arise the different characters of all things and every form of distinguishing knowledge, the basis of *mantra* and vision. *Amitābha,* the embodiment of 'distinguishing' or Discriminating Wisdom of inner vision (like his active reflex, *Amitāyus,* who represents the boundlessness of life), is therefore conceived as the Lord of this Centre. His seed-syllable is HRĪḤ.[1]

The fifth and highest storey, corresponding to the Brain or Crown Centre, is represented by a blue flaming drop (*bindu*; Tib.: *thig-le*), the symbol of the element 'Space' or 'Ether' (*ākāśa*; Tib.; *nam-mkhaḥ*). Its Lord is *Vairocana,* who embodies the 'Wisdom of the Universal

[1] 'H' is the sound of the breath, the symbol of all life; 'R' is the sound of fire ('RAṀ'). The 'Ī', being the vowel of the highest intensity or rate of vibration, stands for the highest spiritual activity and differentiation. The aspirated after-sound (*visarga*), following the 'Ī', though being written in Tibetan script, is omitted in pronunciation, so that the seed-syllable could be rendered phonetically as 'HRĪ' (as often done).

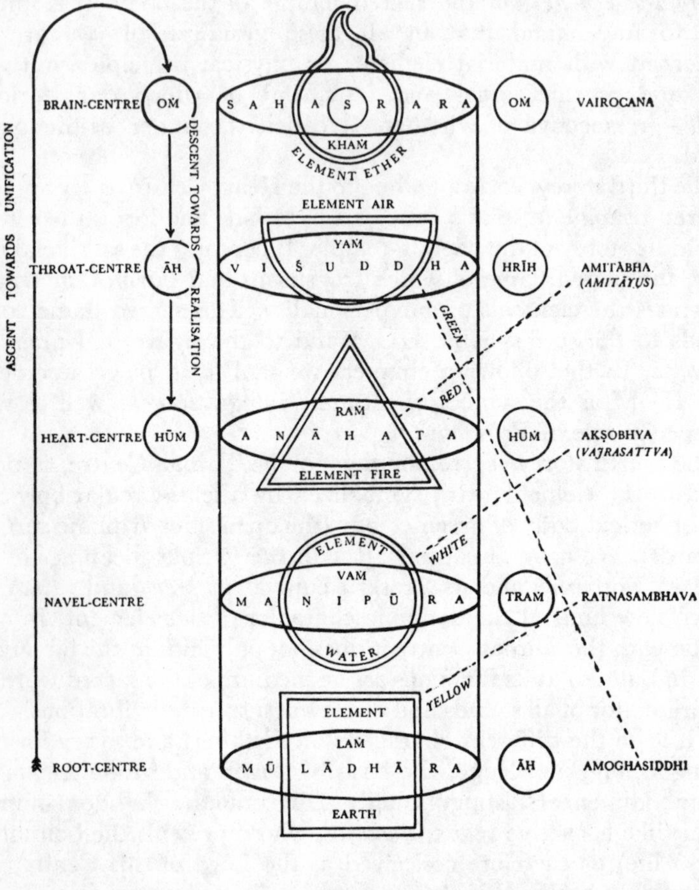

RELATIONS BETWEEN CENTRES, SEED-SYLLABLES, ELEMENTS AND DHYĀNI-BUDDHAS

Law' and who is embraced by the 'Mother of Heavenly Space'. His seed-syllable is 'OṀ'.

The 'OṀ-ĀḤ-HŪṀ' on the left side of the diagram illustrating the relationship between Centres, elements, seed-syllables, and *Dhyāni-Buddhas* corresponds to the three principles of 'Body' (*kāya*; Tib.: *sku*), 'Speech' (*vāk*; Tib.: *gsuṅ*), and 'Mind' (*citta*; Tib.: *thugs*), which – after the unification of all psychic qualities and forces of the meditator – are transformed into:

1. The principle of the all-embracing universal body ('OṀ'), realized in the Crown Centre;

2. The principle of all-embracing, i.e., mantric speech (Tib.: *gzuṅs*) or creative sound ('ĀḤ'), realized in the Throat Centre;

3. The principle of the all-embracing love of the Enlightened Mind (*bodhi-citta*; Tib.: *byaṅ-chub-sems*) of all Buddhas ('HŪṀ'), realized in the Heart Centre. (More about this in the last chapter of this part.)

The broken lines on the right side of the diagram show the relationship between *Dhyāni-Buddhas* and elements in a category of symbols, based on the identity of colours, as found in the *maṇḍala* of the *Dhyāni-Buddhas* in the previous main part.

If the symbols of the five elements, as shown in the present diagram of the five Centres of the Buddhist yoga-system, are placed one upon the other in their corresponding three-dimensional forms, they demonstrate the essential structure of Tibetan 'Chortens' (*mchod-rten*),[1] religious monuments developed from the Indian *stūpa*, which originally served as a receptacle for the relics of the Buddha and his chief disciples.[2] In Tibet, however, they are purely symbolical structures: plastic *maṇḍalas*.

The most beautiful and impressive example of such a *maṇḍala* is the *Chorten* of the 'Hundred-thousand Buddhas' (*sku-ḥbum*, pronounced 'Kumbum') in Gyantse, which forms an imposing terraced pagoda-like temple, containing about a hundred chapels, of which each again forms a *maṇḍala* of its own. The bigger of these chapels contain *maṇḍalas* in which thousands of figures are combined (in form of frescoes as well as of sculptures). One of them contains not less than eight thousand figures!

The cubic forms of the lower storeys correspond to the element 'Earth', the round central part to the element 'Water', the conical

[1] See drawing at the end of this chapter.

[2] As to the development and symbolism of the *Stūpa*, see my monograph *Some Aspects of Stūpa Symbolism* (Kitabistan, Allahabad and London, 1940), as well as my essay on *Solar and Lunar Symbolism in the Development of Stūpa Architecture* ('Marg', Bombay, 1950). Furthermore: *Giuseppe Tucci "Mc'od rten" e "Ts'a ts'a" nel Tibet Indiano ed Occidentale*, Roma, 1932.

(gilt) upper-structure to the element 'Fire', the umbrella above it to the element 'Air'.[1] The flaming drop of the element 'Ether' rests on the vessel with the 'Elixir of Life' (*amṛta-kalaśa*; Tib.: *bum-pa*, or *tse-bum*), which crowns the honorific umbrella.

12

SYMBOLISM OF THE SEED-SYLLABLE HŪṂ AS SYNTHESIS OF THE FIVE WISDOMS

As we have seen in the 'Yoga of the Inner Fire', the meditative experience takes place in different phases. The first is characterized by the taking possession and penetration of the *Maṇipūra-Cakra* by the heat of the Inner Fire, whereby all bodily, elementary, or 'earth-bound' forces of the lower region (Tib.: *smad*) are concentrated and sublimated. (For this reason the Navel Centre is regarded as the actual starting-point or the main organ of psychic

[1] The symbols of the Four Great Elements play a particular part in *Milarepa's* biography. His Guru, *Marpa*, in order to make him expiate his former misdeeds and the bad karmic effects, which stood in the way of his spiritual progress, ordered him to build with his own hands four houses and to destroy each of them after its completion, excepting the last. The ground-plan of the first house was circular, that of the second semi-circular or crescent-shaped, that of the third triangular, and that of the fourth one square. In other words, *Milarepa* was made to concentrate upon the psychic Centres of the elements, Water, Air, Fire, and Earth, which represent, as the text says, the four types of action, namely, the peaceful (*źi-ba*), the grand or far-reaching (*rgyas-pa*), the powerful or fascinating (*dbaṅ*), and the stern (*drag-pa*). He had thus to undo all his former actions by first reconstructing them and then dissolving them, right down to the foundation, the *Mūlādhāra*, the element 'Earth'. Then only was he allowed to build the lasting edifice of his new spiritual life.

Plate 5

KUṀBUM
The Temple of the Hundred-Thousand Buddhas

heat [*gtum-mo*].) After the hindrances of the lower realms have thus been removed, the meditation can proceed on a safe foundation and can turn without hindrance towards the main aim: the becoming *one* in the spirit.

This takes place in the second phase of this meditation, in the attainment of universal consciousness, in which all self-limitation, all duality of 'self' and 'non-self' is extinguished.

The third phase, however, consists in the return to the human plane, on which all attainments are translated into life and deed. The place of this experience is the human heart, in which the 'Diamond Being', i.e. *Vajrasattva*, is realized and becomes an ever-present force in the seed-syllable HŪṀ.

He is the active reflex of *Akṣobhya*, or that side of his being which is turned towards the world. In *Vajrasattva* the highest reality of the Dharma-sphere is reflected and rendered *conscious* on the individual plane. He is the active ray of the 'Wisdom of the Great Mirror', which reflects the Void as well as the things, which mirrors the 'emptiness' in the things, and the things in the 'emptiness'. He is the knowledge of the universal background, the knowledge which recognizes the totality of the world in each form of appearance, the knowledge of the infinite in the finite, the timeless in the apparently transient. He is the Vajra of the Heart, the immutable, indestructible – the spiritual certainty that flows from the direct experience of reality, in which all Wisdoms are fused into one by the flame of an all-embracing feeling of solidarity (we may call it love, sympathy, benevolence, or whatever we like) and the urge to act for the benefit of all living beings.

If OṀ is the ascent towards universality, then HŪṀ is the descent of universality into the depth of the human heart. And just as the OṀ precedes the HŪṀ, and the OṀ (as the centre of the *maṇḍala*) potentially contains all other seed-syllables, and can only be experienced after all these seed-syllables have become actualities in the process of meditation, in the same way HŪṀ contains the experience of OṀ and becomes the living synthesis of all the five Wisdoms. This is not a knowledge which can be defined in words, but a state of mind (as opposed to a mental 'object').[1]

The *Demchog Tantra*, therefore, says that HŪṀ represents the

[1] 'Yoga is the overcoming of outer perception in favour of inner awareness. All essential experience cannot be anything other than self-exploration of life. The living whole of the world may perceive and arrange itself as if it were something external; it may conceive its play within itself as an objective reality confronting it, it may conceive the relationships which exist between its force-formations, as valid rules – in this way science is created. Knowledge arises through inner awareness. As to the communicability and the general recognition of its experiences, knowledge, therefore, is in a less favourable position than

'mind free from all thought-contents or concepts' (*ḥzin-daṅ-bral-paḥi sems*). The five parts of which HŪṀ is composed in its visible form (in Indian as well as in Tibetan script) correspond to the five *Dhyāni-Buddhas* and their Wisdoms.

The vowel 'ū' which forms the lower part of the HŪṀ corresponds, according to the text of this scripture, to the Wisdom of *Amoghasiddhi*, which 'accomplishes all works' (*bya-ba grub-paḥi ye-śes*). The body of the letter 'H' corresponds to the 'Distinguishing Wisdom' (*so-sor-rtogs-paḥi ye-śes*) of *Amitābha*; the head of the 'H' (the horizontal bar which is common to all letters and represents the throne of the deity or the creative power dwelling in every mantric sound) corresponds to the 'Wisdom of Equality' (*mñam-pa-ñid-kyi ye-śes*) of *Ratnasambhava*. The crescent corresponds to the 'Mirror-like Wisdom' (*me-loṅ lta-buḥi ye-śes*) of *Akṣobhya*, and the flaming drop (*thig-le*) to the *Dharmadhātu* Wisdom (*chos-kyi- dbyins-gyi ye-śes*) of *Vairocana*.

Each of these three parts possesses a colour corresponding to its *Dhyāni-Buddha*. The vowel-sign is green, the body of the 'H' red, the head yellow, the crescent white, and the flaming drop blue.

This is an example of the aliveness of the mantric symbol, which is not only audible and speakable, i.e., inner and outer sound, but also visible form and finally divine appearance, which confronts the *Sādhaka* like a spatially-objective being.

Furthermore it is said in the above-mentioned text, that the seed-syllable HŪṀ emits rays of blue, green red, and yellow light, and that these rays are to be regarded as issuing from the four faces of the central deity (*bde-mchog*; Skt.: *Mahāsukha*, the embodiment of highest bliss, into whose form the HŪṀ is transformed) and finally fill the whole universe (*ḥjig-rten-gyi-khams thams-cad*). It should be noted that the white radiation is omitted. The reason is that the white light represents the inner nature of *Mahāsukha*, who herewith reveals himself as a form of *Vajrasattva*, the immanent, all-pervading reality of the adamantine voidness.

Hereto the meditator must return, after he has brought to life the mantric symbol through inner vision, and after he has identified it with his own body and mind. In order to realize this adamantine voidness, he must reverse the process of meditation (*rdzogs-rim*) and dissolve the vowel-sign 'ū' by letting it sink into the body of the

---

science. With the elimination of the opposite side the conventionally valid corporeality of form is annihilated and the world of names deprived of its habitual meaning, because the world of names is valid only from the point of view of perception, not of that of inner awareness. From the latter point of view it is valid only in the sense of a simile, i.e., it is both valid and non-valid.' (Translated from *Ewiges Indien* by Heinrich Zimmer, p. 111.)

'H', the body of the 'H' into the head, the head of the 'H' into the crescent, and the crescent into the flaming drop – until finally the drop dissolves and disappears into empty space or vibrates as a pure mantric sound, until it merges into silence.

Here we have reached the limit of what words can express, and therefore it is safer to remain in the symbolic language of the Tantras, whose similies will help us to penetrate into the mysteries that go beyond words.

Symbolism of the Seed-Syllable HŪM
as quintessence of the Five Wisdoms

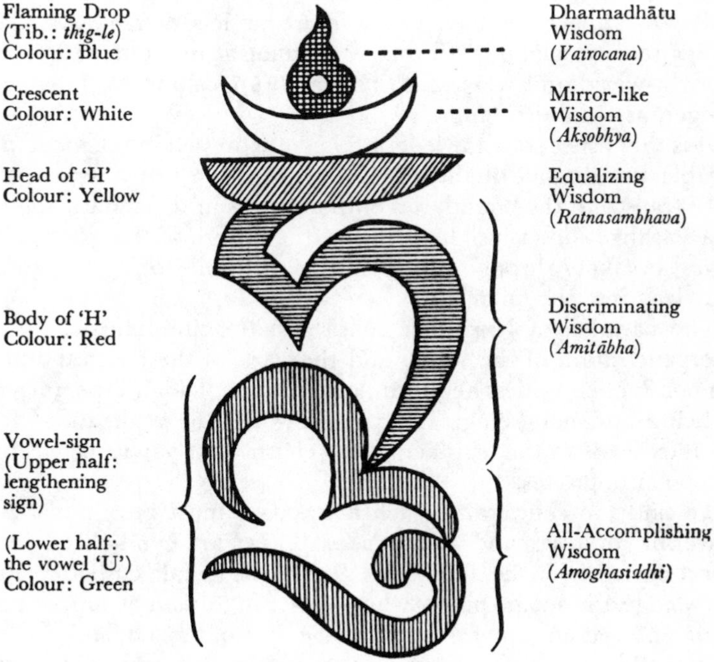

13

THE SEED-SYLLABLE *HŪṀ* AND THE IMPORTANCE OF THE *ḌĀKINĪ* IN THE PROCESS OF MEDITATION (*ḌĀKINĪ* VERSUS *KUṆḌALINĪ*)

If we want fully to understand the profound significance of the seed-syllable HŪṀ in the mantric and meditative practice of the *Vajrayāna*, we must devote ourselves to an aspect of this system, which is particularly foreign to Western thought and feeling, and which therefore is misunderstood even more than all the other features of Tantric Buddhism. We allude here to a class of beings, forces, or symbols, whose nature is closely related to the seed-syllable HŪṀ, and who appear to the outsider more or less demoniacal. These beings seem to embody all that we cannot fit into our well-ordered thought-world and which for this reason appears to us threatening, dangerous, and terrifying.

It is that aspect of knowledge which is expressed in the incommensurable, undefinable quality of HŪṀ, which can only be experienced if we transcend the boundaries of thought, as in the ecstatic moment of a flashlike direct insight into the true nature of things or of ourselves, breaking through the tension of our inner being and forcing us to leap into the unknown.

The paradox of *Vajrasattva* consists in the simultaneousness, the interpenetration of the whole and the part, of the timeless and the temporal, of emptiness and form, of the individual and the universal, of being and non-being. The path towards the realization of this paradox leads to the leap across the chasm that yawns between the two polar opposites.

To find the courage for such a leap, we must be stimulated by powerful impulses and experiences. These are symbolized in the secret doctrines of the Tantras as *Ḍākinīs*, as female embodiments of knowledge and magic power who – either in human or super-human form – played an important role in the lives of the *Siddhas*.

In the biography of *Padmasambhava*, written exclusively in the symbolical language characteristic of *Siddha* literature, we find the description of his initiation into the secrets of the Buddhist *Cakra-Yoga* by a *Ḍākinī*.[1]

[1] '*U-rgyan gu-ru pa-dma-ḥbyuṅ-gnas-gyi rnam-thar*,' translated (in extracts) by S. W. Laden La, edited by W. Y. Evans-Wentz in *The Tibetan Book of the Great Liberation* (Oxford University Press, 1954), p. 131 f.

She dwelt, as the text tells us, in a sandal-wood garden, in the midst of a cemetery, in a palace of human skulls. When *Padmasambhava* arrived at the door of the palace, he found it closed. Thereupon a servant-woman appeared, carrying water into the palace; and Padma sat in meditation so that her water-carrying was halted by his yogic power.[1]

Thereupon, producing a knife of crystal, she cut open her breast, and exhibited in the upper portion of it the forty-two Peaceful and in the lower portion of it the fifty-eight Wrathful Deities. Addressing Padma, she said: 'I observe that thou art a wonderful mendicant, possessed of great power. But look at me; hast thou not faith in me?' Padma bowed down before her, made apology, and requested the teachings he sought. She replied: 'I am only a maidservant. Come inside.'

Upon entering the palace, Padma beheld the *Ḍākinī* enthroned on a sun and moon throne, holding in her hands a double drum and a human-skull cup, and surrounded by thirty-two *Ḍākinīs* making sacrificial offerings to her. Padma made obeisance to the enthroned *Ḍākinī* and offerings, and begged her to teach him both esoterically and exoterically. The one hundred Peaceful and Wrathful Deities then appeared overhead. 'Behold,' said the *Ḍākinī*, 'the deities. Now take initiation.' And Padma responded, 'Inasmuch as all the Buddhas throughout the aeons have had *gurus*, accept me as thy disciple.'

Then the *Ḍākinī* absorbed all the deities into her body. She transformed Padma into the syllable HŪṀ. The HŪṀ rested on her lips, and she conferred upon it the *Buddha Amitābha* blessing. Then she swallowed the HŪṀ, and inside her stomach Padma received the secret *Avalokiteśvara* initiation. When the HŪṀ reached the region of the Root Centre, she conferred upon him initiation of Body, Speech, and Mind.

This story contains much valuable information, but in order to understand its meaning, we have first to clarify the position of the *Ḍākinīs* in the Tibetan system of meditation. In the classical Sanskrit *Ḍākinīs* were mainly conceived as demoniacal beings hostile to humans and haunting cremation grounds and similar lonely and uncanny places, where unknown dangers lurked.

But just these places, which were shunned by common men, were preferred by Yogis as being most suitable for solitary contemplation and religious ecstasy. These were hallowed places to them, where

[1] This is a motive found already in the *Lalitavistara*, where it is described how the young *Siddhārtha* fell into a state of deep trance while sitting under a rose-apple tree, and how five ascetics, gifted with supernatural powers, were flying through the air over that very spot and were stopped by the power of *Siddhārtha*'s concentration. They were able to continue their journey only after having paid obeisance to the future Buddha.

they listened to the voice of the silence and of the liberation from worldly fears and hopes. What caused fear to the worldly-minded, filled the Yogi with tranquillity and determination, and became a source of strength and an incentive to proceed on the path of realization.

Thus *Ḍākinīs* became the genii of meditation, spiritual helpers, who inspired the *Sādhaka* and roused him from the illusion of worldly contentment. They were the forces that awakened the dormant qualities of mind and soul.

This change in the conception of *Ḍākinīs* under the influence of Buddhist schools of meditation (especially those of the sixth and seventh century A.D.) is reflected in the Tibetan rendering of the word *Ḍākinī* as '*Khadoma*' (*mkhaḥ-ḥgro-ma*): '*mkhaḥ*' means 'space' as well as 'ether' (Skt.: *ākāśa*), the fifth element, according to Buddhist definition; in other words, that which makes *movement* possible (Symbol: 'Wind', Tib.: *rluṅ*) and makes forms appear (Tib.: *snaṅ-ba*), without being itself movement or appearance. Its numerical symbol is zero, its philosophical and metaphysical equivalent is *śūnyatā* (Tib.: *stoṅ-pa-ñid*), the 'Great Void', its psychological equivalent the highest spiritual consciousness or Mind (Tib.: *sems*), of which it is said that one should conceive it as equal to the space of heaven (Tib.: *nam-mkhaḥ*).

'*Ḥgro*' (pronounced 'dō') means 'to go', 'to move about'. According to popular conception a *Khadoma* is therefore a heavenly being of female appearance (as indicated by the suffix '*ma*'), who partakes of the luminous nature of space or ether, in which she moves. She is gifted with higher knowledge and appears to the earnest seeker, especially to the practising *Yogi*, in human or divine, demoniacal or fairy-like, heroic or lovely, terrifying or peaceful form, in order to lead him on the way of higher knowledge and conscious realization.

In the sense of meditation and in the language of *Yoga*, however, they are not 'beings' existing outside ourselves, but spiritual impulses and realization of all those forces and conformations, which until then were dormant and hidden in the darkness of the subconsciousness. The impetus, dwelling behind this process of increasing awareness and consciousness, grows in proportion to its progress; it urges on irresistibly until the hidden light of knowledge reveals its secrets. This knowledge is frightening for those who are still slaves to the world of things, but liberating for those who are strong enough to face the highest truth.

The *Khadomas* of the highest order are therefore represented as being naked: they are the embodiment of the knowledge of unveiled reality; and in order to express the fearlessness which is required for facing the naked truth, they are conceived as heroic in character and attitude. They are not blind forces of nature, but the faculties which make use of them and direct them. They combine the forces of nature, of primordial spontaneity, with conscious awareness and perfect knowledge. They are the flashes of inspiration, which transform the power of nature into the creative consciousness of the genius.

Thus, in the Buddhist Yoga the emphasis is not on the power-aspect, the *śakti*, but on the knowledge-aspect, the *prajñā*; and for this reason the *Śakti Kuṇḍalinī* is not even mentioned in the Buddhist system – still less is she made the subject of meditation. The attempt to trace the Buddhist system of meditation to the *Kuṇḍalinī Yoga* of Tantric Hinduism, is therefore as misleading as calling it *Kuṇḍalinī Yoga*. In the '*Yoga of the Six Doctrines of Nāropā*' the seat of the *Kuṇḍalinī* is excluded from the path of visualization, and the *Sādhaka* is advised: 'Meditate on the four *cakras*, of which each is formed like an umbrella or the wheel of a chariot.'[1] The four *cakras*, however, which form the wheels of the fiery chariot of the spirit (which reminds one of the fiery chariot in which the prophet Elias went to heaven!) are: the Crown and Throat Centres, as the front, the Heart and Navel Centres, as the rear pairs.

In place of the *Kuṇḍalinī Śakti* the opposite principle occupies the centre of the meditation, namely that of the *Ḍākinī*: in this case the *Khadoma Dorje Naljorma* (*rdo-rje rnal-ḥbyor-ma*; Skt.: *Vajra-Yoginī*). This does not mean that the Buddhist Tantrics denied or underrated the importance or the reality of the forces connected with the *Kuṇḍalinī*, but only that their methods were different, and that the use which they made of these forces was different. They did not use them in their natural state, but through the influence of another medium.

Water-power, which in a waterfall appears in its crude, untamed form, can be tamed, directed, distributed and utilized on different levels. In a similar way in the Buddhist *Tantra Yoga* concentration is not directed upon the *Kuṇḍalinī* or the Root Centre, but on the channels, the main power-currents whose tension (or 'gravitational' force) is regulated through a temporal damming-up and modification of the energy-content in the upper Centres.

Instead of the natural power of the *Kuṇḍalinī*, the inspirational impulse of consciousness (*prajñā*) in form of the *Khadoma* and her

[1] The classical definition of a *cakra* is found in the *Muṇḍaka Upaniṣad*: '*Arā iva rathanabhau saṁhatā yatra nāḍyaḥ*'. 'Where the *nāḍis* meet like the spokes in the nave of a chariot-wheel." (2, 2, 6.) One hundred subsidiary *nāḍis* meet in the Heart Centre while the *suṣumṇā* runs perpendicularly through the centre of the *cakra*.

mantric equivalents is made the leading principle, which opens the entrance into the *suṣumṇā* by removing the obstructions and by directing the inflowing forces.

Khadomas, like all female embodiments of '*vidyā*', or knowledge, have the property of intensifying, concentrating, and integrating the forces of which they make use, until they are focused in *one* incandescent point and ignite the holy flame of inspiration, which leads to perfect enlightenment. The *Khadomas*, who appear as visions or as consciously produced inner images in the course of meditation, are therefore represented with an aura of flames and called up with the seed-syllable HŪṀ, the mantric symbol of integration. They are the embodiment of the 'Inner Fire', which in *Milarepa*'s biography has been called 'the warming breath of *Khadomas*', which surrounds and protects the saint like a 'pure, soft mantle'.[1]

Just as knowledge has many degrees and forms, so the *Khadomas* assume many shapes, from those of the human *Jigten Khadomas* (*ḥjig-rten*, the world of sense-perception) to the female forms of *Dhyāni-Buddhas*, who as '*Prajñās*' are united with the latter in the aspect of '*Yab-Yum*'.

In the process of meditation, *Khadomas* may correspond to such preliminary experiences as the becoming conscious of the body in the first stage of the four fundamental exercises of mindfulness (in the Pāli Scriptures known as '*Satipaṭṭhāna*'). The *Demchog Tantra*[2] therefore says that one should regard the *Khadoma* as the mindfulness with regard to the body (*mkhaḥ-ḥgro-ma ni lus-rjes-su dran-paḥo*), and that all divine forms of appearance are to be understood as the experiences which constitute the path of meditation (*lha-rnams lam-gyi ṅo-bor dran-par byaḥo*).

The reality of *Khadomas*, like that of 'demons' and 'deities', rests on such experiences, and not on some external facts or data. It is a reality which from the Buddhist point of view is far greater than that of the so-called material objects, because it is a reality, which springs directly from spiritual awareness and not from the roundabout way of peripherical senses and their organs.

The highest, i.e., the most perfect, form of a *Khadoma* is she who embodies the synthesis of all Buddha Wisdoms in the adamantine

[1] In Lama Kazi Dawa Samdup's and Evan-Wentz's poetical rendering:

'The warming breath of angels wear
As thy raiment pure and soft.'

(W. Y. Evans-Wentz: *Tibet's Great Yogi Milarepa*, Oxford University Press, 1928, p. 170.)

[2] Cf. A. Avalon, *Tantric Texts*, London, 1919, Vol. VII. All quotations from '*dpal-ḥkhor-lo bde-mchog*' are derived from a hand-written copy of the Tibetan Text. The text edited by Avalon has long been out of print.

sphere of *śūnyatā*, like the various aspects of the *Vajra-Ḍākinī*, especially *Vajra-Yoginī* (*rdo-rje rnal-ḥbyor-ma*), in whom the meditative experience reaches its culmination. Such a *Ḍākinī* forms the centre of *Padmasambhava's* initiation.

14

PADMASAMBHAVA'S INITIATION

WHAT is the esoteric meaning of *Padmasambhava's* initiation by a *Ḍākinī*?

The sandal-wood garden in the midst of a cemetery is the *saṁsāric* world: pleasant in appearance, but surrounded by death and decay. The *Ḍākinī* lives in a palace of human skulls: the human body, composed of the inheritance of millions of past lives, the materialization of past thoughts and deeds, the *Karma* of the past.

When *Padmasambhava* arrives, he finds the door of the palace closed: he has not yet found the key to the meaning of corporeality. The true nature of the body was not yet known to him.

Then appears a maidservant, carrying water into the palace. 'Water' signifies life-force, *prāṇa*. *Padmasambhava* thereupon arrests this force by the power of his meditation, i.e., he brings it under his control through *prāṇāyāma*. Therefore it is said that her water-carrying was halted by his yogic power.

The maidservant, thereupon, produces a knife of crystal (the clear, razor-sharp, penetrating insight of analytical knowledge), cuts open her breast, i.e., she reveals the hidden inner nature of corporeality (like that *Khadoma* in the *Demchog Tantra*, who represents the insight into the body) – and *Padmasambhava* perceives the *maṇḍalas* of the peaceful and wrathful forms of the *Dhyāni-Buddhas*. He now recognizes that this body, in spite of its transitoriness, is the temple of the highest forces and attainments.

He bows down before the maidservant, who has thus revealed herself as a *Ḍākinī*, and asks for her teachings, whereupon she allows him to enter the palace. Thus humility and the readiness to see things as they really are, opened the hitherto closed door of the palace: his own body, whose secret forces had been inaccessible to him.

Now he beholds the chief *Ḍākinī* (a form of *Vajra-Yoginī*) seated on a sun and moon throne. 'Sun' and 'Moon' represent, as we have seen before, the psycho-cosmic solar and lunar energies, polarized in *pingalā* and *iḍā-nāḍī*. These forces are under the control of the chief *Ḍākinī*. The double drum (*ḍamaru*) in her right hand is the symbol of the eternal rhythm of the universe and of the transcendental sound of the *Dharma*, at which the Buddha hinted, when in his first utterance after his enlightenment he spoke of the 'drum of immortality' (*amata-dundubhin*), which he wanted to be heard throughout the world.

In her left hand the *Ḍākinī* holds a skull-bowl filled with blood, the symbol of knowledge which can be gained only at the price of death.

She is surrounded by thirty-two lesser *Ḍākinis*, reminiscent of the thirty-two marks of physical perfection, which characterize the body of an Enlightened One.

When *Padmasambhava* asks for her teachings, the two *maṇḍalas* of *Dhyāni-Buddhas*, which had been revealed to him by the *Ḍākinī's* maidservant, appear now in their full reality overhead; as if projected into space. But in the moment of initiation they are absorbed into the chief *Ḍākinī*, who thus becomes the embodiment of all the Buddhas and is therefore also called '*Sarvabuddha-Ḍākinī*'.

Padmasambhava, however, is transformed into the seed-syllable HŪṀ and becomes one with the object of his devotion. In other words, the *Sādhaka*, by completely identifying himself with the *Mantra*, which spearheads his meditation, becomes one with the inspirational force (the urge towards enlightenment) of all the Buddhas, and thus confers upon all the Centres of consciousness the bliss of Buddhahood, transforming them into vessels of enlightenment.

The Centres, which are alluded to here, are:

1. that in which *Amitābha* is realized (when the HŪṀ is 'on the lips'), i.e., the Throat Centre (*viśuddha-cakra*), from which emerges the mantric sound;

2. that in which *Avalokiteśvara* (symbolized by the 'jewel', *maṇi*) is realized: the Navel Centre (*maṇipūra-cakra*);

3. the Root Centre (*mūlādhāra-cakra*), the meeting-place of the three *nāḍīs* (trijunction, Tib.: *gsum-mdo*), in which the creative forces of the body are transformed into spiritual potentialities, thus bringing about the regeneration of body, speech, and mind.

These are the three initiations, which the *Ḍākinī* confers in the three Centres of psychic power.

The threefold potentiality of the highest *Ḍākinī* and her integral nature, which comprises all Buddha-Wisdoms, is also expressed in the oldest known mantric formula of the *Vajra-Yoginī*, as found in the *Sādhanamālā*, a Sanskrit work of the Buddhist Tantras.

The formula runs:

'*OṀ OṀ OṀ Sarva-buddha-ḍākinīye Vajra-varṇanīye*

Vajra-vairocanīye HŪṀ HŪṀ HŪṀ PHAṬ PHAṬ PHAṬ Svāhā!'[1]

The threefold *OṀ*, *HŪṀ*, and *PHAṬ* corresponds to the three main forms of *Vajra-Yoginī* on three different planes of experience or, more cautiously expressed (in case 'planes' might suggest the idea of 'higher' or 'lower' qualities, or greater or lesser degrees of reality, which is not intended here), in three different connexions, from three different points of view of meditative experience.

As *Sarva-buddha-ḍākinī*, i.e., as 'genius' (daimon) of all Buddhas, she embodies the inspirational impulse, which urges the Buddhas towards the realization of Buddhahood, towards Perfect Enlightenment, and is the driving force of all aspects of wisdom.

As *Vajra-varṇanī* she represents the true nature (*varṇa*, lit. 'colour') of the *vajra*: being transparent, pure, object-free, non-dual, indestructible and immutable, like the Great Void. For this reason it is said at the beginning of the treatise on *gTum-mo*-practice that one should visualize the body of *Vajra-Yoginī* as empty, transparent, and the like – in short, as a symbol of reality, which is Voidness according to its true nature.

As *Vajra-vairocanī* she represents the outward-directed activity of the *vajra*, its radiation: the active consciousness of the adamantine sphere, the *Dharma*-Reality.

The seed-syllable HŪṀ is common to all forms of appearance of the *Vajra-Yoginī* and to her male counterparts, known as *Herukas*, with whom she is united in the *yab-yum* aspect (the union of Father and Mother). *Herukas* are the embodiment of the 'male' qualities of Buddhahood: the dynamic aspect of Enlightenment.

'HŪṀ' is the quintessence of the *vajra*-order, in its mild and peaceful (*śānta*; Tib.: *ẓi-ba*) as well as in its terrifying (*bhairava*; Tib.: *drag-pa*) forms of appearance.

The mantras of the latter often add to the HŪṀ the onomatopoeic exclamation *Phaṭ*, which, according to the context and the circumstances, serves as a protection from inimical influences, as well as for the removal of inner hindrances, or for the strengthening of the *Sādhaka's* power of concentration, like a rallying-cry to call up the forces of the mind.

Svāhā is an expression of goodwill and auspiciousness, like 'Hail', 'May it be for the good, may it be blessed, may it be auspicious'. It is an expression used in offering sacrificial gifts and prayers or formulae in praise of gods or enlightened beings. Like the Christian 'Amen', it stands at the end of mantric formulae.

Phaṭ Svāhā is thus at the same time a defence against evil and a

[1] *Sādhanamālā*, p. 453 (Gaekwad; Oriental Series No. XLVI); Benoytosh Bhattacharyya *An Introduction to Buddhist Esoterism*, p. 160.

welcoming of beneficial forces, a removal of hindrances and an act of opening oneself towards the light.

And if it is said at the end of *Padmasambhava's* initiation that he received the 'initiation of body, speech, and mind', it means that his body became the body of all the Buddhas, his speech the sacred word of all Enlightened Ones, and his mind the *bodhi-citta* (Tib.: *byaṅ-chub-sems*) the enlightened mind of all the Buddhas. Therefore the *Demchog Tantra* says: 'When pronouncing the word "*kāya*", we think of the body of all [Buddhas and their divine forms of appearance] (Tib.: *kā-ya śes brjod-pas thams-cad-kyi sku*); when saying "*vāk*", we think of the speech of all [Buddhas]; when saying "*citta*", we think of the mind of all [Buddhas], and that all these are inseparable from each other' (*vak-yis gsuṅ daṅ tsi-tta-yis thugs rnams dbyer mi-phyed-par bsams*).

15

THE ECSTASY OF BREAKING-THROUGH IN THE EXPERIENCE OF MEDITATION AND THE *MAṆḌALA* OF THE KNOWLEDGE-HOLDING DEITIES

JUST as the *Ḍākinīs* represent the inspirational impulses of consciousness, leading to knowledge and understanding, so the *Herukas* (the male qualities of the Buddha-nature) represent the active aspect of *karuṇā*, of unlimited compassion, in the ecstatic act of breaking through the confines of egohood to the universal state of the all-comprising essentiality (*Vajrasattva*). In this aspect all hindrances are annihilated: the own illusory 'I' as well as all ideas of selfhood and separateness – in short, all intellectual thought and ratiocination. Intuitive knowledge and spontaneous feeling merge here into an inseparable unity – as inseparable as the union of *Ḍākinī* and *Heruka* in the aspect of *yab-yum*, which only emphasizes in visible form, what is present in every process of enlightenment and in each symbol of Buddhahood, even though it may be put into the form of the male aspect only.

The peaceful (*śāntā*, Tib.: *źi-ba*) forms of *Dhyāni-Buddhas* represent the highest ideal of Buddhahood in its completed, final, static condition of ultimate attainment or perfection, seen retrospectively as it were, as a state of complete rest and harmony.

The *Herukas*, on the other hand – like all ecstatic emanations of the Tantric pantheon of the *Vajrayāna*, which are described as 'blood-drinking' (Tib.: *khrag-ḥthuṅ*), 'angry' (*krodha*, Tib.: *khro-ba*), or 'terrifying' (*bhairava*, Tib.: *drag-pa*) deities – are merely the dynamic aspect of enlightenment, the *process of becoming* a Buddha, of attaining illumination, as symbolized by the Buddha's struggle with the hosts of *Māra*.

The ecstatic figures of heroic and terrifying deities express the act of the *Sādhaka*'s breaking through towards the 'Unthinkable' (*acintyā*), the intellectually 'Unattainable' (*anupalabdha*), as mentioned in *Subhūti's* answer in the *Prajñāpāramitā-Sūtra*, when the Buddha had asked him whether the highest enlightenment (*anuttara-samyak-sambodhi*) could be described, or whether the Buddha had ever taught such a thing: 'As I understand the teaching of the Lord Buddha, there is no such thing as *Anuttara-samyak-sambodhi*, nor is it possible for the *Tathāgata* to teach any fixed *Dharma*. And why? Because the things taught by the *Tathāgata* are, in their essential nature, inconceivable and inscrutable; they are neither existent nor non-existent; they are neither phenomena nor noumena. What is meant by this? It means that the Buddhas and Bodhisattvas are not enlightened by fixed teachings but by an intuitive process that is spontaneous and natural.'[1]

It is the uncompromising realization and continuation of this tradition of the *Prajñāpāramitā*, which finds its visible expression in the ecstatic figures of the *Vajrayāna* and especially in the mystic path of *Vajrassattva* (the active reflex of *Akṣobhya*), the path of transformation and integration. The manifold forms of divine figures, which we meet on this path, especially the specifically Tantric, ascetic-naked embodiments of unveiled reality, like *Ḍākinīs*, *Vīras*, and *Herukas*, are particularly important from the point of *yoga*, because they depict experiences of meditation, events on the path of realization and deliverance.

The growing multitude of figures of the Tantric pantheon was therefore not due to a progressively polytheistic tendency of a 'degenerate' Buddhism, which in an excess of religious emotion and imagination searched for ever new objects of veneration and raised the products of human speculation to the status of gods – on the contrary, it was due to the tendency of replacing religious speculation by practical experience. And just as every new discovery of science not only contributes to the wealth of data and the widening of our field of knowledge, but leads to further discoveries and to a re-appraisal of former data, in the same way each new experience of meditation opens new horizons and creates new methods of practice and realization. The human mind cannot stop at any point on its way

[1] Translation by Bhikshu Wai-tao and Dwight Goddard in *A Buddhist Bible*, p. 102.

towards knowledge. Standstill means death, rigidity and decay. This is the law of all life and of all consciousness. It is the law of the spirit, from which life and consciousness flow.

Just as in mathematical thought each dimension necessarily demands another, higher one, until we are forced to the conclusion that there must be an infinite series of dimensions – in the same way each further extension of our spiritual horizon hints at new, undreamt-of dimensions of consciousness.

The fact that each experience points beyond itself and can therefore not be defined or limited as something that exists in itself, but only in relationship to other experiences; this fact is circumscribed in the concept of '*śūnyatā*', the emptiness of all determinations, the non-absoluteness, the infinite relationship of all experience. And this 'super-relativity' contains at the same time the unifying element of a living universe, because infinite relationship becomes all-relationship and therewith a metaphysical magnitude, which can neither be described as 'being' nor as 'non-being', neither as movement nor as non-movement.

Here we have reached the boundary of thought, the end of all that is thinkable and conceivable. Like movement, which in its ultimate extreme, in its highest form, cannot be distinguished from perfect rest and immobility, thus relativity in the highest sense of universal relationship is indistinguishable from the 'absolute'. 'The eternally constant can only be represented in the changeable; the eternally changeable only in the constant, the whole, the present moment.' (Novalis.)

For this reason *śūnyatā* and *tathatā* (suchness) are identical in their nature. The former characterizes the negative, the latter the positive side of the same reality. The realization of the former starts from the experience of transitoriness, momentariness, temporal and spatial relativity – the latter from the experience of timelessness, of completeness, of the whole, the absolute. This, however, does not mean that *śūnyatā* exhausts itself in the quality of relativity, nor that *tathatā* is to be identified with the absolute. We use these expressions only as a bridge leading from the Western to the Eastern, or, more correctly, from the logical-philosophical to the intuitive-metaphysical mode of thinking.

D. T. Suzuki is therefore right when he denounces the intellectual shallowness which tries to equate the modern conception of relativity with that of *śūnyatā* on purely logical grounds. 'Emptiness is the result of an intuition and not the outcome of reasoning. The idea of Emptiness grows out of experience, and in order to give it a logical foundation the premise is found in relativity. But, speaking strictly logically, there is a gap between relativity and Emptiness. Relativity does not make us jump over the gap; as long as we stay with relativity we are within a circle; to realize that we are in a circle and that therefore we must get out of it in order to see its entire aspect presupposes our once having gone beyond it.'[1]

This leap over the chasm, which yawns between our intellectual surface-consciousness and the intuitive supra-personal depth-consciousness, is represented in the ecstatic dance of the 'blood-drinking deities', embraced by *Ḍākinīs*. The inspirational impulse of the *Ḍākinīs* drives us from the protected, but narrowly fenced circle of our illusory personality and our habitual thought, until we burst the boundaries of this circle and of our egohood in the ecstatic thrust towards the realization of totality. In this ecstatic thrust, all bonds, all worldly fetters, all prejudices and illusions are destroyed, all conventional concepts are swept away, all craving and clinging is cut off at the root, past and future are extinguished, the power of *karma* is broken, and the Great Void is experienced as the eternal present and ultimate Reality and Suchness. The violence and power of this 'breaking through' can only be visualized in a superhuman, demoniacal, many-armed and many-headed figure, as a many-dimensional, all-seeing being, penetrating simultaneously all directions, transforming the 'three times' (indicated by three eyes in each face) into a timeless present.

Such a being cannot appear other than 'terrifying' on the plane of mundane consciousness, because in the warlike symbols which it wields, and which indicate the inner struggle, the worldly man does not see tools of liberation, but weapons of destruction, which annihilate all that belongs to his world.

In all these ecstatic or 'blood-drinking' deities (as they are called, because, like the *Ḍākinīs* with whom they are united, they hold in their hands skull-cups filled with blood) the knowledge-principle is predominant, because blood symbolizes the red solar energy, leading to consciousness and self-awareness, which turns into the poison of mortality in those who stagnate in the narrow vessel of their egohood, while to those, who are willing to give up their illusory self, it turns into liberating knowledge. The 'blood-drinking deities' are therefore generally shown in the *yab-yum* aspect, i.e., united with their *Prajñā*. Their starting-point is the cognizing consciousness, the solar principle, which has its seat in the Brain Centre.

The highest and correspondingly most terrifying aspects of the 'blood-drinking deities' belong therefore to the Brain Centre and are represented in the *Bardo Thödol* as the five *Herukas* and their

[1] D. T. Suzuki: *Essays in Zen Buddhism*, III, p. 241.

Prajñās in the traditional colours of the directions of space, while the peaceful forms of the *Dhyāni-Buddhas* belong to the Heart Centre, and to the 'Knowledge-holding Deities' (*vidyādhara*; Tib.: *rig-ḥdzin*), who stand in the middle between these two extremes, belong to the Throat Centre, the Centre of Mantric Sound.

These 'Knowledge-Holders' are depicted in human figures of heroic mien, ecstatically dancing with raised skull-bowls, filled with blood, and embraced by *Ḍākinīs.* They are a milder aspect of the Blood-drinking Deities, so to say, their reflex on the highest level of individual or humanly conceivable knowledge, as attained in the consciousness of great *Yogis*, inspired thinkers and similar heroes of the spirit (*vīra*; Tib.: *dpaḥ-bo*). It is the last step before the 'breaking through' towards the universal consciousness – or the first on the return from there to the plane of human knowledge.

According to the *Bardo Thödol* the appearances of the peaceful forms of the *Dhyāni-Buddhas* are therefore followed on the seventh day of the Intermediate State (*bardo*) by the 'Knowledge-Holding Deities'. They appear in the form of a *maṇḍala*, the centre of which is formed by the radiating figure of the 'Supreme Knowledge-Holder of Karmic Results' (Tib.: *rnam-par-smin-paḥi rig-ḥdizn*), who perceives the effects (*smin*=Skt.: *vipāka*) of all actions. He is surrounded by an aura of rainbow-colours. He is called the 'Lord of Dance', i.e., the lord of all that moves and is moved, because the psychic Centre, which he governs, is that of the element of motion (Tib.: *rluṅ*), which is characterized by the qualities of 'air', 'wind', 'breath', and regarded as the vehicle of life, of creative sound, of the sacred word and knowledge, of spiritual activity and unfoldment.

The wisdom, which perceives the results of all actions and which 'accomplishes all works', is an attribute of *Amoghasiddhi*, who is associated with the element 'wind' or 'air' (*rluṅ*). However, the *Ḍākinī*, united with him here, is of red colour, and his title 'Lord of Dance' is preceded by the word '*Padma*' (*Padma-gar-gyi-dbaṅ-phyug*). Both these facts reveal that these two figures are associated with the *Padma*-order of *Amitābha*, and that the qualities of *Amoghasiddhi* and *Amitābha* are combined in them.

Amitābha is connected with the life-aspect of breath as well as with the knowledge-aspect of the mantric sound, which creates the visualizing and the distinguishing knowledge, because *Amitābha* is the embodiment of the 'distinguishing Wisdom of Inner Vision', and in his active aspect or reflex, as *Amitāyus*, he is the Lord of Boundless Life (Skt.: *āyus*=life, duration of life). These may be the main reasons why *Amitābha* (or *Amitāyus*) is associated with the Throat Centre.

The four petals of the *maṇḍala* contain:

In the east the white Knowledge-Holder, 'having the earth-element as his abode' (Tib.: *sa-la gnas-paḥi rig-ḥdzin*), embraced by the White *Ḍākinī*;

in the south the yellow 'Knowledge-Holder, who has power over the duration of life' (Tib.: *tshe-la dbaṅ-paḥi-rig-ḥdzin*), embraced by the Yellow *Ḍākinī*;

in the west the red 'Knowledge-Holder of the Great Symbol' (Tib.: *phyag-rgya-chen-poḥi rig-ḥdzin*), embraced by the Red *Ḍākinī*;

in the north the green 'Knowledge-Holder of Spontaneous Realization' (Tib.: *lhag-gyis-grub-pa rig-ḥdzin*), embraced by the Green *Ḍākinī*.

Here we have a transposed *maṇḍala*, i.e., a system in which two

Maṇḍala of the Knowledge-Holding Deities according to the Bardo Thödol

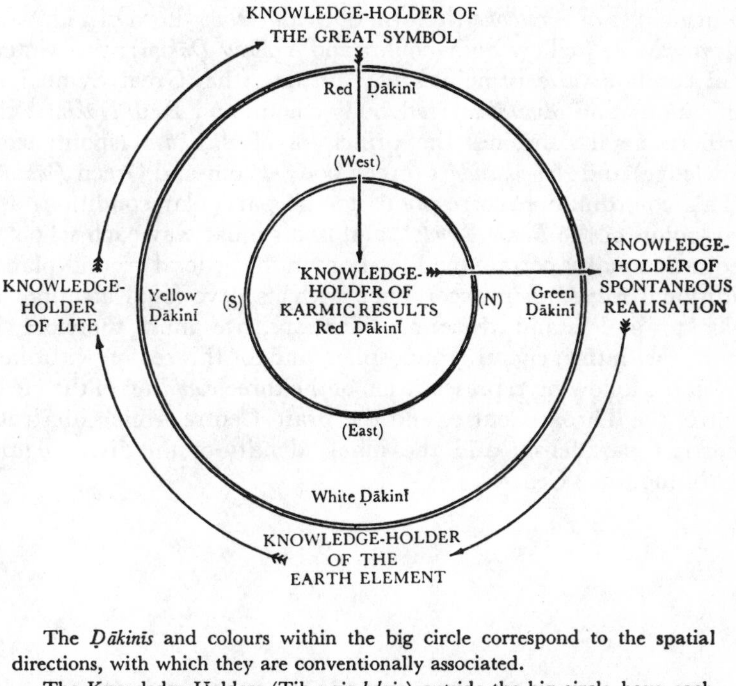

The *Ḍākinīs* and colours within the big circle correspond to the spatial directions, with which they are conventionally associated.

The Knowledge-Holders (Tib.: *rig-ḥdzin*) outside the big circle have each been shifted from their usual places by one unit. The arrows point to the places which they occupy conventionally, as may be seen in the following diagram of the three *maṇḍalas* of the Heart, the Throat, and the Brain Centre.

categories or sets of symbols are combined, and of which one set, by shifting the place of its symbols by one unit within the structure of the *maṇḍala*, enters into a new combination with the other set. This is in no way exceptional in the Tibetan practice of meditation, but is done in many *maṇḍalas* and has a definite purpose, which cannot be explained easily, as it would require a deeper and more detailed investigation of this subtle matter at the hand of many examples. We confine ourselves therefore in the present case upon the hint that in the *Bardo Thödol* tradition *Amitābha* occupies a special position, and that *Padmasambhava*, the originator of this tradition, is looked upon as the earthly reflex (*nirmāṇa-kāya*) of *Amitābha*, as may seem from the dedicatory verse at the beginning of the *Bardo Thödol*. The present *maṇḍala* is therefore seen through the eyes, or from the point of view, of *Amitābha*.

The centre of the *maṇḍala* represents a combination of the principles of *Amitābha* and *Amoghasiddhi*; the eastern petal combines the principles of *Ratnasambhava* (Earth-Element) and *Vajrasattva-Akṣobhya* (white body-colour and White *Ḍākinī*); the southern petal combines the principles of *Amitābha* (in form of *Amitāyus*, as 'Lord of Life') and *Ratnasambhava* (yellow body-colour and Yellow *Ḍākinī*); the western petal combines the principles of *Vairocana* (the 'Great Symbol' of unification) and *Amitābha* (red body-colour and Red *Ḍākinī*); the northern petal combines the principles of *Akṣobhya* (spontaneous knowledge) and *Amoghasiddhi* (green body-colour and Green *Ḍākinī*).

This co-ordination corresponds to the particular conditions and view-points of the *Bardo Thödol*; and in a similar way each school of meditation makes certain modifications in the general ground-plan of traditional *maṇḍalas* in accordance with its devotional attitude. In order to understand these modifications, we must therefore be familiar with the general ground-plan, and for this reason we adhere to it in the following representation of the three *maṇḍalas* of the Heart Centre, the Throat Centre, and the Brain Centre, which illustrates the strict parallelism and the inner identity of the divine figures inhabiting these Centres.

REALM OF UNIFICATION (OṀ) AND OF THE UNIVERSAL BODY: MAṆḌALA OF THE BRAIN CENTRE

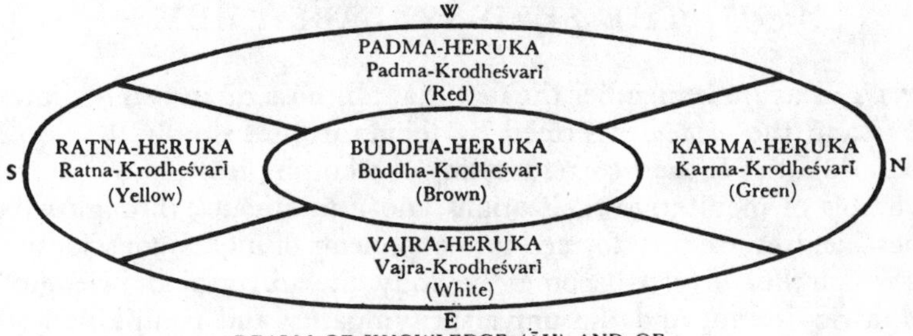

REALM OF KNOWLEDGE (ĀH) AND OF THE CREATIVE SOUND: MAṆḌALA OF THE THROAT CENTRE

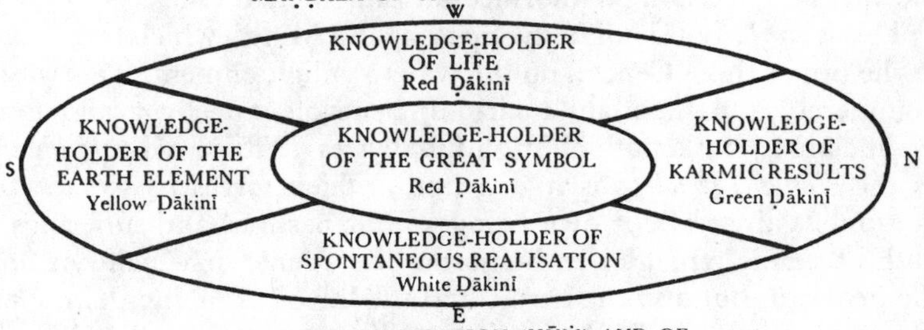

REALM OF REALISATION (HŪṀ) AND OF THE ENLIGHTENED MIND: MAṆḌALA OF THE HEART CENTRE

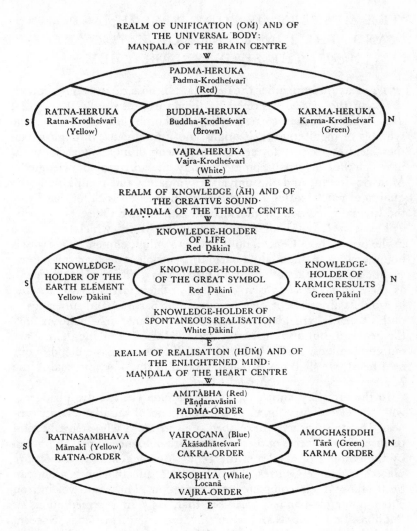

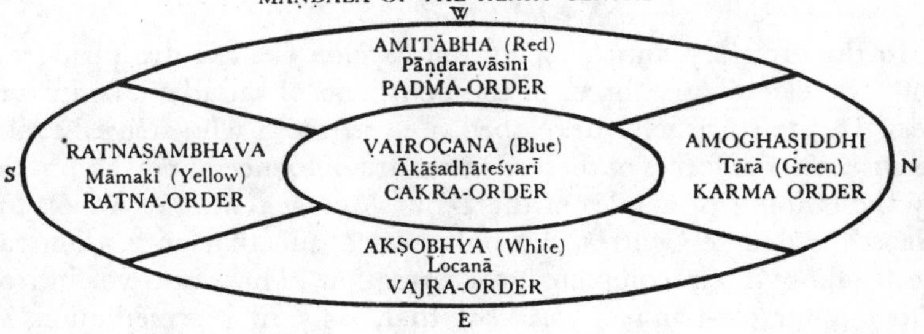

16

'THE MYSTERY OF BODY, SPEECH, AND MIND' AND 'THE INNER PATH OF *VAJRASATTVA*' IN THE SEED-SYLLABLE HŪṂ

LET us again remember the fact that all those divine embodiments and the *maṇḍalas* formed by them, are not simply the natural qualities of their corresponding psycho-physical Centres, but the symbols of meditative realizations and attainments, through which these centres are transformed into exponents of higher consciousness, in which the universe becomes the Body, the universal knowledge the Mantric Sound, and the universal sympathy and compassion (the quality of participating in and identifying oneself with all that lives) the Living Spirit, which informed all Enlightened Ones.

This is the 'Mystery of Body, Speech, and Mind', which takes place in the upper three Centres on the way to enlightenment. This way is not merely a path of mild virtues, benevolent feelings and tame renunciation, but a path of 'frightful abysses' (Tib.: *ḥjigs-paḥi phraṅ*), as the *Bardo Thödol* calls it – a path, which forces us to face the bottomless abyss of our own being, of our passions and sufferings, a path of heroic struggles and ecstatic liberations, in which not only the peaceful, but also the heroic and the 'blood-drinking deities' are our companions. And if we do not sacrifice to them the blood of our own heart, we shall never reach the end of this way and realize the Mystery of Body, Speech, and Mind.

In the ordinary human being the psychic Centres are filled only with the elementary forces of the body and of mundane consciousness. In the spiritually developed, i.e., in those who strive beyond themselves, the forces of these Centres are influenced and sublimated by the guiding principles of the *Dhyāni-Buddhas*, whose symbols are placed into these Centres. But only perfect spiritual unification can bring about their complete transformation. Therefore we find on Tibetan temple-banners (*thaṅ-ka*) that, only in representations of Buddhas, Bodhisattvas and saints, the seed-syllables of Body, Speech, and Mind, namely, OṂ – ĀḤ – HŪṂ, are written on the reverse side of the painting on the places corresponding to the three higher psychic Centres.

The meaning of these three seed-syllables, therefore, goes beyond that of individual symbolical figures like *Vairocana*, *Amoghasiddhi*, or *Akṣobhya*; in other words, they are applied to the highest plane of experience, in which all separate aspects of *Dhyāni-Buddhas* are fused and disappear. In the same way the three higher Centres take over the psychic functions of the remaining Centres: *Amoghasiddhi's* functions are fused (as we saw) with those of *Amitābha* in the Throat Centre, so that the seed-syllable ĀḤ, which now takes the place of HRĪḤ, becomes the exponent of the whole *maṇḍala* of the Knowledge-Holding Deities. The HŪṀ, however, comprises all the aspects of integration, from *Ratnasambhava's* synthetic 'Wisdom of the Oneness of all Beings' (which otherwise would be associated with the Navel Centre) and *Akṣobhya's* 'Wisdom of the Great Mirror', in which the formless as well as the forms of all things are contained, up to *Vajrasattva's* integration of all *Dhyāni-Buddhas* in the adamantine reality and activity of his spontaneous way.

Thus the same mantric sound can have various meanings, according to the connexions in which it appears, and according to the plane of consciousness, on which it is used or to which it is applied. We are, so to say, dealing with different degrees of intensity or different potentialities of the same principle; and the reduplication of the same sound (as for instance HŪṀ) not only expresses its intensification or its relationship towards two different aspects of the same symbolic figure, but often also the same experience on two different levels of reality.

We therefore must distinguish between the simple HŪṀ of *Akṣobhya* and the HŪṀ in its highest potentiality as symbol of the integration of all *Dhyāni-Buddhas*, be it in the active form of *Vajrasattva* or that of *Samantabhādra* (the highest Buddha-form of the *Nyingma* sect) or of *Vajradhāra* (the highest Buddha-form of the *Kargyütpas*). The latter two are, like *Vajrasattva*, the essence of the *Dhyāni-Buddhas*, but are represented in the passive aspect of pure '*tathatā*' or 'suchness', and are therefore called '*Ādibuddhas*'. They are actually the *dharmakāya* of *Vajrasattva*, or the potential Buddhahood inherent in every being (but not a kind of Creator-God, from whom the universe has evolved, as some scholars seem to believe).

In order to make the nature of a Buddha or the quality of Buddhahood humanly understandable, we must distinguish and visualize its different aspects, like those of the sunlight in a prism. From this analytical mode of understanding, however, we have gradually to return to the synthesis. This begins with meditative visualization, which is the way of *Amitābha* and is brought to its perfect fulfilment on the way of ultimate integration, the way of *Vajrasattva-Akṣobhya*. Therefore the *Bardo Thödol* says that the Path of *Vajrasattva* consists in the combined lights of the united Wisdoms.

This experience of inner unification is expressed in the endeavour of all schools of meditation to combine the five *Dhyāni-Buddhas* in one figure, be it in the form of an *Ādibuddha* or in a corresponding *Heruka*-form (like *Mahāsukha*; Tib.: *bDe-mchog*), in whom the 'breaking-through' towards perfection, or the moment of attainment, is symbolized.

After this 'breaking-through' towards unification and universality (OṀ) has been achieved, the consciousness flows back upon the human plane and turns into action in the HŪṀ of the Heart Centre. Thus HŪṀ unites both sides of reality: the living, pulsating presence of individual existence and the supra-individual timelessness beyond all dualities. It is the highest principle, the highest experience-form of inner reality, immanent in all beings. Therefore it has been said: 'The Mind of all the Buddhas of the three times,[1] which is from origin pure[2] and spontaneous,[3] and which goes beyond word, thought, and speech,[4] rises as the indestructible,[5] empty, radiating body of the Five Wisdoms in the form of HŪṀ, clear and perfect[6] in all its organs and fields of activity.[7]

'The five poisons[8] transform themselves into the imperishable, self-

[1] The 'three times' are past, present, and future. In order to show that the Buddhas perceive the three times and the three worlds (namely, the sense-world, the world of pure [abstract] form, and the world of non-form, known as *kāma-loka*, *rūpa-loka*, and *arūpa-loka*) the *Heruka*-forms of the Buddhas are represented with three eyes (in each of the four faces); Tib.: *khams-gsum-la gzigs-śiṅ dus-gsum-gyi dṅos-po mkhyen-pas śal re-re śiṅ spyan gsum-gsum-pa*' (*dpal-ḥkhor-lo bDe-mchog*).

[2] *ka-dag*.

[3] *lhun-grub*.

[4] *smra-bsam-brjod-med*; '*brjod-med*' can also be rendered by 'transcendental'.

[5] *ma-ḥgags*. Dr. H. V. Guenther drew my attention to a mistake in the German edition of this book, in which I had rendered the term *ma-ḥgags* as 'unobstructed' instead of 'imperishable' or 'indestructible'. '*ma-ḥgags*', as he rightly points out, is a synonym for '*anirodha*', while 'unobstructed' would be rendered with *ḥgegs-med*, Skt.: '*avirodha*', 'absence of impediment'.

[6] In all Tibetan meditations great stress is laid upon the clarity of form-perceptions. Here no haziness or indistinctness is tolerated, and nothing is left to chance. Each sound, each colour, each form, must be clearly defined and filled with life. Tibetan mysticsm has nothing to do with the 'mystic darkness' or uncertain individual visions of spiritistic mediums or emotionally unstable minds. It is founded on spiritual discipline, which encourages neither excess of emotion nor of speculative thought or of unbridled imagination.

'Yoga is the way to put a stop to the spontaneous, ever-changing play of consciousness; to dam the rushing stream and to transform it into an immovable, clear mirror; to keep the reflections of the world away from it, and to gain power over movements, which from within might distort its surface, and to determine with sovereign power, what should be mirrored in its stillness as inner vision–indeed, whether anything should be mirrored.' (Zimmer, *Ewiges Indien*, p. 115.)

[7] *skye-mched*=Skt.: *āyatana*.

[8] The traditional 'five poisons' of the human mind are:

Ignorance	(*avidyā*	Tib.: *ma-rig*)
hatred	(*dveṣa*	,, : *że-sdaṅ*)
pride	(*māna*	,, : *ṅa-rgyal*)
passionate desire	(*rāga*	,, : *ḥdod-chags*)
envy	(*īrṣā*	,, : *phrag-dog*).

luminous Wisdoms through the practice of the creative[9] and re-absorptive[10] process of meditation in the Yoga of the Inner Fire.[11] With the maturing of the Four Bodies[12] and the Five Wisdoms, may the Vajra of the Heart[13] be realized even in this life.'[14]

Thus we return from the plurality of visions and forms to inner completeness, to the oneness of all Buddhas and to the realization of Buddhahood within ourselves, here and now.

[9] *bskyed-rim.*

[10] *rdzogs-rim.*

[11] The expression '*zuṅ-ḥjug*' is used here as a technical term for *gTum-mo* practice, i.e., the 'Yoga of the Inner Fire', which aims at the unification of the psychic currents (*iḍā* and *piṅgalā*) in the middle *nāḍī* (*suṣumṇā*).

[12] The 'Four Bodies' are: the *Dharmakāya*, the *Sambhogakāya*, the *Nirmāṇakāya*, and the *Vajrakāya*. They are the subject of Part V.

[13] *thugs-kyi-rdo-rje.*

[14] The Tibetan text, upon which my translation is based, has been reproduced in W. Y. Evans-Wentz: *Tibetan Yoga and Secret Doctrines*, Plate VIII. (Oxford University Press, London, 1935.)

Part Five

OṀ MAṆI PADME HŪṂ

THE PATH OF THE GREAT MANTRA

Plate 6

THE THOUSAND-ARMED AVALOKITEŚVARA
the Embodiment of Active Compassion

I

THE DOCTRINE OF THE 'THREE BODIES' AND THE THREE PLANES OF REALITY

We have become acquainted with the experience of universality in the sacred syllable OṀ, with the luminosity of the immortal mind in the 'MAṆI', its unfoldment in the lotus-centres of consciousness ('PADMA'), and its integration and realization in the seed-syllable HŪṀ.

The way towards the realization of OṀ is the way of universality, the way of the Great Vehicle, the *Mahāyāna*. The way from the OṀ to the HŪṀ is that of realizing the universal in the individual. It is the way of the *Vajrayāna*, or the inner (mystic) path of *Vajrasattva*, who accomplishes the transformation of our earthly, 'material' world into the deeper, invisible reality from which the visible springs, the reality of the inaudible that pervades and motivates sound, of the intangible that pervades touch, and the thought-transcending awareness that pervades and motivates thought.

And just as *Vajrasattva* represents the active force of *Akṣobhya* so *Avalokiteśvara* represents the dynamic aspect of *Amitābha* on the plane of human experience and activity. For every Buddha manifests himself on three planes of reality: the universal, the ideal and the individual.

Thus we discern in the figure of the Buddha three 'bodies' or principles:

1. that, in which all Enlightened Ones are the same: the experience of completeness, of universality, of the deepest super-individual reality of the *Dharma*, the primordial law and cause of all things, from which emanates all physical, moral and metaphysical order;

2. that which constitutes the spiritual or ideal character of a Buddha, the creative expression or formulation of this universal principle in the realm of inner vision: the *Sambhogakāya*, the 'Body of Bliss' (rapture or spiritual enjoyment), from which all true inspiration is born;

3. that, in which this inspiration is transformed into visible form and becomes action: the *Nirmāṇakāya*: the 'Body of Transformation', the human embodiment or individuality of an Enlightened One.

In the *Dharmakāya*, the universal principle of all consciousness, the totality of becoming and being is potentially contained – comparable to the infinity of space, which embraces all things and is the *conditio sine qua non* of all that exists. Yet we can neither say that space is identical with things, nor that it is different from them. As little as we can become conscious of space without its opposite pole, i.e., form, so the *Dharmakāya* cannot become reality for us without descending into forms.

This happens in two ways: in the realm of pure form, or pure mental perception, i.e., in the realm of ideas – and in the realm of action, of individuality, of materialization or embodiment.

In states of rapture, trance and highest intuition, as characterized by the stages of deep absorption in meditation (*dhyāna*), we experience the *Dharmakāya* as the luminous forms of purely spiritual perception – as pure, eternal principles of form, freed from all accidentals – or as the exalted visions of a higher reality. In them the *Sambhogakāya*, 'the Body of Bliss' is realized. From it flow all immortal art, all deep wisdom, all profound truths (*dharma*, in the sense of formulated or proclaimed truth). Its enjoyment is of two kinds, like that of every great work of art: the rapture of the creative act and the enjoyment of those who contemplate the completed work by retrospectively experiencing and reliving the act of creation.

A rapture, comparable to the first of these two kinds, is experienced by all the Buddhas and Bodhisattvas in the course of their *sādhanā* and in the practice of the highest virtues (*pāramitā*)[1], as demonstrated by their lives – while a rapture, comparable to the second kind, is felt by all those who contemplate the significance of these lives and relive them in their mind and their deeds.

Therefore two kinds of *Sambhogakāya* are discerned with regard to Buddhas: the '*svā-sambhoga-kāya*' and the '*para-sambhoga-kāya*': The first is the body of 'pure form' (*rūpa-kāya*), 'which is extremely perfect, pure, eternal and universal, which is boundless and possesses true attributes, due to the effects of immeasurable virtue and knowledge, which have been accumulated by all the *Tathāgatas* in the course of

[1] These *pāramitās* or perfections are: 1. the perfection of giving (*dāna-pāramitā*), culminating in self-sacrifice; 2. the perfection of morality (*śīla-pāramitā*), culminating in all-embracing love; 3. the perfection of forbearance or patience (*kṣānti-pāramitā*), culminating in forgiveness and eradication of ill-will; 4. the perfection of energy (*vīrya-pāramitā*), culminating in the unshakable determination to attain enlightenment; 5. the perfection of meditation or inner vision (*dhyāna-pāramitā*) culminating in the awareness of Reality, the realization of the Mind itself; 6. the perfection of Wisdom (*prajñā-pāramitā*), culminating in Perfect Enlightenment.

Later Pāli Scriptures, like *Buddhavaṁsa* and *Cariyapiṭaka*, probably under the influence of the *Mahāyāna*, mention ten *pāramitās*, namely: Perfection in giving, morality, renunciation (*nekkhamma*), wisdom, energy, forbearance, truthfulness (*sacca*), resolution (*adiṭṭhāna*), unselfish love (*mettā*), and equanimity (*upekkhā*).

countless *kalpas*. It will quietly continue till the end of time: it will always experience within itself the bliss of the *Dharma*.

The second is the *parasambhoga-kāya* (the body that causes enjoyment to others). It is the subtle body with the attribute of purity, which all *Tathāgatas* show on account of their Knowledge of Equality (*samatā-jñāna*).'[1] – Such is the realization of the *Dharmakāya* within the human mind.

Since it is the mind that creates the human body, it follows that the more the mind reflects and is filled with the *Dharmakāya* the more it will be able to influence and to transform the material body. This transformation attains its highest perfection in the Fully Enlightened One. Therefore it is said that the body of the Buddha is adorned with the thirty-two signs of perfection. Hence the name '*Nirmāṇa-kāya*', the 'Body of Transformation'.

This *Nirmāṇakāya* (Tib.: *sprul-sku*; pron. 'tülkū' or 'tūkū') of the Buddha has often been called an illusory body or even a 'phantom body', a concept which is as misleading as the current interpretation of the *māyā*-doctrine. If Indian thinkers define this world as *māyā*, this does not mean that the world is deprived of all reality, but only that it is not what it appears to us; in other words, that its reality is only relative or represents a reality of a lesser degree which, compared with the highest reality (accessible only to a perfectly Enlightened One) has no more existence than the objects of a dream, a cloud-formation or the lightnings flashing up within it.

Seen from the opposite direction, however, even the most impermanent of those phenomena are not mere hallucinations, i.e., they are neither arbitrary nor meaningless, but expressions of an inherent law, whose reality is undeniable. Even if this our world and what we call our personality are mind-made and illusory, this does not mean that they are unreal. They are as real as the mind that creates them. The body, which we have created, does not disappear the moment we recognize it as a product of our mind or when we get tired of it. As soon as the products of our mind have taken material shape, they obey the laws of matter, or whatever we may call the laws governing them. Even a saint cannot arbitrarily change or annihilate the material properties and functions of the body. He can only transform them step by step by controlling them in their initial states or in the moment they come into existence. Materialization can be influenced, directed and modified only while it is still in the process of formation.

[1] *Vijñapitmātra-siddhi-śāstra X*; cfr. Jiryo Masuda *Der individualistische Idealismus der Yogacāra-Schule*, p. 59 f.; *Vijñaptimātratāsiddhi, la Siddhi de Hiuan-Tsang*, translated by Louis de La Vallée Poussin, Vol. 2, pp. 705–6, Paris, 1929.

The theory of the transformed body of a Buddha is therefore not in contradiction to its reality, and the realism of earlier as well as later Theravādins and their belief in the historical human personality, in no way contradicts their faith in his super-human powers and perfections. *Buddhaghosa* speaks of 'that *Bhagavā*, who is possessed of a beautiful *rūpakāya*, adorned with eighty minor signs and thirty-two major signs of a great man, and possessed of a *dhammakāya* purified in every way and glorified by [the five *khandhas*] *śila*, *samādhi*, [*paññā*, *vimutti*, and *vimuttiñānadassana*], full of splendour and virtue, incomparable and fully awakened.'[1]

In the introductory discourse to his *Atthasālinī*, *Buddhaghosa* describes the multi-coloured radiance which issues from the body of the Buddha. The classical beauty of this description could not be surpassed by any *Mahāyāna* text on this subject, which plays such an important role, especially in the conception and *sādhanā* of the *Dhyāni-Buddhas*. 'Rays of six colours – indigo, golden, red, white, tawny and dazzling – issued from the Teacher's body, as he was contemplating the subtle and abstruse Law by his omniscience. . . . The indigo rays issued from his hair and the blue portions of his eyes. Owing to them the surface of the sky appeared as though besprinkled with collyrium powder, or covered with flax and blue lotus-flowers, or like a jewelled fan swaying to and fro, or a piece of dark cloth fully spread out. The golden rays issued from his skin and the golden portions of his eyes. Owing to them the different quarters of the globe shone as though besprinkled with some golden liquid, or overlaid with sheets of gold, or bestrewn with saffron powder and bauhinia-flowers. The red rays issued from his flesh and blood and the red portions of his eyes. Owing to them the quarters of the globe were coloured as though painted with red-lead powder. . . . The white rays issued from his bones, teeth, and the white portions of his eyes. Owing to them the quarters of the globe were bright as though over-flowing with streams of milk poured out of silver pots, or overspread with a canopy of silver plates. . . . The tawny and dazzling rays issued from the different parts of his body. Thus the six-coloured rays came forth and caught the great mass of the earth.' Then follows a beautiful description how the earth, the water, the air, the space beyond and all the heavenly regions and millions of world-systems are penetrated by the Buddha's golden light; and the description ends with the significant words (hinting at the transformation or sublimation of the physical body): 'But the blood of the Lord of the world became clear as he contemplated such a subtle and abstruse Law. Likewise

[1] Quoted by Nalinaksha Dutt in *Aspects of Mahāyāna Buddhism and its Relation to Hīnayāna*, p. 101.

the physical basis of his thought and his complexion. The element of colour, produced by the caloric order, born of the mind, steadily established itself with a radius of eighty cubits.'[1]

Not only was such powerful radiance ascribed to the Buddha in Pāli literature, but even the creation of *Nimmita-Buddhas,* i.e., of mental projections of himself (a kind of *Dhyāni-Buddhas* in his own form) during the time of his absence from the world, when preaching the *Abhidharma* to his mother in the Tuṣita heaven.

All this shows clearly that, though the doctrine of the 'three bodies' was not yet formulated in Pāli-Buddhism, the properties of these bodies and the spiritual qualities on which they are based, were recognized even by those who stressed the historical and human personality of the Buddha. To them a human being was not only a physical reality, because the concept of Man included the infinite possibilities of the Spirit and the boundlessness of the universe. Thus the contradistinction between realism and idealism did not yet exist.

2

MĀYĀ AS THE CREATIVE PRINCIPLE AND THE DIMENSIONS OF CONSCIOUSNESS

FROM the aforesaid it will have become evident that we are not concerned here with a subjective idealism, based on logical speculations, concepts and categories, but with a doctrine which is founded upon the reality of the mind and its deepest experiences.

If we call *māyā* a reality of a lower degree, we do this because illusion rests on the wrong interpretation of a partial aspect of reality. Compared with the highest or 'absolute' reality, all forms, in which this reality appears to us, are illusory, because they are only partial aspects, and as such incomplete, torn out of their organic connexions and deprived of their universal relationship. The only reality, which we could call 'absolute', is that of the all-embracing whole. Each partial aspect must therefore constitute a lesser degree of reality – the less universal, the more illusory and impermanent.

To a point-like consciousness the continuity of a line is inconceivable. For such a consciousness there exists only a continual and apparently unrelated origination and passing-away of points.

[1] *The Expositor* (*Atthasālinī*), p. 17 f. Translated by Maung Tin. Pāli Text Society, London, 1920.

To a linear consciousness – we could call it a one-dimensional consciousness, in contrast to the non-dimensional point-like consciousness – the continuity of a plane would be inconceivable, because it can only move in one direction and only comprehend a linear relationship of points following each other.

To a two-dimensional consciousness the continuity of a plane, i.e., the simultaneous existence of points, straight lines, curves, and designs of all kinds are conceivable, but not the spatial relationship of planes, as they form for instance the surface of a cube.

In three-dimensional space-consciousness, however, the relationship of several planes is co-ordinated to form the concept of a body, in which the simultaneous existence of different planes, lines and points can be conceived and grasped in their totality.

Thus the consciousness of a higher dimension consists in the co-ordinated and simultaneous perception of several systems of relationship or directions of movement, in a wider, more comprehensive unity, without destroying the individual characteristics of the integrated lower dimensions. The reality of a lower dimension is therefore not annihilated by a higher one, but only 'relativized' or put into another perspective of values.

If we perceive and co-ordinate the different phases in the movement of a point proceeding in one direction, we arrive at the perception of a straight line.

If we perceive and co-ordinate the different phases in the movement of a straight line, travelling in a direction not yet contained in it, we arrive at the conception of a plane.

If we perceive and co-ordinate the different phases in the movement of a plane, in a direction not yet contained in its dimension, we arrive at the perception of a body.

If we perceive and co-ordinate the different phases in the movement of a body, we arrive at the perception and understanding of its nature, i.e., we become conscious of its inherent laws and mode of existence.

If we perceive and co-ordinate organically the inner movement (growth, development; emotional, mental, and spiritual movement, etc.) of a conscious being, we become aware of its individuality, its psychic character.

If we perceive the manifold forms of existence, through which an individual has to pass, and observe how these forms arise, according to various conditions, and depending on a multitude of inherent factors, we arrive at the perception and understanding of the law of action and re-action, the law of *karma*.

If we observe the various phases of a karmic chain-reaction in their relationship to other sequences of karmic action and reaction, as this is said to have been observed by the Buddha, we become conscious of a supra-individual karmic interrelatedness, comprising nations, races, civilizations, humanity, planets, solar systems and finally the whole universe. In short, we arrive at the perception of a cosmic world-order, an infinite mutual relationship of all things, beings and events, until we finally realize the universality of consciousness in the *Dharmakāya*, when attaining Enlightenment.

Seen from the consciousness of the *Dharmakāya*, all separate forms of appearance are *māyā*. *Māyā* in the deepest sense, however, is reality in its creative aspect, or the creative aspect of reality. Thus *māyā* becomes the *cause* of illusion, but it is not illusion itself, as long as it is seen as a whole, in its continuity, its creative function, or as infinite power of transformation and universal relationship.

As soon, however, as we stop at any of its creations and try to limit it to a state of 'being' or self-confined existence, we fall a prey to illusion, by taking the effect for the cause, the shadow for the substance, the partial aspect for ultimate reality, the momentary for something that exists in itself.

It is the power of *māyā* which produces the illusory forms of appearance of our mundane reality. *Māyā* itself, however, is not illusion. He who masters this power, has got the tool of liberation in his hand, the magic power of *yoga*, the power of creation, transformation and re-integration. (Skt.: *laya-krama*; Tib.: *rdzogs-rim.*)

'The power of our inner vision produces in Yoga forms and worlds, which, while we become aware of them, can fill us with such a feeling of incredible reality, that compared with it, the reality-content of our sensuous and mental everyday world fades away and evaporates. Here we experience (as in the enjoyment of love) something that means nothing to our thought and that yet is true; that reality has degrees or steps. That the way of the Divine outwardly and inwardly, towards fullness of form and towards inner awareness, is graded, and that Yoga is the power to ascend and to descend these steps. . . .'[1]

Those who think that form is unimportant, will miss the spirit as well, while those who cling to form lose the very spirit which they tried to preserve. Form and movement are the secret of life and the key to immortality. Those who only see the transitoriness of things and reject the world because of its transitory character, see only the change on the surface of things, but have not yet discovered that the form of change, the manner in which change takes place, reveals the spirit that inspires all form, the reality that informs all phenomena. With our physical eye we see only change. Only our spiritual eye is capable

[1] Heinrich Zimmer, *Ewiges Indien*, p. 151.

of seeing stability in transformation. Transformation is the *form* in which the spirit moves: it is life itself. Whenever material form cannot follow the movement of the spirit, decay appears. Death is the protest of the spirit against the unwillingness of the formed to accept transformation: the protest against stagnation.

In the *Prajñāpāramitā-Sūtra* all phenomena are regarded as being *śūnyatā* according to their true nature – and *śūnyatā* as not being different from form, feeling, perception, mental formations and consciousness; i.e., *śūnyatā* is here equated with *māyā*. And just as *śūnyatā* is not only emptiness from all designations of a limited self-nature, but also an expression of ultimate reality, in the same way *māyā* is not only the negative, the veiling, the phenomenal form, but also the dynamic principle, which produces all forms of appearance and which never reveals itself in the single, completed end-product, but only in the process of becoming, in the living flow, in infinite movement.

Māyā, as something that has become, that is frozen and rigid in form and concept, is illusion, because it has been torn from its living connexions and limited in time and space. The individuality and corporeality of the unenlightened human being, trying to maintain and preserve its illusory selfhood, is *māyā* in this negative sense.

Also the body of an Enlightened One is *māyā*, but not in the negative sense, because it is the conscious creation of a mind that is free from illusion, unlimited, and no more bound to an 'ego'.

Only for the unenlightened worldling, who is still enmeshed in ignorance and delusion, the visible form or personality of a Buddha is *māyā* in the ordinary sense of the word. Therefore the *Mahāyāna-Śraddhotpāda-Śāstra*; says 'The harmonizing activities of the *Tathāgatas*, that are no activity in the worldly sense, are of two kinds. The first can be perceived by the minds of common people . . . and is known as *Nirmāṇakāya* . . . the second kind can only be perceived by the purified minds . . . it is the *Dharmakāya* in its aspect of Spirit and Principle. It is the *Sambhogakāya*, which possesses a vast and boundless potentiality.

'That of the *Dharmakāya* which can be perceived by the minds of common people, is only a shadow of it, and takes on different aspects, according as it is considered from the different viewpoints of the six different realms of existence. Their crude perception of it does not include any conception of its possibilities for happiness and enjoyment; they see only its reflection in the *Nirmāṇakāya*.

'But as the Bodhisattvas advance along the stages (on their way towards Enlightenment) their minds become purified, their conceptions of it (the *Dharmakāya*) more profound and mysterious, their harmonizing activities more transcendental, until, when they have attained the highest stage they will be able to realize intuitively its reality. In that final realization all traces of their individual selfness... will have faded away and only a realization of one undifferentiated Buddhahood will remain.'[1]

3

THE *NIRMĀṆAKĀYA* AS THE HIGHEST FORM OF REALIZATION

THE body of an ordinary human being is *māyā*, and also the body of an Enlightened One is *māyā*. But that does not mean that the body of an ordinary man can be called a *Nirmāṇa-kāya*. The difference is, that the body of an Enlightened One is his conscious creation, that of an unenlightened one, the creation of his subconscious drives and desires. Both are *māyā*, but the one is conscious the other unconscious. The one is the master of *māyā*, the other its slave. The difference consists in the knowledge (*prajñā*).

The same holds good for the *Dharmakāya*. It is all-embracing, and therefore omnipresent, whether we are conscious of it or not. But only when we raise the *Dharmakāya* from its subconscious, potential state into that of full consciousness, by opening our spiritual eye to its light, as revealed by the radiance of the *Sambhogakāya* – then only can its nature become an active force in us and free us from our death-bringing isolation.

This, however, is synonymous with the transformation of the mind-and-body combination, i.e., of our whole personality, into the *Nirmāṇakāya*. Only in the *Nirmāṇakāya* can we realize the *Dharma-kāya* effectively, by converting it into an ever-present conscious force, into an incandescent, all-consuming focus of experience, in which all elements of our personality are purified and integrated. This is the transfiguration of body and mind, which has been achieved only by the greatest of saints. The *Nirmāṇakāya*, therefore, is the highest form of realization, the only one in fact, that can open the eyes even of the spiritually blind worldling. It is the highest fruit of perfection, for the sakes of which the Buddhas have exerted themselves in innumerable previous existences over vast periods of time (even *kalpas*, or whole 'world-cycles', according to Buddhist tradition). The Buddha's significant remark in the *Mahāparinibbāṇa-Sutta* (*Dīgha-Nikāya*), that he could continue his bodily existence

[1] Translated by Bhikshu Wai-tao and Dwight Goddard in *A Buddhist Bible*, p. 383 f.

until the end of this *kalpa*, if he wished, can only be understood in context with the *Nirmāṇakāya*.

Seen from the outside, i.e., from the point of view of conceptua thought, the *Sambhogakāya* and the *Nirmāṇakāya* are manifestations of the *Dharmakāya* and are contained in the latter, which in this sense presents itself as the higher or more universal principle.

Seen from within, i.e., from the point of view of experience, the *Sambhogakāya* and the *Dharmakāya* are contained in the *Nirmāṇakāya* (as this may be seen from the iconographical descriptions of certain *Nirmāṇakāya* forms, like that of the thousand-armed *Avalokiteśvara*, which we shall discuss in one of the later chapters). Only in the *Nirmāṇakāya* can the other two 'bodies' be experienced and realized.

The first point of view is that of the philosophy of the *Mahāyāna*, the second that of the practice of the *Yogācāra*, and especially that of the *Vajrayāna*. The latter, therefore, places the *Nirmāṇakāya* into the centre of interest, be it in the form of *Vajrasattva* or that of *Avalokitevśara*.

The *Nirmāṇakāya* in its aspect of actual experience (and not merely looked upon as an external form of appearance) in which all three bodies co-exist and are experienced simultaneously, is therefore also called '*Vajrakāya*' or the 'fourth body',[1] or – as we may say with a certain justification: 'the body of the fourth dimension'. This 'dimension', however, should not be understood in a mathematical but in a psychological sense, namely, as the fourth dimension of consciousness on the Buddhist path of realization: integrating the dimension of individual corporeal experience with the experience of the infinity of the *Dharmakāya* and the spiritual creativeness and rapture of the *Sambhogakāya*.

The experience of this fourth dimension as the integration of the universal, the spiritual and the individual, has been convincingly described in the *Gaṇḍavyūha* (belonging to the *Avataṁsaka Sūtras*, Tib.: *phal-po-che*), in the simile of the tower of the *Bodhisattva Maitreya*, which is visited by the pious pilgrim *Sudhana*. This description confirms our definition, that each higher dimension contains the characteristics of all preceding dimensions and combines them in a higher unity, i.e., in a new kind or direction of movement.

Maitreya's tower is the symbol of the *Dharmadhātu*, the realm of *Dharma* in its universal aspect, in which all things are contained and in which at the same time there is perfect order and harmony. This is described in the following words: 'The objects are arrayed in such

[1] Therefore: 'With the maturing of the *Four Bodies* and the Five Wisdoms, may the Vajra of the Heart be realized in this very life.' (See page 209.)

a way that their mutual separateness no more exists, as they are all fused, but each object thereby never losing its individuality, for the image of the *Maitreya*-devotee ([*Sudhana*], i.e., the individuality of the *sādhaka* experiencing this state of *dhyāna*) is reflected in each one of the objects, and this not only in specific quarters but everywhere all over the tower, so that there is a thorough-going mutual inter-reflection of images.'

The poetically beautiful and profound description concludes with the words: '*Sudhana*, the young pilgrim, felt as if both his body and mind completely melted away; he saw that all thoughts departed away from his consciousness; in his mind there were no impediments, and all intoxications vanished.'[1]

The perfect mutual penetration of forms, things, beings, actions, events, etc., and the presence of the experiencing individual in them all – in other words, the simultaneous existence of differentiation and unity, of *rūpa* and *śūnyatā*, form and emptiness, is the great discovery of *Nāgārjuna* in his philosophy of the Middle Way (*Mādhyamika*), which expresses the nature of reality as being beyond 'being' and 'non-being'.

This way is based on a new orientation of thought freed from the rigidity of the concept of substance and of a static universe, in which things and beings were thought of as arising and passing away more or less independently of each other, so that concepts like 'identity' and 'non-identity' could form the basis of thought. But where everything is in a state of flux, such concepts cannot be adequate, and therefore the relationship of *rūpa* and *śūnyatā*, of form and emptiness, cannot be conceived as a state of mutually exclusive opposites, but only as two aspects of the same reality, which co-exist and are in continual co-operation.

If this were not the case, one would be compelled to ask, how from a perfect, homogeneous, undifferentiated state of emptiness, form, differentiation and movement could arise. But we are not concerned here with an 'earlier' or 'later', a 'higher' or a 'lower' reality, but with two aspects of the same reality. Form and space condition each other, and therefore it cannot be maintained that formlessness is a higher and form a lower state of reality. This is so only when we conceive form in a static sense, as something that has become, that is strictly limited and existing in itself, and not as an expression of a creative process, of a beginningless and endless motion.

But if we consider the nature of all form and of all that is formed, without confusing it with 'thingness' or materiality, then we shall be able to see the inseparability of *rūpa* and *śūnyatā*. Only from the

[1] D. T. Suzuki: *Essays in Zen Buddhism*, vol. III, p. 138 f.

experience of form can we arrive at the experience of formlessness; and without the experience of 'emptiness' or space the concept of form loses its dynamic, living significance.

The universe and the very faculty of consciousness extend between the ever-present poles of emptiness and form, of space and movement, because living form can only be defined as movement, not as something statically existing (otherwise we are dealing with mere abstractions, and not with reality). Only those who can experience the formless (or that which lies beyond form) in the formed, and who likewise can fathom the form in the formless – in other words, only those who experience the simultaneousness of emptiness and form – can become conscious of the highest reality.

In this knowledge lies the supreme value of the *Prajñā-pāramitā-Sūtra*, the quintessence of which is expressed in the famous words of the *Hṛdaya* (the 'heart' of the *Sūtra*, which every student is supposed to memorize, and which we too cannot repeat often enough): 'Form is emptiness, and emptiness is not different from form, nor is form different from emptiness – in fact: emptiness is form. – Since all things possess the nature of emptiness, they have neither beginning nor end – are neither perfect nor imperfect (i.e., neither self-sufficient nor yet entirely without individual significance in themselves).'

The *Dharmakāya* is therefore not only the experience of undifferentiated emptiness, but the co-existence of all forms in and on account of that quality which is present in all forms and which, in absence of a better word, is indicated by expressions like *śūnyatā*, emptiness, non-substantiality, consciousness-space, dimension, infinity of possibilities of movement, infinity of mutual relationships of all forms, mutability and dynamism of all forms, etc.

By emphasizing the negative side of the *Dharmakāya*, already in the earlier *Mahāyāna* the question had arisen, how the visible forms of appearance or experience are related to the essential emptiness of the *Dharmakāya*. The *Mahāyāna-Śraddhotpāda-Śāstra* formulates and answers this problem in the following way: 'If the Buddha's *Dharmakāya* is free from any perceptions or conceptions of form, how can they manifest themselves as sights and forms? The reply is, that the *Dharmakāya* is the very essence of all sights and forms, therefore can manifest itself in sights and forms. Both the mind and the sights that it perceives are in one and the same unity since beginningless time, because the essential nature of sights and forms is nothing but Mind-only. As the essence of sights possesses no physical form, it is the same as the *Dharmakāya*, formless and yet pervading all parts of the universes.'[1]

[1] Translated by Bhikshu Wai-tao and Dwight Goddard in *A Buddhist Bible*, p. 385.

4

THE *DHARMAKĀYA* AND THE MYSTERY OF THE BODY

FROM the aforesaid it will have become clear that the *Dharmakāya* is not only an abstract principle, but a living reality, which manifests itself in different forms on different planes of experience. The word '*kāya*', 'body', is here used in a metaphorical sense, namely, in that of a realm of conscious reality and spiritual activity, forming an organic whole, comparable to the physical body.

The personality of a spiritually undeveloped human being is confined to its material form of appearance, its physical body. The personality of a spiritually advanced man comprises not only the material part of his form of appearance, but also his mental, psychic and spiritual functions: his 'consciousness-body', which reaches far beyond the limits of his physical body.

In a man, who lives in his ideals or in thoughts, which go beyond the realm of individual interests and experiences, this 'consciousness-body' extends into the realm of universally valid truths, into the realm of the beautiful, of creative power, of aesthetic enjoyment and intuitive insight.

To the enlightened man, however, whose consciousness embraces the universe, to him the universe becomes his 'body', while his physical body becomes a manifestation of the Universal Mind, his inner vision an expression of the highest reality, and his speech an expression of eternal truth and mantric power.

Here the mystery of Body, Speech and Mind finds its ultimate consummation and reveals itself in its true nature: as the three planes of action, on which all spiritual events take place.

The Mystery of the Body is here not that of materiality, of physical embodiment, but the mystery of the boundlessness, the all embracing wholeness, of the 'universal body'.

The Mystery of Speech is more than that of mere words or concepts, it is the principle of all mental representation and communication, be it in form of audible, visible or thinkable symbols, in which highest knowledge is represented and imparted. It is the mystery of creative sound, of mantric speech, of sacred vision, from which flows the *Dharma*-revelation of a saint, an Enlightened One, a Buddha.

The Mystery of the Mind, however, is more than what can be

conceived and grasped by way of thoughts and ideas: it is the principle of spiritualization, the realization of the spirit in the realm of matter, of the infinite in the finite, of the universal in the individual; it is the transformation of the mortal body into the precious vessel of the *Nirmāṇakāya*, into a visible manifestation of the *Dharmakāya*.

Hereby the duality, the discrepancy between mind and body, mundane form and supramundane formlessness, is annihilated. Then the body of the Enlightened One becomes luminous in appearance, convincing and inspiring by its mere presence, while every word and every gesture, and even his silence, communicate the overwhelming reality of the *Dharma*. It is not the audible word through which people are converted and transformed in their innermost being, but through that which goes beyond words and flows directly from the presence of the saint: the inaudible mantric sound that emanates from his heart.[1] Therefore the perfect saint is called '*Muni*', the 'Silent One'. His spiritual radiation, which manifests itself as 'inner sound' and 'inner vision', penetrates the infinity of the universe.

In this connexion we may again remember the words of the *Mahāyāna-Śraddhotpāda-Śāstra*: 'The particular sights which Mind-Essence manifests are in their essential nature devoid of any limitations or points of definition. If conditions are suitable appearances may be manifested in any part of the universes, being solely dependent upon the mind for their appearing. Thus there are vast *Bodhisattvas*, vast *Sambhogakāyas*, vast embellishments, all of which are different from one another and yet are devoid of any spheres of limitation or points of definition, for *Tathāgatas* are able to manifest themselves in bodily forms anywhere and at the same moment that other *Tathāgatas* are able to manifest themselves without any conflict or hindrance. This marvellous interpenetration is inconceivable by any consciousness dependent upon sense-mind, but is a commonplace of the inconceivable, spontaneous activities of Mind-Essence.'[2]

In Tibetan representations of Buddhas in a state of deep meditation or in the act of proclaiming the *Dharma*, the aura, which surrounds the body of the Buddha, consists of innumerable *Dhyāni-Buddhas*. This means that the active force of highest enlightenment (and, in a lesser degree, each process of deep absorption and creative inner vision) is not only a subjective process, but a powerful spiritual radiation or projection in which the realization of the *Dharmakāya* in the

[1] *Rāmana Mahārshi*, the saint of Tiruvannamalai, who passed away only a few years ago, convinced those who came near him by his silent presence, not through words. Those of his sayings, which have been preserved by his pupils, do not rise beyond the traditional formulations of pious Hindus and would as such not explain the enormous effect of his personality. The same can be said of Śrī Rāmakrishna.

[2] *A Buddhist Bible*, p. 385.

individual human consciousness breaks through the limits of individuality and – penetrating the universe in all directions – causes in all responsive centres of consciousness similar vibrations and creative forces.

These are the powerful vibrations of a super-individual experience of reality, sounding through the 'mask' of human individuality and therefore modified by the properties or form-symbols of the 'personality' ('persona', in ancient Greek mystery-plays, was the mask of the actor which represented his character and through which his voice sounded [*sonare*, 'to sound']).

'Personality' in this original sense[1] is more than 'individuality', because herewith no illusory indivisibility and uniqueness of a separate being is postulated, but only the idea that our momentary form of appearance is like a temporarily assumed mask, through which the voice of a higher reality sounds.

From this point of view D. T. Suzuki's remark (strange as it may appear at first sight), that the concept of '*Dharmakāya*' implies the notion of 'personality', may be more easily understandable.[2] 'The highest reality', he says, 'is not a mere abstraction, it is very much alive with sense and awareness and intelligence, and, above all, with love purged of human infirmities and defilements.'

In other words, it is a living force, which manifests itself in the individual and assumes the form of 'personality'. But it goes beyond the individual consciousness, as its origin is in the universal realm of the spirit, the *Dharma*-sphere. It assumes the character of 'personality' by being realized in the human mind. If it were merely an abstract idea, it would have no influence on life, and if it were an unconscious life-force, it would have no spiritual value, i.e., no forming influence on the mind.

This is why Suzuki emphasizes that even the *Dhyāni-Buddhas*, as for instance *Amitābha*, have all the characteristics of personality, in the sense of a living, self-sustaining, conscious force, and that they are not merely 'personifications' of an abstract concept. The human qualities of *Amitābha* are not arbitrarily added attributes, but the transformation of a universal reality in the form of human experience. Only in this way can this reality retain its vital value and effectiveness on the human plane.

Just as high-tension electricity has to be transformed into low-tension current for normal use (without losing thereby its nature),

[1] The distinction between individuality and personality has been pointed out already by Réné Guénon, and D. T. Suzuki seems to take a similar stand, if he sees in the *Dharmakāya* the elements of personality.

[2] D. T. Suzuki: *The Essence of Buddhism* (The Buddhist Society, London, 1947), p. 41.

so universal values have to be transformed into human values, if they are to affect human life.

This principle is applicable to all *Dhyāni-Buddhas* and similar forms of religious or yogic experiences. They are primordial forms (or 'archetypes', as Jung would say) of the human mind. Therefore they are *necessary* for the process of realization and an effective protection against a premature abstraction, intellectualization, or mental anticipation of spiritual aims and values. (Herein lies the danger of a superficial intellectual acceptance or imitation of tantric or zennistic paradoxes, as found in the sayings of *Siddhas* and Zen Masters – the validity of which lies not at the beginning, but only at the end of the spiritual path, where we are capable of dispensing with all tradition, religious forms and logical definitions.)

An abstract idea is in no way 'higher' than its humanized, personified ('personalized') or visualized form-symbol – the formless state not necessarily more valuable or true than the form-possessing. It all depends on whether we are able to see *through* the form and realize the relativity of both form and formless experience. Both have their dangers: the one, that we may take the form as ultimate, the other, that we lose ourselves in generalizations and forget the connexions with the other side of reality, namely, form. In fact, as long as we live exclusively on any one of the three planes of reality, we cannot escape this danger. Hence the necessity of their integration, their becoming simultaneously conscious in the *Vajrakāya*.

5

THE MULTI-DIMENSIONALITY OF THE GREAT *MANTRA*

THE meaning and the effectiveness of a *mantra* consists in its multi-dimensionality, its capacity to be valid not only on one, but on all planes of reality, and to reveal on each of these planes a new meaning – until, after having repeatedly gone through the various stages of experience, we are able to grasp the totality of the mantric experience-body.

Therefore it is said in the *Kāraṇḍa-Vyūha*[1] that *Avalokiteśvara* refused to teach the sacred Six Syllables of the Great Mantra OṀ

[1] *Kāraṇḍa Byūha*, a work on the doctrines and customs of the Buddhists, edited by Satya Bratu Samasrami, Calcutta, 1873. The full title of the Sanskrit text is: *Avalokiteśvara-guṇa-karaṇḍa-vyūha*.

MAṆI PADME HŪṀ without an initiation into the symbolism of the *maṇḍala* connected with it. For the same reason we had to deal at such length with the nature of the *maṇḍala* and the *cakras*.

'If *Avalokiteśvara* does not want to communicate the six syllables without a description of the *maṇḍala*, this has its reason in the fact that the formula as a creation in the realm of sound is incomplete and useless, if its sisters in the realm of inner and outer vision and in the sphere of gestures are not combined with it. If this formula is to transform a being and to lead it to the state of enlightenment, the nature of this formula, the miraculous and ideal nature of *Avalokiteśvara* must be able to occupy all spheres of reality and activity of the initiate: speech, imagination, bodily attitude and movement. The *yantra* – in the case of the *Kāraṇḍa-vyūha* a *maṇḍala* – does not and cannot stand alone functionally; in order to act it requires the knowledge and the practice of those differently-natured manifestations of the 'innermost heart', of a divine being which it makes perceptible even in the sphere of the visible. But even in the realm of the visible it does not remain the only manifestation.'

This 'divine being', however, is none other but the *Sādhaka's* mind in a state of deep absorption and self-forgetfulness. In the act of liberating himself from the illusions and fetters of his ego-consciousness and the impediments of his limited individuality, his body becomes the vessel, the visible manifestation of *Avalokiteśvara*, whose nature is expressed in the *mantra* OṀ MAṆI PADME HŪṀ.

The meaning of such a *mantra* can therefore not be exhausted by the meaning of its component parts. As with all living things and in all fields of creative activity, the whole is more than the sum of its parts. The knowledge of the parts can help us towards the understanding of the whole only when we remain conscious of their organic relationship. The organic relations are so important that it is not sufficient to investigate and analyse each part and to connect them subsequently one after another, but we must view the whole of this simultaneously in direct inner vision. This is achieved by the symbolism of the *maṇḍala* and the realization, nay the *embodiment* of the *maṇḍala* in the 'person' of the *Sādhaka* and on all planes of his consciousness.

In this case *Amitābha* is represented by the seed-syllable OṀ in the *Dharmakāya*, because *Amitābha* is taking here the place of *Vairocana* in the centre of the *maṇḍala*, which at the same time corresponds to the highest psychic Centre.

In the 'MAṆI' *Amitābha* appears as *Amitāyus* in the garb of a Prince of the *Dharma*, in which his virtues and accomplishments are symbolized by the insignia of royalty (like crown and other traditional pieces of adornment), i.e., in the *Sambhogakāya*. As such he represents the active side of his nature as the Giver of Infinite Life, in which the infinite light of *Amitābha* becomes the source of true life, a life that is boundless, no more caught in the narrow confines of the ego, a life in which the multiplicity of apparently separate forms of existence is realized in the oneness of all living beings.

In the 'PADMA' *Amitābha* appears in the *Nirmāṇakāya*, in the unfoldment of infinite forms of activity, as symbolized by the Thousand-Armed *Avalokiteśvara*.

In the 'HŪṀ', finally, *Avalokiteśvara* becomes the 'Diamond Body' (*Vajrakāya*) of the *Sādhaka*, in which the totality of his being is comprised. Thus the mediator becomes the embodiment of *Avalokiteśvara* and the *Nirmāṇakāya* of *Amitābha*.

This is expressed by the integration of the mantric formula in the seal of *Amitābha*, the sacred seed-syllable HRĪḤ. The complete formula thus becomes: OṀ MAṆI PADME HŪṀ:HRĪḤ.

In the advanced practice of meditation, the various forms in which *Amitābha* appears, are transmitted to the corresponding psychic Centres (*cakras*) of the *Sādhaka*. Thus the *Dharmakāya* aspect of *Amitābha* is visualized in the Crown Centre (*sahasrāra-cakra*), *Amitāyus* in the Throat Centre, *Avalokiteśvara* (or a *vajra*-form corresponding to him) in the Heart Centre, and his present embodiment as the totality of the body and the personality of the meditator.

From the point of view of the three Mysteries of Body, Speech and Mind, the formula takes on the following meaning:

In the OṀ we experience the *Dharmakāya* and the mystery of the universal body;

in the MAṆI the *Sambhogakāya* and the mystery of the mantric sound, as the awakener of psychic consciousness, of inner vision and inspiration;

in the PADMA we experience the *Nirmāṇakāya* and the mystery of the all-transforming mind;

in the HŪṀ we experience the *Vajrakāya* as synthesis of the transcendental body of the Three Mysteries;

in the HRĪḤ we dedicate the totality of our transformed personality (which thus has become the *Vajrakāya*) to the service of *Amitābha*. This is the realization of the *Bodhisattva* ideal, symbolized in the figure of *Avalokiteśvara*.

The seed-syllable HRĪḤ is not only the seal of *Amitābha* (just as HŪṀ is the seal of *Vajrasattva Akṣobhya*), but has a special meaning for the realization of the *Bodhisattva* way. HRĪḤ is the inner voice, the moral law within us, the voice of the conscience, of inner knowledge[1]–

[1] What makes us blush is the shame we feel in the presence of our better knowledge

not the intellectual, but the intuitive, spontaneous knowledge – due to which we do the right thing for the sake of the good and not for the sake of any advantage. It is the *leitmotif*, the guiding principle and the special virtue of the *Bodhisattva*, who is bent upon the enlightenment of all, like the sun which shines equally for sinners and saints.

As a sound-symbol HRĪḤ means far more than hinted at by its philological associations. It does not only possess the warmth of the sun, i.e., the emotional principle of goodness, compassion and sympathy – but also the power of illumination, the quality of making things visible, the faculty of perception, of direct vision. HRĪḤ is a mantric solar symbol, a luminous, elevating, upwards-moving sound composed of the prānic aspirate (H), the fiery R (RAṀ is the seed syllable of the element 'fire') and the high 'i'-sound, which expresses upwards-movement, intensity, etc.

In the sphere of universality all these light- and fire-associations are in harmony with *Amitābha*, the Buddha of infinite light, whose symbols are the element 'fire', the red colour and the direction of the setting sun; while the ideological and emotional associations point towards the human sphere and towards *Avalokiteśvara*.

Avalokiteśvara, the 'Down-looking One', the Lord of Compassion, is the embodiment of the love of an Enlightened One towards all living and suffering beings, a love which is free from possessiveness, but consists in an unlimited and undivided active sympathy. Wherever this feeling and this attitude of mind reveals itself in action, there *Avalokiteśvara* reveals himself, embodies himself and becomes reality. Therefore it is said, that *Avalokiteśvara* manifests himself in an infinite number of forms, and may appear in any shape.

Just as the *prajñā*- or knowledge-principle prevails in *Vajrasattva*, the adamantine nature of all consciousness, which is experienced as the imperishable, the deathless, the eternal in man (especially in all those who strive towards liberation) – in the same way the emotional or *karuṇā*-principle of Buddhahood is predominant in *Avalokiteśvara*. Their co-operation represents the perfect path of enlightenment. The mantric formulae of *Avalokiteśvara* finds therefore its fulfilment in the final seal of *Vajrasattva*, the seed-syllable HŪṀ.

---

our conscience. The literal meaning of '*Hrī*' (Pāli: '*hiri*') is 'to blush' (which corresponds tothe colour of *Amitābha*), 'to feel shame'. It goes without saying, that the mantric meaning goes far beyond the word-meaning. The mantric meaning may be said to be the primordial experience, which is the basis of common speech, the source from which the words of daily use are derived. The aspirate (Ḥ), called *Visarga*, which, as already mentioned, is used in Tibet only as a written symbol, without being pronounced, distinguishes the seed-syllable from the ordinary use of the word (as in case of the nasal *anusvara*) and emphasizes its mantric character.

'As long as we remain on the plane of *jñāna* (the plane of transcendental knowledge) the world does not seem to be very real, as its *māyā*-like existence in which it presents itself to *jñāna* is too vapoury; but when we come to the *adhiṣṭhāna* aspect of Bodhisattvahood, we feel as if we have taken hold of something solid and altogether sustaining. This is where life really begins to have its meaning. To live ceases to be the mere blind assertion of a primordial urge, for *adhiṣṭhāna* is another name for *praṇidhāna* (the ethical principle of Bodhisattvahood: the *Bodhisattva*-vow), or it is that spiritual power emanating from the *praṇidhāna* which constitutes with *jñāna* (the higher knowledge) the essence of Bodhisattvahood. – By means of *jñāna* we climb, as it were, and reach the summit of the thirty-three heavens; and sitting quietly we watch the underworld and its doings as if they were clouds moving underneath the feet; they are the whirling masses of commotion, but they do not touch one who is above them. The world of *jñāna* (of transcendental knowledge) is transparent, luminous and eternally serene. But the *Bodhisattva* would not remain in this state of eternal contemplation above the world of particulars and hence of struggles and sufferings, for his heart aches at the sight. He is now determined to descend into the midst of the tempestuous masses of existence.'[1]

According to the well-known legend, *Avalokiteśvara*, looking down upon this suffering world with his all-penetrating eye of wisdom, was filled with such profound compassion, that in his overwhelming desire to lead beings towards liberation his head burst into innumerable heads,[2] and from his body sprang a thousand helping arms and hands, like an aura of dazzling rays. And in the palm of each hand an eye appeared; because the compassion of a *Bodhisattva* is not blind emotion, but love combined with wisdom. It is the spontaneous urge to help others, flowing from the knowledge of inner oneness. Thus wisdom is the pre-condition of this compassion and is therefore inseparable from it; because wisdom consists in the recognition of the inner identity of all beings – and the experience of this solidarity results in the capacity of feeling others' sufferings as one's own.

Thus compassion is not based on the feeling of mortal or mental superiority, but on the essential equality with others: '*Attānam upamaṁ katvā*', 'having made oneself equal to others', as it has been said already in the *Dhammapada* (Pāli). In other words, to recognize oneself in others, is the key to mutual understanding, the foundation of true ethics.

[1] D. T. Suzuki: *Essays in Zen Buddhism*, vol. III, pp. 149–50 (Rider & Co., London, 1953). Brackets are mine.

[2] Iconographically represented by eleven heads.

'The great secret of morals is love, or a going out of our own nature, and an identification of ourselves with the beautiful which exists in a thought, action or person, not our own. A man to be greatly good, must imagine intensely and comprehensively; he must put himself in the place of another and of many others; the pains and pleasures of his species must become his own.' (Shelley.)

Because the compassionate puts himself in the place of the sufferer and experiences his pain, his longings and desires, he can understand him in his deepest nature and offer the help which is most suited under the circumstances and in accordance with the character of the sufferer.

The help of a *Bodhisattva* is therefore not something that comes from outside or that is pressed upon those who are helped, but it is the awakening of a force which dwells in the innermost nature of every being, a force which, awakened by the spiritual influence or the example of a *Bodhisattva*, enables us to meet fearlessly every situation and to convert it into a positive value, an asset, a means of liberation. Indeed, we may not go too far in identifying this force directly with fearlessness.

This fearlessness may even break the power of *karma* – or, as it is put in the language of the *Sūtras*: Even the sword of the executioner breaks into pieces if the condemned prisoner invokes the name of *Amitābha* from the depths of his heart.[1] The executioner is none other than the *karma* of the condemned. But the moment he recognizes and sincerely accepts this fact, by readily taking upon himself the consequences of his actions in the light of that inner certainty, which flows from the message and the example of the Enlightened Ones – the passive victim of blind (ignorance-created) 'fate' turns into an active moulder of his destiny. Feeling himself in the presence of the noble figure of *Avalokiteśvara*, he arouses in his heart the powers of light and of spiritual oneness with all those who attained the state of Enlightenment. This miracle of inner transformation breaks even the sword of the Judge of the Dead (*Yāma*; Tib.: *gśin-rje*), and he reveals himself as the Great Compassionate One: *Avalokiteśvara.*

As a matter of fact, we see among the eleven heads of the thousand-armed *Avalokiteśvara* the terrifying features of the Lord of Death immediately below the benign face of *Amitābha*, who represents the *Dharmakāya*-aspect of *Avalokiteśvara*. As demonstrated by the multi-dimensionality of the Great Mantra, the figure of *Avalokiteśvara* is not exclusively an appearance-form of the *Nirmāṇakāya*, but comprises at the same time the *Dharmakāya* and the *Sambhogakāya*.

This is also expressed by the iconographical description of the

[1] Cf. D T. Suzuki: *The Essence of Buddhism*, p. 54. The Buddhist Society, London, 1947.

thousand-armed *Avalokiteśvara*, which says: 'The thousand arms are divided into eight belonging to the *Dharmakāya* manifestation, forty belonging to the *Sambhogakāya* and nine hundred and fifty-two to the *Nirmāṇakāya* manifestation.'[1] The arms of the *Dharmakāya* manifestation fill the innermost circle, surrounding the body; the forty hands (the arms are not visible) of the *Sambhogakāya* fill the next-following circle – while the hands of the *Nirmāṇakāya* (extended in a gesture of help and, in contrast to the previous ones, not holding any symbolical implements) fill, in steadily increasing numbers, the five outer circles. The further the helping forces of the *Bodhisattvas* hurl themselves into the depths of the world, the greater becomes their differentiation, the more manifold and varied their manifestation.[2]

6

AVALOKITEŚVARA'S DESCENT INTO THE SIX REALMS OF THE WORLD

WHAT is the nature of this world into which the helping forces of the *Bodhisattva* hurl themselves? – According to Buddhist definition it is what we experience as the world: the result of our sense-activities, our thoughts, feelings and actions. So long as this thinking, feeling and acting is motivated by the illusion of our individual separateness, we experience a correspondingly limited, one-sided and therefore imperfect world, in which we attempt in vain to maintain our self-identity, our imaginary ego, against the irresistible stream of eternally changing forms and conditions. The world, therefore, appears to us as a world of impermanence, insecurity and fear; and it is this fear that surrounds each being like a wall, separating it from others and from the greater life.

[1] *Tsao Hsiang Liang-tu Ching*, a Chinese Lamaist text, printed by order of Chang Chia Hu-t'u-k'e-t'u in the thirteenth year of the reign of Emperor Ch'ien-Lung (1748). Quoted by Dr. P. H. Pott in his *Introduction to the Tibetan Collection of the National Museum of Ethnology*, Leiden, 1951.

[2]

Innermost circle	8 arms	(*dharmakāya*)
Second circle	40 arms	(*sambhogakāya*)
Third circle	142 arms	(*nirmāṇakāya*)
Fourth circle	166 arms	
Fifth circle	190 arms	
Sixth circle	214 arms	
Seventh circle	240 arms	
Total	1,000 arms	

The *Bodhisattva*, liberating the beings from this fear by the example of his own fearlessness and boundless devotion, breaks down the separating walls and opens a vision into undreamt realms of freedom, in which the solidarity of all beings is revealed and becomes the natural basis of mutual understanding. Then compassion, good-will, selfless love, pity, etc., will no more be felt as 'virtues', but as the natural attitude of spiritual freedom. Therefore Laotse says in his *Tao Teh Ching* (38): 'The truly virtuous is not conscious of his virtue. The man of inferior virtue, however, is ever anxiously concerned with his virtue, and therefore he is without true virtue. True virtue is spontaneous and lays no claim to virtue. The virtue of the perfect sage does not interfere, it co-operates with an open and sympathetic mind, while the virtue of inferiors acts with intention and under conditions and is influenced by desires.'

If, therefore, it is said in the *Śūraṅgama Sūtra*, that *Avalokiteśvara*, after having attained the transcendental powers of supreme freedom and fearlessness, took the vow to liberate all living beings from their fetters and sufferings, then we have to regard this vow as the expression of a spontaneous urge, arising from the depths of the heart in the knowledge of the essential oneness of all life. With the extinction of the ego-illusion, nay, even with the mere recognition of the fact that there is no such thing as a separate 'I', how can there be anything like one's 'own salvation'? As long as we know about the suffering of our fellow beings and experience it as our own (or, more correctly, if we do not make any more a distinction between 'self' and 'others'), our liberation can only be equated with the liberation of all.

This does not mean a postponement for an unlimited time, but it signifies that the act of liberation includes all living beings, that it is an act of boundless devotion, in which there is no place for any conception of time. It is an act in the realm of *Dharma*-reality, beyond time and space, i.e., in a sphere, in which the polarity of time and space is transcended and is experienced only as an immanent presence and totality. Just as it is said of Christ that he sacrificed himself for the whole of humanity and for each single human being – even for the still unborn generations – in the same way we may say that the Buddha's Enlightenment (as that of any other realized being) included all living beings and will benefit them till the end of time.

This must remain incomprehensible to the intellect, because it goes beyond its dimension. Only from the mystic (i.e., time- and space-freed) experiences of the greatest spirits of humanity, can we get an inkling of the depth of this mystery. It is the mystery of the power of the Enlightened Mind, acting beyond the confines of time and space, and revealing itself in the 'All-Accomplishing Wisdom' of *Amoghasiddhi*. This is symbolized by the *Viśvavajra*, the double-*vajra*, in which the dimensions of time and space are combined in the higher reality of a 'fourth' dimension. It is this dimension of consciousness, in which the transcendental forces of the Enlightened Ones act, and in which all *Bodhisattvas* have their being. And it is here that *Avalokiteśvara*, as the embodiment of active Bodhisattvahood, manifests himself in innumerable forms.

But in order to partake of these forces, our own co-operation is necessary, either in the form of a sincere effort or of spiritual receptivity and preparedness. Just as a flower opens itself to the sun, so we must open ourselves to these forces and turn towards them, if we want to make use of them. For, as little as the sun has the power to penetrate into a flower if the flower does not open itself to the sun, as little can the enlightenment of a Buddha act upon us, if we close ourselves to his influence, or if we direct our attention exclusively upon the satisfaction of material wants and selfish desires.

This problem has been elucidated already in the *Mahāyāna-Śraddhotpāda Śāstra*: 'If all the Buddhas from remotest beginnings have had these transcendental powers of Wisdom, Compassion and command of unlimited expedient means for benefiting all sentient beings, how is it that sentient beings do not recognize and appreciate their goodwill and beneficent activities and respond to them by awakening faith and beginning devotional practices and, in due course, attain enlightenment and Buddhahood? – The reply is, that all Buddhas – having become identified with the pure *Dharmakāya*, pervade all the universes equally and potently and spontaneously, but embracing in their pure Essence all sentient beings, also, and being in eternal relations with them and being of the same self-nature, they wait the willing and inevitable response that is a necessary part of the perfect purity and unity of the *Dharmakāya*.'[1]

Thus the figures of the Enlightened Ones appear in all the realms of existence: in the deepest hells as well as in the highest heavens, in the realms of man and of animals as well as in other realms of non-human beings.

In practically every Tibetan temple a vivid pictorial representation of the six realms of the *saṁsāric* world can be found. And corresponding to the nature of this world, in which the endless cycle of rebirths takes place, the six realms are represented as a wheel, whose six segments depict the six main types of worldly, i.e., unenlightened existence. These forms of existence are conditioned by the illusion of separate selfhood, which craves for all that serves to satisfy or to

[1] Translated by Bhikshu Wai-tao and Dwight Goddard in *A Buddhist Bible*, p. 396.

TIBETAN 'WHEEL OF LIFE'
(Tracing of a Tibetan temple-fresco of Sankar Gompa, Leh)

maintain this 'ego', and which despises and hates whatever opposes this craving.

These three basic motives or root-causes (*hetu*) of unenlightened existence form the nave of the wheel of rebirths and are depicted in the form of three animals, symbolizing greed, hatred and delusion: a red cock stands for passionate desire and attachment (*rāga*; Tib.: *ḥdod-chags*); a green snake is the embodiment of hatred, enmity and aversion (*dveṣa*; Tib.: *źe-sdaṅ*), the qualities that poison our life; and a black hog symbolizes the darkness of ignorance and ego-delusion (*moha*; Tib.: *gti-mug*), the blind urge, that drives beings round and round in the unending cycle of births and deaths.

The three animals are biting each other's tails and are linked in such a way that they too form a circle, because greed, hatred, and delusion condition each other and are inseparably connected. They are the ultimate consequences of ignorance (*avidyā*; Tib.: *ma-rig*) concerning the true nature of things, on account of which we regard transient things as permanent, and unreal things as real and desirable. In mentally and spiritually undeveloped beings, governed by blind urges and subconscious drives, this lack of knowledge leads to confusion, hallucinations and delusion (*moha*) or, as the Tibetan puts it, to mental darkness and gloom (*gti-mug*), which involves us more and more in the rounds of *saṁsāra*, the chasing after ephemeral happiness, the flight from suffering, the fear of losing what has been gained, the struggle for the possession of desirable things and the defence or protection of those that have been acquired. The *saṁsāra* is the world of eternal strife and dissension, of irreconcilable contrasts, of a duality, which has lost its balance, due to which beings fall from one extreme into the other.

Conditions of heavenly joy are opposed by states of infernal tortures; the realm of titanic struggle and lust for power is opposed by the realm of animal fear and persecution; the human realm of creative activity and pride of accomplishment is opposed by the realm of 'hungry spirits' (*preta*; Tib.: *yi-dvags*), in whom unsatisfied passions and unfulfilled desires lead a ghost-like existence.

The Tibetan 'Wheel of Life',[1] as reproduced on the previous page shows in the upper sector the realm of the gods (*deva*; Tib.: *lha*) whose carefree life, dedicated to aesthetic pleasures, is indicated by dance and music. On account of this one-sided dedication to their own pleasures, they forget the true nature of life, the limitations of their existence, the sufferings of other beings as well as their own transiency. They do not know that they live only in a state of temporary harmony, which comes to an end as soon as the causes (their

[1] Tib.: *srid-paḥi ḥkhor-lo*, 'the cycle of worldly states of existence'.

moral merits, according to Buddhist conception), which led them to this happy state, are exhausted. They live, so to say, on the accumulated capital of past good deeds without adding any new values. They are gifted with beauty, longevity and freedom from pain, but just this lack of suffering, of obstacles and exertion, deprives the harmony of their existence of all creative impulses, all spiritual activity and the urge for deeper knowledge. Thus finally they sink again into lower states of existence. Rebirth in heavenly realms, therefore, is not an aim which Buddhists think worth striving for. It is only a temporary suspension, but no solution of the problem of life. It leads to a strengthening of the ego-illusion and to a deeper entanglement in the *saṁsāric* world.

Thus we see in the lowest sector of the Wheel of Life the reverse side of those heavenly pleasures: the realm of infernal pain (*nirāya*; Tib.: *dmyal-ba*). These infernal sufferings, which are drastically depicted in form of various tortures, are not 'punishments' that have been inflicted upon erring beings by an omnipotent god and creator, but the inevitable reactions of their own deeds. The Judge of the Dead does not condemn, but only holds up the mirror of conscience, in which every being pronounces his own judgement. This judgement, which seems to come from the mouth of the Judge of the Dead, is that inner voice, which is expressed in the seed-syllable HRĪḤ, which is visible in the centre of the mirror. Therefore it is said that *Yāma*, the Judge and 'King of the Law' (*dharma-rāja*; Tib.: *gśin-rje-chos-rgyal*), is an emanation of *Amitābha* in the form of *Avalokiteś-vara* who, moved by infinite compassion, descends into the deepest hells and – through the power of the Mirror of Knowledge (which arouses the voice of conscience) – transforms suffering into a cleansing fire, so that beings are purified and can rise to better forms of existence.

In order to make this unmistakably clear to the beholder of the Wheel of Life, *Avalokiteśvara* has been represented once more in his Buddha-form besides his terrifying appearance as *Yāma*, the Judge and Lord of Death. And from *Avalokiteśvara's* hand emerges the purifying flame. In a similar way he appears in all other realms of existence – carrying in his hands the symbol of his special message, according to the nature of the particular realm.

In the realm of the *Devas* he appears with the lute, in order to rouse the gods with the sounds of the *Dharma* from their self-complacency and from the illusions of transient pleasures, and to awaken them to the timeless harmonies of a higher reality.

In the realm of warring Titans, the 'anti-gods' or *Asuras* (Tib.: *lha-ma-yin*), depicted to the right of the *Deva*-world, *Avalokiteśvara* appears with a flaming sword, because the beings of this realm understand only the language of force and strife. Instead of fighting for the fruits of the Wishing Tree (*kalpataru*), which stands between the realm of the gods and the Titans, the *Bodhisattva* teaches the nobler struggle for the fruits of knowledge and desirelessness. The flaming sword is the symbol of the active 'Discriminating Knowledge', which cuts through the darkness of ignorance and the knots of doubt and confusion.

The reverse side of the realm of power-drunken Titans is the realm of fear in the left lower sector (opposite the *asura-loka*). It is the realm of animals, of persecution and surrender to a blind destiny of natural necessities and uncontrollable instincts. Here *Avalokiteśvara* appears with a book in his hands, because animals lack the faculty of articulate speech and reflective thought, which could liberate them from the darkness of subconscious drives and the sluggishness and dumbness of an undeveloped mind.

To the left of the realm of the gods, we see the world of man, the realm of purposeful activity and higher aspirations, in which the freedom of decision plays an essential role, because here the qualities of all realms of existence become conscious, and all their possibilities are equally within reach – and beyond them the chance of ultimate liberation from the cycle of birth and death through insight into the true nature of the world.

It is here, therefore, that *Avalokiteśvara* appears as *Buddha Śākyamuni* with the alms-bowl and the staff of an ascetic, in order to point out the way towards liberation to those 'whose eyes are covered only with little dust'. But only few are prepared to walk the way of final liberation. The majority are entangled in worldly activities, in chasing after possessions and sense-pleasures, power and fame. And thus, opposed to the world of purposeful human activity and proud self-assertion, we find (in the opposite sector) the realm of unfulfilled desire and unreasonable craving.

This is depicted in the right lower sector of the Wheel of Life. Here we see the reverse side of passions in their impotent clinging to the objects of desire without a possibility of satisfaction. The beings of this realm, called *Pretas* (Tib.: *yi-dvags*), are restless spirits, filled with unsatisfied passions, leading a ghost-like, peaceless existence in a world of imaginary objects of their desire. They are beings who have lost their inner balance and whose wrongly directed lust for life produces a correspondingly disharmonious form of existence, which has neither the power of proper material embodiment nor of any kind of spiritualization. They are those beings, entities or forces of consciousness, by which believers in spiritualistic seances are deceived and which, according to popular belief, haunt the places of their former existence, to which they are fettered by their unsatisfied desires. (It is for this reason that they are objects of necromantic exorcism.) They are depicted as ghoulish creatures with spindly, dried-up limbs and bloated bellies, tortured by insatiable hunger and thirst, without being able to satisfy them. Because the little that they are able to swallow through the narrow gullet of their thin neck, causes them unspeakable tortures, since food is indigestible for them and merely bloats up their bellies. And whatever they drink turns into fire: a drastic simile of the nature of passionate craving (*rāga*; Tib.: *ḥdod-chags*), the sufferings of which cannot be stilled by giving in to passion, since this would only increase its force, like a fire upon which oil is poured. In other words: passions are the origin of suffering, because they are unstillable due to their own nature, and every attempt at satisfying them leads to deeper attachment and entanglement and to greater sufferings.

Liberation from such passionate desire is only possible if we succeed in replacing unwholesome objects by wholesome ones (i.e., by transforming *kāma-chanda*, sensual desire, into *dharma-chanda*, desire for truth and knowledge). The Buddha, in whose form *Avalokiteśvara* appears in the realm of the *Pretas*, carries therefore in his hands a receptacle with heavenly treasures (or spiritual food and drink, which will not turn into poison and fire), beside which objects of worldly desire appear paltry, and which thus liberate suffering beings from the tortures of unquenchable desire.

7

THE FORMULA OF DEPENDENT ORIGINATION

WHILE the Six Realms depict the unfoldment of the *saṁsāric* world under the influence of those motives or driving forces, which form the centre of the Wheel of Life, its outer rim shows the unfoldment of these principles in individual life. Ignorance is here represented by a blind woman (because *avidyā* [Tib.: *ma-rig*] is of female gender), feeling her way with a stick. On account of his spiritual blindness man blunders through life, creating an illusory picture of himself and the world, due to which his will is directed upon unreal things, while his character is formed in accordance with this direction of his will, his desire and his imagination.

This form-creating activity (*saṁskāra*; Tib.: *ḥdu-byed*) is adequately symbolized by the picture of a potter. Just as a potter creates the shapes of pots, so we form our character and our destiny or, more correctly, our *karma*, the outcome of our deeds in works, words and

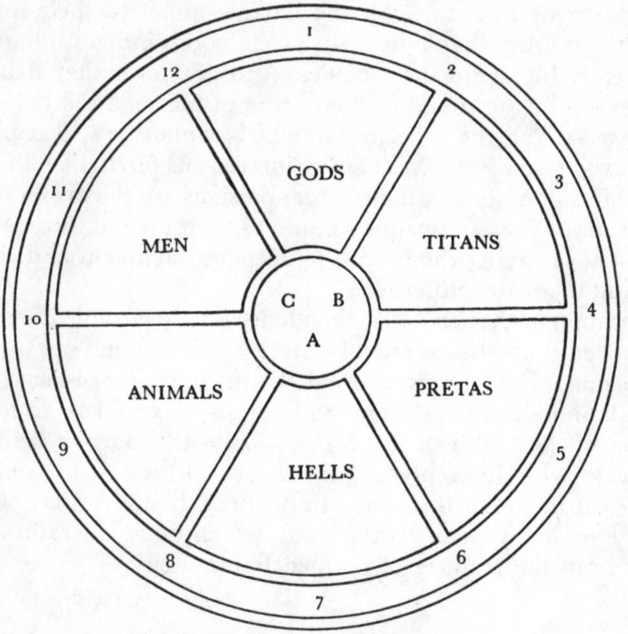

A. Delusion (*moha*); B. Greed (*lobha, rāga*); C. Hatred (*dveṣa*)

1. Blind woman: 'ignorance' (*avidyā*).
2. Potter: 'karmic formations' (*saṁskāra*).
3. Monkey: 'consciousness' (*vijñāna*).
4. Two men in a boat: 'mind-and-body' (*nāma-rūpa*).
5. House with six windows: 'six senses' (*ṣaḍāyatana*).
6. Pair of lovers: 'contact' (*sparśa*).
7. Arrow piercing eye of man: 'feeling' (*vedanā*).
8. Drinker, served by woman: 'thirst' (*tṛṣṇā*).
9. Man gathering fruit: 'clinging' (*upādāna*).
10. Sexual intercourse: 'becoming' (*bhava*).
11. Woman giving birth: 'birth' (*jāti*).
12. Man carrying corpse on his back: 'death' (*maraṇa*).

thoughts. *Saṁskāra* is here volitional action, synonymous with *cetanā* (will) and *karma* (effect-creating deed) in contradistinction to *saṁskāra-skandha*, the group of mental formations, which, as a *result* of those volitional acts, become a cause of new activity and constitute the actively directing principle or character of a new consciousness.

For character is nothing but the tendency of our will, formed by repeated actions. Every deed leaves a trace, a path formed by the process of walking, and wherever such a once-trodden path exists, there we find, when a similar situation arises, that we take to this path spontaneously. This is the law of action and reaction, which we call *karma*, the law of movement in the direction of the least resistance, i.e., of the frequently trodden and therefore easier path. It is what is commonly known as the 'force of habit'.

Just as a potter forms vessels out of formless clay, so we create through deeds, words and thoughts, out of the still unformed material of our life and our sense-impressions, the vessel of our future consciousness, namely that which gives it form and direction.

When departing from one and entering into another life, it is the consciousness thus formed which constitutes the nucleus or germ of the new embodiment. This consciousness (*vijñāna*; Tib.: *rnam-śes*), which stands at the beginning of a new life, is represented in the third picture, in form of a monkey grasping a branch. Just as a monkey restlessly jumps from branch to branch, so the consciousness jumps from object to object.

Consciousness, however, cannot exist by itself. It has not only the property of incessantly grasping sense-objects or objects of imagination, and to let go one object for the sake of another, but it has also the capacity to crystallize and to polarize itself into material forms and mental functions. Therefore it is said that consciousness is the basis of the 'mind-and-body-combination' (*nāma-rūpa*; Tib.: *miṅ-gzugs*), the pre-condition of the psycho-physical organism, in which the close relationship between bodily and mental functions is compared with two people in a boat. This is shown in the fourth picture, in which we see a ferryman propelling a boat with two people in it. (The ferryman, strictly speaking, does not belong to the simile.)

The psycho-physical organism is furthermore differentiated through the formation and action of the six senses (*ṣaḍāyatana*; Tib.: *skye-mched*), namely the faculties of thinking, seeing, hearing, smelling, tasting and feeling (touching). These faculties are like the windows of a house, through which we look upon the world outside. They are therefore generally depicted as a house with six windows. The artist, however, who painted the Wheel of Life which we have reproduced here, took the liberty to depict (in the fifth picture) the front of the temple from whose porch this fresco was traced.

The sixth picture symbolizes the contact (*sparśa*; Tib.: *reg-pa*) of the senses with their objects, in the form of the first contact between lovers.

The feeling (*vedanā*; Tib.: *tshor-ba*), resulting from the contact of the senses with their objects, is represented in the seventh picture by a man whose eye has been pierced by an arrow.

The eighth picture shows a drinker, who is served by a woman. It symbolizes the thirst for life (*tṛṣṇā*; Tib.: *sred-pa*), or craving caused by agreeable sensations. (It goes without saying that the arrow in the eye is not meant to indicate the 'pleasure', but only the intensity of the feeling and perhaps also its future painful consequences, which overtake those who allow themselves to be carried away by agreeable sensations.)

From the thirst for life arises the grasping of and clinging to (*upādāna*; Tib.: *len-pa*) the desired objects. This is symbolized in the ninth picture by a man who plucks fruit from a tree and gathers it in a basket.

Clinging leads to a strengthening of the bonds of life, to a new process of becoming (*bhava*; Tib.: *srid-pa*). This is symbolized by the sexual union of man and wife, as seen in the tenth picture.

Becoming leads to rebirth (*jāti*; Tib.: *skye-ba*) in a new existence. The eleventh picture, therefore, shows a woman who is giving birth to a child. The Tibetan attitude towards sexual things is of a disarming naturalness and objectivity. The Tibetan, therefore, does not hesitate to depict the sexual act and the act of giving birth undisguised and without ambiguity. He lays greater stress upon nearness to life than upon philosophical abstractions. In spite of this he succeeds in his symbolism (of words as well as of visible forms) to express the finest shades of spiritual experience with an astonishing precision. His mysticism is never inimical to life, his philosophy never merely an expression of speculative thought, but the result of practical experience. Due to the same attitude he endeavours to put religious ideas into such visible forms and similies, that even the simplest mind can grasp them and include them into the realm of concrete life. In order to avoid misunderstandings, each of the above-mentioned symbolical pictures bears a short inscription, as for instance: 'monkey – consciousness', 'blind woman – ignorance', etc.

The twelfth picture shows a man, who carries a corpse (with knees drawn up, swathed in cloths, according to Tibetan custom) on his back to the cremation-ground (or the place where dead bodies are disposed of). It illustrates the last of the twelve links of the formula of Dependent Origination (*pratītyasamutpāda*; Tib.: *rten-ḥbrel-gye-yan-lag-bcu-gñis*), which says that all that has been born, leads to old-age and death (*jarā-maraṇa*; Tib.: *rgas-śi*).

Thanks to such pictorial representations this formula, which belongs to the oldest Buddhist tradition, is more popular in Tibet than in any other Buddhist country.[1] It has often been called the twelvefold 'causal nexus', and due to this wrong presupposition many a scholar has cudgelled his brain as to how this causality could be explained according to the laws of logic or of the natural sequence of the constituents of this formula. *Avidyā*, the not-knowing or non-recognition of reality, however, is not a *prima causa*, a metaphysical cause of existence or a cosmogonic principle, but a condition under which our present life develops, a condition that is responsible for our present state of consciousness.

The Buddha spoke only of a *conditioned* or *dependent* origination, not however of a law of causality, in which the single phases of development follow each other in ever the same way with mechanical necessity. He started with the simple question: 'What is it that makes old-age and death possible?' And the answer was: 'On account of being born, we suffer old-age and death!' Similarly, birth is dependent on the process of becoming, and this process would not have been set in motion, if there had not been a will to live and a clinging to the corresponding forms of life. This clinging is due to craving, due to unquenchable 'thirst' after the objects of sense-enjoyment, and this again is conditioned by feeling (by discerning agreeable and disagreeable sensations). Feeling, on the other hand, is only possible by the contact of the senses with their corresponding objects. The senses are based on a psycho-physical organism, and the latter can only arise if there is consciousness! Consciousness, however, in the individually limited form of ours, is conditioned by individual, egocentric activity (during countless previous forms of existence), and such activity is only possible as long as we are caught in the illusion of our separate egohood.

The twelvefold formula of Dependent Origination has rightly been represented as a circle, because it has neither a beginning nor an end. Each link represents the sum total of all other links and is the precondition as well as the outcome of all other links. The Commentaries generally distribute the formula over three consecutive existences, so that the first two links (*avidyā* and *saṁskāra*) correspond to the past, the last two links (birth and death) to the future, and the remaining links (3–10) to the present existence. This shows that *avidyā* and *saṁskāra*

[1] The cave-temples of *Ajanta* (second century B.C. until seventh century A.D.) contained such a Wheel of Life, fragments of which were still to be seen when I visited these caves some years ago. At that time they were generally mistaken for a representation of the zodiac, which likewise is divided into twelve compartments. Sarat Chandra Das mentions in his Tibetan Dictionary a Tibetan tractate (*rten-ḥbrel-gyi-ḥkhor-lo-mi-ḥdra-ba-bco-rgyad*) which, as the title says, contains eighteen different descriptions of the 'Wheel of Life as illustrations of the *pratītyasamutpāda*. The earliest of these illustrations is said to be the work of *Nāgārjuna*, according to the *bsTan-ḥgyur*, *go* 32.

represent the same process, which in the present existence is differentiated into eight phases, and which for the future existence is hinted at by the words 'birth, old-age and death'. In other words, the same process is described once from the standpoint of higher knowledge (1 and 2), another time from the point of view of a psychological analysis (3–10), and a third time from the point of view of a physiological phenomenon (11 and 12). In order to understand this, we must keep in mind the original question of the Buddha, which starts from the plane of the concrete physical existence, i.e., from the problem of old-age, death and birth, and slowly goes deeper: first into the realm of psychology and finally into that of spiritual reality, which reveals the illusoriness of the ego-concept, and thus the nature of ignorance and its karmic consequences.

It is actually of no great importance, whether we distribute the formula of Dependent Origination over three consecutive existences or over three consecutive moments or periods within one and the same life, because, according to the teachings of the *Abhidharma*, 'birth and death' is a process which takes place in every moment of our life.[1]

This formula, therefore, is neither concerned with an abstract-logical, nor with a purely temporal causality, but with the interdependence of various conditions, with a living, organic correlation, which

[1] More about this in my *The Psychological Attitude of Early Buddhist Philosophy, Patna University, 1937*; Rider & Co., 1961.

The following table may be useful in showing at a glance the temporal and causal connexions and aspects of the twelve links of the formula of Dependent Origination, according to *Abhidhamma* tradition:

Time-Aspect	Links of the *Pratītyasamutpāda*	Causal Aspect
Past	1. Ego-Illusion (*avidyā*) 2. Karma-Formations (*saṁskāra*)	Karmic Cause
Present	3. Consciousness (*vijñāna*) 4. Mind and Body (*nāma-rūpa*) 5. Sense-Organs (*ṣaḍāyatana*) 6. Contact (*sparśa*) 7. Feeling (*vedanā*)	Karmic Effect
	8. Craving (*tṛṣṇā*) 9. Clinging (*upādāna*) 10. Becoming (*bhava*)	Karmic Cause
Future	11. (Re-)Birth (*jāti*) 12. Old-Age, Death (*jarā-maraṇa*)	Karmic Effect

can be interpreted as a succession in time, as well as a timeless or simultaneous co-existence and interpenetration of all its factors and phenomena.

All phases of this Dependent Origination are phenomena of the same illusion, the illusion of egohood. By overcoming this illusion, we step beyond the circle in which we imprisoned ourselves, and we realize that no thing and no being can exist in itself or for itself, but that each form of life has the whole universe as its basis and that therefore the meaning of individual form can only be found in its relationship to the whole.

The moment in which the human individual becomes conscious of this universality, he ceases to identify himself with the limits of his temporal embodiment and feels flooded with the fullness of life, in which the distinction between past, present and future does not exist any more. From the depth of this experience *Milarepa* could sing:

> '*Accustomed, as I've been, to meditating on this life and the future life as one,*
> *I have forgot the dread of birth and death.*'[1]

This fearlessness is the characteristic quality of a *Bodhisattva*, who – because he himself is free from the illusion of birth and death – is willing to descend into the suffering world of mortals, in order to spread the happy tidings of final liberation from the fetters of karmic bondage.

8

THE PRINCIPLE OF POLARITY IN THE SYMBOLISM OF THE SIX REALMS AND OF THE FIVE *DHYĀNI-BUDDHAS*

In accordance with his various functions, *Avalokiteśvara* assumes a different form in each realm of the *saṁsāric* world:

In the heavenly world he appears under the name 'the Powerful One of the Hundred Blessings' (Tib.: *dbaṅ-po-brgya-byin*) in the form of a *white* Buddha;

in the hellish regions of the purgatory he appears under the name '*Dharma-rāja*' (Tib.: *chos-kyi-rgyal-po*) in the form of a *smoke-coloured* Buddha;

[1] *Tibet's Great Yogi Milarepa*, p. 246. Translated by Lama Kazi Dawa Samdup, edited by W. Y. Evans-Wentz, Oxford University Press, London, 1928.

in the human world he appears under the name 'the Lion of the *Śākyas*' (Tib.: *śā-kya-seṅge*) in the form of a *yellow* Buddha;

in the *Preta*-world he appears under the name 'Flaming Mouth' (Tib.: *kha-ḥbar-ma*) in the form of a *red* Buddha;

in the *asuric* world of Titans he appears under the name of 'the Heroic-Good One' (Tib.: *thag-bzaṅ-ris*=Skt.: *vīrabhadra*) in the form of a *green* Buddha;

and in the animal kingdom he appears under the name 'the Steadfast Lion' (Tib.: *seṅge-rab-brtan*) in the form of a *blue* Buddha.

The colours contained in this list are those of the generally accepted iconographical tradition, as found in *thaṅkas* and temple-frescoes (like the one reproduced on p. 237). This tradition has given rise to the misunderstanding that the colours of these Buddhas correspond to the colour-radiations which emanate from each of these realms.[1] This, however, is not the case. The colours of the Buddhas are completely independent and, as far as possible, different from those of the realms in which they appear (with the exception of the highest and the lowest realms, which do not possess any colour in the strictest sense of the word, and represent in their pure contrast between light and darkness, white and black, the extreme limits of the possibilities of mundane existence).

Besides, there can be no doubt that these Buddha-figures represent a later iconographical development and were subsequently inserted into the original Wheel of Life in order to illustrate the activity of *Avalokiteśvara* in the six realms of existence. This could therefore not have any influence upon the original symbolism of the six realms. To make the body-colours of the Buddhas the starting-point or basis of the symbolism of the Wheel of Life, would result in a complete reversal of the whole system of relations and of its logical, historical, and ideological development. The very fact that the text of the *Bardo Thödol* mentions only the names but not the colours of the Buddhas of the six realms, shows that these colours were not regarded as essential or as part of the original system.

The fundamental symbolism rests on the principle of polarity, as

[1] Lama Kazi Dawa Samdup, for instance, is of the opinion that the colours of the six realms should correspond to the colours of the Buddhas appearing in these realms, namely, *deva-loka*: white, *asura-loka*: green, human world: yellow, animal world: blue, *preta-loka*: red, hells: smoke-coloured or black. Without giving any reasons for this, he declares that 'the Block-Print is wrong in all save the first and last; and the MS. is wrong in assigning dull blue to the human and black or smoke-coloured to the animal world. (*The Tibetan Book of the Dead*, p. 124, n. 2.) Proceeding from this arbitrary presupposition, Lama Dawa Samdup replaces the version of the officially recognized Block-Print by a colour-symbolism of his own choice. It is therefore necessary to lay bare the original principles of this symbolism in accordance with the authorized and generally accepted Tibetan text, if we want to gain a deeper psychological understanding.

can be seen from the *Bardo Thödol*'s description of colours, psychological causes, conditions and qualities of the six realms and of their relationship to the qualities and radiations of the five *Dhyāni-Buddhas*.

The text says that on the first day of the experiencing of reality in the after-death state (*chos-ñid bar-do*) the deep-blue light of the *Dharmadhātu*-Wisdom radiates from the heart of *Vairocana* with such power that the eyes are blinded. 'At the same time the dull white light of the gods (*lhaḥi-ḥod dkar-po bkrag-med*) shines upon you. Due to the power of bad *karma* the radiant blue light causes you fear and the desire to flee, while the dull white light of the gods pleases you.' – 'Do not get attached to it; do not be weak! If, due to overwhelming delusion (*gti-mug drag-pa*) you give in to this attachment, you will go to the realm of the *devas* and, getting involved in the rounds of the six worlds, you will be diverted from the path of liberation.'

On the second day of the 'Bardo of Reality', it is said that the radiant white light of the Mirror-like Wisdom emanates from the heart of *Vajrasattva* (*-Akṣobhya*), and that at the same time there appears the dull, smoke-coloured light of the purgatory (*dmyal-baḥi-ḥod du-kha bkrag-med*). 'Due to the power of hatred (*źe-sdaṅ-gi dbaṅ-gis*) you will be frightened by the radiant white light and desire to flee, while you feel attracted by the dull, smoke-coloured light of the hells. – If you allow yourself to be attracted by it, you will fall into hellish worlds and suffer unbearable tortures, and for long you will be detained from the path of liberation.'

On the third day the radiant yellow light of the Wisdom of Equality emanates from the heart of *Ratnasambhava*, and simultaneously there appears the dull blue light of the human state of existence (*miḥi-ḥod sṅon-po bkrag-med*). 'Due to the power of pride (*ṅa-rgyal-gyi dbaṅ-gis*) you will then be frightened by the radiant yellow light [of the Wisdom of Equality] and try to flee from it, while you feel attracted by the dull blue light of the human world. If you allow yourself to be attracted by it, you will be reborn in the human realm (*miḥi gnas*) and you will have to endure the sufferings of birth, old-age, illness and death.'

On the fourth day the radiant red light of the Distinguishing Wisdom will emanate from the heart of *Amitābha*, and simultaneously there appears the dull yellow light of the *Pretas* (*yi-dvags-kyi ḥod ser-po bkrag-med-pa*). 'Due to the power of passionate craving (*ḥdod-chags draṅ-poḥi dbaṅ-gis*) you will then feel frightened by the radiant red light of the Distinguishing Wisdom and wish to flee from it, while you feel attracted by the dull yellow light of the *Pretas*. – If you allow yourself to be attracted by it, you will fall into the realm of the *Pretas* (*yi-dvags-kyi-gnas*) and suffer unbearable tortures through hunger and thirst.' (This realm may therefore be called 'the world of hungry spirits' – hunger and thirst being the symbols of unquenchable craving and lust for life.)

On the fifth day the radiant green light of the All-Accomplishing Wisdom emanates from the heart of *Amoghasiddhi*, and simultaneously there appears the dull red light of the *Asuras* (*lha-ma-yin-gyi ḥod dmar-po bkrag-med-pa*). 'Due to violent envy (*phrag-dog-drag-pos*) you will then be frightened by the radiant green light of the All-Accomplishing Wisdom and try to flee from it, while you will feel attracted by the dull red light of the *Asuras*. – If you allow yourself to be attracted by it, you will fall into the realm of the *Asuras* (*lha-ma-yin-gyi-gnas*) and suffer unspeakable miseries of strife and warfare.'

On the sixth day appear the radiant lights of the combined Five Wisdoms of the *Dhyāni-Buddhas*, the protective deities (the gate-keepers of the *maṇḍala*) and the Buddhas of the Six Realms (whose names we mentioned at the beginning of this chapter). 'Simultaneously with the radiant lights of the combined five Wisdoms appear the dull lights of the six realms (*rigs drug*): White from the *Devas*, red from the *Asuras*, blue from the humans, green from the animals, yellow from the *Pretas*, and smoke-coloured from the hells.' This emphatically repeated statement of the colours associated with the six realms should remove any possible doubts in this matter.

On the seventh day there appears the fivefold radiance of the 'Knowledge-Holding Deities' together with the dull green light of the animal-world (*dud-ḥgroḥi-ḥod ljaṅ-khu bkrag-med*). 'Due to the power of illusory attachments (*chags-ḥkhrul-paḥi dbaṅ-gis*), you will be frightened by the brilliance of the fivefold radiance and wish to flee from it, while you will feel attracted by the dull light. – If you allow yourself to be attracted by it, you will sink into the spiritual darkness (*gti-mug*) of the animal kingdom (*dud-ḥgroḥi gnas*) and suffer infinite miseries of bondage, dumbness, and torpor.'

As we see from this summary of the Tibetan text, the principle of polarity is not only applied to the symbolism of the six realms and their juxtaposition in the Wheel of Life, but also to the relationship between the qualities and Wisdoms of the *Dhyāni-Buddhas* and the psychological causes of the six states of existence.

Beings who are not in tune with the spiritual qualities of the *Dhyāni-Buddhas*, shrink back from the latter's pure radiance and are attracted by those realms of existence which correspond to their own qualities and are diametrically opposed to those of the *Dhyāni-Buddhas* in question. The symbolism of 'lights' or of colour-radiations, which appear side by side in each phase (designated as 'day' in our text) of the experience of reality, can therefore not be of equal or similar colours (as, for instance, a radiant green besides a dull green – as

Lama Dawa Samdup tries to maintain), but simultaneously with the radiant light of each *Dhyāni-Buddha* there always appears the dull light of an opposite or (if that is not possible) totally different colour. (Since there are six realms, but only five *Dhyāni-Buddhas* to counteract them, an absolute polarity is not possible.) The forces of the *Dhyāni-Buddhas* are thus the remedies for the elimination of the five poisons – delusion, hatred, greed, envy, and pride – the causes of worldly or *saṁsāric* states of existence. The Buddhas are therefore called the great healers or physicians of mind and soul (Tib.: *bcom-ldan-ḥdas-sman-bla*, which has led to the ugly but often used expression 'Medicine Buddhas'. They are in reality none other than the *Dhyāni-Buddhas* in eight different *mudrās* and colours, and conceived as exponents of the highest powers of healing or salvation from the ills of the world protecting us in the eight directions of space.)

According to the prevalence of the one or the other of these five poisons, beings are reborn in the one or the other realm of existence. Ignorance of the illusory nature of worldly happiness and of the transiency of individual existence (even in its highest forms), is the characteristic feature of the world of gods, while hatred, which leads to the opposite extreme, is the main cause for a hellish existence. The characteristic quality of the human form of existence is pride, ego-conceit (Skt.: *asmi-māna*), while the helpless bondage to insatiable craving (Skt.: *rāga*) is characteristic for the *Preta*-world. The main quality of the ever-fighting and quarrelling *Asuras* is envy (Skt.: *īrṣā*), while in the animal-world delusion, ignorance in its grossest form (Skt.: *avidyā*, *moha*) prevail, on account of a less developed consciousness and the lack of intellectual faculties (reflection, reasoning, logic, thinking, etc.).

The means for the annihilation of these 'five poisons' are the five Wisdoms of the *Dhyāni-Buddhas*. The *Dharmadhātu*-Wisdom, which reveals the realm of highest reality, eliminates the illusion of the *Devas* and the desire for such a form of existence; the unshakable and impartial equanimity of the Mirror-like Wisdom, which shows things and beings in their true nature (Skt.: *yathābhūtam*), annihilates hatred, which leads to hellish forms of existence; the Wisdom of the essential Equality of all beings destroys the ego-conceit of the human form of existence; the Wisdom of Discriminating Vision eliminates passionate craving, which leads to the *Preta*-world; and the profound compassion and loving kindness of the All-Accomplishing Wisdom eliminates envy, which leads to the *Asura*-world.

Thus:

(1) *Vairocana*'s deep-blue radiance counteracts the dull white light of the *Devas* (—1);

(2) *Vajrasattva-Akṣobhya's* white radiance counteracts the blackish or smoke-coloured light of the purgatories (—2);

(3) *Ratnasambhava's* yellow radiance counteracts the dull blue light of the human world (—3);

(4) *Amitābha's* red radiance counteracts the dull yellow light of the *Preta*-world (—4);

(5) *Amoghasiddhi's* green radiance counteracts the dull red light of the *Asura*-world (—5).[1]

The spiritual torpor of the animal world (—6) is counteracted by the five-coloured radiations of the Knowledge-Holding Deities (*rig-ḥdzin-gyi-lha-tshogs*).

Thus the principle of polarity extends to all planes of spiritual activity, beginning with the realms of existence, in which

(—1) heavenly joy and hellish torture (—2),
(—3) human activity and powerless craving (—4),
(—5) titanic power and animal fear (—6),

are opposed to each other like the corresponding

(—1) dull white and dull black (—2),
(—3) dull blue and dull yellow (—4),
(—5) dull red and dull green (—6),

until we come to the mutual interaction of transcendental factors, supramundane visions and worldly states of existence, qualities and colour-radiations of *Dhyāni-Buddhas* and those of the Six Realms.

All these relations are illustrated in the diagram, reproduced on the opposite page. It demonstrates the inner relationship of the Great Six-Syllabled Mantra to the six realms of existence, the subject of the following chapter.

9

THE RELATIONSHIP OF THE SIX SACRED SYLLABLES TO THE SIX REALMS

NOTHING has done more harm to the progress of Tibetology than the overbearing attitude of those scholars who could see in Tibetans nothing more than a people steeped in primitive shamanism and superstitious fear, a people 'whose practical religion

[1] The positive numbers indicate the lights of the *Dhyāni-Buddhas* in the sequence of their appearance in the '*Bardo Thödol*'. The negative numbers indicate the simultaneously appearing dull lights emanating from the Six Realms. The light of the animal-world (—6) appears in the *Bardo* on the seventh day.

RELATIONSHIP OF THE DHYĀNI-BUDDHAS AND THE SIX SACRED SYLLABLES TO THE SIX REALMS OF THE SAMSARIC WORLD

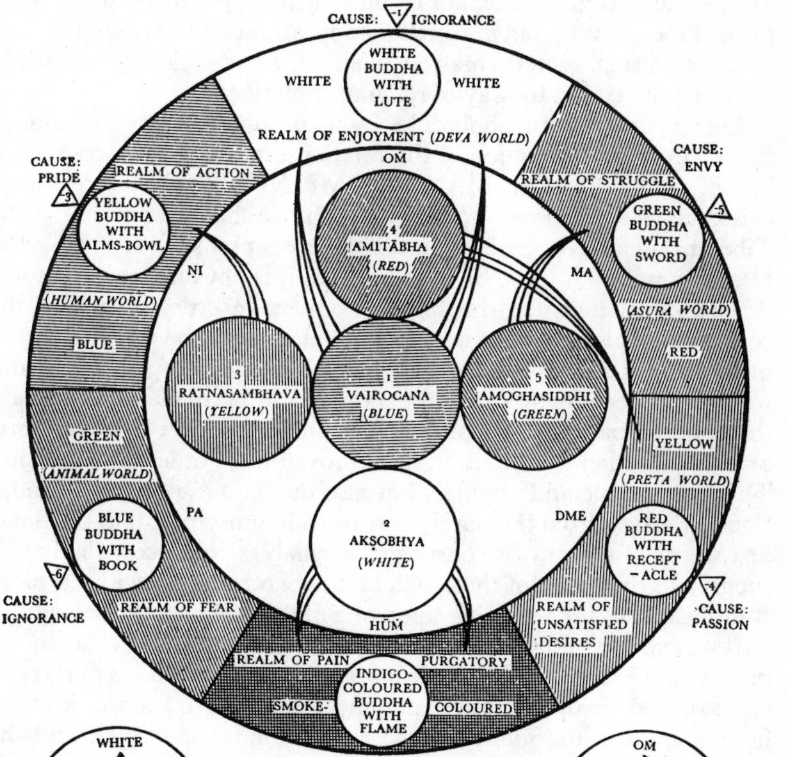

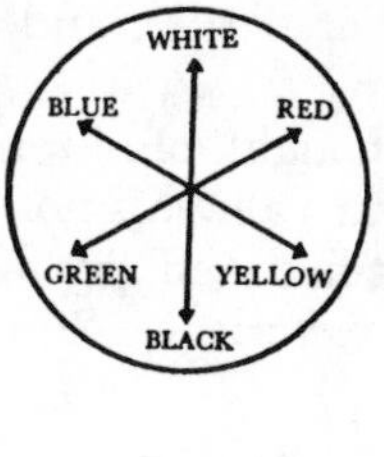

Complementary arrangement of the colours of the Six Realms

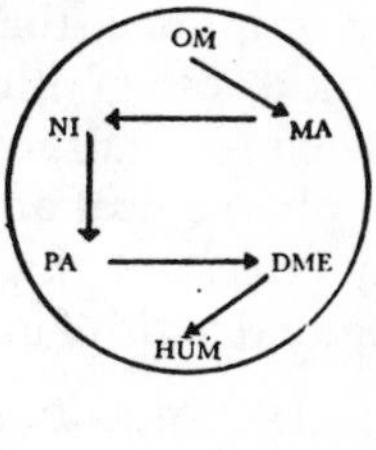

Way of the Mantra through the Six Realms

chiefly consists in the performance of certain rites and ceremonies',[1] 'whose mysticism is a silly mummery of unmeaning jargon and "magic circles" ',[2] 'whose philosophy makes but a mockery of truth, by identifying it with a negation of reality',[3] and 'whose Yoga is a parasite, whose monster outgrowth crushed and cankered most of the little life of purely Buddhist stock yet left in the *Mahāyāna*'.[4]

Scholars who were biased by such prejudices, while trying to translate and to interpret Tibetan literature, could neither understand nor appreciate its significance, nor communicate anything of the spiritual life of Tibet, as revealed in its religion, its art, and its philosophy – not to mention such esoteric matters like mantric tradition, which could only be understood by way of religious practice.

Even so deserving a scholar like Jäschke is unable to see any sense in the Tibetan interpretation of the relationship of the six sacred syllables of the mantra OṀ MAṆI PADME HŪṀ to the six realms of existence. He dismisses the matter with the following words: 'The Tibetans themselves are ignorant of the proper sense of these six syllables, if sense at all there be in them, and it is not unlikely that some shrewd priest invented this form of prayer, in order to furnish the common people with a formula or symbol, easily to be retained by the memory, and the frequent recital of which might satisfy their religious wants. – The numerous attempts that have been made to explain the Ommanipadmehum satisfactorily, and to discover a deeper sense or even a hidden wisdom in it, have proved more or less unsuccessful. The most simple and popular, but also the flattest, of these explanations is derived from the purely extrinsic circumstance, that the Sanskrit words of the prayer consist of six syllables, and accordingly it is suggested, that each of these syllables, when pronounced by a pious Buddhist, conveys a blessing upon one of the "six classes of beings".'[5]

If we want to understand the thoughts and feelings of a Tibetan, we must first of all put aside our own opinions and prejudices and try to enter the sphere of religious experience, from which the words of the holy scriptures, the sounds of the *mantras*, the sacred rites, and the attitude of the faithful derive their meaning.

Then we shall see that the logic of syllogistic thought, of historical and philological analysis, of abstract concepts and values, is not the only one, and that there exists an equally justified and far more profound logic of growth in the realm of spiritual experience. 'First of

[1] Jäschke: *Tibetan-English Dictionary*, p. 607.
[2] Waddell: *Lamaism*, p. 15.
[3] Jäschke: op. cit., p. 271.
[4] Waddell: op. cit., p. 14.
[5] H. A. Jäschke: op. cit., p. 607.

all we should not forget,' as Otto Strauss says in his classical work on Indian Philosophy, 'that spiritual practice can never be understood properly from books alone. Experiences ought to be experienced, or at least be understood by a psychology, the like of which Europe has only just now begun to explore.'

It is not the flatness or superficiality of Tibetan thought which used purely external circumstances in order to establish a relationship between the six syllables of the formula and the six realms of existence, but it is the inner nature of *Avalokiteśvara*, which made such an interpretation possible and raised the significance of each syllable to such heights. In other words, it is the experience-content which gives meaning to a *mantra*, and not the original or philological word-meaning.

A merely historical or philological interpretation of a *mantra* is indeed the most superficial and senseless way of looking at it, since it takes the shell for the kernel and the shadow for the substance; because words are not dead things, which we toss at each other like coins and which we can put away, lock up in a safe or bury underground, and which we can take out again unchanged, even after centuries, when it pleases us. They are rather like symbols or hieroglyphs of a steadily growing and expanding consciousness and field of experience. They are what we make of them and what we bring to them by way of associations, either consciously or unconsciously.

Just as *Avalokiteśvara* descends into the world, and as each ray of his compassion is like a helping hand stretched out towards those in need of help, so each syllable of his *mantra* is filled with the power and devotion of his love. It is therefore perfectly natural that the six sacred syllables are conceived in juxtaposition to the six realms, whose sufferings they are meant to relieve by liberating the beings from their illusions and attachments. For those who open themselves to the power of the *mantra*, i.e., for those who not only believe in its efficacy, but who fill it with the power of their own devotion, it is not sufficient to keep in mind their own salvation only, but they must likewise be moved by the desire to contribute to the possibilities of liberation of all other living beings.

For this reason the *Sādhaka* – after having traversed the various planes and stages of spiritual reality, contained in the *mantra* – turns his mind towards the different classes of beings, and while pronouncing each of the six sacred syllables, he directs his attention on one of the six realms.

Thus each syllable becomes a vehicle for the realization of the compassionate power of *Avalokiteśvara*, and at the same time the *Sādhaka* becomes conscious of the unsatisfactory nature of each of these states of existence. Therefore it is said that when one recites the sacred formula with a sincere heart, this will not only be a blessing for all living beings, but it will at the same time close the gates of rebirth in those realms for the *Sādhaka*. Because states of existence, which arouse our compassion, have lost their attraction for us, however great our sympathy may be. That, from which we wish to liberate others, can no more be the object of our desire.

Thus, while uttering OṀ, we direct our mind upon the world of gods, who are enmeshed in the illusion of their own permanence and perfection; and while opening for them the gates of liberation by the power of this *mantra*, we shut for ourselves the entrance into this realm of rebirth.

In a similar way we direct our mind upon the beings of the other realms: while uttering 'MA', upon those of the *Asura*-world who, driven by envy, are engaged in a perpetual struggle against the powers of light; while uttering 'ṆI', upon the world of men, who are blinded by ego-conceit. While uttering 'PA', we direct our mind upon the realm of animals, moving about in spiritual darkness and dumbness; while uttering 'DME' we direct it upon the hungry spirits of the *Preta*-world; and while uttering 'HŪṀ', we send our compassionate thoughts to all those beings, who endure hellish tortures in the deepest abyss of existence.

Thus OṀ MAṆI PADME HŪṀ embodies the happy tidings of liberation, of the love towards all living beings, and of the Way that leads to final realization. In uttering these sacred syllables in all sincerity and in full awareness of their meaning, the radiant figure of the Great Compassionate arises in the heart of the *Sādhaka*, transforms his mortal body into the *Nirmāṇakāya* of *Avalokiteśvara* and fills his mind with the boundless light of *Amitābha*. Then the horrors of *Saṁsāra* change into the sounds of the six syllables. Therefore it is said in the *Bardo Thödol* that, if in the moment of the Great Recognition in the intermediate state between death and rebirth 'the primordial sound of Reality reverberates like thousandfold thunder, may it happen that it is transformed into the sound of the Six Syllables'.

And likewise we read in the *Śūraṅgama Sūtra*: 'How sweetly mysterious is the transcendental sound of *Avalokiteśvara*. It is the 'primordial sound of the universe' (the pure Brahman Sound). It is the subdued murmur of the sea-tide setting inward. Its mysterious sound brings liberation and peace to all sentient beings, who in their distress are calling for aid; it brings a sense of permanency to those who are truly seeking the attainment of *Nirvāṇa's* peace.'

The deep devotion with which this hopeful message was accepted and taken to heart by the people of Tibet, is demonstrated by the innumerable rock-inscriptions and votive-stones, on which the sacred formula of *Avalokiteśvara* (Tib.: *spyan-ras-gzigs*, pron. 'chä-ray-zee', with the accent on the first syllable) is millionfold engraved. It is on the lips of all pilgrims, it is the last prayer of the dying and the hope of the living. It is the eternal melody of Tibet, which the faithful hears in the murmuring of brooks, in the thundering of waterfalls and in the howling of storms, just as it greets him from rocks and *maṇi*-stones, which accompany him everywhere, on wild caravan tracks and on lofty passes. Thus he knows himself always to be in the presence of the Enlightened Ones and is conscious of the precious jewel which awaits its awakening in the lotus of his heart. Life and death, dangers and troubles, become immaterial in such an exalted presence, and the eternal dissonance between *saṁsāra* and *nirvāṇa* fades away in the light of this knowledge.

And out of the deepest conviction he would repeat the words which in the *Kāraṇḍa-vyūha* are spoken by the *Bodhisattva Sarva-nīvaraṇa-viśkambhin*, 'the Remover of all Hindrances': 'To him, who would give me the Great Wisdom of the Six Syllables, I would present the four continents of the world filled with sevenfold jewels. And if he could not find birch-bark to write upon, nor ink and paper, he should make ink out of my blood, take my skin instead of birch-bark, split one of my bones and make it into a pen. And all this would not cause pain to my body. He would be to me like father and mother and the most venerable of venerables.'[1]

[1] *Avalokiteśvara-guṇa-kāraṇḍa-vyūha*, published under the title: '*Kāraṇḍa Byūha*, a work on the Doctrines and Customs of the Buddhists' edited by Satya Bratu Samasrami, Calcutta, 1873

Epilogue and Synthesis

ĀḤ
THE PATH OF ACTION

Plate 7

AMOGHASIDDHI
who embodies the All-Accomplishing Wisdom

I

AMOGHASIDDHI: THE LORD OF THE ALL-ACCOMPLISHING WISDOM

We have dealt, one by one, with the *Dhyāni-Buddhas Vairocana, Ratnasambhava, Amitābha*, and *Akṣobhya*, and with their corresponding symbols – the wheel, the jewel, the lotus, and the *vajra* – since each of them is related to one of the four main themes of the *mantra* OṀ MAṆI PADME HŪṀ. The role of the fifth *Dhyāni-Buddha, Amoghasiddhi*, we have only touched in passing. Yet he too is contained in our *mantra*, though in a less obvious way; for, if OṀ represents the Way of Universality, MAṆI the way of Unity and Equality of all beings, PADMA the Way of Unfolding Vision, and HŪṀ the Way of Integration – then it must be said, that behind all of them stands the act of realization, the mysterious spiritual power (Skt.: *siddhi*), which not only encourages us to proceed on the chosen way, but which transforms us while proceeding, until we ourselves have become the aim of our striving. This again shows that the teaching of the Buddha is not some nebulous idealism, a chasing after eternal but unattainable ideals, but a doctrine of self-realization, of action, a practical doctrine, a path that can be trodden by all who are seriously bent on its aim.

The idea of the Way, of going, of movement, was from the start one of the basic features of Buddhism, as we may see from expressions like 'the eightfold path' (*aṣṭāṅgika-mārga*), the 'middle way' (*madhyamā pratipad*), the small and the big 'vehicle' (*hīnayāna, mahāyāna*), the 'crossing of the stream' or the sea to the 'other shore' (*pāragataṁ*), the 'entering into the stream of liberation' (*sotāpatti*), the Buddha as one who has 'thus come' or 'thus gone' (*tathāgata*), etc. In these expressions the dynamic character of Buddhism is revealed, and in no other *Dhyāni-Buddha* is this more strongly emphasized than in *Amoghasiddhi*. While *Akṣobhya* embodies the reflective clarity of a perfectly stilled consciousness, or the 'Wisdom of the Great Mirror', *Ratnasambhava* the deep feeling of the solidarity of all beings, and *Amitābha* the inner vision, through which the illusory nature of 'I' and 'world' is revealed – *Amoghasiddhi* converts these experiences and their resulting knowledge into action, into the perfect deed, the deed of ultimate perfection, which makes the adept into an Enlightened One. Then the power of his will which for so long fettered him to the restless cycle of rebirths, is transformed into the spontaneous, purpose-free action of the saint, the *Bodhisattva*, whose life is no more based on the thirst for existence, but on all-embracing compassion – whose body is converted into the 'Body of Transformation' (*nirmāṇakāya*), the sacred vessel of perfection – whose mind is the Mind of all the Buddhas, and whose speech becomes the wakening sound, the expression of highest wisdom (*dharma*) and of mantric power.

Amoghasiddhi is the *Dhyāni-Buddha* of the fulfilment and realization of the *Bodhisattva*-Path, the *Dhyāni-Buddha* of the *Nirmāṇakāya* par excellence, in whom the *Sambhogakāya* and the *Dharmakāya* have taken visible shape and have become a living presence. This unique position of *Amoghasiddhi* explains that strange statement in the *Bardo Thödol*, in which it is said that on the sixth day only the radiances of the combined *four* Wisdoms appear, in spite of the presence of the complete *maṇḍalas* of the five *Dhyāni-Buddhas* and their retinue. 'The green light of the All-Accomplishing Wisdom', we are told, 'will *not* shine upon you, since the faculties of spiritual perception (or wisdom) are not yet perfectly developed.' This clearly shows that the realization of *Amoghasiddhi's* All-Accomplishing Wisdom is the ultimate and highest step of the path to enlightenment within the realm of human embodiment.

This is also expressed in *Amoghasiddhi's viśva-vajra*, which is an intensification of *Akṣobhya's vajra*, not merely in the sense of a reduplication, but in that of a new perspective, a new plane of activity, a new dimension. The Inner Way of *Vajrasattva*, according to the *Bardo Thödol*, consists in the combination of the rays of the Wisdoms of the above-mentioned four *Dhyāni-Buddhas* and in their absorption within one's own heart – in other words, in the recognition that all these radiances are the emanations of one's own mind in a state of perfect tranquillity and serenity, a state in which the mind reveals its true universal nature. This Inner Way leads into the mystery of *Amoghasiddhi*, in which the inner and the outer world, the visible and the invisible, are united, and in which the spiritual takes bodily shape, and the body becomes an exponent of the spirit. For *Amoghasiddhi* is the Lord of the great transformation, whose vehicle is the winged man, the man in transition towards a new dimension of consciousness. He is the Lord of the element 'air' or 'wind', the principle of motion, of living breath, of life-force. In this quality he merges with the figure of *Amitāyus*, the emanation of *Amitābha* in the centre of the *maṇḍala* of the Knowledge-Holding Deities, under the name 'the Lotus-Lord of Dance'. This *maṇḍala* is visualized in the Throat Centre.

The meaning of this 'dance' may be elucidated by a chapter of the *Śūraṅgama Sūtra*, in which various *Bodhisattvas* describe their way towards spiritual awakening. Each of them was led towards liberation by practising concentration upon a certain object of meditation: one through concentration upon the element 'Earth', another by concentrating upon the element 'Water', a third one through contemplating the element 'Fire', a fourth through the element 'Air'. The latter, the *Bodhisattva-Mahāsattva Vejurya*, embodies more or less the features of *Amoghasiddhi* and reveals the essential character of this element as the dynamic principle at the basis of all life and existence.

'In my practice of *Dhyāna* I concentrated on this and reflected on how the great world was upheld in space, on how the great world was kept in perpetual motion, on how my body was kept in motion, moving and standing, on the rhythmic vibration of its life established and maintained by breathing, upon the movement of the mind, thoughts rising and passing. I reflected upon these various things and marvelled at their great sameness without any difference save in the rate of vibration. I realized that the nature of these vibrations had neither any source for their coming, nor destination for their going, and that all sentient beings as numerous as the infinitesimal particles of dust in the vast spaces, were each in his own way topsy-turvy balanced vibrations, and that each and everyone was obsessed with the illusion that he was a unique creation.'[1]

This almost sounds like a modern world-description, based on the latest discoveries of nuclear physics, and may give us an idea of the profundity of the inner vision of which people in a distant past were capable, and which only now we begin to appreciate – without, however, being able to draw the last consequences from these discoveries, which defy all our notions of the substantiality and reality of our 'material' world.

In the somewhat clumsy dialectics of the *Prajñāpāramitā Sūtras*, the Buddhist thinkers of India have drawn the epistemological conclusions, which however went so far beyond the capacity of human language, that the scholars of that time were compelled to take refuge in paradoxes, beyond which no further philosophical development was possible. The human mind had arrived at the boundaries of thought.

Thus only the way beyond thought remained: the way of an extended or enlarged consciousness, reaching beyond the frontiers of

[1] Translated from the Chinese by Bhikshu Wai-tao and Dwight Goddard, in *A Buddhist Bible*, p. 243.

discursive thought into the realm of intuitive experience through inner vision (*dhyāna*) and spiritual unification (*yoga*). The language of discursive thought was replaced by the language of sound-symbols, in which the vibrations of light and sound were combined in a scale of new experience-values and became mutually exchangeable.

This is demonstrated by the amalgamation of *Amitābha* and *Amoghasiddhi*, the exponents of mystic vision and mystic sound in the Centre of the Knowledge-Holding Deities, in the process of realizing the Inner Path of *Vajrasattva*. In this Centre the *prāṇa* of *Amoghasiddhi*, rising from the Root Centre, becomes the principle of spiritual life and the vibration of mantric sounds – just as *Amitābha's* infinity of light-pervaded consciousness is converted in this Centre into *Amitāyus's* infinity of life.

These things can only be hinted at, but not explained in their deepest meaning. One thing, however, should become clear from our discussion, namely, that the nature of *Amoghasiddhi* presupposes the experience of the other *Dhyāni-Buddhas*, since *Amoghasiddhi* dynamically unites many essential qualities of the former. (We already mentioned the mysterious dark green of *Amoghasiddhi*, which unites the blue of *Akṣobhya*, as well as the blue radiance of *Vairocana's Dharmadhātu*-Wisdom, with the yellow light of *Ratnasambhava's* Wisdom of Equality.)

The four *Dhyāni-Buddhas* of the periphery of the *maṇḍala* become here representatives of *Rinzai's* fourfold contemplation.[1] In the Wisdom of the Great Mirror we destroy the subject (and the subjective conception of the world) in favour of the object (the objective 'suchness');[2] in the Wisdom of Equality we destroy the object (the separating differentiation of the outer world of appearance) in favour of the subject (the living being); in the analytical Wisdom of Inner Vision we destroy the subject and the object (in the final experience of *śūnyatā*); and in the All-Accomplishing Wisdom we neither destroy the subject nor the object, i.e., we have reached that ultimate freedom, in which we, like the Buddha after his enlightenment, can return into the world for the benefit of all living beings, and this without danger to ourselves, because we do not cling any more to the world. Then 'the mountains are for us again mountains, and the

[1] *Rinzai's* 'fourfold contemplation' (*Katto-Shu*, part II, folio No. 27b–28a), quoted by Ohasama-Faust in *Zen, der lebendige Buddhismus in Japan*, Perthes A.G., Gotha, Stuttgart, 1925, p. 45.

[2] In the *Vijñaptimātra-siddhi-śāstra*, X, we find the following definition: 'The consciousness which is connected with the Knowledge of the Great Mirror reflects the characteristics of all objects clearly and correctly—just as a big mirror reflects the images of various forms (*rūpa*).' (Jiryo Masuda.)

waters again waters', as a master of meditation once said,[1] because here we have reached the last great synthesis, in which the perfect emptiness (*śūnyatā*) and the concrete reality of the world are grasped in their deepest sense. The Buddha's teaching does not attempt to deny the importance of differentiation in favour of absolute oneness, or to proclaim the undifferentiated equality of all things. It does not strive after the destruction or devaluation of contrasts, but after the recognition of their relativity within a unity existing simultaneously with them, within them and beyond them.[2] Each phenomenon is a unique expression of the whole, unique in its spatial, temporal, and causal position. We, therefore, can neither speak of identity, nor of non-identity, neither of 'existence' nor of 'non-existence' with regard to forms of appearance, beings, things, or conditions of life.

2

AMOGHASIDDHI'S ALL-ACCOMPLISHING WISDOM AS LIBERATION FROM THE LAW OF KARMA

AMOGHASIDDHI is the embodiment of that highest freedom, in which an Enlightened One moves through this world, without creating new karmic bonds by his actions, i.e., without the formation of egocentric tendencies (*saṁskāra*). He transforms these tendencies in the crucible of an all-encompassing love and compassion into the selfless impulse of an enlightened helper.

[1] 'A Master said: "Before one studies Zen the mountains are mountains and the waters waters to him. If, however, he gets an insight into the truth of Zen through the instruction of a good Master, then to him the mountains are no more mountains and the waters no more waters; but later on when he has really reached the abode of peace (i.e., when he has attained *satori*), the mountains are again mountains to him and the waters waters!"' (D. T. Suzuki: *Essays in Zen Buddhism*, Vol. I, p. 12.)

[2] 'The *Prajñāpāramitā* may be said to be standing on the line which divides the absolute aspect of existence from its relative aspect, and this line is a geometrical one just marking the boundary and having no dimension. Even then we must not conceive the *Prajñā* as looking this way or that way when it wants to survey the two realms of existence. If the *Prajñā* were to take *Śūnyatā* alone without its *Aśūnyatā*, or *Aśūnyatā* alone without its *Śūnyatā*, it would no more be *Prajñā*! To symbolize this, the Indian gods are furnished with one extra eye cut straight up between the two ordinary ones. This is the *Prajñā*-eye (the eye of wisdom). By means of this third eye the enlightened are enabled to perceive Reality *yathābhūtam*, without splitting it into two and then unifying them, for this splitting and unifying is the work of abstract thinking. The *Prajñā*-eye, placing itself on the boundary line of Oneness and Manyness, of *Śūnyatā* and *Aśūnyatā* . . . takes in these two worlds at a glance as one Reality.' (D. T. Suzuki: *Essays in Zen Buddhism*, Third Series, p. 269. Rider & Co., London, 1953.)

The conflict between law and free will seems to arise from the over-specialization of one particular centre of our consciousness in which the reflective and egocentric tendencies prevail. By over-emphasizing these tendencies, we forget our real nature, lose the connexion with other equally important centres, and thus the spiritual balance which is founded on the harmonious co-operation of all our inner forces is disturbed. The one-sided intellectualization of the individual does not express its real nature, but only stresses the peripheral self-consciousness, a mere by-product of the process of reasoning, which requires a fixed point of reference. But this hypothetical point of reference does not contain anything which is characteristic for the qualities of any particular individual; in fact it is the least individual feature, as it is common to all thinking beings.

Every individual represents a certain position in space and time. Even if its consciousness has become all-embracing, by breaking down all limitations (or by no more identifying itself with individual limitations), it retains the character of its position or its starting-point as a particular centre of experience.

This explains why each Buddha, in spite of the essential sameness of Buddhahood, preserves his particular character, and why even the *Dhyāni-Buddhas* are conceived as embodying or emphasizing different qualities or characteristics, and why different spacial positions are symbolically assigned to them. In this sense, individual character is not a fetter, a karmic bondage, in which the *saṁskāras* of the past hold sway over the present and the future. In an Enlightened One, the conflict between law and free will does not exist any more, because in the light of full knowledge, the own 'will' and the laws governing the universe coincide or complement each other. One's own nature, if properly understood and freed from the illusion of egohood, proves to be a modification and conscious embodiment of universal law (*dharma-kāya*) or the harmony of universal forces (a living, continual process of readjustment), as it might be called as well.

Harmony, as we know it from music, is the best example of an experience in which law and freedom are fused, and in which these expressions lose their contradictory meaning. A musician does not feel any compulsion in following the laws of musical harmony. On the contrary, the more perfect he is able to express them in his play or his compositions, the more he feels the joy of creative freedom. He is no more a slave to law, but its master, because he has understood and realized it so profoundly, as to become one with it and to make it the most perfect expression of his own being. Through knowledge we master the law, and by mastering it, it ceases to be necessity, but becomes an instrument of real self-expression and spiritual freedom.

Only retrospectively can we conceive it as a law, i.e., under the aspect of time, of the past.

In Buddhist parlance, karma loses its power and is dissolved in the light of perfect knowledge. As long as karma remains the force of the dark and impenetrable past, it is a fixed and unalterable magnitude, which we feel as 'the power of fate', against which we struggle in vain. In the moment of profound intuition or enlightenment, the past is transformed into a *present* experience, in which all the moving forces and circumstances, all inner and outer connexions, motives, situations, causes and effects, in short the whole dependent origination, the very structure of reality, is clearly perceived. In this moment the Enlightened One becomes master of the law, the master-artist, in whom the rigid necessity of law is transformed and dissolved into the supreme freedom of harmony.

The experience of this harmony is not to be confounded with that of unqualified one-ness, absolute unity or sameness, because harmony, in spite of its all-embracing nature, does not annihilate diversity (without which unity becomes meaningless uniformity, the equivalent of dullness) and is capable of infinite variation.

Though all musical harmony is based on the same laws, there are not two composers who compose the same music. This means that individual law and creativeness are neither superseded nor absorbed by universal law, but that individual and universal law complement each other. If this were not so, there could be no justification or sufficient reason for the existence of differentiation and individuality, self-consciousness and free will.

'An element of freedom of choice pervades the Universe: how better can we describe the fact, that from the galaxies to the atom, from the amoeba to man, every individual differs from every other individual? How better describe the indeterminacy said to exist within the atom itself; the irregularity of the molecular movement of liquids and gases; the variations of movements of chromosomes; the variability of living organisms; the variation in the modes of giving effect to their instincts by insects and animals, of the same species; the personal variation in the chemical composition of all the tissues, and the functions of the body? How better describe the fact of the innumerable directions which life has taken; the tendency throughout the universe to diversity, variability, division; the exceptions to the general order which are apparent at every stage and in every sphere of becoming? How better record man's freedom of choice; the sentiment of freedom which we have within ourselves?'[1]

' "The universe is finite but unbounded." – It is finite in the sense

[1] **Frank Townshend, *Becoming*,** p. 88. **Allen &** Unwin ,London, 1939.

that it is pervaded by a hierarchy of order, outside of which it is impossible to go. It is unbounded in the sense that it is pervaded by an element of freedom of choice.'[1]

This hierarchy of order is at the same time a hierarchy of causality, a causality of different planes of existence, in which each higher plane offers a greater number of possibilities, a greater number of solutions to each problem, and hence a greater opportunity of choice, self-determination or free will.

Utilizing the simile of vibration, we might speak of different planes of vibration, or of higher and lower orders, grosser and finer mediums of vibration, etc. In the realm of solid, inorganic matter, mechanical causality (complete or absolute determinism) prevails, because here vibration takes place on one plane only. In the realm of organic life, this determinism becomes less rigid, while in the spiritual realm, vibrations of many planes are combined: some of them determined, others not. The different realms correspond to different dimensions or different types of mathematics, of which the higher ones allow several solutions to the same problem, while the lower types confine themselves to one solution only.

The German scientist and philosopher, Alwin Mittasch, speaks of a 'gradation of causality' in nature, showing that causality is of many different grades, the highest of which is 'opposed to the simpler mechanical causality, which is fundamentally calculable, and is to be observed when a whole is somehow or other stimulated, i.e., when its total condition together with the conditions of its system are disturbed, and respond to the disturbance *actively* and *selectively* in accordance with its own store of energy.'[2]

'The concept of a gradation of impulse-causality within the totality-causation of the organism also opens up prospects of the problem of body and soul in so far as the unconscious and conscious will appear as the highest form of an impulse-causality which has here become a *directive*, *guiding* and *expanding* causality on a grand scale with continuously increasing manifoldness.'[3]

Here causality is transformed into an inner, self-regulating and self-preserving force, which may be stimulated by external happenings, but which can no more be conceived in the form of an external or general law. If we speak of causality in this case, we have to admit that it is only a retrospective mental construction, in which we try to define the continuity and coherence of an otherwise indeterminable course of actions or reactions. 'The fact of the existence of a

[1] Op. cit. p. 89.

[2] *Research and Progress*, Vol. IV, p. 239.

[3] Op. cit., p. 240 f.

gradation presents the possibility of following up the system of causation either by ascending from below or by descending from above. Viewed from below, all is cause and effect, reason and consequence; regarded from above, however, all is aim, arrangement and guidance. A genuine and universal determinism which has nothing to do with mechanical determinism, then embraces *necessity* and *liberty*, limitation and definiteness; a causation from below, or outwards, according to causal laws, and a causation from above, or inwards, according to aim and purpose, plan and sense.' (p. 240 f.)

The 'guidance' of which Mittasch speaks, naturally cannot be any outside agent or supernatural force (like a god), otherwise it could not be associated with liberty; nor can 'aim and purpose, plan and sense' be imposed from outside – but each conscious being has to create his own inner order and to give sense and meaning to his own existence and to the world which he conceives in his mind. And the only guidance that there can be, is the guidance by that inner light, the power of consciousness, which gradually through discrimination and understanding, grows into knowledge and wisdom. Even the guidance of a spiritual teacher, or Guru, consists in nothing other than the awakening of that inner light. And the clearer this light, the more perfect is the insight into the nature of reality.

If, therefore, the results of this inner knowledge become more and more similar the further we advance, it is not on account of an inherent uniformity of individual qualities or of spiritual forces in which the individual partakes passively, like a crystal in the light of the sun, but it is a positive ('intelligent') reaction, by which each individual finds his way (his own way) towards the same reality. Consciousness, as the latent spark of light, is inherent in all life, but it has many degrees of intensity and as many hues of colour as there are living beings. The more individually limited they are, the more outspoken is the 'colour' of their light. And just as each colour has its own law of vibration, so each individual creates and follows his own law. Only when the fullness of Enlightenment is attained, in which all the colours are merged and integrated into supreme splendour, the mind becomes free to vibrate in all directions, encompassing and mastering all the hierarchies of order.

Then only does it become possible, as Krishnamurti says, 'to meet an experience wholly, completely, without bias or prejudice – without being caught up in the wave of memory', in the wave of the past. 'When your action is incomplete, when you do not meet an experience fully, but through the barriers of tradition, prejudice or fear, the action is followed by the quavering of memory. As long as there is this scar of memory, there must be the division of time as past, present and future. As long as the mind is tethered to the idea that action must be divided into past, present and future, there is identification through time and therefore a continuity from which arises the fear of death, the fear of the loss of love. To understand timeless reality, timeless life, action must be complete. But you cannot be aware of this timeless reality by searching for it.'

This timeless reality is what I call 'the experience of the present', because the present has no (temporal) extension and is therefore timeless. It is the irrational boundary line between the two directions of time. The present has no extension but intensity. It knows no causality, which can only be thought of in time, but a simultaneous relationship which can exist in a spatial dimension only.

As thinking can only take place in time, causality is a necessary quality of thought. Vision, however, is bound up with space of a higher dimension, and therefore timeless. For this reason the Seer takes a higher place than the thinker. The artist does not think out his creations, but he visualizes them spontaneously. The creative act is an intense experience of the present, and as such, timeless.

Causality, on the other hand, is a thought-expectation ('Denkerwartung', as Mittasch puts it), based on the past, namely the memory of former experiences. These experiences as such are facts, but the perspective of time in which we see them, foreshortens their proportions and their relative value, and replaces their real relations by a temporal succession which excludes all other inherent possibilities.

In other words, it is the reflective and discursive mind, our mode of thinking, which selects and determines the standpoint, on which the perspective and its resulting laws depend. If our consciousness is pure and unbroken by reflection, free from the past, and completely dwelling in the present, then this temporal perspective cannot exist, and with it the self-imposed law of causality vanishes and the true relationship of things with its infinite possibilities of interaction reveals itself. While in the past everything is final, rigid, unalterable law, causality – the present is living relationship, which is alterable, fluid and nowhere final. Thus the present is the liberation from causality.

In this connexion it might be useful to keep in mind what we said previously about the dynamic character of the formula of Dependent Origination (*pratītyasamutpāda*), namely that we are here concerned with neither a purely temporal nor a purely logical causality, but a living, organic relationship, a simultaneous correlation, juxtaposition and succession of all the links, in which each, so to say, represents the transverse summation of all the others, and bears in itself its whole past as well as all the possibilities of its future. And precisely on this account the entire chain of Dependent Origination at every moment and from every phase of it, is removable, and is neither tied to 'causes lying in an unreachable distant past', nor yet referred to a future beyond the limits of vision in which perhaps, some time, the effects of these causes will be exhausted.

Only thus is the possibility of becoming free conceivable, for how could causes heaped up from beginningless time, and working on with natural necessity, ever come to an end? The idea that the consequences of all deeds, whether of a mental or corporeal kind, must be tasted to the very last morsel, and that through every most trivial action, through the slightest motion of the heart, one is further involved in the inextricable net of fate, is assuredly the most frightful spectre that the human intellect has ever conjured up; for only the subsequent conceptualization and concretizing of the vital connexions of destiny could, out of the living law of our inmost being, manufacture the blind necessity of mechanical law. Mechanical laws are applicable only to inert 'things' or to conceptual units, i.e., mental abstractions, but not to living, growing organisms, which are units only in the sense of their continuity (*santāna*) and direction of transformation. This does not mean that the law of cause and effect is to be eliminated from the realms of psychology and biology, but only that it is restricted and modified, and can operate only under certain conditions. The *pratītyasamutpāda* is in fact the Middle Way, avoiding the extremes of rigid necessity – with which free will would be incompatible – and blind chance, which would make development and progress towards a higher goal impossible.

This Middle Way is neither a theoretical compromise nor an intellectual escape, but the recognition of both sides of our existence, of which the one belongs to the past, the other to the present. With our intellect, our thought-activities (and even our bodily functions) we live in the past; in our intuitive vision and spiritual awareness we live in the timeless present.

Thus we are able to overcome thought by vision (*dhyāna*), the past by the realization of the present, the illusion of time by the experience of space. This space, however, is not the external 'visible' space, in which things exist side by side, but a space of higher dimensions, which includes and goes beyond the three-dimensional one. In such a space, things do not exist as separate units but rather like the interrelated parts and functions of one organism, influencing and penetrating each other.[1] It is a space which is not only visualized but *felt*

[1] This is the central idea of the *Avataṁsaka* philosophy (as epitomized in the symbolism of the *Gaṇḍavyūha*, quoted in part V, chapter 3), on which *Ch'an* or *Zen* Buddhism is based and without the knowledge of which *Zen* becomes an intellectual plaything or at the best a psycho-analytical experiment. Most of the apparently paradoxical statements are not arbitrarily coined witticisms or expressions of a momentary mood or situation,

at the same time, a space filled with consciousness, a conscious space: the realization of cosmic consciousness.

In such a consciousness the problem of free will ceases to exist, because in spite of differentiation there is no duality; for here the awareness of differentiation does not lead to the illusion of egohood, and therefore greed and aversion can find no foothold. It is the liberation from passion-dictated will, a will struggling in vain against self-imposed barriers; it is the freedom from a will which is not in accordance with reality.

Thus the problem of free will is dissolved in the rays of knowledge, because will is not a primary quality, which can be treated as an independent element, but it is the ever-changing expression of our respective degree of insight. If this insight is perfect, our will is perfect, i.e., it is in harmony with the forces of the universe, and we are free from the karmic bondage of the past, free from the will that opposes and finds opposition in reality.

So long, however, as we have not attained this highest state, we may know at least 'that nothing can happen to us that does not intrinsically belong to us', as Rainer Maria Rilke says in his *Letters to a Young Poet*, and we may exclaim with another great poet and Seer: 'Do I not choose myself all my destinies since eternity?' (Novalis.)

3

THE FEARLESSNESS OF THE *BODHISATTVA*-PATH

THE certainty 'that nothing can happen to us that does not belong to us in our innermost being' is the foundation of the fearlessness, which *Avalokiteśvara* proclaims, which is expressed in *Amoghasiddhi*'s gesture (*abhaya mudrā*) and embodied in the nature of *Maitreya*, the Great Loving One, the Buddha to come, whose human incarnation will reflect the qualities of *Amoghasiddhi*.

---

nor are they merely meant to baffle the mind of the pupil, but they are based on definite symbols and key-words contained in Buddhist tradition. Without this background *Zen* loses its meaning and its deeply metaphysical and religious significance. The very fact that all *Zen* Masters laid great stress on traditional *Koans* and *Mondos* (as subjects of meditation), which have been meticulously collected and preserved through many centuries, proves the importance of living tradition in *Zen*, which modern imitators try to minimize or to disregard.

Plate 8

AMOGHASIDDHI
The Gesture of Fearlessness

Fearlessness is the quality of all *Bodhisattvas* and of all those who tread the *Bodhisattva*-Path. For them life has lost its horrors and suffering its sting, for they imbue this earthly existence with new meaning, instead of despising and cursing it for its imperfections, as so many do, who in the teachings of the Buddha try to find a pretext for their own negative conception of the world. Is the smiling countenance of the Buddha, which is millionfold reflected by countless images in all Buddhist countries, the expression of an attitude that is inimical to life, as modern intellectual representatives of Buddhism (especially in the West) so often try to make out?

To condemn life as evil, before having exhausted its possibilities for a higher development, before having penetrated to an understanding of its universal aspect, and before having realized the highest qualities of consciousness in the attainment of enlightenment, the noblest fruit and ultimate fulfilment of all existence, such an attitude is not only presumptuous and unreasonable, but utterly foolish. It can only be compared to the attitude of an ignorant man who, after examining an unripe fruit, declares it uneatable and throws it away, instead of giving it time to mature.

Only one who has reached that supra-individual state of Perfect Enlightenment can renounce 'individuality'. Those, however, who only suppress their sense-activities and natural functions of life, before they even have tried to make the right use of them, will not become saints but merely petrefacts. A saintliness, which is built merely on negative virtues, merely on avoidance and escape, may impress the crowd and may be taken as proof of self-control and spiritual strength; however, it will lead only to spiritual self-annihilation, but not to Enlightenment. It is the way of stagnation, of spiritual death. It is the liberation from suffering at the price of life and of the potential spark of Illumination within us.

The discovery of this spark is the beginning of the *Bodhisattva*-Path, which achieves the liberation from suffering and from the fetters of egohood not by a negation of life, but by service to our fellow-beings, while striving towards Perfect Enlightenment.

Therefore it is said in *Śāntideva*'s immortal work 'The Path towards Enlightenment' (*Bodhicaryāvatāra*):

'*He who wants to avoid the hundredfold pain of existence,*
who wants to still the sufferings of sentient beings,
who wants to enjoy the hundredfold happiness [*of the spirit*],
such a one must never abandon the Thought of Enlightenment.

As soon as the Thought of Enlightenment takes root in him,
the miserable one who is fettered by passions to the prison

of existence, becomes immediately a son of the Buddhas.
He becomes worthy of veneration in the world of men and of gods.

As soon as this thought has taken possession of this unclean body
it transforms it into the precious gem of a Buddha's body.
Therefore, take hold of this elixir, which causes this wonderful transformation,
and which is called the Thought of Enlightenment.'[1]

Bodhi-citta (Tib.: *byaṅ-chub-sems*) is here the spark of that deeper consciousness, which in the process of enlightenment is converted from a latent into an active all-penetrating and radiating force. Before this awakening has taken place, our existence is a senseless running about in circles; and since we cannot find any meaning within ourselves, the world around us appears equally meaningless.

Before we pass judgement on the meaning of life and the real nature of the universe, we should ask ourselves: 'Who is it after all, who assumes here the role of a judge? Is not the judging, discriminating mind itself a part and product of that world which he condemns? If we deem our mind capable of judgement, then we have already conceded to the world a spiritual value, namely the faculty of producing a consciousness that goes beyond the mere necessities and limitations of a transient life. If this, however, is the case, we have no reason to doubt the further possibilities of development of such a consciousness or of a deeper kind of consciousness, which lies at the very root of the universe, and of which we only know a small superficial section.

If, on the other hand, we take the view that consciousness is not a product of the world, but that the world is a product of consciousness (which is the view of the *Mahāyāna* in general), it becomes obvious that we live in exactly the type of world which we have created and therefore deserved, and that the remedy cannot be an 'escape' from the 'world' but only a change of 'mind'. Such a change, however, can only take place, if we know the innermost nature of this mind and its power. A mind which is capable of interpreting the rays of heavenly bodies, millions of light-years distant, is not less wonderful than the nature of light itself. How much greater is the miracle of that inner light, which dwells in the depths of our consciousness!

The Buddha and many of his great disciples have given us an insight into this deeper (universal) consciousness. This fact in itself is of greater value than all scientific and philosophical theories, because it shows to humanity the way of the future. Thus there can be only *one* problem for us: to awaken within ourselves this deeper consciousness and to penetrate to that state, which the Buddha

[1] *Bodhicaryāvatāra* I, 8–10 (Tib.: *Byaṅ-chub-sems-dpaḥi-spyod-pa-spyod-pa*).

called the 'Awakening' or 'Enlightenment'. This is the *Bodhisattva-Mārga*, the way to the realization of Buddhahood within ourselves.

That such a realization should no more be possible in our present world, as has been maintained in certain circles of Buddhist orthodoxy, or that the attainment of perfect enlightenment (*samyak-sambodhi*) could only be possible for a single individual within a period of thousands of years, so that it would be utterly senseless to strive after such an aim, this indeed is nothing but an admission of spiritual bankruptcy and dogmatic ossification. A religion, whose ideal is only a matter of the past or of the most distant future, has no living value for the present.

The main fault in such a view lies in the separation of the Buddha's teaching from the living personality of the Teacher, on account of which his doctrine becomes de-humanized, and is sterilized and converted into a pseudo-scientific system of pure negations and abstractions. In such a system meditation merely turns into a morbid, analytical, dissecting attitude, in which everything is taken to pieces and finally disintegrates into putrid matter or empty functions of a senseless mechanism.

If we would examine a master-work of art, say a painting, with a microscope and come to the conclusion that it is nothing but some sort of fibrous matter combined with some coloured substance, and that all this can again be reduced to mere elementary vibrations – this would not bring us one step nearer to the phenomenon of beauty or to the understanding of its significance, its meaning or its message; it would only reveal the senselessness of such a philosophy of 'nothing-but-ism' and its methods of 'objective' analysis. (In reality it is neither 'objective', i.e., unprejudiced, nor an analysis of the thing in question, because it is an intentional arbitrary suppression of all non-material factors, without which the particular form and composition of matter could not exist.)

Nevertheless there are people who in this way try to investigate the nature of life, of corporeality and of psychic and physical functions. We only need to remember in this connexion those passages in post-canonical Buddhist literature, in which the analysis of the body and its functions proceeds on the basis of a naïve realism (which from the start anticipates the conclusions which are to be proved by a seemingly objective analysis), without the slightest attempt to see the inner connexions of spiritual and physical functions or to understand the underlying unity of physiological, vital, psychological and spiritual phenomena.

As long as we look upon the body and its organs as if it were a 'bag filled with various kinds of grain or pulses', arbitrarily or accidentally thrown together, we not only by-pass the real problem, but we deceive ourselves. It is a similar self-deception to create an artificial aversion against the body by the contemplation of corpses in various states of decay. As long as we feel aversion against the body, we have not overcome it. We overcome it only if we grow beyond it. And we can only grow beyond it, if we can *see* beyond it, i.e., if we can see the body in connexion with its antecedents, the forces that built it up and keep it going, the world in which it moves, in short, in connexion with the whole, in its universal perspective. The analysis gets its meaning only from the synthesis; without it it degenerates into a meaningless process of disintegration. 'We then have merely the parts in our hand, while missing their spiritual connexion',[1] the very essence and *conditio sine qua non*, due to which they constitute a living organism.

All this does not mean, however, that we should close our eyes to the unpleasant aspects of existence. The masters of the *Vajrayāna* often used cemeteries and cremation-grounds for practising meditation – not, however, in order to produce aversion against life, but in order to get acquainted with all its aspects and, last but not least, because in these places, which were avoided by others, they could devote themselves undisturbed to their *sādhanā*.

For the beginner such places and the particular meditations connected with them, are a way towards fearlessness, towards the overcoming of aversion and the attainment of equanimity. Even the Buddha relates, that during his spiritual training, he frequented lonely and uncanny places in order to overcome fear.

The contemplation of corpses and similar exercises, which may appear extreme to the layman, have a meaning only when they lead to that fearlessness which enables the *Sādhaka* to come face to face with reality and to see things in their true nature, without attachment and without aversion. He who fights desire by creating aversion and disgust, only replaces one evil by another. We do not feel aversion against dead leaves or dried flowers. And we do not enjoy flowers less because we know that they are transient. On the contrary: the knowledge of their impermanence makes their flowering all the more precious to us – just as the fleetness of the moment and of human life gives each of them their special value. To make this perishable body the abode of the Imperishable, the temple of the Mind – just as the flower makes its impermanent form the abode of timeless beauty – this is the task of man according to the teaching of the Adamantine Vehicle (*Vajrayāna*).

[1] '. . . dann haben die Teile wir in der Hand, fehlt leider nur das geistige Band!' (Goethe, *Faust*.)

In a similar way we should look upon our spiritual and intellectual functions. Then the ego loses its importance automatically and naturally, without any effort on our part, in trying to destroy it by force (which would only strengthen its illusory reality) and without trying to deny its relative existence (which would only lead to hypocrisy or self-deception). As long as every act of ours tends towards our self-preservation, and as long as every thought circles round our own personal interests, all our protestations against the existence of an 'ego' are meaningless. In fact it would be truer in that case to admit that we still possess an ego, or rather that we are possessed by it (as a drunkard is possessed by some persistent hallucination) and that we in our present state can only hope and try to get rid of it in course of time.

The surest way to this end is to see ourselves in the proper perspective to the rest of the world, i.e., in the universal perspective, which has been opened to us by the teachings of the Enlightened Ones, illustrated by their lives and emphasized by the teachers of the Great Vehicle. As long as we see life only through the pin-point of our ordinary human consciousness, it seems to make no sense, while, if we would see the 'whole picture' of the universe, as mirrored in the mind of an Enlightened One, we would discover its meaning. And this meaning, or what we might call 'ultimate reality', would probably no more be expressible in human words, except in symbols like '*samyak-sambodhi*', or '*nirvāṇa*', or '*prajñā-pāramitā*', etc., which cannot be explained and which the Buddha refused to define – insisting that we should experience it for ourselves! The meaning of this our life and of the universe that it reveals, lies in the fact of consciousness itself, but nowhere outside ourselves.

Whether life in itself has a meaning or not: it is up to us to *give* it a meaning. In the hands of an inspired artist a worthless lump of clay turns into a priceless work of art. Why should we not likewise try to make something worth-while out of the common clay of our lives, instead of lamenting about its worthlessness? Our life and the world, in which we live, have as much meaning as we choose to give them.

'Man is exactly as immortal as his ideal and exactly as real as the energy with which he serves it.' These words of Count Keyserling point in the right direction. The problems of value and reality are matters of attitude and creative realization, not of conceptual objectivity.

The Buddhas, therefore, or the state of Buddhahood, represent the highest reality, and those who want to realize it, have to follow the example of the Buddhas: the *Bodhisattva*-Path, in which there is no place for escapism, no running away from discomfort and suffering, but, on the contrary, the recognition, the understanding and acceptance of the fact that perfect enlightenment cannot be attained without the readiness to take upon oneself the suffering of the world. It is exactly this point in which the Buddha went beyond the teachings of the *Vedas* and *Upaniṣads* and through which his doctrine, instead of merely becoming one more sect of Hinduism, grew into a world-religion.

To take upon oneself the suffering of the world, does not mean that one should seek suffering, or that one should glorify it, or inflict it upon oneself as penance, like certain ascetics among Hindus and Christians. This is an extreme, which should be avoided as much as the over-emphasis of our own well-being. The Buddhist attitude flows from the inner urge to identify oneself with all living and suffering beings.

This attitude does not only prevent us from laying too much stress on our own suffering – which would only strengthen our ego-consciousness – but it actually helps us to overcome it and to minimize our own suffering.

Did not the Buddha himself point out this way to *Kisā Gautamī*,[1] when he made her realize that death was a universal affliction and that she was not alone in her grief? – He who accepts suffering in this spirit, has already won half the battle – if not the whole!

The Buddha did not teach a merely negative avoidance of suffering, otherwise he would have chosen the short-cut to liberation, which was within his reach in the times of Buddha *Dīpaṅkara*, and would have saved himself from the sufferings of innumerable rebirths. But he knew that only by going through the purifying fires of suffering can one attain highest enlightenment and become fit to serve the world.

His way was not to escape suffering, but to *conquer* it (this is why the Buddhas are called '*Jinas*' or 'Conquerors'), to *overcome* suffering by facing it bravely and seeing it not only as a personal affliction but in its totality, as the common fate of all living beings.

It is in this spirit that the Bodhisattva's vow is taken by all those who want to follow the sacred path of the Buddhas:

'I take upon myself the burden of all suffering, I am determined to endure it. I do not turn back, I do not flee, neither do I tremble. I fear

[1] A young mother, whose only child had died so suddenly, that she could not believe in its death, came to the Buddha with the dead child in her arms and asked him for a remedy. The Buddha, who realized her state of mind, answered: 'Go into the town and bring me some mustard seeds from a house where nobody has ever died.' The young woman did as she was told, but could not find a single house which had not been visited by death. Thereupon she realized that she was not alone in her grief, returned to the Buddha, gave up the body of her child and found her inner peace.

not, I yield not, neither do I hesitate. – And why? – Because the deliverance of all beings is my vow. . . .

'I am working for the establishment of the incomparable realm of knowledge among all beings. I am not only concerned with my own salvation. All these beings must be rescued by me from the ocean of *saṁsāra* by the vessel of perfect knowledge.'[1]

The attainment of this state of salvation implies the overcoming of all narrow individual limitations and the recognition of super-individual realities within one's own mind. It is the most universal experience the human mind can attain, and from the very outset it demands a universal attitude; for he who strives for his own salvation, or merely with a view of getting rid of suffering in the shortest possible way, without regard for his fellow-beings, has already deprived himself of the most essential means for the realization of his aim.

Whether it is objectively possible to liberate the whole world is beside the point – firstly, because there is no such thing as an 'objective world' for the Buddhist, since we can only speak of the world of our experience, which cannot be separated from the experiencing subject; secondly, the state of enlightenment is no temporal state, but an experience of a higher dimension, beyond the realm of time.

Therefore, even if Buddha *Śākyamuni*'s enlightenment took place at a certain point in the history of mankind, yet we cannot identify the process of enlightenment with this point in time. Just as, according to the Buddha's own words, his consciousness penetrated countless world-periods of the past, in the same way it penetrated countless world-periods of the future; in other words, the infinity of time, irrespective whether we call it past or future, became for him the immediate present.

What appears to us as the gradually unfolding consequences of this event in temporal sequence, is what was present in the Buddha's mind as an accomplished reality. Expressed in the language of our mundane consciousness, the universality of the Buddha-Mind created such a far-reaching effect, that its presence can be felt until the present day, and that the torch of liberating wisdom, which he lit two and a half milleniums ago, still radiates and will continue to radiate, as long as there are beings who yearn for light.

It is in the very nature of enlightenment that it tolerates no exclusiveness (which, indeed, is the root of all suffering), neither on the way towards its realization, nor after its attainment – because it radiates without limits and without exhausting itself, allowing others to participate in it – like the sun which gives its light without restriction to all

[1] From the *Vajradhvaja Sūtra*, quoted in *Śāntideva's Śikṣāsamuccaya*, XVI.

who have eyes to see and sensitiveness to feel its warmth, or organs to absorb its life-giving forces.

And just as the sun, while illuminating the universe impartially, acts in different ways upon different beings, in accordance with their own receptivity and qualities, so the Enlightened One – though he embraces all living beings without distinction in his mind – knows that not all can be liberated at the same time, but that the seed of enlightenment, which he is sowing, will bear fruit sooner or later according to the readiness or maturity of each individual.

But since to an Enlightened One time is as illusory as space, he anticipates in the supreme experience of enlightenment the liberation of all. This is the universality of Buddhahood and the fulfilment of the *Bodhisattva*-vow through the 'Wisdom which accomplishes all works', the Wisdom of *Amoghasiddhi*.

This All-Accomplishing Wisdom consists in the synthesis of heart and mind, in the union of all-embracing love and deepest knowledge, in the complete self-surrender to the highest ideal of human striving, which finds the force for its realization in the fearless acceptance of life's sufferings. For fearlessness is the gesture of *Amoghasiddhi*.

He who, inspired by this attitude, takes upon himself the *Bodhisattva*-vow at the feet of the Buddha, in the eternal presence of all the Enlightened Ones, may remember Tagore's deep-felt words:

'Let me not pray to be sheltered from dangers
but to be fearless in facing them.
Let me not beg for the stilling of my pain
but for the heart to conquer it.
Let me not look for allies in life's battlefield
but to my own strength.
Let me not crave in anxious fear to be saved
but hope for patience to win my freedom.'

SARVAMAṄGALAM!

Blessings to ALL!

APPENDIX

1 Notes, concerning:
   A. Plates of Tibetan Statues;
   B. Examples of Indian and Tibetan Scripts;
   C. Symbols

2 Method of Transliteration and Pronunciation of Indian and Tibetan words.

3 Bibliography of Works on Indian and Tibetan Literature and of Original Texts quoted in this book

4 Index

I

NOTES

A. PLATES OF TIBETAN STATUES

THE over-life-size gilt statues, seen in the frontispiece and Plates Nos. 1, 2 and 8, belong to the temples of *Tsaparang* (Western Tibet), the foundation of which is ascribed to the *Lotsava Rinchen Zangpo* (965?–1054). These statues belong to the best examples of early Tibetan sculpture, which attained its climax during this period, when *Tsaparang* and *Tholing* (*mtho-ldiṅ*) formed the centre of Tibetan civilization and the strongholds of the rulers of Western Tibet. The author's *Tsaparang Expedition* (1947–9) served the exploration of the art-treasures of this long-forgotten ruined city, which had been abandoned centuries ago.

The giant statue of *Amitābha* (Plate 3) and *Amoghasiddhi* (Plate 7), dating probably from the beginning of the fifteenth century A.D., are in the *Kumbum*, the temple of the 'Hundred Thousand Buddhas' (*sku-ḥbum*) in *Gyantse* (Central Tibet). *Amitābha* and *Amoghasiddhi* are shown here in the richly adorned *Sambhogakāya*.

The thousand-armed *Avalokiteśvara* (Plate 6) is a modern statue in the temple of the Tibetan monastery of *Yi-Gah Chö-Ling* (Ghoom), near Darjeeling.

The basic material of these statues is hardened clay, which in the dry atmosphere of Tibet attains almost the hardness and durability of stone. An exception is the giant statue of *Akṣobhya* (Plate 4) which is made of metal.

B. EXAMPLES OF INDIAN AND TIBETAN SCRIPTS

All mantric words and syllables have their origin in Sanskrit and are generally written in Tibetan book-characters (*dbu-can*, pron. 'oo-chan') or in the particularly decorative and traditionally hallowed Indian script of the seventh century A.D. (*Lantsa*), a kind of *Devanāgarī*, the 'Script of the Gods' (*lhaḥi yi-ge*), as the Tibetans still call it. Examples of this script are the OṀ MAṆI PADME HŪṀ at the head of the title-page and the HRĪḤ in the circle at the bottom, as well as the five seed-syllables of the four-petalled lotus on the title-page of Part III (p. 87). All other specimens of Tibetan script belong to the above-mentioned book-characters (*dbu-can*).

C. SYMBOLS (used on title-pages)

Part I (p. 15) The 'Wheel of the Law' (*Dharma-cakra*), which comprises the universal as well as the spiritual law and its ethical application in the life of the individual (formulated in the teachings of the Buddha), is the symbol of *Vairocana*, who is represented in the gesture of 'Setting in Motion the wheel of the Dharma' (*dharma-cakra-pravartana mudrā*), i.e., as spiritual promoter and inspirer. His seed-syllable is OṀ, the primordial sound, which expresses the experience of universality and freedom. Therefore OṀ stands in the centre of the Wheel, whose eight spokes represent the Eightfold Path of the Buddha, which leads from the periphery of mundane existence, from the world of eternal recurrence, to the centre of liberation (in the OṀ). The Noble Eightfold Path (*ārya aṣṭāṅgika mārga*) consists in the following steps:

1. perfect understanding (*samyag dṛṣṭi*)
2. perfect aspirations (*samyak samkalpa*)
3. perfect speech (*samyak vāk*)
4. perfect action (*samyak karmānta*)
5. perfect livelihood (*samyag ājīva*)
6. perfect effort (*samyag vyāyāma*)
7. perfect mindfulness (*samyak smṛti*)
8. perfect absorption (*samyak samādhi*)

I am using the word 'perfect' here, not in a final, static or absolute sense, but in that of a *completeness* of action and of mental attitude (we might call it a 'singleness of mind'), that can be established in every phase of life, on every stage of our spiritual development. That is why each of the eight steps of the Path is characterized by the word *samyak* (Pāli: *sammā*; Tib.: *yaṅ-dag*). This is a word whose importance has been consistently overlooked and which has generally been rendered by the weak and nebulous adjective 'right', which introduces into the formula a taste of dogmatic moralism, quite foreign to Buddhist thought. Concepts like 'right' and 'wrong' have always been bones of contention, and will lead us nowhere. What is 'right' to one person may be 'wrong' to another. But *samyak* has a much deeper, stronger, and more definite meaning: it signifies perfection, completeness, fullness of an action or a state of mind, in contrast to something that is half-hearted, incomplete, or one-sided. A *Samyak-Sambuddha* is a 'perfectly, fully, completely Enlightened One' – not a 'rightly Enlightened One'!

Samyag dṛṣṭi, therefore, means more than what is commonly called 'right views', or the agreement with a certain set of established religious ideas. It means a perfectly open and unprejudiced attitude of mind, which enables us to see things as they are,[1] i.e., not only *one* side of them (and especially not only our own!), but to see them from *all* sides: fully, completely, without flinching, without bias, in order to arrive at a perfectly balanced view, which leads to perfect understanding. Thus, instead of closing our eyes to what is unpleasant and painful, we face the fact of suffering, and by facing it, we discover its causes, and finally, by discovering that these causes are within us, we are able to overcome them. Thus we arrive at the knowledge of the supreme aim of liberation and of the way that leads to its realization. In other words, *samyag dṛṣṭi* is the experience (not only the intellectual recognition or acceptance) of the Buddha's Four Noble Truths (of suffering, of its cause, its overcoming, and the way that leads to its overcoming). Only from this attitude can perfect aspirations grow and give birth to perfect speech, action, and livelihood, as well as to perfect or full effort (in which the whole of the human personality is engaged), perfect mindfulness and perfect concentration or absorption, which leads to Full Enlightenment (*samyak sambodhi*).

Part II (p. 49). The 'threefold jewel' (*tri-ratna*) is the symbol of *Ratnasambhava*, who is shown in the gesture of giving (*dāna-mudrā*). He is the giver of the Three Jewels: '*Buddha, Dharma, Saṅgha*', i.e., of himself, his teaching, and the community of those who have *realized* this teaching (not those who merely belong to the Order). The 'threefold jewel', as seen on the title-page of Part II, grows from a lotus, which forms its base. The middle tip of the jewel bears *Ratnasambhava*'s seed-syllable TRAṀ. At the basis of the jewel stand the syllables MA and ṆI. The flames emanating from the jewel are a symbol of wisdom.

Part III (p. 87). The lotus is the symbol of *Amitābha*, who is represented in the gesture of meditation (*dhyāna-mudrā*). (Plate 3 shows *Amitābha* with his hands resting one upon the other in his lap, palms upwards. A fully-opened lotus-flower lies in the palm of his right hand.) His seed-syllable is HRĪḤ. The latter, therefore, is seen in the centre of the *maṇḍala* of *Amitābha*. As ruler of the *maṇḍala*,

[1] To see things 'as they are in their true nature' (*yathābhūtam*) is therefore the first and basic wisdom, the 'Wisdom of the Great Mirror' (as mentioned on p. 251).

Amitābha takes the place of *Vairocana* in the centre of the lotus, while *Vairocana's* OṀ takes the place of *Amitābha* on the western (upper) petal. On the eastern (lower) petal rests *Akṣobhya*'s HŪṀ, on the southern (left) petal *Ratnasambhava*'s TRAṀ, and on the northern (right) petal *Amoghasiddhi*'s ĀḤ. In all Tibetan *maṇḍalas* the four directions of space are given in this way:

W

S N

E

Part IV (p. 127). The symbol of *Akṣobhya* is the *vajra* (Tib.: *rdo-rje*), his seed-syllable is HŪṀ, his gesture the 'touching of the earth' (*bhūmisparśa-mudrā*). The *vajra* is often shown in his right hand, with which he is touching the ground, or as standing upright on his left hand, which is resting on his lap.

Part V (p. 211). The six-petalled lotus, bearing the six sacred syllables OṀ MA ṆI PA DME HŪṀ on its petals and the HRĪḤ in the centre, is the symbol of *Avalokiteśvara*, who is also known as *Padmapāṇi*, 'Lotus-Holder'. He belongs to the 'Lotus Order' of *Amitābha*. The *mantra of Avalokiteśvara* is engraved in this form on millions of *maṇi*-stones all over Tibet.

Epilogue (p. 259). The double-*vajra* (*viśva-vajra*) is the symbol of *Amoghasiddhi*, whose seed-syllable ĀḤ appears in the centre of the double-*vajra*. *Amoghasiddi* is represented in the gesture of fearlessness (*abhaya-mudrā*). The outward-turned palm of his raised right hand is sometimes adorned with the outlines of the *viśva-vajra*, as seen on Plate 7.

2

METHOD OF TRANSLITERATION AND PRONUNCIATION OF INDIAN AND TIBETAN WORDS

THE method of transliteration commonly used for Sanskrit and Pāli has also been applied to the Tibetan language, since the Tibetan script, in spite of its different pronunciation, is based on the Indian alphabet, which is reproduced here phonetically and in its systematic structure, together with the five exclusively Tibetan consonants.

VOWELS

'a i u ṛ (=ri)' are short
'ā ī ū e ai o au' are long

CONSONANTS

A. The Five Classes

	Surds		Sonants		Nasal
		Aspirates		Aspirates	
Gutturals	*k*	*kh*	*g*	*gh*[1]	*ṅ*
Palatals	*c*	*ch*	*j*	*jh*[1]	*ñ*
Cerebrals	*ṭ*[1]	*ṭh*[1]	*ḍ*[1]	*ḍh*[1]	*ṇ*[1]
Dentals	*t*	*th*	*d*	*dh*[1]	*n*
Labials	*p*	*ph*	*b*	*bh*[1]	*m*

[1] Only in Pāli and Sanskrit

B. Consonants outside the Five Classes

ts	*tsh*	*dz*	*ź*	*z*

Only in Tibetan

y *r* *l* *v*

ś *ṣ* *s* *h* (*ḥ* *ṁ*)

ḥ represents in Sanskrit the voiceless sound of breathing out, and is called *visarga*. In Tibetan the sign corresponding to it is not spoken and merely serves as basis for a vowel or as an indication that the '*a*'-sound inherent in the previous consonant is lengthened into a full '*ā*' (transcribed as *aḥ*).

ṁ (only in Sanskrit and Pāli), called *anusvāra*, nasalizes the preceding vowel, and is pronounced like the English 'ng' in 'long' or as the humming after-sound of 'm' (as for instance in OṀ).

ṅ corresponds to the English 'ng' (as above). In Sanskrit and Pāli it is used only within the word, in Tibetan also as termination.

In all *aspirates* the 'h' following the consonant is audibly pronounced. *th* should *never* be pronounced like the English 'th', but as two distinct sounds, like 't' and 'h' in 'ra*t-h*ole'. Similarly: *ph* like in 'sa*p-h*ead', *dh* like in 'ma*d-h*ouse', *kh* like in 'bloc*k-h*ead', *jh* like in 'sle*dge-h*ammer'.

c corresponds to the English 'ch', like in '*ch*ur*ch*',

ch to 'ch-h' in 'mat*ch-h*ead'.

j corresponds to the English 'j', as in '*j*ar'.

ñ corresponds to the initial sound in 'new', or the Spanish 'ñ' as in 'mañana'.

The *cerebral* consonants *ṭ, ṭh, ḍ, ḍh, ṇ* require the tongue to be placed against the roof of the mouth, while in case of the *dentals* (t, th, d, dh, n) the tongue touches the teeth.

ś represents a sharp *palatal* like a forcefully pronounced 'sh'.

ṣ is a soft *cerebral* 'sh', while *s* corresponds to a sharp 's' or 'ss', as in 'cro*ss*'.

The vowels correspond more or less to the Italian pronunciation, though the short *a* sounds somewhat less open, and in Sanskrit and Pāli the difference between short and long vowels is of greater importance, since it may completely change the meaning of a word. It is therefore as objectionable to leave out the necessary diacritical marks in quotations from these languages as it would be to quote French words or passages without accents. The often-repeated excuse that the scholar knows the correct spelling anyway, and that to the layman it does not matter, is an insult to the reader's intelligence.

In Indian languages the accent of a word generally lies on the long vowel (for instance: *Ā'nanda, tathā'gata, asmimā'na, nikā'ya*). In words consisting of several syllables and short vowels, the third-last syllable carries the accent (for instance: *máṇḍala, dássanaṁ*). If the last but one syllable of a word contains a long vowel or a short one followed by a double-consonant, then this vowel takes the accent

(*Mahāyā'na, svarū'pa, visā'rga*). In words of three syllables, in which the first and third syllable contain long vowels, the first syllable is accentuated (*védanā, śūnyatā*). If two or several words have been combined, each word retains its original accent (*Rátna-sámbhava, Anáṅga-vájra, bodhi-sáttva*). In words of two syllables and short vowels the first syllable is accentuated (*vájra, dhárma, mántra*, in contrast to *vidyā,' mudrā'*).

PECULIARITIES OF TIBETAN PRONUNCIATION

The letters *ts, tsh, dz, ź, z*, which occur only in Tibetan words, are pronounced in the following way:

ts as in 'heigh*ts*'
tsh=ts+h, as in 'knigh*ts-h*all'
ź like French 'j' in '*j*our'
z as in English '*z*ero'.

The main difficulty of Tibetan pronunciation is due to the fact that Tibetan orthography, which was fixed more than a thousand years ago, differs widely from the modern pronunciation, and the latter again is different in each part of Tibet. Western Tibet and Khams (in the east) are nearest to the original pronunciation, while that of Central Tibet, especially of Lhasa (which is regarded to be the most cultured), has moved farthest away from its origin. The following hints, in which only the most important modifications of modern pronunciation can be mentioned, may give the reader an approximate idea of the living language, which has nothing of the apparent tongue-twisting clumsiness of the transcribed script.

1. *Mute Initial Consonants*

In words which begin with a group of two or three consonants, the following initial consonants are mute:

g, d, b, m, ḥ, and likewise: *r, l, s* (these three are mute as prefixes as well as between two consonants).

Examples

gsaṅ='sang' ('*a*' as in 'f*a*ther') (secret)
dgu='gu' ('u' like *oo* in 'book') (nine)
bla-ma=Lāma (Superior, spiritual teacher, etc.)

mchod-rten='chörten' ('*ö*' as in German 'K*ö*rper') (Stūpa)
ḥkhor-lo='khorlo' (wheel)
rluṅ='lung' (wind)
sgom='gom' (meditation)
brda='da' (sign)
brliṅ-ba='ling-wa' (sure)
bstan-pa='tämpa' ('*ä*' as in German) (doctrine)

Exception

lha (god), in which the *h* is audibly pronounced after the *l*

2. *Modified Consonants*

y after *p, ph, b, m* modifies the pronunciation of these consonants in the following way:

py=*c* ('ch')	*phy*=*ch* ('ch+h')
by=*j*	*my*=*ñ* ('ny')

Examples

spyan='chä' (eye), as in *spyan-ras-gzigs*='chä-rä-zee'; Skt.: *Avalokiteśvara*

phyag='chag' (hand), as in *phyag-rgya* ('chag-gya'); Skt.: *mudrā* (gesture)

byaṅ-chub (enlightenment), as in *byaṅ-chub-sems*; Skt.: *bodhicitta* (enlightenment-consciousness) and *byaṅ-chub-sems-dpaḥ* = 'jang-chup-sempa'; Skt.: *Bodhisattva* (a being filled with the consciousness of enlightenment)

gy is sometimes (in certain cases) pronounced like 'ja': for instance in *bstan-ḥgyur*=*Tanjur* ('Tänjoor'), the translated (*ḥgyur*) teaching (*bstan*); or in *bkaḥ-ḥgyur*=*Kanjur* ('Kānjoor'), the translated word (of the Buddha).

dmyal-ba='nyalwa' (hell); *mya-ṅan*='nya-ngan' (suffering).

r after *k, kh, g, d, p, ph, b* converts these consonants into cerebrals:

kr and *pr*=*ṭ*
khr and *phr*=*ṭh*
gr, dr, br=*ḍ*

Examples:

bkra-śis (bliss; Skt.: *maṅgalam*) = 'ṭashi' as in 'Tashi-Lama')
sprul-sku = 'ṭu(l)ku' (transformation-body; Skt.: *nirmāṇa-kāya*)
khro-ba = 'ṭho-wa' (terrifying; Skt.: *bhairava*)
ḥphraṅ = 'ṭhrang' (narrow path above a precipice)
grub-pa = 'ḍuppa' (state of realization, attainment), as in
grub-thob = 'ḍup-thob' (a saint; Skt.: *siddha*)
dril-bu = 'ḍi(l)bu' (ritual bell; Skt.: *ghaṇṭa*)
brag = 'ḍag' or 'ḍa' (rock).

3. *Final Consonants and Modified Vowels*

d, l, s are mute as final consonants, but they modify the preceding vowel (with the exception of '*i*' and '*e*'). In this way *a* is transformed into an open 'e' or 'ä', *u* into 'ü', and *o* into 'ö'. The three modified vowels 'ä, ü, ö' are pronounced like the corresponding 'umlaut' in German.

n as final consonant has the same effect upon the preceding vowel, but is clearly pronounced.

Examples:

rgyud = 'gyü' (Tantra)
vod = 'yö' (is)
ḥod = ö (light); as in *ḥod-dpag-med*, 'Öpamé' (Skt.: *Amitābha*)
skad = 'kä' (language)
bod = 'pö' (Tibet)
sgrol-ma = 'Dö(l)ma'
dṅul = 'ngü' (silver)
ras = 'rä' (cotton)
lus = 'lü' (body)
chos = 'chö' (Skt.: *dharma*)
śes-rab = 'shé-rab' (wisdom; Skt.: *prajñā*)
saṅs-rgyas = 'sangyä' (Buddha)
gdan = 'den' (seat, throne)
bdun = 'dün' (seven)
dpon-po = 'pömpo' (official, master)
slop-dpon = 'lobön' (teacher; Skt.: *ācārya*)

g as final consonant is hardly audible and shortens the preceding vowel. If, however, the second syllable of the same word begins with a consonant, the final *g* of the first syllable is clearly pronounced and has no influence upon the preceding vowel.

In the Tibetan language the accent is generally upon the first syllable of the word (i.e., on the root).

These rules can only give a very general idea of the pronunciation of 'high' Tibetan. The more commonly known Tibetan names, book-titles, etc., occurring in this work, have been rendered according to their generally accepted pronunciation (for instance: *Milarepa*, *Bardo Thödol*, *Kargyütpa*, *Khadoma*, etc.), and their orthographic transcription has only been added at their first mentioning. All technical terms related to the Buddhist doctrine or to Indian Yoga-systems have been rendered in Sanskrit (unless otherwise indicated).

3

BIBLIOGRAPHY

of works of Indian and Tibetan literature and of original texts quoted in this book

Aggañña-Sutta (*Dîgha-Nikaya*), 76

Anangavajra: "*Prajñopâya-viniścaya-siddhi*" (Sanskrit), 101

"*Aṅguttara-Nikâya*" (*Sutta-Piṭaka*, Pâli-Canon), 32

"*Âṭânâṭiya-Sutta*" (*Digha-Nikâya*, *Sutta-Piṭaka*, Pâli-Canon), 32

"*Atthasâlinî*", Buddhaghosa's commentary on the *Dhammasangaṇi*, the first book of the *Abhidhamma Piṭaka* (Pâli-Canon), 217

Aurobindo, Sri, "*The Synthesis of Yoga*", Sri Aurobindo Ashram, Pondicherry, 1955; 70, 131, 134, 138

"*Avalokiteśvara-guṇa-karaṇḍa-vyûha*" (Sanskrit), edited by Satyavrata Sâmûśramî, Calcutta, 1873; 228, 257

Avalon, Arthur, "*The Serpent Power*", two works on Tantrik Yoga (*Saṭ-cakra-nirûpaṇa* and *Pâdukâ-pañcaka*), translated from the Sanskrit with introduction and commentary, Luzac & Co., London, 1919; 143

"*Bar-do-thos-grol*" (Bardo Thödol), Tibetan block-print, 125, 248

Bhattacharyya, Benoytosh, "*An Introduction to Buddhist Esoterism*", Oxford University Press, Bombay, 1932; 95f., 197

"*Bodhicaryâvatâra*" by Sântideva (Sankrit), 274

"*Buddhavaṁsa*" (Pāli), 214

"*Buddhist Bible*", edited by Dwight Goddard, containing selections from Pâli, Sanskrit, Chinese, and Tibetan sources, translated by Nyanatiloka, Rhys Davids, Chao Kung, Goddard, Wai-tao, Suzuki, Wong Mou-lam, Evans-Wentz and Lama Dawa Samdup. (1938; Reprint, Harrap, London, 1957), 74, 118, 167, 199, 221, 224, 226, 236, 263

"*Byaṅ-chub-sems-dpaḥi-spyod-pa*", Tibetan version of Śântideva's "*Bodhicaryâvatâra*" (block-print), 274

"*Cariyapiṭaka* (Pāli), 214

"*Chāndogya Upaniṣad*" (Sanskrit), 21, 158

"*Chos-drug bsdus-paḥi-zin-bris*" (Tibetan block-print), Nâropâ's "Six Doctrines", compiled by Padma Karpo, 103, 157, 167

Das, Sarat Chandra, "A Tibetan-English Dictionary", Calcutta, 1902;245

David-Neel, Alexandra, "*Tibetan Journey*", 26

"*With Mystics and Magicians in Tibet*" (Penguin Books, London, 1937), 26, 160

Demchog-Tantra, see "*dPal-ḥKhor-lo bDe-mchog*"

"*Devendra-paripṛccha-Tantra*" (Sanskrit), 172

"*Dhammapada*" (*Khuddaka-Nikâya*, *Sutta-Piṭaka*, Pâli Canon), 66, 102, 154, 159

"*Dhâmmapada-Aṭṭhakatâ*" (Pâli Commentary), 177

Digha Nikâya, 58, 76, 221

Dutt, Nalinaksha, "*Aspects of Mahâyâna Buddhism and its Relation to Hînayâna* (Calcutta Oriental Series, No. 23), Luzac & Co., London, 1930; 216

"*Expositor, The,*" English translation of "*Atthasâlinî*" (Buddhaghosa), by Maung Tin; Pâli Text Society, London, 1920; 216f

Evans-Wentz, W. Y., and Lama Kazi Dawa-Samdup:

"*The Tibetan Book of the Dead*", with a Psychological Commentary by Dr. C. G. Jung, Introductory Foreword by Lama Anagarika Govinda, and Foreword by Sir John Woodruffe (Third Edition, 1957), 115, 125, 248

"*Tibet's Great Yogi Milarepa*" (1928), 167. 194, 247

"*Tibetan Yoga and Secret Doctrines*" (1935), 103, 157, 209

"*The Tibetan Book of the Great Liberation*", with a Psychological Commentary by Dr. C. G. Jung. (1954), 190

(All these works have been published by the Oxford University Press London)

"*Gaṇḍavyûha*", one of the *Avataṁsaka-Sûtras* (Sanskrit), 222, 271

Glasenapp, H. von, "*Der Buddhismus in Indien und im Fernen Osten*", Atlantis-Verlag, Berlin/Zürich, 1936; 44

"*Die Entstehung des Vajrayâna*". Zeitschrift der deutschen Morgenländischen Gesellschaft, Band 90, Leipzig, 1936; 93, 100

Goddard, Dwight, "*A Buddhist Bible*", Thetford, Vermont, 1938. (Reprint: Harrap, London, 1957), 74, 118, 167, 199, 221, 224, 226

Govinda, Lama Anagarika, "*The Psychological Attitude of Early Buddhist Philosophy*" (according to Abhidhamma Tradition). Patna University, 1937; Rider & Co. 1961

"*Some Aspects of Stûpa Symbolism*" (Kitabistan, Allahabad and London, 1940; 185

"*Solar and Lunar Symbolism in the Development of Stûpa Architecture*" Marg, Bombay, 1950; 185

The following publications have partly been incorporated in more or less modified form in the corresponding chapters of this book:

"*The Significance of OṀ and the Foundations of Mantric Lore.*" 'Stepping Stones', Kalimpong, 1950–1; 17–47

"*The Philosopher's Stone and the Elixir of Life.*" 'The Maha Bodhi Journal', Calcutta, 1937; 51–61

"*Masters of the Mystic Path.*" 'The Illustrated Weekly of India Bombay, 1950; 51–61

"*Principles of Tantric Buddhism.*" '2,500 Years of Buddhism', Publications Division, Government of India, Delhi, 1956; 94–104

"*The Tibetan Book of the Dead*". 'The Times of India Annual', Bombay, 1951; 122–125

"*Time, Space, and the Problem of Free Will*", Part II: "*The Hierarchy of Order: Causality and Freedom.*" 'The Maha Bodhi Journal', Calcutta, 1955; 266–272

"*Grub-thob brgyad-cu-rtsa-bżiḥi rnam-that*" (Tibetan block-print) belonging to the *bsTan-hgyur* (*rgyud*), 57

Guénon, Réné, "*Man and His Becoming, According to the Vedânta*", Luzac & Co., London, 1945; 154, 227

Guenther, H. V., "*Yuganaddha*, the Tantric View of Life", Chowkhamba Sanskrit Series, Benares, 1952; 99, 172

"*Guhyasamâja Tantra*" (Sanskrit), Gaekwad's Oriental Series, No. LIII, 94, 101

"*mGur-ḥbum*" (Tibetan block-print), "The Hundred Thousand Songs" of Milarepa, 170

rGyud, an important section of the *bKaḥ-ḥgyur* ("Kanjur"), the Tibetan Canonical Scriptures, dealing with Tantrik teachings, 93

Hui-Neng, "*Sûtra Spoken by the Sixth Patriarch*" (Chinese, translated by Wong Mou-lam in "A Buddhist Bible"), 118

Indrabhûti: "*Jñânasiddhi*" (Sanskrit), Gaekwad's Oriental Series, No. XLIV, 109, 113

"*Îśâ-Upaniṣad*" (Sanskrit), 130

Jäschke, H. A., "*A Tibetan-English Dictionary*", Routledge & Kegan Paul, London, 1949; 254

"*Jâtaka*" (Pâli), Stories of the Buddha's former lives, 40

"*rJe-btsun-bkaḥ-bum*" (Tibetan block-print), Milarepa's Hundred Thousand Verses, 167

"*rJe-btsun-rnam-thar*" (Tibetan block-print), Milarepa's Biography, 167, 170

"*bKaḥ-ḥgyur*", the Tibetan Canonical Scriptures (the "Buddha's Word"), 133

"*Kâraṇḍa-Vyûha*", see *Avalokiteśvara-guṇa-kâraṇḍa-vyûha.*

"*Kaṭhopaniṣad*" (Sanskrit), 169

"*Kevaddha-Sutta*" (*Dîgha-Nikâya*, Pâli-Canon), 58

"*Khuddakapâtha*" (*Sutta-Piṭaka*, Pâli-Canon), 32

Krishna Prem, Srî, "*The Yoga of the Bhagavat Gîta*", John M. Watkins, London, 1951; 23

"*Kṣurikâ Upaniṣad* (Sanskrit), 158

"*Kulacûdâmaṇi-Tantra*" (Sanskrit), 97

"*Lalitavistara*" (Sanskrit)

"*Laṅkâvatâra-Sûtra*" (originally in Sanskrit), translated from the Chinese by D. T. Suzuki and D. Goddard in "A Buddhist Bible", 73ff, 78

"*Mahâparinibbâna-Sutta*" (*Dîgha-Nikâya*, Pâli-Canon), 221

"*Mahâ-Prajñâpâramitâ Hṛdaya*" (Sanskrit), 84

"*Mahâyâna-Samparigraha-Śâstra*" (Sanskrit), 74

"*Mahâyâna-Śraddhotpâda-Śâstra*" (originally in Sanskrit), translated from the Chinese by Bhikshu Wai-tao and Dwight Goddard in "A Buddhist Bible", 79, 224, 225, 236

"*Maitrâyaṇa-Upaniṣad* (Sanskrit), 22, 158

"*Majjhima-Nikâya*" (*Sutta-Piṭaka*. Pâli-Canon), 32, 72, 150, 158

"*Mâṇḍûkya-Upaniṣad*" (Sanskrit), 23

"*Mañjuśrîmûlakalpa*" (Sanskrit), 94

Masuda, Jiryo, "*Der individualistische Idealismus der Yogâcâra-Schule*", 10. Heft der Materialien zur Kunde des Buddhismus, Heidelberg, 1926; 84, 215, 264

"*Muṇḍaka-Upaniṣad*" (Sanskrit), 23, 169, 175, 193

Nyâṇaponika, Mahâthera, "*Satipaṭṭhâna, the Heart of Buddhist Meditation*", The Word of the Buddha Publishing Committee, Colombo, 1954; 152. Rider & Co. 1962.

Ohasama-Faust: "*Zen, der lebendige Buddhismus in Japan*", Perthes, Gotha, 1925; 264

"*dPal-gsaṅ-ḥdus-pa*", Tibetan version of the *Guhyasamâja Tantra*, 94
"*dPal-ḥKor-lo bDe-mchog*", Tibetan version of the *Śrî-Cakra-Samvara Tantra* (extant only in Tibetan), 166, 194, 198, 208
Pott, H. P., "*Introduction to the Tibetan Collection of the National Museum of Ethnology*", Leiden, 1951; 234
"*Prajñâpâramitâ-Sûtra*" (Sanskrit) Translated into Chinese and Tibetan. English translation from the Chinese by Bhikshu Wai-tao and D. Goddard in "A Buddhist Bible", 199, 224, 263
"*Prajñopâya-viniścaya-siddhi*" by Anaṅgavajra (Sanskrit), Gaekwad's Oriental Series, XLIV, 101
Rhys-Davids, C. A. F., "*Sakya, or Buddhist Origins*", Kegan Paul, Trench, Trubner & Co., London, 1931; 45
Rosenberg, Otto, "*Die Probleme der buddhistischen Philosophie*", Materialien zur Kunde des Buddhismus, Heft 7–8, Heidelberg, 1924 (Harassowitz, Leipzig), 110
Ṛgveda (Sanskrit), 21f
"*Sâdhanamâlâ*" (Sanskrit), Gaekwad's Oriental Series, No. XLVI, 197
"*Sâmaveda*" (Sanskrit), 21f.
"*Saṃyutta-Nikâya*" (*Sutta-Piṭaka*, Pâli-Canon), 131
Śântideva: "*Bodhicaryâvatâra*" (Sanskrit), 273
Byaṅ-chub-sems-dpaḥi-spyod-pa" (Tibetan), 274
"*Śikṣâsamuccaya*" (Sanskrit), 279
"*Satipaṭṭhâna-Sutta*" (*Majjhima-Nikâya* 10 and *Dîgha-Nikâya* 22, *Sutta-Piṭaka*, Pâli-Canon), 150, 152, 194
"*Ṣaṭ-cakra-nirûpaṇa*" (Sanskrit), a work on the six centres of the body by Purnananda Swami. Tantrik Texts, vol. II, edited by Arthur Avalon, 143, 158
"*Śikṣâsamuccaya*" by Śântideva (Sanskrit). English translation by Cecil Bendall and W. H. D. Rouse; John Murray, London, 1922; 279
"*Shrichakrasambhara*", (*Śrî-Cakra-Samvara*), a Buddhist Tantra, edited by Kazi Dausamdup (Lama Kazi Dawa Samdup). Vol. VII of Arthur Avalon's Tantrik Texts, 194
"*Subhâṣitasamgraha*" (*Devendra-paripṛcchâ-Tantra*) (Sanskrit), 172
"*Śûraṅgama-Sûtra*" (originally Sanskrit, preserved only in Chinese), translated into English by Bhikshu Wai Tao and Dwight Goddard in "A Buddhist Bible", 47, 167, 263
"*Sûtra of the Sixth Patriarch*" (Wei-Lang, also known as Hui-Nêng), translated from the Chinese by Wong Mou-lam in "A Buddhist Bible", 118
Suzuki, D. T.: "*Essays in Zen Buddhism*" (3 volumes), Rider & Co., London, 1953; 201, 223, 232, 265
"*The Essence of Buddhism*", The Buddhist Society, London, 1947; 227, 233
"*rTen-ḥbrel-gyi-ḥkhor-lo-mi-ḥdra-ba-bco-rgyad*" (a Tibetan text belonging to the *bsTan-ḥgyur*), 245
"*bsTan-ḥgyur*" ("Tanjur") 225 volumes of philosophical, commentarial, and Tantric works, forming the second part of the Tibetan Sacred Scriptures, 245
"*Tsao-Hsiang Liang-tu Ching*", a Chinese Lamaist text, 234
Tucci, Giuseppe, "*Mc'od rten*" *e* "*Ts'a ts'a*" *nel Tibet Indiano ed Occidentale*, Roma, 1932; 185

"*Udâna*" (*Khuddaka-Nikâya, Sutta-Piṭaka*, Pâli-Canon), 58
"*U-rgyan gu-ru pa-dma-ḥbyuṅ-gnas-gyi rnam-thar*" (Tibetan block-print). Biography of Guru Padmasambhava, 190
"*Vajracchedikâ-Prajñâpâramitâ-Sûtra*", No. 9 of the Great Prajñâpâramitâ-Sûtra, called "the Diamond Saw", translated from the Sanskrit into Chinese by Kumarajiva (A.D. 384–417) and from Chinese into English by Bhikshu Wai-tao and Dwight Goddard in 1935; published in "A Buddhist Bible", 62
"*Vajradhvaja-Sûtra*" (Sanskrit), quoted in Śântideva's *Śikṣâsamuccaya*, 279
Veltheim-Ostrau, Baron von, "*Der Atem Indiens*", Claassen Verlag, Hamburg, 1955; 164
"*Vidyâdhara-piṭaka*" (Sanskrit), belonging to the Canon of the Mahâsânghikas, 31
"*Vijñapti-mâtra-siddhi-śâstra*" (Sanskrit), French translation by Louis de la Vallée Poussin, Librairie Orientaliste Paul Geuthner, Paris, 1928; 84, 109, 215, 264
"*Visuddhimagga*" (Pâli) by Buddhaghosa, 72
Vivekânanda, Swâmi, "*Râja-Yoga*", 157
Waddell, L. A., "*The Buddhism of Tibet or Lamaism*", London, 1895; 28, 254
"*Yogâvachara's Manual*" or "*Manual of a Mystic*", translated from Pâli and Sinhalese by F. L. Woodward, edited by Mrs. Rhys Davids, Pâli Text Society, London, 1916; 140
"*Yogaśikhâ Upaniṣad*" (Sanskrit), 158
Zimmer, Heinrich, "*Ewiges Indien*", Müller & Kiepenheuer Verlag, Potsdam, Orell Füssli Verlag, Zürich, 1930; 19, 188, 219
"*Kunstform und Yoga im Indischen Kultbild*", Frankfurter Verlags-Anstalt AG, Berlin, 1926; 98, 105

NOTE: All Pâli texts mentioned in this list have been published for the *Pâli Text Society* by the Oxford University Press, London.

Most of the Upaniṣads are available in the *Sanskrit Scriptures Series* of the Sri Ramakrishna Math, Mylapore, Madras.

INDEX

A

Absolute, the, 131, 179
Adamantine Vehicle, 276
Aggañña-Suttanta, 76
Air, element, 140, 183
All-accomplishing Wisdom, 86, 122, 250, 262, 264, 280
Alphabet, letters of, sacred symbols, 19
Arahans, 38, 40, 41
Arnold, Edwin, 81
Aspects of Mahāyāna Buddhism and its Relation to Hīnayāna, 216 *fn.*
Aurobindo, Sri, 70 *fn.*, 131 *fn.*, 138 *fn.*
Avalon, Arthur, 28, 143
Avataṁsaka Sūtras, 222

B

Becoming, 267 *fn.*
Bhattacharya, Benoytosh, 95, 96
Blood-drinking deities, 201, 202, 206
Blue Buddha, 248
Bodhicaryāvatāra, 273
Bodhisattva, nature of world to, 234–5
Bodhisattva ideal, the, 40 *et seq.*
Bodhisattva Path, fearlessness of, 272–80
Bodhisattva Way, 46
Bodhisattva-vow, 45, 85, 112, 232, 280
Bodhisattvahood, essence of, 232
Body, human—
  a replica of the universe, 155
  currents of force in, 155 *et seq.*
  speech and mind, the mystery of, 206 *et seq.*
  spiritual development of, 163–5
  the Dharmakāya and the mystery of the, 225–8
  value and meaning of physical, 149–50
Body functions, 153–5
Body of Bliss, 148, 213
Body of Inspiration, 148
Body of Transformation, 213, 262
Brahmanism, 31, 34
Brain Centre, 176, 183, 201
Breath, importance among bodily functions of prāṇa, 152
Breathing—
  basis of meditation, 150–1
  spiritual functions in, 151
Buddha, the, 33, 34, 45, 58, 61, 167, 168, 199
  and metaphysics, 110
  and the reality of the external world, 72
  definition of world, 66
  lotus legend of, 89
  multi-coloured radiance of, 216
  the attraction of, 129–30
  the teachings of, 36–8
Buddha-Eye, 109
Buddha-knowledge, 113
Buddha-Mind, universality of, 279
Buddhahood, 42
Buddhism—
  as living experience, 35–9
  emergence as a world religion, 45
  four elements of, 57–8
  mantric tendencies of early, 31–5
  methods of teaching, 36
  restores significance of Oṁ, 31
  Schools of, 26
  universality of, 40
Buddhism of Tibet or Lamaism, The, 28 *fn.*, 95 *fn.*
Buddhist Bible, A, 47 *fn.*, 74 *fn.*, 78 *fn.*, 118 *fn.*, 167 *fn.*, 199 *fn.*, 221 *fn.*, 224 *fn.*, 226 *fn.*, 236 *fn.*, 263 *fn.*
Buddhist Tantras, 158
  not Śaktism, 96

C

Centres, psychic, 140 *et seq.*
Ch'an Buddhists, 53, 117
Chortens, 185
Christianity and the Word, 26
Clear Light, Doctrine of the, 167
Colours, properties and spiritual associations of, 115–25
Completeness, 149
  realization of, 80 *et seq.*
Consciousness, 243
  dimensions of, 217 *et seq.*
  doctrine of, 70 *et seq.*
  kinds of, 71
  luminous, 148
  space a property of, 116
  three planes of, 23
Conversion, inner, 75, 77 *et seq.*
Cosmic consciousness, 23
Council of Vaiśālī, 44
Creative sound, the idea of, 25–9
Crown Centre, 171, 173, 175, 177, 183, 185
Currents of force in human body, 155 *et seq.*
Curtis, A. M., 141

N

O

P

R

S

Symbols, mantric, 25–6
Synthesis of Yoga, The, 70 *fn.*, 131 *fn.*, 138 *fn.*

T

Tagore, Rabindranath, 46, 130 *fn.*, 280
Tantras—
  anthropomorphic symbolism of, 91–4
  Buddhist, 133–4, 158
  Hindu, 28, 133, 134, 158
Tantric Buddhism, influence on Hinduism, 94
Tantric Yoga, 135
Tao Teh Ching, 235
Temple-banners, 206
Thought-moments, 67, 68
Thousand-petalled Lotus, 141, 143, 156, 160, 169, 173, 177
'Three Bodies', Doctrine of the, 213–17
Three-dimensional space-consciousness, 218
Three Jewels, 109, 119
Three-fold jewel, 61
Throat-Centre, 140, 173, 183, 185, 202, 206, 263
Tibetan Book of the Dead, The, 115 *fn.*, 125 *fn.*, 248 *fn.*
Tibetan Book of the Great Liberation, The, 190 *fn.*
Tibetan Journey, 26
Tibetan Yoga and Secret Doctrine, 103 *fn.*, 157 *fn.*
Tibet's Great Yogi Milarepa, 34 *fn.*, 167 *fn.*, 247 *fn.*
Townshend, Frank, 267
Tractate of the Six Doctrines, 157, 170
Transcendental Intelligence, 74
Transcendental knowledge, plane of, 232
Transference of Consciousness, Doctrine of, 167
Transformation, 80 *et seq.*
  metabolic functions of, 154
Tree of Enlightenment, 43
Tree of Knowledge, 176
Truth, the (dharma), 61
Twilight language, 53
Twin Miracle, 177
Two-dimensional consciousness, 218

U

Ultimate State, 169
Universal consciousness, 73, 74
Universal Mind, 74, 118, 225
Universal Path, 44 *et seq.*
'Unloosening of the knots', 167
Unthinkable, The, 199

V

Vibration, theory of, 25–9
Vijñapti-mātra-siddhi-śāstra, 84, 109, 113
Vision—
  as creative reality, 104–8
  Bardo Thödol and creative, 122–5
Visuddhimagga, 58
Void, 187

W

Waddell, L. A., 28 *fn.*, 95
Wai-Tao, Bhikshu, 47
Waking consciousness, 23
Warren, H. C., 72 *fn.*
Water, element, 140, 178, 179
Wheel of Life, 236–41
Wheel of the Law, 83
Wisdom of Discriminating Clear Vision, 109, 120, 251
Wisdom of Equality, 109, 120, 182, 188, 249, 264
Wisdom of the Inner Vision, 202, 264
Wisdom of the Great Mirror, 131, 180, 187, 207, 264
Wisdom of the Oneness of All Beings, 207
Wisdom of the Universal Law, 183, 185
Wisdoms—
  synthesis of the five, 186 *et seq.*
  the four, 113
With Mystics and Magicians in Tibet, 160 *fn.*
Woodward, F. L., 140 *fn.*
Word, magic of the mantric, 33
Words—
  essential nature of, 17
  seals of the mind, 17

Y

Yellow Buddha, 248
Yoga, 31, 134–5, 138
  anatomy and physiology of, 147
  meaning of term, 22
  psycho-physical processes in, 166 *et seq.*
  psychological aspects of, 179
Yoga of the Inner Fire, 149
  centre of psychic forces in, 173 *et seq.*
Yuganaddha, the Tantric View of Life, 99 *fn.*

Z

Zen Buddhism, 53, 118
Zimmer, H., 19 *fn.*, 28, 98 *fn.*, 105 *fn.* 219 *fn.*

INDEX

OF INDIAN AND TIBETAN TECHNICAL TERMS AND PROPER NAMES

This index follows the English alphabet for the convenience of the majority of readers, who are not acquainted with the Indian and Tibetan alphabets. Pāli words are marked by (P), Tibetan words by (T). All other words are Sanskrit. Diacritical signs (like ¯ ´ . · ˜) and consonants before Tibetan words have not been taken into account in the alphabetical order.